OBJECT-ORIENTED
SOFTWARE
CONSTRUCTION

Prentice Hall International
Series in Computer Science

C. A. R. Hoare, Series Editor

BACKHOUSE, R. C., *Program Construction and Verification*
BACKHOUSE, R. C., *Syntax of Programming Languages: Theory and practice*
DE BAKKER, J. W., *Mathematical Theory of Program Correctness*
BIRD, R., AND WADLER, P., *Introduction to Functional Programming*
BJÖRNER, D., AND JONES, C. B., *Formal Specification and Software Development*
BORNAT, R., *Programming from First Principles*
BUSTARD, D., ELDER, J., AND WELSH, J., *Concurrent Program Structures*
CLARK, K. L., AND MCCABE, F. G., *micro-Prolog: Programming in logic*
DROMEY, R. G., *How to Solve it by Computer*
DUNCAN, F., *Microprocessor Programming and Software Development*
ELDER, J., *Construction of Data Processing Software*
GOLDSCHLAGER, L., AND LISTER, A., *Computer Science: A modern introduction (2nd edn)*
HAYES, I. (ED.), *Specification Case Studies*
HEHNER, E. C. R., *The Logic of Programming*
HENDERSON, P., *Functional Programming: Application and implementation*
HOARE, C. A. R., *Communicating Sequential Processes*
HOARE, C.A.R., AND SHEPHERDSON, J. C. (EDS), *Mathematical Logic and Programming Languages*
INMOS LTD, *occam Programming Manual*
INMOS LTD, *occam 2 Reference Manual*
JACKSON, M. A., *System Development*
JOHNSTON, H., *Learning to Program*
JONES, C. B., *Systematic Software Development using VDM*
JONES, G., *Programming in occam*
JONES, G., *Programming in occam 2*
JOSEPH, M., PRASAD, V. R., AND NATARAJAN, N., *A Multiprocessor Operating System*
LEW, A., *Computer Science: A mathematical introduction*
MACCALLUM, I., *Pascal for the Apple*
MACCALLUM, I., *UCSD Pascal for the IBM PC*
MEYER, B., *Object-oriented Software Construction*
PEYTON JONES, S. L., *The Implementation of Functional Programming Languages*
POMBERGER, G., *Software Engineering and Modula-2*
REYNOLDS, J. C., *The Craft of Programming*
SLOMAN, M., AND KRAMER, J., *Distributed Systems and Computer Networks*
TENNENT, R. D., *Principles of Programming Languages*
WATT, D. A., WICHMANN, B. A., AND FINDLAY, W., *ADA: Language and methodology*
WELSH, J., AND ELDER, J., *Introduction to Modula-2*
WELSH, J., AND ELDER, J., *Introduction to Pascal (2nd edn)*
WELSH, J., ELDER, J., AND BUSTARD, D., *Sequential Program Structures*
WELSH, J., AND HAY, A., *A Model Implementation of Standard Pascal*
WELSH, J., AND MCKEAG, M., *Structured System Programming*
WIKSTRÖM, Å., *Functional Programming using Standard ML*

OBJECT-ORIENTED SOFTWARE CONSTRUCTION

Bertrand Meyer

Interactive Software Engineering,
Santa Barbara, California
and
Société des Outils du Logiciel,
Paris

CLASS		005.1
NO.		30975
AUTHOR	SUBJECT	DATE
		1988
		21.95 ✓
✓	✓	₩ᴀᴢ ɔɪ

PRENTICE HALL

NEW YORK   LONDON   TORONTO   SYDNEY   TOKYO   SINGAPORE

Pour Annie, Caroline, Isabelle-Muriel,
Laurent, Raphaël et Sarah

First published 1988 by
Prentice Hall International (UK) Ltd,
66 Wood Lane End, Hemel Hempstead,
Hertfordshire, HP2 4RG
A division of
Simon & Schuster International Group

© 1988 Bertrand Meyer

Printed and bound in Great Britain at
the University Press, Cambridge.

Library of Congress and British Library Cataloging-in-
Publication Data are available upon application to the
publisher.

11 92 91

ISBN 0-13-629049-3
ISBN 0-13-629031-0   PBK

Contents

Preface

Born in the ice-blue waters of the festooned Norwegian coast; amplified (by an aberration of world currents, for which marine geographers have yet to find a suitable explanation) along the much grayer range of the Californian Pacific; viewed by some as a typhoon, by some as a tsunami, and by some as a storm in a teacup – a tidal wave is reaching the shores of the computing world.

"Object-oriented" is the latest *in* term, complementing or perhaps even replacing "structured" as the high-tech version of "good". As is inevitable in such a case, the term is used by different people with different meanings; just as inevitable is the well-known three-step sequence of reactions that meets the introduction of a new methodological principle: (1) "it's trivial"; (2) "besides, it won't work"; (3) "anyway, that's how I did it all along". (The order may vary.)

Let's make it clear right away, lest the reader think the author takes a half-hearted approach to his topic: I do not think object-oriented design is a mere fad; I think it is not trivial (although I shall strive to make it as limpid as I can); I know it works; and I believe it is not only different from but even, to a certain extent, incompatible with the software design methods that most people use today – including some of the principles taught in most programming textbooks. I further believe that object-oriented design has the potential for significantly improving the quality of software, and that it is here to stay. Finally, I hope that as the reader progresses through these pages, he will share some of my excitement about this promising avenue to software design and implementation.

"Avenue to software design and implementation". The view of object-oriented design taken by this book is definitely that of software engineering. Other perspectives are possible: there has been much interest in applying object-oriented methods to Artificial Intelligence, graphics or exploratory programming. Although the presentation does not exclude these applications, they are not its main emphasis. We study the object-oriented approach as a set of principles, methods and tools which can be instrumental in building "production" software of higher quality than is the norm today.

Object-oriented design is, in its simplest form, based on a seemingly elementary idea. Computing systems perform certain actions on certain objects; to obtain flexible and reusable systems, it is better to base the structure of software on the objects than on the actions.

Once you have said this, you have not really provided a definition, but rather posed a set of problems: What precisely is an object? How do you find and describe the objects? How should programs manipulate objects? What are the possible relations between objects? How does one explore the commonalities that may exist between various kinds of objects? How do these ideas relate to classical software engineering concerns such as correctness, ease of use, efficiency?

Answers to these issues rely on an impressive array of techniques for efficiently producing reusable, extendible and reliable software: inheritance, both in its linear (single) and multiple forms; dynamic binding and polymorphism; a new view of types and type checking; genericity; information hiding; use of assertions; programming by contract; safe exception handling. Efficient implementation techniques have been developed to allow practical application of these ideas.

In the pages that follow, we shall review the methods and techniques of object-oriented software construction. Part 1 (chapters 1 to 4) describes the software engineering issues leading to the object-oriented approach, and the basic concepts of object-oriented design. Part 2 (chapters 5 to 16) reviews object-oriented techniques in detail; this part of the book relies on the object-oriented language **Eiffel**. Part 3 (chapters 17 to 20) looks at the implementation of object-oriented concepts in other environments: classical, non-object-oriented languages such as Fortran, Pascal and C; modular but not really object-oriented languages such as Ada and Modula-2; object-oriented languages other than Eiffel, such as Simula 67 and Smalltalk. Part 3 concludes with a brief review of current issues such as concurrency and persistency. Part 4 contains a number of appendices, particularly on details of Eiffel.

Eiffel plays an important part in this book and its use deserves a few comments. Attempts to discuss issues of software design independently of any notation may seem commendable, but are in fact naive, and bound to yield superficial results. Conversely, many discussions of what appear to be language problems are in fact discussions of serious software engineering problems. Object-oriented design is no exception; to describe it thoroughly, one needs a good notation. For me, Eiffel is that notation, which I designed because no existing language was up to my expectations. In other words, Eiffel is used in this book to support the concepts rather than the other way around. My estimate is that 90% of the material will be useful to readers interested in object-oriented design, even if they never approach the Eiffel programming environment. The remaining 10% is mainly concentrated in the appendices and syntactic notes at the end of each chapter. Part 3 explains how the concepts may be transposed to other languages.

Some of the chapters of part 2 include a "discussion" section explaining the design issues encountered during the design of Eiffel, and how they were resolved. Being the language designer, I felt this was some of the most useful information I could try to convey. I hope the reader will see in these discussions not attempts at self-justification, but candid insights into the process of language design, which holds much in common with the process of software design. I often wished, when reading descriptions of well-known programming languages, that the designers had told me not only what solutions they chose, but why they chose them.

The use of a programming notation should not lead the reader to believe that object-oriented techniques only cover the implementation phase. Quite to the contrary, much of this book is about **design**. Software design is sometimes mistakenly viewed as an activity totally secluded from actual implementation. A tendency has even arisen recently to present simple graphical notations, perhaps adequate for *expressing* designs, as "design methods" (or better yet, "methodologies"). In reality, design involves the same intellectual mechanisms and the same intellectual challenges as programming, only at a higher level of abstraction. Much is to be gained from an approach that integrates both activities within the same conceptual framework. Eiffel was conceived with this goal in mind; such language features as deferred classes, information hiding and assertions address it directly. Several chapters (especially 3, 4, 7, 9, 12 and 14) specifically discuss issues of high-level design.

Although I take full responsibility for any flaws in this book and the design of Eiffel, I acknowledge with great pleasure the help received from many people. The foremost influence has been that of Simula, which introduced most of the concepts twenty years ago, and had most of them right; Tony Hoare's remark about Algol 60 – that it was such an improvement over most of its successors – applies to Simula as well. The staff of Interactive Software Engineering helped tremendously. Jean-Marc Nerson contributed numerous insights and implemented some of the tools of the Eiffel environment; his constant support has been decisive. He and Reynald Bouy, as the first Eiffel programmers, provided feedback and suggestions at a crucial time. The first implementation of Eiffel was started by Deniz Yuksel and brought to completion by Olivier Mallet, Frédéric Lalanne and Hervé Templereau; in this process they came up with many brilliant insights, regarding not only implementation techniques but the language itself. Key contributions were also made by Pascal Boosz. The help of Ruth Freestone and Helen Martin from Prentice-Hall International in bringing the manuscript to production was much appreciated. I am also indebted to Peter Lohr, W. Rohdewald and especially David Yost for pointing out a number of errors in the first printing. Finally, I have given short courses and lectures on the topics of this book on three continents, and the participants' questions and comments have considerably enriched my understanding of the field, as have the many suggestions contributed by the commercial and academic users of Eiffel.

Santa Barbara   B.M.
July 1988

Acknowledgments

Some of the material in appendix B appeared in part in "Eiffel: Programming for reusability and extendibility", *SIGPLAN Notices*, 22, 2, February 1987, pp. 85-94.

Some of the material in chapters 3 and 12 appeared in part in "Reusability: The Case for Object-Oriented Design", *IEEE Software*, 4, 2, March 1987, pp. 50-64

Some of the material in chapter 19 appeared in part in "Genericity vs. Inheritance", Proc. OOPSLA Conference, ACM, October 1986; revised version to appear in *Journal of Pascal, Ada and Modula-2*.

Some of the material in chapter 4 and appendix A appears in part in "Eiffel: A Language and Environment for Software Engineering", *The Journal of Systems and Software*, 1988.

Trademarks used in this book: Ada (US Department of Defense); Eiffel (Interactive Software Engineering, Inc.); Objective-C (Productivity Products International); Simula 67 (Simula AS); Smalltalk (Xerox); Unix (AT&T Bell Laboratories).

Author's addresses

Interactive Software Engineering, Inc.
270 Storke Road, Suite 7 Goleta, CA 93117 - USA

Société des Outils du Logiciel
Centre d'Affaires 3 MPP, 4 rue René Barthélémy 92120 Montrouge - France

Syntax notation

The following notation, a simple variant of BNF (Backus-Naur Form), is used in the syntactical descriptions found at the end of each chapter on Eiffel and in Appendix C.

Language structures are defined as "constructs", whose names start with a capital letter and are written in normal (roman) font, as Class, Instruction etc. The syntactical form of the instances of a construct is given by a production of the form:

Construct = Right_hand_side

Every syntactical construct appears on the left-hand side of exactly one production, except for the lexical constructs (Identifier, etc.) which are defined separately.

The right-hand side of a production is a sequence of constructs and/or terminals, where a terminal represents an actual language element (keyword such as **class**, operator such as +, etc.). Terminals are written as follows:

- Keywords appear in boldface and stand for themselves, for example **class**, **loop** etc.

- Predefined types, entities or routines such as *INTEGER, Result* or *Create* appear in italic font and stand for themselves.

- Special symbols are enclosed in double quotes, for example ";", ":", etc. The double quote character is written in simple quotes as '"' (the simple quote character is written as "'").

Alternative right-hand sides are separated by vertical bars, as in

Type = *BOOLEAN* | *INTEGER* | *CHARACTER* | *REAL* |
Class_type | Association

where the first four alternatives are terminals and the last two are references to non-terminals defined elsewhere.

Two notational simplifications are used in right-hand sides:

- [comp] denotes the optional presence of an optional component comp;
- {Construct § ...} describes sequences of **zero or more** instances of Construct, separated from each other, if more than one, by the separator §.
- {Construct § ...}[+] describes sequences of **one or more** instances of Construct, separated from each other, if more than one, by the separator §.

Note that special symbols are quoted, so that there is no danger of confusion between the meta-symbols of this notation, such as [, {, + etc., and corresponding symbols in the language described, which will appear as "[", "{", "+" etc.

As an example of this notation, the following describes a trivial language with instructions "skip" and "goto", each instruction being possibly labeled, and separated from the next by a semicolon.

Warning: this is not the syntax of Eiffel!

Program	=	{Instruction ";" ...}
Instruction	=	[Label ":"] Simple_instruction
Simple_instruction	=	Skip | Goto
Skip	=	**skip**
Goto	=	**goto** Label
Label	=	Identifier

PART 1

Issues and principles

1

Aspects of software quality

The principal aim of software engineering is to help produce quality software. This book introduces a set of techniques which have a dramatic potential for improving the quality of software products.

Before we consider these techniques, we must clarify their goals. Software quality is not so simple an idea; it is best viewed as a multi-faceted notion, described by a set of factors. This chapter analyzes some of these factors, shows where improvements are most sorely needed, and points to the directions where we shall look for solutions in the rest of our journey.

1.1   EXTERNAL AND INTERNAL FACTORS

We all want our programs to be fast, reliable, easy to use, readable, modular, structured and so on. But these qualifiers describe two different sorts of qualities.

On one side, we are considering such qualities as speed or ease of use, whose presence or absence in a software product may be detected by users of the product. Such qualities may be called **external** quality factors. To provide a broad enough view, we should include under "users" not only the persons who actually interact with the final products (for example an airline clerk using a flight reservation system) but also those who purchase the software or contract out its development and evolution (such as the airline executive in charge of acquiring flight reservation systems). Thus the ease with which the software may be adapted to changes of specifications (*extendibility*) falls in the category of external factors.

Other qualities applicable to a software product, such as being modular, or readable, are **internal** factors, only perceptible to computer professionals.

Clearly, only external factors really matter in the end: when I use a spreadsheet or a nuclear plant control system, little do I care whether the source program is readable or not if my computations take ages to complete, or if a wrong input blows the nuclear plant off. However the internal factors are the key to ensuring that external factors are satisfied: for users to enjoy the visible qualities, the designers and implementors must have applied internal techniques that will ensure the hidden ones.

The rest of this book is devoted to the presentation of a set of modern techniques for obtaining internal quality. However we should not lose track of the global picture; the internal techniques are not an end in themselves, but a means to reach external software qualities. The most important of these qualities will now be presented.

1.2   EXTERNAL QUALITY FACTORS

1.2.1   Correctness

> **Definition**: Correctness is the ability of software products to exactly perform their tasks, as defined by the requirements and specification.

Correctness is clearly the prime quality. If a system does not do what it is supposed to do, then everything else about it matters little. This goal is more easily stated than achieved, however, if only because meeting it demands that system requirements be expressed in a completely formal way.

1.2.2   Robustness

> **Definition**: Robustness is the ability of software systems to function even in abnormal conditions.

Robustness has to do with what happens in abnormal cases. This is different from correctness, which defines the system's behavior in cases that are explicitly addressed by the specification.

Robustness is by nature a more fuzzy notion than correctness. At issue is what happens in any case not explicitly covered by the specification. It is not possible to say, as with correctness, that the system should "perform its tasks" in such a case, since by definition these tasks are not known; were they to be specified more precisely, the abnormal case would become part of the specification and we would be back in the province of correctness. But there will always be cases that the specification does not explicitly address. The role of the robustness requirement is to make sure that if such cases do arise, the system does not cause catastrophic events to occur; it should terminate its execution cleanly, or enter a so-called "graceful degradation" mode.

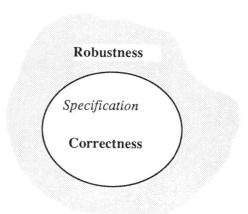

Figure 1.1   Robustness vs. correctness

The term "reliability" is sometimes used for robustness; but it connotes a more general concept and is best interpreted as covering both correctness and robustness.

1.2.3   Extendibility

> **Definition**: Extendibility is the ease with which software products may be adapted to changes of specifications.

Software is supposed to be "soft", and indeed it is in principle; nothing is easier than to take a program element and change it.

The problem of extendibility is one of scale. Change is usually not a serious issue with small programs, but characterizes what is known as *programming-in-the-large*. As programs grow bigger, they become harder and harder to adapt. It often seems that a large software system is a giant but fragile construction in which pulling out any one brick will cause the whole edifice to collapse.

Although many of the techniques that improve extendibility may be introduced on small examples or in introductory courses, their relevance only becomes clear for larger projects.

Two principles are essential for improving extendibility:

• *Design simplicity*: a simple architecture will always be easier to adapt to changes than a complex one.

• *Decentralization*: the more autonomous the modules in a software architecture, the higher the likelihood that a simple change will affect just one module, or a small number of modules, rather than trigger off a chain reaction of changes over the whole system.

Simplicity and decentralization are indeed two of the main recurring themes in the discussions which follow.

1.2.4   Reusability

> **Definition**: Reusability is the ability of software products to be reused, in whole or in part, for new applications.

The need for reusability comes from the observation that many elements of software systems follow common patterns; it should be possible to exploit this commonality and avoid reinventing solutions to problems that have been encountered before.

The importance of reusability is obvious. Note in particular that reusability has an influence on all other aspects of software quality, for solving the reusability problem essentially means that less software must be written, and hence that more effort may be devoted (for the same total cost) to improving the other factors, such as correctness, robustness etc.

Chapter 3 is entirely devoted to the reusability issue; the discussion there will lead us to the techniques of object-oriented design.

1.2.5   Compatibility

> **Definition**: Compatibility is the ease with which software products may be combined with others.

Compatibility is important because software products are not developed in a vacuum: they need to interact with each other. But they too often have trouble interacting because each product makes conflicting assumptions about the rest of the world. An extreme example is the wide variety of incompatible file formats supported by many operating systems. A program can directly use another's result as input only if the file formats are compatible.

The key to compatibility lies in homogeneity of design, and in agreeing on standardized conventions for inter-program communication. Examples of solutions include:

- Standardized file formats, as in the Unix system, where every text file is simply a sequence of characters.
- Standardized data structures, as in Lisp systems, where all data, and programs as well, are represented by binary trees (called lists in Lisp).
- Standardized user interfaces, as in the Smalltalk system, where all tools rely on a unique paradigm for communication with the user, based on windows, icons, graphics etc.

More general solutions are obtained by defining standardized access protocols to all important entities manipulated by the software. This is the idea behind abstract data types (chapter 4) and the object-oriented approach.

1.2.6 Other qualities

The qualities seen so far are the ones that stand to benefit the most from the techniques of object-oriented design and will be the focus of the discussions that follow. But we should not neglect other aspects of software quality.

Efficiency is the good use of hardware resources, such as processors, internal and external memories, communication devices. Although there may have been an over-emphasis on low-level efficiency in early discussions of programming, good use of the available resources, both in space and time, is of course an essential requirement on any software product.

Portability is the ease with which software products may be transferred to various hardware and software environments.

Verifiability is the ease of preparing acceptance procedures, particularly test data, and procedures for detecting failures and tracing them to errors during the validation and operation phases.

Integrity is the ability of software systems to protect their various components (programs, data, documents) against unauthorized access and modification.

Ease of use is the ease of learning how to use software systems, operating them, preparing input data, interpreting results, recovering from usage errors.

1.2.7 Tradeoffs

In this review of external software quality factors, we have encountered requirements that may not be totally compatible. How can one get perfect integrity without introducing protections and barriers of various sorts, which will inevitably hamper ease of use? Similarly, optimal efficiency would require perfect adaptation to a particular hardware and software environment, which is the opposite of portability, and perfect adaptation to a particular specification, whereas extendibility and reusability push towards solving problems more general than the one initially given.

In many cases, solutions may be found to reconcile apparently conflicting factors. Sometimes, however, tradeoffs must be made. It is important in such cases that the criteria be expressed clearly.

1.3   ABOUT SOFTWARE MAINTENANCE

Often, discussions of software and software quality consider only the development phase. But the real picture is wider. The hidden part, the side of the profession which is not usually highlighted in programming courses, is maintenance. It is widely estimated that 70% of the cost of software is devoted to maintenance. No discussion of software quality can be satisfactory if it neglects this aspect.

What does "maintenance" mean for software? A minute's reflection shows this term to be a misnomer: a software product does not wear out from repeated usage, and thus need not be "maintained" the way a car or a TV set does. In fact, the word is used by software people to throw a veil over some noble and some not so noble activities. The noble part is modification: as the specifications of computer systems change, reflecting changes in the external world, so must the systems themselves. The less noble part is late debugging: removing errors that should never have been there in the first place.

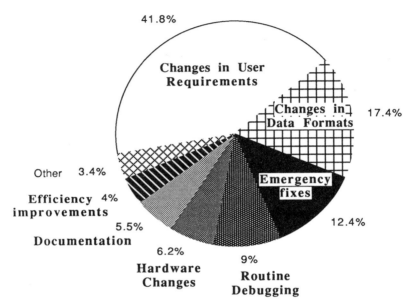

Figure 1.2   Breakdown of maintenance costs (source: [Lientz 1979])

The above chart sheds some light on what the catch-all term of maintenance really covers. Based on a survey of 487 installations developing software of all kinds, it shows the breakdown of maintenance costs. More than two-fifths of maintenance activities, according to this study, are extensions and modifications requested by users. This seems to be what we have called the noble part of maintenance, which is also the inevitable part. However the magnitude of this proportion seems to reflect the lack of extendibility of commonly implemented software: systems are much harder to change than they should be. One of the key benefits of the techniques studied in this book will be to make software easier to modify.

The second item by order of magnitude is particularly interesting: effect of changes in data formats. When the physical structure of files and other data items change, programs must be adapted. For example, when the US Post Office, a few years ago, introduced the "5+4" postal code for large companies (using nine digits instead of the standard five), numerous programs that dealt with addresses and "knew" that a postal code was exactly five digits long had to be rewritten, at great cost to the industry.

The issue is not that some part of the program knows the physical structure of data: this is inevitable since the data must eventually be accessed for internal handling.

But with most current software design techniques this knowledge is spread out over too many parts of the system. Thus when the physical data structure changes (as is bound to happen sooner or later), the effect on system structure is out of proportion; too many parts of the system are affected. The theory of abstract data types, studied in chapter 4, provides the key to this problem, by allowing programs to access data by external properties rather than physical implementation.

Another significant item in the distribution of activities is the low percentage (5.5%) of documentation costs. Remember that these are costs of tasks done at maintenance time. The observation here is that documentation is either done as part of system development, or not done at all. This book emphasizes a design style in which documentation is not thought of as separate from the software proper; most of the documentation (excluding perhaps the diagrams describing the architecture at the highest level) is embedded within the programs. Special tools are available (see chapters 9 and 15) to extract the documentation from the code.

The next items in Lientz and Swanson's list are also interesting, if less directly relevant to the topics of this book. Emergency bug fixes (done in haste when the program is not producing the expected results or behaves in some catastrophic way) cost more than routine, scheduled corrections. This is not only because they must be performed under heavy pressure, but also because they disrupt the orderly process of delivering new releases and tend to introduce new errors. The last two activities account for small percentages. One is efficiency improvements; this seems to show that once a system works, project managers and programmers are not eager to disrupt its delicate balance in the remote hope of performance improvements. The other is transfer to new environments; it appears that commonly written systems are either very portable by nature, or so dependent on specific hardware as to defeat any hope of portability. The choice between these interpretations is left to the reader.

1.4 THE KEY QUALITIES

The rest of this discussion will highlight the first five qualities discussed above: **correctness, robustness, extendibility, reusability and compatibility**. They reflect the most serious difficulties with today's software development practices. Programs too often do not do what they are supposed to do. They are not well equipped enough to deal with abnormal situations. They are too difficult to change. Their construction does not rely enough on previous efforts. They do not combine well enough with each other.

As we look for solutions to these issues, two subgroups will clearly appear in this list. On the one hand, reusability, extendibility and compatibility demand architectural techniques that produce flexible, decentralized designs, made of coherent modules connected by well-defined interfaces. The object-oriented approach provides the best known solution. Correctness and robustness, on the other hand, are favored by techniques that support systematic software development based on the precise specification of requirements and constraints. As will be shown below, such techniques can be made to blend harmoniously with other aspects of object-oriented design.

1.5   KEY CONCEPTS INTRODUCED IN THIS CHAPTER

- The object of software engineering is to find ways of building quality software.

- Software maintenance, which consumes a large proportion of software costs, is penalized by the difficulty of implementing changes in software products, and by the over-dependence of programs on the physical structure of the data they manipulate.

- Rather than a single criterion, quality in software is best viewed as a tradeoff between a set of different goals.

- External factors, perceptible to users and clients, should be distinguished from internal factors, perceptible to designers and implementors.

- What matters is the external factors, but they can only be achieved through the internal factors.

- A list of ten basic external factors was presented. Those for which current software is most badly in need of better methods are the safety-related factors, correctness and robustness, and those which require more decentralized software architectures: reusability, extendibility and compatibility.

1.6   BIBLIOGRAPHICAL NOTES

Several authors have proposed definitions of quality; one of the first to rely on a systematic study was due to a TRW group [Boehm 1978]; see also an earlier article by Hoare [Hoare 1972].

The distinction between external and internal factors was introduced in a 1977 General Electric study commissioned by the US Air Force [McCall 1977]. McCall uses the terms "factors" and "criteria" for what we have called external factors and internal factors. The ten factors introduced in this chapter are close to McCall's; one of McCall's factors, maintainability, was dropped, because (for reasons explained in section 1.3) it is adequately covered by extendibility and verifiability. McCall's study also discusses a number of internal factors (called criteria) as well as *metrics*, or quantitative techniques for assessing satisfaction of the internal factors. However the internal factors and metrics introduced in this study are too closely linked with programming techniques that are obsolete by the standards of object-oriented design. Carrying over this part of McCall's work to the techniques developed in this book would certainly be a worthwhile endeavor.

The chart of maintenance costs (figure 1.2) comes from [Lientz 1979]. See also [Boehm 1979].

The expression *programming-in-the-large* was introduced by [DeRemer 1976].

2

Modularity

Chapter 1 has emphasized the need for flexible system architectures in order to achieve the goals of software extendibility, reusability and compatibility. One word springs to mind: we should make our software more *modular*.

Like "structured" or "user-friendly", "modular" is one of the favorite buzzwords in software engineering, but precise definitions do not abound. Modular programming was once taken to mean the construction of programs as assemblies of small pieces, usually subroutines. But such a technique cannot bring real benefits in terms of extendibility and reusability unless the resulting pieces – the *modules* – are autonomous, coherent and organized in robust architectures. Any comprehensive definition of modularity must address these issues.

As it turns out, a single definition would be insufficient; as with software quality, we must look at modularity from more than one perspective. We will use a set of five "criteria" and five "principles". The criteria are independent: it is possible to attain some while violating the others. The principles are just as important in practice as the criteria, but they follow logically from them.

The purpose of this discussion is to assess what it means for a *software construction method* to be modular, in the sense of helping designers produce software systems made of autonomous elements connected by a coherent, simple structure. The most important consequences of modularity are felt at the design level; thus we are interested in looking not only at *program* modules but also at *design* modules.

The form of the modules is not yet decided at this stage. Our aim is precisely to lay down a basis for deciding on a form of module. The simplest form is the equivalent of a subroutine (or procedure), representing a step of the task to be performed by the software. But the subroutine will soon appear to be less than satisfactory for the purposes of modularity, and more advanced forms of modules will be introduced.

2.1   FIVE CRITERIA

The five criteria help evaluate design methods with respect to modularity. They are termed:

- modular decomposability
- modular composability
- modular understandability
- modular continuity
- modular protection

2.1.1   Modular decomposability

The Modular Decomposability criterion is met by a design method if the method helps in the decomposition of a new problem into several subproblems, whose solution may then be pursued separately.

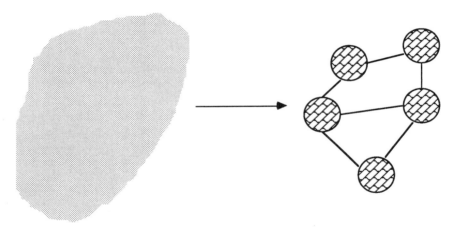

Figure 2.1   Decomposability

The picture symbolizes the idea: the method should help reduce the apparent complexity of an initial system description by decomposing it into a set of less complex subsystems connected by a simple structure. In general, the process will be repetitive: subsystems must themselves be decomposed.

Meeting this criterion is essential for the modular development of non-trivial systems. The criterion is more demanding than might appear at first sight, since it implies that the different subproblems obtained from the decomposition may be handed over to different people for separate work. This is a stringent requirement.

- *Example: top-down design.* The top-down design method directs designers to start with a most abstract description of the system's function, and then to refine this view through successive steps, each subsystem being decomposed at each step into a small number of simpler ones, until all elements obtained are of a sufficiently low level of abstraction as to allow for direct implementation. The process may be modeled as a tree. This approach clearly favors decomposability.

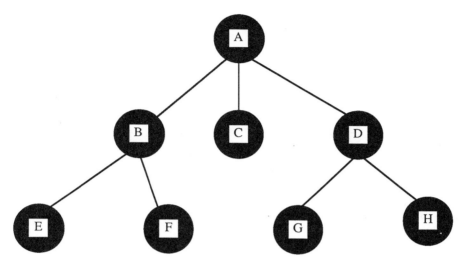

Figure 2.2   A top-down hierarchy

- *Counter-example: initialization module.* Many modules require some kind of initialization: some actions, such as assigning initial values to certain variables, opening files etc., need to be taken before the module may perform its first useful tasks. It may seem a good idea to concentrate all such actions, for all modules of the system, in a single initialization module that initializes everything for everybody. Such a module will exhibit good "temporal cohesion" in that all its actions are executed at the same stage of the system's execution. (The term "temporal cohesion" comes from the method known as structured design; see the bibliographical notes.) However such an initialization module will have to access the data structures of all the modules it initializes, requiring constant interplay between the initialization module and others. This is contradictory with the decomposability criterion.

2.1.2   Modular composability

A method satisfies the criterion of Modular Composability if it favors the production of software elements which may be freely combined with each other to produce new systems, possibly in an environment quite different from the one in which they were initially developed.

Where decomposability was concerned with the derivation of software elements from specifications, composability addresses the reverse process: ensuring that existing software elements may be applied to the construction of new systems.

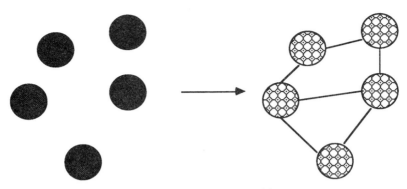

Figure 2.3   Composability

Composability is directly connected with the reusability problem: the aim is to find ways to design pieces of software performing well-defined tasks and usable in widely different contexts.

This criterion reflects an old dream: transforming the software design process into a construction box activity, whereby programs would be built by combination of existing standard elements.

• *Example 1: Subprogram libraries.* Subprogram libraries are designed as sets of composable elements. One of the areas where they have been successful is numerical computation, where carefully designed libraries of subroutines are routinely used to solve classical problems in linear algebra, finite elements, differential equations etc.

• *Example 2: Unix shell conventions.* Basic Unix commands operate on an input viewed as a sequential character stream, and produce an output with the same standard structure. This makes them potentially composable; the composition operator is written as |, so that A | B represents a program which will take A's input and have it processed by A, A's output being sent to B as input and processed by B. Such a systematic convention favors the composability of software tools.

• *Counter-example: preprocessors.* One popular way to "extend" the facilities of programming languages (and sometimes to correct some of their most blatant deficiencies) is to use "preprocessors" which will accept an extended syntax as input and map them into the standard form of the language. For example, Fortran has variously been extended to accept graphical primitives, "structured programming" control structures or database operations. Usually, however, such extensions are not compatible; then the preprocessors may not be combined with each other, which results in unsolvable dilemmas, such as having to choose between graphics and adequate control structures.

The composability criterion is independent from the previous one, decomposability. In fact, they are often at odds. For example, top-down design does not take composability into account and tends to produce modules that are *not* reusable. This is because modules are developed to fulfill a specific requirement, corresponding to a particular subproblem obtained at some point in the refinement process symbolized by figure 2.2; the method provides neither hints towards making the module more general than this subproblem, nor incentives to do so.

2.1.3 Modular understandability

A method favors Modular Understandability if it helps produce modules that can be separately understood by a human reader. At worst, the reader should be required to look at just a few neighboring modules.

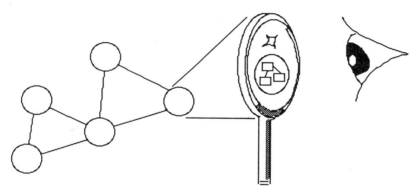

Figure 2.4 Understandability

This criterion is important with respect to the maintenance problem. Most maintenance activities, whether of the noble or not-so-noble category (see chapter 1), involve having to dig into existing software elements. The method can hardly be called modular if documents may not be understood separately.

Recall that this discussion has design, rather than programming, as its main focus; thus the elements that should be separately understandable may be design modules just as well as program units.

- *Counter-example: sequential dependencies.* If a set of modules has been so designed that its correct functioning depends on these modules being activated in a certain prescribed order, then they will not be individually understandable.

2.1.4 Modular continuity

A design method satisfies Modular Continuity if a small change in a problem specification results in a change of just one module, or few modules, in the system obtained from the specification through the method. Such changes should not affect the *architecture* of the system, that is to say the relations between modules.

This criterion reflects the extendibility problem: as mentioned in chapter 1, almost all specifications change as the project progresses. Continuity means that small changes should affect individual modules in the structure of the system rather than the structure itself.

The term "continuity" is drawn from an analogy with the notion of a continuous function in mathematical analysis where, roughly speaking, a function is continuous if a small change in the argument will yield a small change in the result. Here the function considered is the design method, viewed as a mechanism for obtaining systems from specifications:

design_method: Specification → *System*

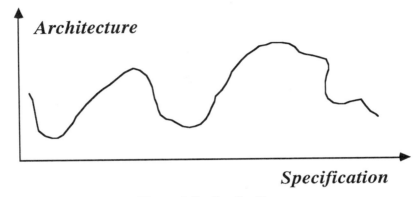

Figure 2.5   Continuity

In spite of the mathematical analogy, of course, we are dealing with non-rigorous concepts; it is hard to define precisely what "small" or "large" means in the context of changes to program architecture, let alone specifications. However the concept of continuity is intuitively clear, and reflects an important requirement on any method that claims to be modular.

• *Example 1: Symbolic constants.* Some programming projects enforce the rule that no numerical or textual constant should ever be used in the instructions of a program: all constants must be used through symbolic names, whose associated value only appears in a constant definition clause (*PARAMETER* in Fortran 77, **constant** in Pascal or Ada). If the value has to change, only the definition is impacted. This is a very wise precaution as regards continuity.

• *Example 2: The Principle of Uniform Reference.* Let x be the name of a program object, and a the name of an attribute of x. For example, x might be a variable representing a bank account, and a the "current balance" attribute of bank accounts.

How do you denote the value of the attribute a for x? In many design or programming languages, this depends on whether this value is stored along with x or computed when needed. For example, the balance of an account may be either a field of the record object representing the account, or the result of computing a function (based on some other fields of the record, such as the lists of withdrawals and deposits to the account). In Pascal or Ada, the notation is $x.a$ in the first case and $a(x)$ in the second.

Choosing between these two representations is a space-time tradeoff; one economizes on computation, the other on storage. How to resolve this tradeoff is the kind of decision that is often reversed at least once during a project's lifetime. Thus the continuity criterion favors any notation that is immune to such changes. This is an example of the principle of Uniform Reference, which in its general form may be stated as follows: the services offered by a module should be available through a uniform notation, regardless of whether the service is implemented through storage or through computation.

In Algol W, for example, both function calls and field access are written $a(x)$; in Simula 67 or Eiffel, both are written $x.a$. In each case the convention is uniform, satisfying the principle. In contrast, Pascal or Ada, as we saw, use different notations.

• *Counter-example 1: Using physical representations.* A method in which program designs are patterned after the physical implementation of data will yield designs that are very sensitive to slight changes in the environment.

• *Counter-example 2: Static arrays.* Languages such as Fortran or Pascal, which do not allow the declaration of arrays whose bounds will only be known at run-time, make program evolution much harder.

2.1.5   Modular protection

A method satisfies the Modular Protection criterion if it yields architectures in which the effect of an abnormal condition occurring at run-time in a module will remain confined to this module, or at least will propagate to a few neighboring modules only.

The underlying issue, that of failures and errors, is a central one in software engineering. The errors considered here are run-time errors, resulting from hardware failures, erroneous input or lack of needed resources (like exhaustion of available storage). The criterion does not address the avoidance or correction of errors, but the aspect that is directly relevant to modularity: their propagation.

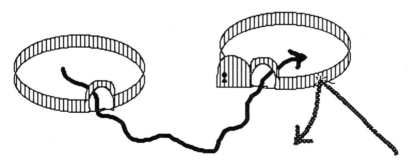

Figure 2.6   Protection

- *Example: Validating input at the source*. A method which imposes that every module inputing data is also responsible for checking their validity is good for modular protection.

- *Counter-example: Undisciplined exceptions*. Languages such as PL/I, CLU and Ada have the notion of exception. An exception is a special signal that may be "raised" by a certain instruction and "handled" in another, possibly remote part of the system. When the exception is raised, control is transferred to the handler. (Details of the mechanism vary between languages; Ada or CLU are more disciplined in this respect than PL/I.) Such facilities may have some merits with respect to simplifying the structure of programs, as they make it possible to uncouple the algorithms for normal cases from the processing of erroneous cases. But they tend to separate the detection and handling of errors and hence to hinder modular continuity. A disciplined exception mechanism, which does not violate the criterion of modular protection, will be studied in chapter 7.

2.2 FIVE PRINCIPLES

From the above set of criteria, certain principles follow which must be observed to ensure proper modularity. The five principles examined are:

- linguistic modular units
- few interfaces
- small interfaces (weak coupling)
- explicit interfaces
- information hiding

The first principle has to do with notation; the next four all address the essential issue of communication between modules. Obtaining good modular architectures requires that communication occur in a controlled and disciplined way.

2.2.1 Linguistic Modular Units

The principle of linguistic modular units expresses that the formalism used to express designs, programs etc. must support the view of modularity retained:

> Modules must correspond to syntactic units in the language used.

The language mentioned may be a programming language, a program design language, a specification language etc. In the case of programming languages, modules should be separately compilable.

What this precludes is the possibility of having the module structure described from the outside, with no correspondence with the linguistic structure of the program (for example by saying that module X extends from lines 47 to 203 and 542 to 597 of procedure P).

This principle follows from several of the criteria given in the previous section:

• Decomposability: if you want to divide system development into separate tasks, then every one must result in a clearly delimited syntactic unit, and, in the case of program units, they must be separately compilable.

• Composability: how can you combine anything other than closed units?

• Protection: you can only hope to control the scope of errors if modules are syntactically delimited.

The principle removes any hope that good modular policies may be implemented without the appropriate language support. Developers subject to practical external constraints sometimes believe that they can apply advanced modular concepts as a guide to design but still use whatever language is imposed by the environment. This is the often heard phrase "I will design in an Ada-like [or object-oriented, etc.] modular style and then implement in C [or Pascal, or Fortran]". This approach cannot work for significant developments; the gap between ideas and their realization is too broad, as it becomes painfully clear when the time comes for maintenance and evolution.

2.2.2 Few Interfaces

The "few interfaces" principle restricts the overall number of communication channels between modules in a software architecture:

> Every module should communicate with as few others as possible.

Communication may occur between modules in a variety of ways. Modules may call each other (if they are procedures), share data structures etc. The "Few Interfaces" principle limits the number of such connections.

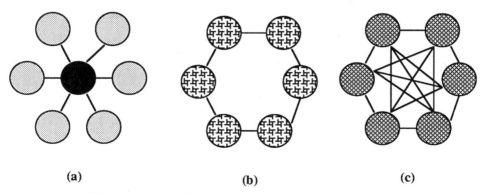

| (a) | (b) | (c) |

Figure 2.7   Types of module interconnection structure

More precisely, if a system is composed of n modules, then the number of intermodule connections should remain much closer to the minimum, $n-1$, shown as (a) on the figure, than to the maximum, $n(n-1)/2$, shown as (c).

This principle follows in particular from the criteria of continuity and protection: if there are too many relations between modules, then the effect of a change or of an error may propagate to a large number of modules. It is also connected to composability (if you want a module to be usable by itself in a new environment, then it should not depend on too many others), understandability and decomposability.

Figure 2.7 (a) shows a way to reach the minimum number of links, $n-1$, through an extremely centralized structure: one "boss", everybody else talks to it and to it only. But there are also much more "libertarian" structures, such as (b) which has about the same number of links. In this scheme, every module just "talks to" its two immediate neighbors, but there is no central authority. Such a style of design is a little surprising at first since it does not conform to the traditional model of functional, top-down design. But it may be used to obtain interesting, robust architectures; this is the kind of structure that object-oriented techniques tend to yield.

2.2.3　Small Interfaces (Weak Coupling)

The "Small Interfaces" or "Weak Coupling" principle relates to the size of intermodule connections rather than to their number:

> If any two modules communicate at all, they should exchange as little information as possible.

Using an expression from electrical engineering, what this principle says is that all channels must be of limited bandwidth. This requirement stems in particular from the criteria of continuity and protection.

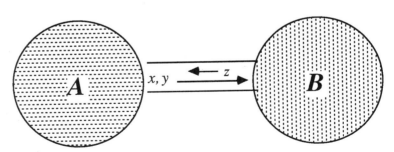

Figure 2.8　Intermodule communication

An extreme counter-example is a Fortran practice which some readers will recognize: the "Garbage Common Block". Programmers who use this technique find it very convenient to put at the beginning of every program unit an identical *COMMON* directive which lists all significant data objects (variables, arrays), so that every unit may directly use every piece of data. The problem is that every unit may also misuse the common data, and hence that units are tightly coupled to each other; the problems of continuity (propagation of changes) and protection (propagation of errors) are particularly nasty.

Nevertheless this time-honored technique remains a favorite of Fortran programmers; program debugging is so much fun...

Programmers in languages with block structure can have their share of the excitement too by just declaring all variables at the topmost level. (Similarly, C programmers may introduce all variables as external.) Block structure, as introduced by Algol, is in fact quite dangerous with respect to the Small Interfaces principle. Any block has access to all the objects belonging to higher level enclosing blocks, including many which are of no interest to it. This introduces the risk of unjustified accesses.

2.2.4   Explicit Interfaces

With the fourth principle, we go one step further in enforcing a totalitarian regime upon the society of modules: not only do we require that everyone talks with few others, and that any such conversation be limited to the exchange of a few words; we also impose that it be held in public and loudly!

> Whenever two modules A and B communicate, this must be obvious from the text of A or B or both.

Behind this principle stand the criteria of decomposability and composability (if a module is to be decomposed into or composed with others, any outside connection should be clearly marked), continuity (what other element might be impacted by a change should be obvious) and understandability (how can one understand A by itself if its behavior is influenced by B in some tricky way?).

One of the problems in applying the Explicit Coupling principle is that there is more to intermodule coupling than procedure call; in particular, data sharing is an important source of indirect coupling.

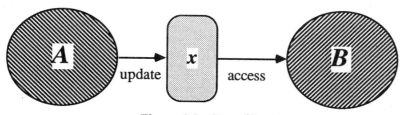

Figure 2.9   Data Sharing

Assume for example that module A modifies and module B uses the same data element x. Then A and B are in fact strongly coupled through x even though there may be no apparent connection, such as procedure call, between them.

2.2.5   Information Hiding

The Information Hiding principle may be stated as follows:

> All information about a module should be private to the module unless it is specifically declared public.

Application of this principle assumes that every module is known to the rest of the world (that is to say, to designers of other modules) through some official description, or **interface**. Of course, the whole text of the module itself (program text, design text) could play the role of interface: by definition, it provides a correct view of the module. However the principle states that this should not in general be the case: the interface should include only some of the module's properties. The rest should remain private.

The fundamental reason behind this principle is the continuity criterion. If a module changes, but only in a way that affects its private elements, not the interface, then other modules who use it, called *client modules*, will not be affected. (The inverse of a client is called a *supplier*.) The smaller the interface, the higher the chances are that changes to the module will indeed be without effect on clients. A module implemented with information hiding may be pictured as an iceberg; only the tip – the interface – is visible.

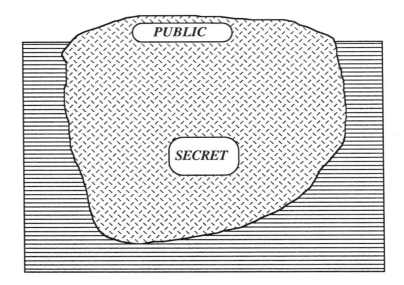

Figure 2.10   Information hiding

Although there is no absolute rule for deciding what should be in the interface and what should be secret, the general idea is clear: the interface should be the description of the module's function or functions; anything that relates to the *implementation* of these functions should be kept private, so as to preserve other modules from later reversals of implementation decisions.

A typical example is a procedure used for retrieving the attributes associated with a key in a certain table, for example a personnel file or the symbol table of a compiler. The procedure will internally be very different depending on how the table is stored (sequential array or file, hash table, binary or B-Tree etc.). Information hiding implies that uses of this procedure should be independent of the particular implementation chosen. Thus user modules will not suffer from any change in implementation.

It should be noted that information hiding does not imply *protection* in the sense of security restrictions – physically restricting client designers from accessing the internal text of the module. Client designers may well be permitted to read all the details they want; but they should be unable to write client modules whose correct functioning depends on private information. Assume for example that table searching is done using binary search trees; if this property is not part of the interface, a module using the table should not be allowed to take advantage of this knowledge.

Information hiding emphasizes the need to separate function from implementation. Apart from continuity, it is also related to the requirements of decomposability, composability and understandability: to separately develop the modules of a system, to combine various existing modules, or to understand individual modules, it is indispensable to know exactly what each of them may and may not expect from the others.

The information hiding principle, a fundamental component of programming methodology, provides guidelines but also raises questions as to how interfaces should be conceived. This issue, set in the context of object-oriented design, is the subject of chapter 9.

2.3   THE OPEN-CLOSED PRINCIPLE

A satisfactory modular decomposition technique must satisfy one more requirement: it should yield modules that are *both* open and closed.

- A module will be said to be open if is still available for extension. For example, it should be possible to add fields to the data structures it contains, or new elements to the set of functions it performs.

- A module will be said to be closed if is available for use by other modules. This assumes that the module has been given a well-defined, stable description (the interface in the sense of information hiding). In the case of a programming language module, a closed module is one that may be compiled and stored in a library, for others to use. In the case of a design or specification module, closing a module simply means having it approved by management, adding it to the project's official repository of accepted software items (often called the project *baseline*), and publishing its interface for the benefit of other module designers.

Consider a simple example at the programming language level. Assume we are dealing with a library handling system, which has a data structure representing publications. The type declaration may be:

```
type PUBLICATION =
    record
            author, title: STRING;
            publication_year: INTEGER
        case pubtype: (book, journal, conference_proceedings) of
            book: (publisher: STRING);
            journal: (editor: STRING);
            conference_proceedings: (editor, place: STRING)
    end
```

(The Pascal-Ada notion of record type with variants is used to describe sets of data structures with some fields common to all instances, and some specific to particular variants. An equivalent construct would be obtained with the union types of C or Algol 68.)

As long as the module is considered open, new fields or new variants may be added to this record type. Closing it implies a decision that the fields and variants given are the only relevant ones.

The two properties – being open and being closed – appear contradictory, but effective software project management requires both. The openness requirement is inescapable, because we seldom grasp all the implications of a subproblem when we start solving it. This means we inevitably overlook important aspects when we write a module, and must be prepared to add new items later on. But closing modules is just as indispensable: we cannot wait until all the information is in to make a module available to others. If we did, no multi-module software would ever be produced, as work on every module would be hanging on the completion of work on the suppliers.

In classical design approaches, the solution is to close modules when it appears that they have reached a reasonable level of stability, and then, when a modification is needed, to reopen them. But if you reopen a module, you must also reopen all its clients to update them, since they rely on the old version.

For example, if you realize later in the project that the library also needs to handle a type of publication not previously considered, like technical reports, with its specific fields, the above declaration must be changed. All client modules must be recompiled; besides, they must probably be changed, as most of them were likely to contain discriminations of the form

```
case p.pubtype of
        book: ... ;
        journal: ...;
        conference_proceedings: ...
    end
```

to which a new case must be added. The problem is by no means confined to this example of data structures with variants; it arises every time a module must be extended by a new function or data element, triggering changes in direct and indirect clients.

This phenomenon is a major source of disarray in software development, and one of the prime reasons why it is so difficult to keep software projects under control. The unattainable dream of any project manager is to be able to close parts of the project for good, and force all project members to keep their hands off the closed parts. But this does not work for the reason mentioned above: one seldom gets the whole picture the first time.

By using software engineering tools called **configuration management systems**, developers may keep track of inter-module dependencies and obtain reports about the state of the project: which modules are up-to-date and which are not. But the configuration management system will only find the modules which must be reopened, and will not by itself carry out the needed modifications. The most it will do is to recompile a module if no modification is needed. In any case, this does not address the real problem, which is the very need to reopen modules that should have been frozen long ago.

With classical approaches to design and programming, there is no way to write modules that are both open and closed. Only with inheritance as offered by the object-oriented method can we solve this apparent dilemma. The techniques will be introduced in chapter 10.

2.4   KEY CONCEPTS INTRODUCED IN THIS CHAPTER

- Modularity is the key to achieving the aims of reusability and extendibility.

- Modular concepts apply to programming as well as to specification and design.

- A comprehensive definition of modularity must take several perspectives; the various requirements may sometimes appear at odds with each other, as with decomposability (which pushes towards top-down methods) and composability (which favors a bottom-up approach).

- Controlling the amount and form of communication between modules is a fundamental step in achieving modular architectures.

- The long-term integrity of modular system structures can only be achieved through information hiding, which enforces a rigorous separation of interface and implementation.

- A closed module is one that may be used, through its interface, by client modules.

- An open module is one that is still subject to extension.

- Effective project management requires support for languages that are both open and closed. But classical approaches to design and programming do not permit this.

2.5   BIBLIOGRAPHICAL NOTES

One design method that emphasizes the importance of modular structures is "structured design" [Yourdon 1979]. The method is based on an analysis of module "cohesion" and "coupling". However the view of modules implicit in the discussion is very much influenced by the traditional notion of subroutine, which limits the scope of the discussion.

The principle of uniform reference is described in [Geschke 1975].

Information hiding was introduced in a milestone article by David Parnas [Parnas 1972].

Configuration management tools that will recompile the modules of a system that are impacted by modifications in other modules, provided the programmer has prepared a list of module dependencies, are based on the ideas of the Make tool available under Unix [Feldman 1979].

EXERCISES

2.1   Modularity in programming languages

Examine the modular structures of any programming language which you know well and assess how, if in any way, they support the criteria and principles developed in this chapter.

2.2   The open-closed principle (for Lisp programmers)

Many Lisp implementations support dynamic binding of names to functions. Does this feature make Lisp more supportive of the open-closed principle (page 23) than more static languages?

2.3   Limits to information hiding

Can you think of circumstances where information hiding should *not* be applied to a module?

2.4   Metrics for modularity (*Term project*)

The five principles of section 2.2 were introduced through qualitative definitions. The four principles that have to do with communication (all but the first) appear amenable to quantitative analysis.

Devise a set of modularity metrics that will make it possible to evaluate the modularity of a software architecture according to these principles. The metrics should be size-independent: increasing the size of a system without changing its modular structure should not change its complexity measures.

Apply the metrics you have developed to existing systems. Can you draw clear correlations between the results of these measurements and intuitive assessment of structural complexity or, if available, data about debugging and modification costs?

3

Approaches to reusability

"Why isn't software more like hardware? Why must every new development start from scratch? There should be catalogs of software modules, as there are catalogs of VLSI devices: when we build a new system, we should be ordering components from these catalogs and combining them, rather than reinventing the wheel every time. We would write less software, and perhaps do a better job at that which we do get to develop. Wouldn't then some of the problems that everybody laments – the high costs, the overruns, the lack of reliability – just go away? Why isn't it so?"

You have probably heard this kind of remark before; perhaps you have uttered them yourself. As early as 1968, in the now famous NATO workshop on the software crisis, D. McIlroy was advocating "mass-produced software components". Reusability, as a dream, is not new.

This chapter discusses some of the progress that must be achieved if this dream is to become reality.

3.1 REPETITION IN PROGRAMMING

Anyone who observes software development cannot but be impressed by its repetitive nature. Over and over again, programmers weave a number of basic patterns: sorting, searching, reading, writing, comparing, traversing, allocating, synchronizing.... Experienced programmers know this feeling of *déjà vu* which is so characteristic of their trade.

3.1.1   A naive question

One good way to assess this situation is to honestly answer the following question –
again assuming you develop software, or direct people who do. Consider the general
problem of table searching: an element of some kind, say x, is given, as well as a set t
of similar elements, and the program should determine whether or not x appears in t.
The question is the following: *How many times over the past six months did you, or
people working for you, write some program fragment for table searching?*

Chances are the answer will be one or more. But what is truly remarkable is that,
most likely, this fragment will have been written at the lowest reasonable level of
abstraction, namely as code in some programming language, rather than by calling
existing routines. Yet table searching is one of the best researched areas of computer
science: excellent books describe the fundamental algorithms, and it would seem that
nobody should need to code a searching algorithm any more, at least in standard cases
– in the same way that electronic engineers do not design standard inverters: they buy
them.

3.1.2   Non-technical obstacles

Why then is reuse not more common?

Some of the obstacles are economical. If, as a contractor, you deliver to your
customers software which is overly general and reusable, you will not be able to get
the next job from them – because they will not need a next job! If reuse is to succeed
on a large scale, incentives must be found to reward companies that develop reusable
products and, within a company, to programmers whose work exhibits good reusability.

There are also serious organizational issues. The best reusable components in the
world are useless if nobody knows they exist, if it takes a long time to obtain them, or
if they cost too much. The practical success of reusability techniques requires the
development of adequate databases of software components, which may be searched by
appropriate keywords so that a potential user will find out quickly whether some
existing component satisfies a particular need. Network services must also be
available, allowing electronic ordering and immediate downloading of selected
components. A price structure must be found to allow users to try out components at a
low price, but reward component manufacturers fairly in case of widespread and
repeated use.

Finally the psychological difficulties should not be underestimated. The "Not
Invented Here" complex is well known. What it means in practice for reusability is
that reusable components should bring a significant advantage over home-brewed ones
in terms of quality, ease of access and cost. A marginal advantage will not be enough
to convince programmers to use somebody else's mousetrap rather than invent their
own.

Efforts to address these issues have been undertaken in the US by the "STARS"
program (*Software Technology for Adaptable, Reliable Systems*), one of whose goals is
to provide library of reusable Ada components, and in Japan by the "software
factories" installed by some large companies.

Important as these questions are in the long term, it is a mistake, in my opinion,
to concentrate on them in the current state of the technology. Organizational solutions

to the reusability problem are only meaningful if you are starting from the appropriate basis. Today, however, the main roadblocks are technical: we simply do not have the appropriate notion of module.

The rest of this chapter shows why common notions of module are not appropriate for large scale reusability. Better module structures are presented in the subsequent chapters.

3.1.3 Change and constancy

The technical difficulties of reusability become apparent if one takes a closer look at the nature of repetition in software development. Such an analysis reveals that although programmers do tend to do the same kinds of things time and time again, these are not *exactly* the same things. If they were, the solution would be easy, at least on paper; but in practice so many details may change as to render moot any simple-minded attempt at capturing the commonality.

> A telling analogy is provided by the works of the Norwegian painter Edvard Munch, the majority of which may be seen in the museum dedicated to him in Oslo. Munch was obsessed with a small number of profound, essential themes: love, anguish, jealously, dance, death.... He drew and painted them endlessly, using the same pattern each time, but continually changing the technical medium, the colors, the emphasis, the size and other details.

Such is the software engineer's plight: time and time again composing a new variation that elaborates on the same basic themes.

Take table searching again. True, the general form of the code is going to look the same each time: start at some position in the table t; then start exploring the table from that position, each time checking whether the element found at the current position is the one that is being sought, and, if not, moving to another position. The process terminates when either the element has been found, or all the interesting positions of the table have been unsuccessfully probed.

```
search (x: ELEMENT, t: TABLE_OF_ELEMENT) return boolean is
        -- Does element x appear in table t?
    pos: POSITION
begin
    pos := INITIAL_POSITION (x, t);
    while not EXHAUSTED (pos, t) and then not FOUND (pos, x, t) do
        pos := NEXT (pos, x, t);
    end;
    return not EXHAUSTED (pos, t)
end -- search
```

Figure 3.1   Pattern for table searching

This paradigm is more or less applicable to all possible cases of data representation (unsorted or sorted array, unsorted or sorted linked list, sequential file, binary tree, B-tree, hash table etc.). It may be expressed more precisely by the following program schema, where elements in capital letters correspond to details that will vary from one instance of the problem to the next.

The problem of coming up with a general software element for searching is apparent here. Even though the pattern is fixed, there remains a considerable amount of variation: what type of table elements you are dealing with (*ELEMENT*), how the initial position is selected (*INITIAL_POSITION*), how you proceed from one position to the next (*NEXT*), and so forth.

Not only is it hard to implement a general-purpose searching module: because of the large amount of variability in searching situations, it is almost as hard to *specify* the module in such a way that clients could rely on it without knowing about its implementation. (Recall that a client of a module is any other module that uses its facilities.)

3.2 SIMPLE APPROACHES

In spite of the above obstacles, it would be unfair to say that no reuse ever occurs in software. Several approaches have been applied with some success.

Source code reusability is common in academic environments. Much of the Unix culture, for example, has spread in universities and laboratories thanks to the on-line availability of the source code, enabling users to study, imitate and extend the system. This is also true of many Lisp environments. It is unlikely, however, that this form of reusability could be widely generalized to more traditional industrial contexts. Beyond the economical and psychological obstacles to source code dissemination, this technique does not support information hiding, an essential requirement for large-scale reuse.

Reusability of personnel is a form of reusability widely practiced in industry: by transferring software engineers from project to project, companies avoid loss of know-how and ensure that previous experience is applied to new developments. However this non-technical approach to reusability is obviously limited in scope, if only because of the high turnover in the data processing professions.

Reusability of designs, rather than implementations, has been advocated. The idea is that a company should accumulate a repository of blueprints describing accepted design structures for the most common applications it develops. For example, a company developing aircraft guidance systems will have a set of model designs summarizing its experience in this area. Such documents describe module patterns rather than actual modules. This does not appear to bring much beyond the just mentioned reuse of know-how and experience. The very notion of designs as independent software products, having their personal lives separate from those of the corresponding implementations, seems dubious: perpetual consistency between design and code, which software engineering textbooks rightly promote as a desirable goal, is notoriously hard to maintain throughout the evolution of a software system. Thus if only the design is reused there is a strong risk of reusing incorrect or obsolete elements. Of course, the picture changes in approaches which eliminate the frontier between design and implementation; more on this later.

Note that all of the above approaches, however limited in their applicability, serve to show important aspects of the reusability problem:

- The notion of source code reusability serves as a reminder that, once everything has been said, software is defined by code. A satisfactory policy for reusability must ultimately produce reusable programs.

- Personnel reusability is necessary if not sufficient. The best reusable components are useless unless programmers are properly trained and have acquired sufficient experience to recognize a situation in which existing components may provide help.

- Design reusability emphasizes the necessity for a reusable component to be of sufficiently high conceptual level and generality − not just a solution to a specific problem. We shall see how the classes of object-oriented languages may be viewed as design modules as well as implementation modules.

3.3　FIVE REQUIREMENTS ON MODULE STRUCTURES

How can we find module structures that will yield appropriate reusable components? The table searching case provides a good example of the stringent requirements imposed on any solution. Look again at the template for a general-purpose searching routine (figure 3.1). This example shows five issues that must be solved before we can hope to produce practically reusable modules.

3.3.1　Variation in types

The searching module should be applicable to different instances of the type *ELEMENT*. You will want to use the same module to search for an integer in a table of integers, an employee record in the corresponding table etc.

3.3.2　Variation in data structures and algorithms

The above scheme is very general and must be adapted to many different data structures and associated search algorithms: sequential tables (sorted or unsorted), arrays, binary search trees, B-trees, files of various structures etc. The primitives *INITIAL_POSITION*, *EXHAUSTED* and *NEXT* are different in each case. How can we account for such variability?

3.3.3　Related routines

To know how to search a table, one must know how the table was created, how elements are inserted, deleted etc.

Thus a searching routine is not enough by itself. It must be coupled with routines for table creation, insertion, deletion etc.

3.3.4   Representation independence

A truly flexible modular structure should enable clients to specify an operation without knowing how it is implemented. For example, it should be possible for a client module to contain a call of the form

  present := search (x, t)

without knowing what kind of table *t* is at the time of the call. If various searching algorithms have been provided, the underlying mechanisms should be able to find the appropriate ones without client intervention.

In its most simple form, this requirement is simply a natural extension of the information hiding principle (2.2.5), essential for smooth development of large systems: implementation decisions will often change, and clients should be protected.

The idea goes further, however. Taken to its full consequences, the principle of representation independence does not just mean that representation changes should be invisible to clients during the *project lifecycle*: clients should also be immune from changes *during execution* – a much smaller time frame! In the above example, we want *search* to adapt itself automatically to the run-time form of table *t*, even if that form has changed since the last call. Only when we reach this stage shall we be able to boast that we have achieved true representation independence.

Why is this requirement so important? The criterion here is not just reusability but extendibility. If *t* may indeed change form at run-time, then somewhere in the system a decision must be taken to use a specific version of *search* among all possible ones. In other words, unless there is an automatic mechanism to make this decision, the code must somewhere contain a control structure of the form

> **if** *t* is of type A **then**
>   "apply searching algorithm A"
> **elsif** *t* is of type B **then**
>   "apply searching algorithm B"
> **elsif** ...
> (etc.)

This decision structure must be either in the module itself or in client code. Neither solution is satisfactory:

- If the decision is in the module, this module must know about all available implementations of tables. Such a policy would lead to huge, unmanageable modules, subject to constant change and revision (the code must be adapted every time a new form of table is brought in).

- Letting the client choose is no better. The client may specify that *t* should be a table of a certain form, but should not be required to say anything more: this information is sufficient to determine which variant of the *search* operation must be used.

The second point is not just a simple matter of programming convenience, but a key aspect of the extendibility issue. If clients must do the discrimination between table forms, it means that every request for the *search* operation (and every *insert*, *delete* etc.) will be expressed by a large conditional instruction of the above form. Any addition of a new form will require updating and recompiling a considerable amount of client code.

This problem is one of the crucial obstacles to extendibility. If, as said in chapter 1, software is not "soft" enough (remember the 42% of software maintenance costs devoted to implementing changes), it is for a large part because too many modules must know about all the possible forms of objects they can manipulate. Typical code is filled with lengthy case analyses of the form

> **if** "t is of form 1" **then**
>   "Appropriate treatment 1"
> **elsif** "t is of form 2" **then**
>   "Appropriate treatment 2"
> **elsif** ...
> (etc.)

Not only is this windy and complex, always a bad sign in software, but also any addition of a new form – a common occurrence indeed during the lifetime of a project – results in a chain reaction of changes, all over the software system. As the process is repeated, the "entropy" of the system (in less pompous terms, its messiness) grows ceaselessly. Every new change is more difficult to achieve.

You are entitled to feel puzzled if you have followed this discussion carefully. We have seen the inadequacy of letting either the supplying module or the clients adapt operations to the current representation. But surely someone must make the decision?

Unfortunately, a solution may not yet be presented. Roughly speaking, we shall strive towards decentralized module architectures, in which various modules, built by successive incrementation and modification, and connected by well-defined relationships, provide rival versions of variable operations such as *search*; a supporting mechanism, known as **dynamic binding**, performs the selection automatically. But this mechanism relies on inheritance, the marvels of which will only be revealed in chapter 10.

3.3.5 Commonality within subgroups

The last item in our list of technical issues in reusability affects the design of reusable modules themselves, not their clients. But this issue is also fundamental because it determines the possibility of writing well-structured collections of modules, without undue repetition. If there is too much repetition among related modules, their conceptual integrity is hard to maintain; configuration management soon becomes an impossible problem, as changes must be carried over to many different elements.

The issue is how module implementors may take advantage of the strong commonality that may exist within a subgroup of the set of possible implementations of a data structure. In the table searching case, a typical example is the subgroup comprising all sequential tables, be they implemented as sequential arrays, linked lists or sequential files. The algorithm may be expressed more precisely in this case than the general form given above. The algorithm is really the same for all sequential implementations; the only remaining differences affect a small set of primitive operations used by the algorithm: starting at first position, advancing to the next position, testing for final positions. The figures below show the general sequential algorithms and some possible implementations of the primitive operations.

```
search (x: ELEMENT, t: SEQUENTIAL_TABLE): boolean is
        -- Does element x appear in table t?
    pos: POSITION
begin
    START_SEARCH; -- Does not depend on x
    while not EXHAUSTED and then not FOUND (pos, x, t) do
        MOVE_TO_NEXT        -- Does not depend on x
    end;
    return not EXHAUSTED
end -- search
```

Figure 3.2   Pattern for sequential table searching

	Sequential Array	Linked List	Sequential File
START_SEARCH	i := 1	l := head	rewind
MOVE_TO_NEXT	i := i+1	l := l.next	readnext
EXHAUSTED	i > size	l = null	end_of_file

Figure 3.3   Implementations variants for primitive operations

The challenge here is to find a way to capture the commonality within this specific group of table searching implementations. Ideally, we should be able to work by marginal increments, giving the overall pattern of all searching implementations at the most general level, then adding the properties of sequential search at the level of the sequential group, and finally filling in the last remaining details for each specific implementation in this group (linked list etc.). We do not want the same code to be repeated over many different modules.

For ease of reference in subsequent discussions, the above five constraints are summarized and given a number in the following table.

1. Variation in types
2. Variation in data structures and algorithms
3. Not just one operation but several related operations
4. Requesting an operation without knowing its implementation
5. Commonality between groups of implementations

Figure 3.4   Issues in devising module structures

3.4   ROUTINES

The classical approach to reusability is to build libraries of routines; the term "routine" is used here to cover what in the literature is also variously called procedure, function, subroutine, subprogram etc. Each routine in such a library implements a well-defined operation.   An area where this approach has been quite successful is scientific computation: excellent routine libraries are commonly used for solving problems in linear algebra, differential equations and other fields.   Decomposition of software systems into routines is also what one obtains through the method of top-down, functional decomposition.

The routine library approach indeed seems to work well in areas where a (possibly large) set of individual problems may be identified, subject to the following limitations.

A.   • Each problem should admit a simple specification, in the sense that every instance of the problem may be defined by a small set of parameters.

B.   • The individual problems should be clearly distinct from each other: the approach does not allow putting to good use any significant commonality that might exist – except by reusing some of the design.

C.   • No complex data structures should be involved: they would be distributed among the routines using them, and the conceptual autonomy of each module would be lost.

The limitations of the routine approach appear clearly if you consider the table searching problem. You have the choice between writing a single routine or a set of routines, each corresponding to a specific case. However the number of possible cases is so great that the overall complexity is going to make actual reuse very difficult in practice:

• In the first solution, the single routine will have a considerable number of arguments and will probably be structured like a gigantic set of **case** instructions; its complexity and inefficiency will in all likelihood make it unusable. Worse yet, the addition of any new case will imply modifying and recompiling the whole routine.

• In the second solution, there will be a large number of routines; many will look very similar (as in the example of sequential arrays and sequential linked lists), but there is no simple way for the implementors to make use of this similarity. Designers and implementors of client modules (called *client programmers* in the sequel) will have to find their way through a maze of routines.

An even more serious limitation of the subroutine approach in this case and many others is that it fails to address issue 3: a searching routine says nothing about table creation, insertion or deletion, which must be covered by different routines. Another way of looking at this deficiency is to note that condition C above is not satisfied: the various routines must act on a common data structure, the table, which is entirely ignored by the design.

3.5   PACKAGES

Modular languages such as Modula-2 and Ada offer a first step towards more appropriate solutions.

These languages have a notion of module (variously called module or package) providing a higher-level program structuring facility than the routine. Such modules – the Ada term *package* will be retained for this discussion – may contain more than one routine together with declarations of types, constants or variables. A package may thus be devoted to a whole data structure and associated operations.

Packages correct some of the most blatant deficiencies of the routine approach by allowing a module to contain a group of related operations, rather than just one; the implementation of the data structure to which the operations apply is also described in the package.

In the searching example, our module will not just be *search* any more but a whole implementation of the table concept and associated operations. An example, describing the implementation of binary search trees of integers, would be a module *INT_BINARY_TREES* containing the following elements:

- A type declaration: the type *intbintree* of binary trees of integers.
- A set of routines: *Create*, *search*, *insert* etc.

Client code may use the type and operations defined in *INT_BIN_TREES* to create and manipulate binary search trees of integers. A notation is needed to allow clients of a module M to reference an element e (type, constant, variable or operation) defined in M. Let us use the notation $M\$e$, imitated from the CLU language. (The Ada notation would be $M.e$.) Client code using binary trees could look like the following:

> x: **integer**; b: **boolean**;
>> -- Declarations of auxiliary variables
>
> t: *INT_BINARY_TREES\$intbintree*;
>> -- Declaration of t as a variable of type *intbintree*,
>> -- defined in module *INT_BINARY_TREES*
>
> *INT_BINARY_TREES\$Create* (t);
>> -- Apply routine *Create*, from *INT_BINARY_TREES*, to t
>
> *INT_BINARY_TREES\$insert* (x, b);
> b := *INT_BINARY_TREES\$search* (x, p)
>> -- Operations from *INT_BINARY_TREES*

Actual languages provide various syntactic facilities to avoid repeating the name of the module, here *INT_BINARY_TREE*, whenever one of its elements is used. (The Ada facilities are described in chapter 18.)

A minor annoyance is the need to invent two kinds of related names, one for the module (here *INT_BINARY_TREES*) and the other for its main data type (*intbintree*). One of the key steps towards object-orientedness will be to actually merge the module and the type. But let's not anticipate.

The package approach makes it possible to gather related elements (types, variables, routines) under one roof. It is consistent with the principle of linguistic modular units (2.2.1). The improvement it brings to encapsulation mechanisms is significant to both module implementors and client programmers:

- The advantage for module implementors is that all program entities that relate to an important conceptual part of the system are at the same place, compiled together. This facilitates maintenance and evolution. In contrast, with separate subroutines there is always a risk of forgetting to update some of the routines when making a change of implementation (such as updating *Create*, *insert* and *search* but forgetting to change *delete*).

- For client programmers, it is easier to find and use a set of facilities if they are all collected in one place.

The details of the package approach will be presented in chapter 18 in the Ada case. From the reusability standpoint, packages address issue 3, the need to tackle more than one operation at a time. They are clearly better than subroutines when there is an important data structure aspect to the problem (see condition C as given on page 35): in this case the data structure is described together with the operations.

Packages do not, however, solve the other reusability issues. Further techniques are needed to make modules more flexible (issues 1 and 2), to free clients from choices of representation (4), and to exploit commonalities within groups of implementations (5).

3.6 OVERLOADING AND GENERICITY

3.6.1 Overloading

A further degree of flexibility is made possible by name overloading, as it exists in Algol 68 or Ada.

Overloading may be defined as the ability to attach more than one meaning to a name appearing in a program.

Names of operations are typical candidates for overloading. For example, if you write several table implementations, each defined by a separate type declaration, overloading allows you to give the same name, say *search*, to all the associated search procedures; in this way, a search operation will always be invoked as $b := search\ (x, t)$ regardless of the implementation chosen for t. This works well in a strictly typed language such as Ada or Algol 68, where the compiler has enough type information about x and t to choose the appropriate version of *search*.

This is a facility for client programmers: they may use the same name when requesting different implementations of a given operation.

3.6.2 Genericity

A companion technique is genericity as provided in Ada or CLU.

Genericity is the ability to define parameterized modules. Such a module, called a *generic* module, is not directly usable; rather, it is a module pattern. In the most common case, the parameters (called **formal generic parameters**) stand for types. Actual modules, called **instances** of the generic module, are obtained by providing actual types (**actual generic parameters**) for each of the formal generic parameters.

A typical generic module is

BINARY_TREES [*T*]

where the formal generic parameter *T* represents the type of the binary tree elements. Thus instead of a number of very similar modules, one for each kind of element type – module *INT_BINARY_TREES*, module *REAL_BINARY_TREES* etc. – you can now have a single generic *BINARY_TREE* [*T*] module. As mentioned, this is more accurately described as a module pattern; actual modules are obtained by providing actual generic parameters, for example:

BINARY_TREES [*INTEGER*]
BINARY_TREES [*REAL*]

The declaration of the generic module will resemble that of *INT_BINARY_TREES* above, with the difference that *T* will be used instead of *INTEGER* . For example:

type *intbintree* =
    record
       info: T;
       left, right: intbintree
    end;

search (*x* : *T* , *t* : *intbintree*) **return boolean is**
       -- Does element *x* appear in binary tree *t* ?
    begin
       ... *Implementation of search* ...
    end

-- etc.

This technique is a definite advance in flexibility as it allows the writing of parameterized modules that may be adapted to various types.

3.6.3   An assessment of genericity and overloading

Overloading and genericity provide symmetric possibilities:

   • Overloading is a facility for *client programmers*: it makes it possible to write the *same client code* when using *different implementations* of a data structure, as provided by different modules.

   • Genericity is for *module implementors*: it allows them to write the *same module code* to describe all instances of the *same implementation* of a data structure, applied to various types of objects.

What do these techniques bring us in terms of reusability? Genericity is a solution to issue 1 (accounting for various types). Overloading appears to be an attack on 2, (accounting for variations in data structures and algorithms), and 4 (enabling clients to request an operation without knowing its implementation). On closer look, however, the result is disappointing.

First, we have not made any progress towards solving issue 5: capturing fine grains of commonality between groups of implementations of the same general data structure. Overloading does not help; neither does genericity, as it provides only two levels of modules:

- Generic modules, which are parameterized, and thus open to variation, but not usable directly.

- Module instances, usable directly but no longer open to refinement.

Thus we cannot describe a complex hierarchy of representations, with different levels of parameterization.

The techniques also suffer from another major limitation. Neither allows a client to use various implementations of a data structure (say the table) without the client programmer knowing which implementation is used in each instance:

- A generic module, as pointed out, is usable by clients not directly, but through its instances. These instances have lost all flexibility, since the formal generic parameters have been filled in by actual types.

- Overloading, on the other hand, is no more than a syntactic facility which relieves programmers from having to invent different names for different implementations of an operation and, in essence, places that burden on the compiler. But this does not solve issues 2 and 4. Each invocation of an overloaded operation name – say *search* (x, t) – refers to just one version of the operation; the client programmer who writes the invocation knows exactly (as does the compiler which analyzes it) which version is being invoked.

Note that client programmers do not actually need to know *how* each version is implemented, since in most languages with generic packages (such as Ada) modules may be used through an interface describing the available routines independently of their implementation. But they do need to decide explicitly in each case *which* version is used. In other words, if your modules use various kinds of tables, you do not need to know how to implement binary trees, indexed sequential files and the like, but you must say which one of these representations you want each time you use a table operation.

To achieve true representation-independence, we need to be able to write an invocation such as *search* (x, t) and mean: "look for x in t, using the appropriate algorithm for **whatever kind of table** t **happens to be at the time the invocation is executed**". To reach this degree of flexibility, essential for the construction of reusable software elements, we must turn to object-oriented design.

3.7   KEY CONCEPTS INTRODUCED IN THIS CHAPTER

- Programming is a highly repetitive activity, involving frequent use of common patterns. However there is considerable variation in the way these patterns are used and combined, defeating simplistic attempts to develop programs from off-the-shelf components.

- Putting reusability into practice raises economical, psychological and organizational problems. The last in particular are serious as databases of reusable modules must be made available in a convenient way. Even more important, however, are the underlying technical problems: commonly accepted notions of module are simply not adequate to support serious reusability. These technical problems must be solved before organizational solutions become of any use.

• Simple approaches, like source code reusability, reusability of personnel, reusability of designs and subroutine libraries have experienced some degree of success in specific contexts. They all fall short, however, of providing a basis for a systematic attack on the reusability problem.

• Packages provide a better encapsulation technique than routines, as they collect together a data structure and the associated operations.

• Two techniques extend the flexibility of packages: overloading, or the reuse of the same name for more than one operation; genericity, or the availability of modules parameterized by types.

• Neither genericity nor overloading solves all the issues of reusability. Overloading is essentially a syntactic facility; genericity only addresses type parameterization.

• What is needed is techniques for capturing commonalities within groups of related data structure implementations, and techniques for isolating clients from internal module representations.

3.8   BIBLIOGRAPHICAL NOTES

The first published discussion of reusability in programming was probably McIlroy's 1968 paper cited at the beginning of this chapter, republished as [McIlroy 1976].

A special issue of the IEEE *Transactions on Software Engineering* [Biggerstaff 1984] contains a number of interesting articles examining reusability from different viewpoints. See in particular, from this issue, [Horowitz 1984], [Jones 1984], [Curry 1984], [Standish 1984] and [Goguen 1984]. [Wegner 1984] provides a good complement.

Another approach to reusability, based on concepts from artificial intelligence, is embodied in the MIT Programmer's Apprentice project [Waters 1985]. Rather than actual reusable modules, this system uses patterns (called *clichés* and *plans*) representing common program design strategies.

The STARS project of the US Department of Defense emphasizes reusability, with emphasis on the organizational aspects of the problem, and use of Ada as the language for software components. A number of contributions on this approach may be found in the proceedings of the 1985 STARS DoD-Industry conference [NSIA 1985].

The argument for waiting until execution-time to choose the appropriate variant of an operation, based on the form of the object to which it applies (see 3.3.4), may be found in [Cox 1986].

4

The road to
object-orientedness

We have studied the aims that modular design methods should strive to attain. This chapter shows how, by reversing the traditional focus of software design, one may get more flexible architectures, furthering the goals of reusability and extendibility.

4.1 PROCESS AND DATA

A software system is a set of mechanisms for performing certain actions on certain data.

When laying out the architecture of a system, the software designer is confronted with a fundamental choice: should the structure be based on the actions or on the data? In the answer to this question lies the difference between traditional design methods and the object-oriented approach.

> Hybrid approaches might be advocated, since in the end both data and actions play a part in the structure of a program. The question of most importance, however, is what to use as the primary criterion when describing the highest level decomposition structures. This question may not be easily evaded: the designer must choose.

The discussion will use interchangeably the words "function", "action" or "process" when considering the first approach, and similarly "data" or "objects" when considering the second.

As the quick-witted reader may have guessed, the rest of this discussion will advocate the second approach: basing system structure on data structure. Arguments for this approach will now be stated – positive arguments, as well as negative ones showing why traditional, function-based methods are unsatisfactory.

4.2 FUNCTIONS, DATA AND CONTINUITY

Perhaps the key element in answering the question "should we structure around functions or around data?" is the problem of extendibility and more precisely, the principle called *continuity* in chapter 2. Recall that continuity is satisfied by a design method if it yields architectures that will not need to be changed abruptly for every small change in the system requirements.

Continuity is a long-term concern. If you just view the software construction process as starting with requirements definition and ending with the first operational system release, then continuity is perhaps not so important (although change is an inescapable feature of even this restricted process). But continuity becomes crucial if you consider the full life-cycle, extending over the evolution and adaptation phase.

Any successful system inevitably undergoes numerous changes over its lifetime. To consider the software lifecycle only up to the first delivery of a more or less working version is to neglect the whole afterlife of change and revision that follows. This is as remote from real life as those novels which stop when the hero marries the heroine − in reality, the time when the really interesting part begins.

To evaluate the quality of an architecture (and the method that produced it), we should not just consider how easily this architecture is initially obtained: it is just as important, and perhaps more, to ascertain how well the architecture will weather the process of change. Here objects have a decisive edge over functions.

In the evolution of a system, the functions performed tend to be the most volatile part. A successful system will soon be asked to perform new tasks. For example, a payroll program that was initially used to produce paychecks from time cards will, after a while, be extended to gather statistics, produce tax information, maintain a repository of employee data etc.; its initial function may be modified (to produce, say, monthly rather than bi-weekly checks) and often will in the end be just one among many services rendered by the system. Taking examples from other fields: A nuclear code that initially just applied some numerical algorithm to produce tables of numbers from batch input will be extended to handle graphical input and output or maintain a database of previous results. A compiler that initially just translated correct source into object code will after a while be used also as a syntax verifier, static analyzer, prettyprinter etc.

Often, in such cases, the change process is incremental. The new requirements evolve from the initial ones in a continuous way. The new system is still, in many respects, the same as the old one; it is still − in the examples mentioned − a payroll system, a nuclear code, a compiler.

If the architecture is overly based on the functions, it seems impossible to ensure that system evolution will be as smooth as the evolution of requirements, as required by the criterion of continuity.

But now consider the data. A payroll program, throughout its diverse avatars, will always more or less manipulate the same sorts of data: employee records, company and social security regulations (or rather computer representations thereof), tax information etc. A compiler will always manipulate source text, lexical tokens, syntax trees, object code and the like.

These remarks are evidence of a common phenomenon. As a system evolves, its tasks may change dramatically. Much more persistency may be found in the classes of data it manipulates, *at least if viewed from a sufficient level of abstraction* (more on this qualification later). This is the key argument for using them, rather than the tasks, as the principal guide for system structuring.

4.3   THE TOP-DOWN FUNCTIONAL APPROACH

Before we bring in more direct arguments for data-based design, it is interesting to examine the traditional approach more closely. Classical design methods typically use the functions, not the objects, as the basis. The best-known method is top-down functional design. Let us look at what it is and how it addresses the concerns of reusability and extendibility.

4.3.1   The top-down method

The top-down method is based on the idea that software should be based on stepwise refinement of the system's abstract function. The process is started by expressing a topmost statement of this function, such as

(C0) *Translate a C program to Motorola 68030 code*

or

(P0) *Process a user command*

and continued by a sequence of steps. Each step must decrease the level of abstraction of the elements obtained; it consists in decomposing every statement obtained into a combination of one or more simpler statements. For example, the next step in the first example could produce the decomposition

(C'1)

>   *Read program and produce sequence of tokens;*
>   *Parse sequence of tokens into abstract syntax tree;*
>   *Decorate tree with semantic information;*
>   *Generate code from decorated tree*

or, using an alternative structure:

(C"1)

>   **while** *not all function definitions processed* **do**
>   *read in next function definition;*
>   *generate partial code*
>   **end;**
>   *Fill in cross references*

(A C program is a sequence of function definitions.)

In either case, the elements obtained ("Read program ...", "not all function definitions processed" etc.) must be repeatedly expanded until all remaining elements are at a level of abstraction low enough to allow direct implementation in the programming language at hand.

The process of top-down refinement may be described as the development of a tree. Nodes of the tree represent elements of the decomposition; branches show the relation "*B* is part of the refinement of *A* ". More precise representations could be devised to also show the control structures involved in various instances of this relation (like sequencing in the first decomposition above and **while** loop in the second).

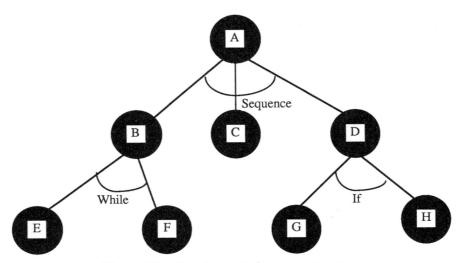

Figure 4.1   Top-down design: tree structure

A strong case may be made in favor of the top-down approach. It is a logical, well-organized thought discipline, encouraging orderly development of systems and helping the designer find a way through the apparent complexity that characterizes the initial stages of system design.

But top-down design suffers from several flaws.

• The method fails to take into account the evolutionary nature of software systems.

• The very notion of a system being characterized by one function is questionable.

• Using the function as basis often means that the data structure aspect is neglected.

• Working top-down does not promote reusability.

The next sections examine these deficiencies in turn.

4.3.2   Functions and evolution

The main trouble with top-down functional design is continuity. As discussed above, functions are not the most stable part of a system. Yet top-down design takes the functional decomposition as the key criterion of the structure. This is trading short-term convenience – a fairly easily obtained initial structure – for long-term disaster: as the system changes, the designers are faced with the prospect of constant redesign.

Consider the example of a program that has two versions, a "batch" one in which every problem is handled in a single big run, and an interactive one in which a session is a sequence of transactions, with a much finer grain of user-system communication. This is typical of large scientific programs, which often have a "let it run a big chunk of computation for the whole night" version and a "let me try out a few things and see the results at once" version.

The top-down refinement of the batch version might begin like the following.

(B0) [Top-level abstraction]

> *Solve a complete instance of the problem*

(B1) [First refinement]
> *Read input values*;
> *Compute results*;
> *Output results*

and so on. The top-down development of the interactive version would go somewhat like this:

(I1)

> *Process one transaction*

(I2)

> **if** *new information provided by the user* **then**
> > *Input information*;
> > *Store it*
> **elsif** *request for information previously given* **then**
> > *Retrieve requested information*;
> > *Output it*
> **elsif** *request for result* **then**
> > **if** *necessary information available* **then**
> > > *Retrieve requested result*;
> > > *Output it*
> > **else**
> > > *Ask for confirmation of the request*;
> > > **if** *yes* **then**
> > > > *Obtain required information*;
> > > > *Compute requested result*;
> > > > *Output result*
> > > **end**
> > **end**
> **else** ... (etc.)

It is clear that top-down development will yield two entirely different structures. The method fails to capture that these are but two different versions of the same program – either developed concurrently, or one evolving from the other.

This example brings to light two of the most dangerous consequences of the top-down approach: its focus on the external interface (implying here an early choice between batch and interactive) and its premature binding of temporal relations (the order in which actions will be executed).

The focus on interfaces is inevitable in a method that asks "What will the system do for me?" as the key question. Answers tend to emphasize the most external aspects. In a large software system, the interface is only one of the components. It tends to be the most volatile, if only because it is difficult to design the interface right the first time: experimentation with prototypes or initial versions of the actual system is almost always required. Initial versions of the interface, as obtained during preliminary design, may be grossly off the mark. Thus healthy design methods will attempt, as much as possible, to separate the interface from the rest of the system, and to use deeper properties as a guide to system structuring. System architecture should be based on substance, not form. But top-down development tends to use the most superficial aspect of the system as a basis for its structure.

The other flaw evidenced here is the premature emphasis on temporal relations. In a functional decomposition, each refinement expands a piece of the abstract structure into more detailed control architecture. Recall the two alternative candidate structures for the first refinement of a compiler:

(C'1)

> *Read program and produce sequence of tokens*;
> *Parse sequence of tokens into abstract syntax tree*;
> *Decorate tree with semantic information*;
> *Generate code from decorated tree*

(C"1)

> **while** *not all functions have been processed* **do**
> > *read in next function*;
> > *generate partial code*
>
> **end**;
> *Fill in cross references*

Here again, two completely different architectures are obtained right from the beginning. Each is defined by a control structure (a sequence of operations in the first case, a loop followed by an operation in the second case), implying strict ordering constraints between the elements of the structure. But freezing such ordering relations at the earliest stages of system design is not reasonable. Issues such as the number of passes in a compiler and the sequencing of various activities (lexical analysis, parsing etc.) may be resolved in many ways; solutions result from space-time tradeoffs and other criteria which are not necessarily under control at the beginning of a project. Much fruitful design and implementation work may be done on the individual components before their temporal relationships are frozen. It is vital to retain as much flexibility as possible, with respect to sequencing constraints, for as long as possible. Top-down functional design does not grant such flexibility.

It should be noted that many design methods that attempt to correct some of the deficiencies of functional top-down design also suffer from this premature binding of temporal relationships. For example, the dataflow-directed methods of Yourdon and DeMarco use the flow of information through a system as the primary structuring criterion. The order in which various things happen to a piece of data is thus considered essential.

In contrast, object-oriented design adopts a more neutral attitude towards ordering: the designer lists the various operations that are applicable to a certain kind of data, and specifies precisely the effect of each operation, but defers for as long as possible the specification of the order in which these operations may be applied. This is what may be called the **shopping list** approach: list needed operations, but not their ordering constraints. The result is much more flexible architectures.

4.3.3 Not just one function

Top-down methods assume that every system may be properly described, at the most abstract level, by its main function. Although textbook examples of algorithmic problems – the Tower of Hanoi, the Eight Queens and the like – are easily characterized by a functional "top", practical software systems are more appropriately described as offering a number of services. Defining these systems by single functions is usually possible, but yields rather artificial answers.

Take an operating system. It is best viewed as a system that offers a number of services – allocating CPU time, managing memory, handling input-output devices, interpreting user's commands etc. A well-organized operating system will be more or less built in modules centered around these groups of functions. But top-down functional decomposition does not naturally yield such an architecture. It forces you, the designer, to first answer the artificial question "what is the topmost function?", and to use the successive refinements of the answer as a basis for the structure. Under torture, you would probably come up with an answer, for example

"Process all user requests"

which could be refined into something like

    while *not crashed* **do**
        read in a user's request and put it into input queue;
        get a request r from input queue;
        process r;
        put result into output queue;
        get a result o from output queue;
        output o to its recipient
    end

One can go on from here. It is highly unlikely, however, that a reasonably structured operating system may ever be developed in such a fashion. This is true of many practical systems. **Real systems have no top.**

Even those types of system that seem to belong to the "one input, one abstract function, one output" category, such as a compiler or a typesetting system, show a more flexible structure on closer examination. The compiler example was mentioned above. To view a typesetting program as just a mechanism for producing typesetter code from input texts is to miss the set of functions that such a tool offers, and the object classes it manipulates (documents, chapters, sections, paragraphs, lines, words, characters, fonts, running heads, titles, figures etc.)

To obtain realistic system structures, and ones that will weather the test of change, we must find a less superficial way of characterizing software than "the" main function.

4.3.4   The data structure aspect

Functional decomposition neglects the data structures of the program. Every data structure must be attached to one or (usually) more functions. In problems which have a strong data component, the influence of the data structure is lost on the program structure.

Table searching, discussed in the previous chapter, is a typical example. Organizing the design around operations such as search, insert, create etc. misses the unifying factor, here the table data structure. The description of this structure will be scattered among the functions that use it.

It is natural to note that, since functions and data play a complementary role in software, the inverse solution – attaching functions to data – carries a symmetric risk: yielding structures in which the importance of functions would not be properly accounted for. As will be seen, however, functions can be given their proper place a data-centered architecture through the use of abstract data types as the basis for modularization.

4.3.5   Reusability

Working top-down means that software elements are developed in response to particular subspecifications encountered in the tree-like development of a system. At a given point of the development, corresponding to the refinement of a certain node, the need for a specific function – say analyzing an input command line – is detected, and the corresponding program element is developed.

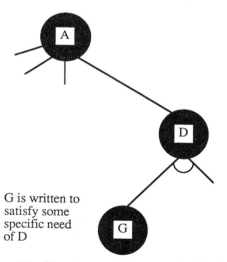

Figure 4.2   Top-down design: graph structure

This approach is good at ensuring that the design will meet the initial specification, but it does not promote reusability. Elements tend to be narrowly adapted to the subproblem that led to their development; they are not naturally general. For example if the need for a command line analyzer was encountered in a precise context, it is unlikely that the result will be usable for analyzing command lines with a different structure.

Of course, top-down design does not in itself force the components to be specific and non-reusable. Designers may always write elements that transcend the particular need which led to their development. In fact, the structure obtained in a top-down design is not constrained to be a pure tree: it can be a more general directed graph, with some elements shared by several refinements.

However such reusable elements are not a natural result of the method. The very notion of top-down design is essentially the contrary of reusability; reusable software implies that systems are developed, to all the extent possible, by combination of existing components, which is the definition of bottom-up design.

4.3.6 An assessment

This discussion of top-down functional design shows this method to be poorly adapted to the development of significant software systems. Top-down design remains a useful paradigm for small programs and individual algorithms; it is certainly a helpful technique to teach in introductory programming courses, enabling students to approach a problem in an orderly way. But it does not scale up to sizable practical systems. The point is *not* that you cannot develop a system top-down: you can. But in doing so you trade short-term convenience for long-term inflexibility, you unduly privilege one function over the others and (often) the interface over the deeper features of the system, you lose sight of the data aspect, and you sacrifice reusability.

4.4 WHY USE THE DATA?

The case for using data (objects) as the key to system modularization is based on some of the quality aims defined in chapter 1: compatibility, reusability, extendibility. In reviewing these aims, many of the arguments that have been made against top-down function-based design reappear as arguments for data-based, bottom-up design.

- **Compatibility** is a significant incentive to use data as the criterion for decomposition. It is difficult to combine actions if the data structures they access are not taken into consideration. Why not instead try to combine entire data structures?

- **Reusability** also suggests arguments. For any application involving non-trivial data structures, it is difficult to build reusable components if they embody actions alone and ignore the data part. The example of table searching is a case in point.

- Finally, we have seen that **continuity** provides the most convincing argument: over time, data structures, at least if viewed at a sufficient level of abstraction, are the really stable aspect of a system.

4.5 OBJECT-ORIENTED DESIGN

4.5.1 A first definition

We have by now accumulated enough background to consider a first definition of object-oriented design.

> **Definition 1**: Object-oriented design is the method which leads to software architectures based on the objects every system or subsystem manipulates (rather than ''the'' function it is meant to ensure).

This is only a broad definition, and it will be refined into a more technical one below. It suffices to characterize the basic property of object-oriented design, whose motto could be expressed as

> *Ask not first what the system does:*
> *Ask WHAT it does it to!*

What a system is supposed to do is of course an important question; to get a working implementation, this question must be answered sooner or later. Better later than sooner, says object-oriented wisdom.

Using object-oriented design, the designers will stay away, as long as possible, from the (ultimately inescapable) need to describe and implement the topmost function of the system. Instead, they will analyze the classes of objects of the system. System design will be based on successive improvements of their understanding of these object classes.

For many programmers, this change in viewpoint is as much of a shock as may have been for some people, in another time, the idea of the earth orbiting around the sun rather than the reverse. It is also contrary to most of the established software engineering wisdom, which tends to present system construction as the fulfillment of a system "function" expressed in a narrow, binding requirements document. Yet this simple idea – look at the data first, forget the immediate purpose of the system – holds the key to reusability and extendibility.

4.5.2 Issues

The above definition provides a general guideline for designing software the object-oriented way. It also raises a number of issues:

- How to find the objects.
- How to describe the objects.
- How to describe the relations and commonalities between objects.

- How to use objects to structure programs.

The rest of this chapter takes a first look at these issues, which are treated in more detail in the following chapters.

4.6 FINDING THE OBJECTS

Newcomers to the object-oriented method often ask how the objects are to be found.

We have not equipped ourselves yet with the necessary mechanisms for a proper answer to this question (not even, in fact, for a proper formulation, which involves *classes* rather than objects). But we may take a first look at it by noting that the answer is, in some practical cases, surprisingly simple.

To understand why, it is useful to take a candid view at what computer programming is about. We use software to obtain answers to certain questions about the outside world (as in a computation designed to solve a problem), to interact with the world (as in a process control system), or to create new world entities (as in a text processing system or a compiler). In every case, the software must be based on some description of the aspects of the world that are relevant to the application, whether physical laws (in a scientific program), salary structures (in a payroll system), income tax regulations, language syntax and semantics (in a compiler) etc.

Thus a well-organized software system may be viewed as an **operational model** of some aspect of the world. Operational because it is used to generate practical results and sometimes to feed these results back into the world; model because any useful system must be based on a certain interpretation of some world phenomenon.

When software design is understood as operational modeling, object-oriented design is a natural approach: the world being modeled is made of objects – sensors, devices, airplanes, employees, paychecks, tax returns – and it is appropriate to organize the model around computer representations of these objects. This is why object-oriented designers usually do not spend their time in academic discussions of methods to find the objects: in the physical or abstract reality being modeled, the objects are just there for the picking! The software objects will simply reflect these external objects.

Nowhere perhaps is this view of software as inescapable as in the area of **simulation**. Thus it is no accident that since Simula 67 simulation has been one of the choice application domains of object-oriented techniques. It seems hard to devise a better structure for simulation programs than one which is directly patterned after the objects whose behavior is being simulated. Simula 67, itself a general-purpose programming language although it includes primitives for discrete-event simulation (20.1), evolved from the earlier language Simula 1 which was specifically devoted to simulation.

There is more to say about finding the classes than this discussion implies (see further remarks in 14.2). But the above simple remarks are often remarkably fruitful: just use as your first software objects representations of the obvious external objects.

4.7   DESCRIBING OBJECTS: ABSTRACT DATA TYPES

4.7.1   Classes

Once you have settled on the kind of objects that your system decomposition is going
to use, the next question is how these objects should be described.

First, when talking about systems being organized around data structures, we are
clearly more interested in *classes* of data structures than in individual objects. The item
of interest in system structuring is not an individual syntax tree, or employee
descriptor, etc., but the class of all syntax trees or employee descriptors.

"Class" is indeed the technical term that will be applied in object-oriented
languages to describe such sets of data structures characterized by common properties.
(Sometimes confusions are made between classes and objects. The difference is the
same as that between a set of items, say the set of all caterpillars, and one element of
the set, as a given caterpillar.)

4.7.2   Implementation variations

How do we characterize a class of objects? We could use some representation. A stack,
for example, is commonly represented by an array and an integer variable whose value
indicates the stack top. A stack operation such as pushing an element onto the top is
represented by instructions as shown on the figure.

last := last+1
space [last] := x

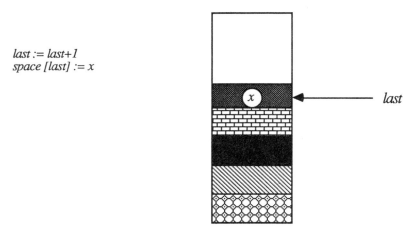

Figure 4.3   Array representation of a stack

Such a way of describing objects is, however, inadequate for our purposes. We
are concerned about flexibility and continuity; yet physical representations are among
the decisions that get changed the most in the evolution of a system. Recall the results
of Lientz and Swanson (section 1.3, figure 1.2): 17.4% of maintenance costs was
found to come from the need to take into account changes of data formats. As was
noted in the commentary to this result, common programs are already too dependent on
the physical structure of the data they manipulate. A design method using the physical
data structure to produce the system architecture would not be likely to yield flexible

software. In fact, we are probably better off with top-down functional design which, at least, encourages abstraction.

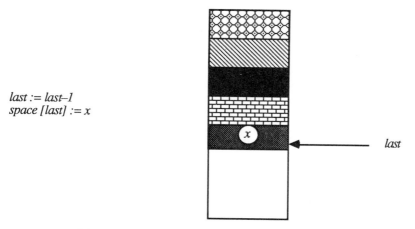

last := last–1
space [last] := x

Figure 4.4   An array stack growing down

An example of the variations in data structures is provided by the stack case. For some reason, systems programmers tend to have their stacks grow down than up; the code fragments for operations such as *push* will be different. Yet another representation uses linked structures; here the code for *push* (shown in Pascal notation) bears almost no apparent relation to the original form.

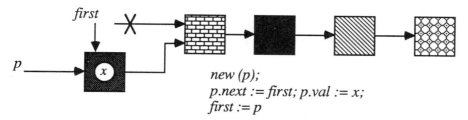

new (p);
p.next := first; p.val := x;
first := p

Figure 4.5   Stack in linked representation

4.7.3   Abstract data types

We are faced with a dilemma. We would like to have complete, precise, unambiguous descriptions of (classes of) data structures; yet we do not want a description based on the physical representation, although it satisfies these criteria: using the representation is too binding and does not allow for later evolution. In other words, it leads to *overspecification*.

How do we retain completeness, precision and non-ambiguity without paying the price of overspecification? The answer is in the theory of abstract data types. Roughly speaking, an abstract data type specification describes a class of data structures not by an implementation, but by the list of *services* available on the data structures, and the formal *properties* of these services. (The words "operations" and "features" will also be used instead of "services".)

A stack, for example, will be seen as a structure on which available services are push a new element, pop the top element, access the top element, test whether the stack is empty etc.; these services should observe the last-in-first-out policy that characterizes stack behavior. A bank account may be opened or closed, money may be deposited to or withdrawn from it etc., with associated properties (exercise 4.2).

A data structure is thus viewed as a set of services offered to the outside world. Using abstract data type descriptions, we do not care (we refuse to care) about what a data structure *is*; what matters is what it *has* – what it can offer to other software elements. This is a utilitarian view, but the only one consistent with the constraints of large scale software development: to preserve each module's integrity in an environment of constant change, every system component must mind its own business. It must only access others' data structures on the basis of their advertized properties, not the implementation that may have been chosen at a certain point of system evolution. This, of course, is in line with the principle of information hiding (2.2.5).

In summary, an abstract data type is a class of data structures described by an external view: available services and properties of these services. The next section gives a more formal definition of this notion.

4.7.4   Formally specifying abstract data types

Below is the complete formal specification of an abstract data type, *STACK*. (The stack example has been used over and over again to the point of becoming a cliché, but since this is because it is excellent, there is no reason to have any second thoughts about using it once more.)

The specification is shown below (figure 4.6). It consists of four parts: types, functions, preconditions and axioms. The first two may be said to express the syntax of the type (its structural properties), the last two its semantics.

4.7.5   The TYPES paragraph

The TYPES paragraph lists the types of the specification. In general, it may be convenient to specify several abstract data types together, although in this example there is only one, *STACK*.

This particular type is introduced as *STACK* [*X*]. This means it is a **generic** abstract data type, having a dummy parameter, *X*, which represents an arbitrary type. Genericity, which has already been encountered in the context of program packages (3.6.2), is used here for an obvious purpose: rather than writing separate but almost identical specifications for stacks of integers, stacks of lexical tokens, stacks of employee records etc., the specification should capture the common properties in a parameterized type. Actual stack types are obtained by providing a type for *X*, as in *STACK* [*INTEGER*] etc.

The rest of the specification describes the properties of such a stack type, viewed as a set of objects (individual stacks), called instances of the type.

TYPES

    STACK [*X*]

FUNCTIONS

    empty: STACK [*X*] $\rightarrow$ *BOOLEAN*

    new: $\rightarrow$ *STACK* [*X*]

    push: X × *STACK* [*X*] $\rightarrow$ *STACK* [*X*]

    pop: STACK [*X*] $\nrightarrow$ *STACK* [*X*]

    top: STACK [*X*] $\nrightarrow$ *X*

PRECONDITIONS

    pre *pop* (*s: STACK* [*X*]) = (**not** *empty* (*s*))

    pre *top* (*s: STACK* [*X*]) = (**not** *empty* (*s*))

AXIOMS

    For all *x: X, s: STACK* [*X*]:

    empty (*new* ())

    not *empty* (*push* (*x, s*))

    top (*push* (*x, s*)) = *x*

    pop (*push* (*x, s*)) = *s*

Figure 4.6   Stacks as an abstract data type

4.7.6 The FUNCTIONS paragraph

The FUNCTIONS paragraph lists the services available on instances of the type. These services are specified as mathematical functions, here *empty*, *new*, *push*, *pop* and *top*.

Each line in this paragraph gives the signature of a function, that is to say the types of its arguments and results. A function *f* with signature

$$A_1 \times A_2 \times \ldots \times A_m \rightarrow B_1 \times B_2 \times \ldots \times B_n$$

takes *m* arguments, of respective types A_1, ..., A_m, and yields *n* results, of respective types B_1, ..., B_n. At least one of the A_i or B_j must be the abstract data type being specified, here *STACK* [*X*]. In practice, all functions considered will have one result set only (*n* = 1). A crossed arrow ($\nrightarrow$) denotes a partial function (see below).

An abstract data type specification is a mathematical description. The notion of command in the programming sense (an action that may modify the objects to which it applies, such as an assignment) is foreign to mathematics. In actual implementations, a stack operation like *push* will usually work by side-effect, modifying its target object. But side-effects do not exist in mathematics. The corresponding mathematical concept is that of a function, which takes one or more arguments and returns one or more results. The cosine function, for example, does not change a number *r* into its cosine, but simply yields a result from *r*, written *cos* (*r*).

Similarly, services such as *push* are mathematically modeled as functions:

push: $X \times STACK\ [X]\ \longrightarrow\ STACK\ [X]$

That is to say, *push* is viewed as a function that will accept two arguments, an X and a stack, and yield a result which is a new stack. Informally, the result is identical to the input stack with one more element on top. If s is a stack and x an X, then the resulting stack is written *push* (x, s).

At the implementation stage, we seldom want to follow such a specification to the letter; this would imply making a complete copy of the stack for every *push* operation (and similarly for *pop*). The functional specification is appropriate, however, as an abstract description of the operations, allowing the specifier to benefit from the well-established features of mathematical specifications; this is necessary in particular to express the properties of the abstract data type simply and rigorously (through the axioms of the type, discussed below). Side-effects may be introduced at the design or implementation stage.

Other functions and their signatures are the following. Function

empty: $STACK\ [X]\ \longrightarrow\ BOOLEAN$

returns a boolean result expressing whether its argument, a stack, is empty or not. Functions *pop* and *top* describe access to the top stack element and removal of this element:

pop: $STACK\ [X]\ \nrightarrow\ STACK\ [X]$
top: $STACK\ [X]\ \nrightarrow\ X$

which, alternatively, could be defined as a single function with two results. Creation of a new empty stack is expressed by the function

new: $\longrightarrow\ STACK\ [X]$

which takes no argument and hence always returns the same result, denoted *new* ().

4.7.7 Categories of functions and partial functions

The functions in the definition of an abstract data type T are classified into three categories:

- A function for which T only appears on the right of the arrow yields new elements of the type (possibly from elements of other types if the left-hand side is not empty). It is called a **constructor** function. Here the only constructor is *new*.

- Functions for which T appears only on the left of the arrow yield attributes of existing elements of the type, expressed as values belonging to other types. They are called **accessor** functions. Here the accessors are *empty* and *top*.

- Finally, if T appears both on the left and on the right, the function yields new elements of the type from previous elements (and possibly other arguments). It is a **transformer** function. The transformers here are *push* and *pop*.

Also note that functions *pop* and *top* are introduced not with a normal arrow $\longrightarrow$ but with a crossed arrow $\nrightarrow$. This means they are **partial** functions, not necessarily defined for every *STACK* object. Indeed, a stack may not be popped, and its top element does not exist, if the stack is empty.

4.7.8   The PRECONDITIONS paragraph

Partial functions are an inescapable fact of programming life (not every operation may be applied to any object) but also a potential source of errors. It is essential to express clearly the requirements on the use of any partial function. This is the aim of the preconditions paragraph, which for every partial function states the condition for its applicability. Here:

1.   **pre** *pop* (*s: STACK* [*X*]) = (**not** *empty* (*s*))
2.   **pre** *top* (*s: STACK* [*X*]) = (**not** *empty* (*s*))

meaning: the precondition that may be satisfied for *pop* to be applicable to a stack *s* is the right-hand side of the first line, namely that *s* be non-empty – and similarly for *top* .

4.7.9   The AXIOMS paragraph

The specification given so far applies to more than just stacks. Any data structure with similar available services would be described by functions with the same signatures: a queue, a priority list etc. To restrict the specification to stacks, we must add semantic properties. This is the role of the axioms.

The first two axioms express the properties of the *empty* function:

For all *x: X, s: STACK* [*X*]:

1.   *empty* (*new* ())
2.   **not** *empty* (*push* (*x, s*))

In other words, a new stack is empty, and any stack obtained by pushing an element *x* onto an existing stack *s* , empty or not, is non-empty.

The last two axioms express the basic last-in-first-out property of stacks:

3.   *top* (*push* (*x, s*)) = *x*
4.   *pop* (*push* (*x, s*)) = *s*

In other words: let *s'* = *push* (*s, x*) be the stack obtained by pushing element *x* onto stack *s* . Then *top* (*s'*) is *x*, the last element pushed, and *pop* (*s'*) is identical to *s* . Or, in a more operational phrasing: pushing an element onto a stack and popping the result yields back the initial stack.

4.7.10   Nothing but the truth

The power of abstract data type specifications comes from their ability to capture the essential properties of data structures without overspecifying. The above stack specification expresses all there is to know about the notion of stack in general, excluding anything that only applies to some particular representations of stacks. In short: the whole truth about stacks, yet nothing but the truth.

This provides a general model of computation with data structures. Complex sequences of operations may be described by mathematical expressions enjoying the usual properties of algebra; the process of carrying out the computation (executing the program) may be viewed as a case of algebraic simplification. In the same way that ordinary laws of trigonometry allow us to find a simplified form for, say, *cos* (2∗*x*), the stack axioms make it possible to simplify an expression such as

> *x* = *top* (*pop* (*push* (*x1*, *pop* (*push* (*x2*, *push*
> (*top* (*pop* (*push* (*x4*, *push* (*x5*, *new* ( ))))),
> *pop* (*push* (*x6*, *push* (*x7*, *push* (*x8*, *new* ( )))))))))))

which is perhaps more clearly understood by using auxiliary expressions:

> *s1* = *new* ( )
> *s2* = (*push* (*x6*, *push* (*x7*, *push* (*x8*, *s2*))))
> *s3* = *pop* (*s2*)
> *s4* = *new* ( )
> *s5* = *push* (*x4*, *push* (*x5*, *s4*))
> *s6* = *pop* (*s5*)
> *y1* = *top* (*s6*)
> *s7* = *push* (*y1*, *s3*)
> *s8* = *push* (*x2*, *s7*)
> *s9* = *pop* (*s8*)
> *s10* = *push* (*x1*, *s9*)
> *s11* = *pop* (*s10*)
> *x* = *top* (*s11*)

The computation described by this expression is easy to follow: create a new stack; push elements *x8*, *x7*, *x6*, in this order, on top of it; remove the last pushed element (*x6*), calling *s3* the resulting stack; create another empty stack; and so on. It is easy to see, by drawing pictures along the way, what the result will be. But the theory yields this result formally without any need for pictures: by applying axioms, successive simplifications may be performed formally. For example, axiom 3 indicates that *s3* = *push* (*x7*, *push* (*x8*, *s2*)), and so on. Successive simplifications, carried out as simply and mechanically as in elementary arithmetic, yield the result (find it!).

These aspects of abstract data types have made them the basis for much of the work in formal specification, symbolic computation, program verification and software prototyping. For the present discussion, abstract data types provide an invaluable answer to the issue of data structure descriptions. In object-oriented design, every module is organized around a class of data structures; to avoid implementation dependencies, the underlying description should be that of an abstract data type.

One particularly satisfying property of this approach is that it reintroduces the **functions** of software systems in a balanced way. As noted at the outset of this chapter, functions and data play an equally important role in software. One of the main criticisms directed at function-based decomposition techniques was that they overlook half of the picture – the data aspect. We have already mentioned a risk with data-based architectures: might they not suffer from the symmetric deficiency – neglecting the functions? With abstract data types, this concern disappears: true, system structure is based on data structure; but the data structure itself is defined *in terms of the abstract functions*. Thus the loop is closed: we have all the elements for a harmonious decomposition technique, guided by the data, but assigning functions their proper place.

4.8   A PRECISE DEFINITION

We are now in a position to provide a more technical definition of object-oriented design. The initial definition (page 50) was "software architectures based on the objects every system manipulates". The following definition expands this notion:

Definition 2: Object-oriented design is the construction of software systems as structured collections of abstract data type implementations.

In an object-oriented architecture, every module will be built on a data abstraction, that is to say on a set of data structures described by the services that are part of its official interface, and the properties of these services.

Note how well these ideas blend with the principle of information hiding. If a module is built on one data abstraction, its interface (the tip of the iceberg) will correspond exactly to the services representing the functions of the abstract data type specification. The interface of a stack module, offering a coherent view of stacks to the rest of the world, will include services *push*, *pop*, *top* and *empty*. The module may contain other auxiliary operations, used internally for implementation purposes; they should not be part of the interface.

As announced earlier, the modules of object-oriented systems are called **classes**. According to the above definition, a class is an abstract data type implementation, *not* the abstract data type itself. This is inevitable for a method targeted to actual design and implementation rather than just specification. For example, the side-effect-free functions of the specification (*push* and the like) may be represented in the class, for efficiency reasons, by procedures working by side-effect.

We shall see, however, that object-oriented techniques allow for classes that cover more than one implementation of an abstract data type. Such classes are called **deferred classes** and will be introduced in chapter 10. The Eiffel language used in the following chapters grants designers flexibility as to the level of abstraction of the classes they write. It is possible to write classes general enough to be very close indeed to a bona fide abstract data type specification.

Another important word in the definition is *collection*. It reflects how classes should be designed: as units which are interesting and useful on their own, independently of the systems to which they belong. Such classes may then be reused in many different systems. System construction is viewed as the bottom-up assembly of existing classes, not as a top-down process starting from scratch.

Finally, the word *structured* reflects the existence of important relationships between classes. Specifically, two relations are noteworthy: *client* and *descendant*.

- A class is a client of another when it makes use of the other class's services, as defined in the interface. For example, a stack implementation could rely on an array for its implementation and thus be a client of the *ARRAY* class.

- A class is a descendant of one or more other ones when it is designed as an extension or specialization of these classes. This is the powerful notion of (multiple) *inheritance*.

Both of these relations will be discussed in much more detail in the following chapters.

4.8.1 Classes and reusability

Since reusability is one of our main concerns, the abstract data type specifications, and the classes that implement them, should be as general and robust as possible. They will indeed provide the reusable software components that are so essential to the object-oriented approach.

One repository of robust and reusable components, the **Eiffel basic library**, will be discussed in the following chapters.

4.9   SEVEN STEPS TOWARDS OBJECT-BASED HAPPINESS

The above definition is used as the basis for the study of object-oriented techniques in this book. Because the term "object-oriented" has been used to describe various techniques – even Ada has been claimed to be an object-oriented language! – it is useful to distinguish the various steps that lead to true object-orientedness. Needless to say, only systems that reach the last step are, in my opinion, worthy of the name.

The first level corresponds to the basic remark that data should provide the fundamental structuring criterion:

> **Level 1** (*Object-based modular structure*): Systems are modularized on the basis of their data structures.

The next step is where abstract data types join the fun:

> **Level 2** (*Data abstraction*): Objects should be described as implementations of abstract data types.

Most current programming languages make it possible to reach this level. Ada and Modula-2 are obvious examples. But even Fortran may be used in this way. On the other hand, languages which do not provide any such possibility are Pascal, Cobol and Basic. More details on the adaptability of classical languages to object-oriented concepts are given in chapters 17 to 19.

The third step is of a less conceptual nature, but reflects an important implementation concern: how objects are created. Programmers should not need to take care of how memory space is reclaimed when the objects that occupy it become useless.

> **Level 3** (*Automatic memory management*): Unused objects should be deallocated by the underlying language system, without programmer intervention.

Here most of our language friends leave us; although this is in a strict sense a property of language systems rather than languages, the language design may help or hinder the implementation of a garbage collector. Pascal and Modula-2 systems do not normally include garbage collection; it is an optional feature in Ada systems. On the other hand, all Lisp systems provide garbage collection, which is part of the reason why Lisp has often been used to implement object-based languages (chapter 20).

The next step is the one which, in our opinion, truly distinguishes object-based languages from the rest of the world. It may be understood by looking at languages which are not object-oriented even though they provide facilities for data abstraction and encapsulation, such as Ada or Modula-2. In such languages, the module is a purely syntactic construct, used to group logically related program elements; but it is not itself a meaningful program element, such as a type, a variable or a procedure, with its own semantic denotation. In contrast, true object-oriented programming all but identifies the notion of module with the notion of **type**. One may say that the defining equation of such languages is the identity

$$module \ = \ type.$$

This fusion of two apparently distinct notions is what gives object-based design its distinctive flavor, so disconcerting to programmers used to more classical approaches. In its dogmatism, it has some drawbacks. But it also gives considerable conceptual integrity to the general approach. We will have more to say, in the following chapter, on the remarkable consequences of this identification.

> **Level 4** (*Classes*): Every non-simple type is a module, and every high-level module is a type.

The qualifier "non-simple" makes it possible to keep predefined types (such as *INTEGER* etc.) which are not viewed as modules; the word "high-level" permits program structuring units such as procedures which are not types.

A language construct combining the module and type aspects is called a **class**.

The next step is a natural consequence from the previous one: if types are identified with modules, then it is tempting to identify the reusability mechanisms provided by both concepts:

- On the one hand, the possibility for a module to directly rely on entities defined in another.

- On the other hand, the concept of subtype, whereby a new type may be defined by adding new properties to an existing type (as a Pascal integer range, whose elements are integers subject to some restrictions).

In object-based languages, this is known as the inheritance mechanism, with which a new class may be declared as an extension or restriction of a previously defined one. Its realization in Eiffel is described in chapters 10 and 11.

> **Level 5** (*Inheritance*): A class may be defined as an extension or restriction of another.

We shall say in such a case that the new class is *heir* to the other.

The above techniques open the possibility of *polymorphism*, whereby a given program entity may refer at run-time to instances of different classes, and *dynamic binding*, whereby the run-time system will automatically select the version of an operation adapted to the corresponding instance. The consequences of this technique, studied in detail in chapter 10, are far-reaching for the construction of robust, extendible systems.

> **Level 6** (*Polymorphism and dynamic binding*): Program entities should be permitted to refer to objects of more than one class, and operations should be permitted to have different realizations in different classes.

This notion may be implemented in different ways. In the design of Eiffel, it is reconciled with the notion of static typing: every Eiffel entity has a static type (class) and the dynamic types it may take are restricted to the descendants of that class. Dynamic binding is implemented in Eiffel by permitting the *redefinition* of a class operation in a descendant, and by having *deferred* operations whose implementation is only given in the descendants.

The next and last step extends the notion of inheritance to enable reuse of more than one context. This is the notion of multiple inheritance.

> **Level 7** (*Multiple and repeated inheritance*): It should be possible to declare a class as heir to more than one class, and more than once to the same class.

If you didn't completely understand the last few levels, do not panic: this list is just a preview of things to come.

4.10   KEY CONCEPTS INTRODUCED IN THIS CHAPTER

- System architecture may be obtained from the functions or from the data.

- Data provide better stability over time.

- Top-down functional design is appropriate for producing an initial version of a software system, but not for the long-term view of continuous change and adaptation.

- Object-oriented design bases the structure of systems on the classes of objects they manipulate.

- In object-oriented design, the primary design issue is not what the system does, but what objects it does it to. The design process defers to the last steps the decision as to what is the topmost function of the system (if any).

- To satisfy the requirements of extendibility and reusability, the data descriptions on which object-oriented software structures are built should be sufficiently abstract. The answer is provided by the theory of abstract data types, reconciling completeness of specifications with the need not to overspecify.

- Abstract data types may be generic and are defined by functions, preconditions and axioms. The preconditions and axioms express the semantics of a type and are essential to a full, unambiguous description.

- An abstract data type specification is a formal, mathematical description. It is side-effect-free.

- Object-oriented systems are built as collections of classes. Every class represents a particular abstract data type implementation, or a group of implementations. Classes should be designed to be as general and reusable as possible; the process of combining them into systems is often bottom-up.

- A class offers a number of services. However no constraints are imposed on the order in which these services may be requested by clients (users) of the class. A class is like a "shopping list" of available services, with no temporal dependencies.

- Classes are connected by two important relations: *client* and *descendant* (inheritance).

- Several levels of object-orientedness may be defined. Of particular importance is level 4, the identification of the concepts of module and type, and level 5, inheritance.

4.11   BIBLIOGRAPHICAL NOTES

The case for object-based decomposition is made, using various arguments, in [Booch 1983, 1986], [Cox 1986] and [Meyer 1978, 1979, 1982, 1987].

The top-down method was introduced by [Wirth 1971] and has been advocated in many books and articles.

Design methods whose rationales start with some of the same arguments that have led us to the exposition of object-oriented concepts, but diverge after a while, include

Jackson's "JSD" [Jackson 1983], a higher-level extension of "JSP" [Jackson 1975]; Warnier's data-directed design method [Orr 1977]; structured design [Yourdon 1979]; structured analysis [DeMarco 1978] [McMenamin 1984] [Page-Jones 1980]; Merise [Tardieu 1984] [Tabourier 1986].

Abstract data types were introduced by Liskov and Zilles [Liskov 1974]; a more algebraic approach was given by [Guttag 1977]. See also [Meyer 1976].

EXERCISES

4.1 Boxers

The members of the ADT Boxing League regularly compete in matches to ascertain their comparative strength. A match is played between two boxers and results in a winner and loser, or is declared a tie. If not a tie, the outcome of a match is used to update the ranking of players in the league: the winner is declared better than the loser and than any boxer b such that the loser was previously better than b. Other comparative rankings are left unchanged.

Specify this problem as a set of abstract data types: *ADT_LEAGUE*, *BOXER*, *MATCH*. (**Hint**: do not introduce the notion of "ranking" explicitly, but model it by a function *better* expressing whether a player is better than another in the league.)

4.2 Bank accounts

Reference was made page 54 to a "bank account" abstract data type. Write a formal specification of this type.

4.3 More stack operations

Modify the abstract data type specification of stacks to account for operations *nb_elements* (returning the number of elements on a stack) *change_top* (replacing the top of the stack by a given element) and *wipe_out* (remove all elements). Include the appropriate axioms.

4.4 Queues and stacks

Describe queues (first-in, first-out) as an abstract data type, in the style used for *STACK*. Examine closely the similarities and differences. Can you conceive and formally specify a more general abstract data type that covers both stack and queue structures?

4.5 Text

Consider the notion of text, as handled by a text editor. Specify this notion as an abstract data type.

PART 2

Techniques of

object-oriented

design and programming

5

Basic elements of Eiffel programming

By now, you have seen the reasons why a better modular design method is needed: reusability and extendibility. You have been shown the limitations of the traditional approaches: lack of flexibility, overly centralized architectures. You have been exposed to some of the theory behind the object-oriented approach: abstract data types. You have heard enough about the issues. Now for the solutions!

In this chapter and the rest of part 2, the techniques of object-oriented design and programming will be introduced, using as a basis the Eiffel language.

We begin by examining the basic constituents of an object-oriented language: objects, classes, references, entities. These are the nuts and bolts of the object-oriented approach. In contrast with the previous discussions, which tackled high-level design issues, we will for a while remain at the implementation level, because we need a clear, solid basis on which to establish the more advanced concepts of the following chapters.

5.1 OBJECTS

Object-oriented programming is, first, what the name implies: writing programs that deal with objects. Throughout the rest of this book, the first question we shall ask whenever we are confronted with the requirements for a software system is: "What objects does it deal with?"

This question is really two-sided. On the one hand, it is about the objects of the physical reality our systems are dealing with: in a graphics system, points, lines, angles, surfaces, solids etc; in a payroll processing system, employees, pay checks, salary scales, and so on. On the other hand, the software does not directly deal with these but with appropriate computer representations, which may also be called objects. Whenever there is a need to distinguish, one may talk about *external* and *internal* objects.

The object-oriented approach uses objects in both senses: at the design stage, the goal is to spell out the classes of external objects whose behavior the system will attempt to model; at the implementation stage, object-oriented languages ensure that systems are written as collections of internal object descriptions, rather than procedures.

In this chapter, we look at the internal objects. We shall first treat them just as records, as they would exist in classical programming languages. Then we shall see how a set of objects with a common behavior may be described by a powerful abstraction − a class.

5.1.1 Records

At an elementary level, internal objects are simply like records as may exist during the execution of a Pascal or C program. (The C term is "structure".) Like a record, an object is a structure occupying some memory space during system execution, and made of a certain number of constituents, called **fields**. The object pictured below has three fields: two integers and a string.

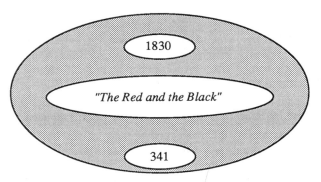

Figure 5.1 Simple object

The external object of which this is a partial model could be a book, with its title, number of pages and date of publication.

5.1.2 References

It is often convenient to introduce internal objects (called just objects from now on) which, beyond the simple fields shown above (numbers, characters etc.), include fields that refer to other objects. For example, an object representing a book should probably include information relative to the author. The author himself, or any other person, is also represented by an object, with fields representing first and last names, birth and death year etc.

One technique is to allow objects to contain other objects, as pictured below.

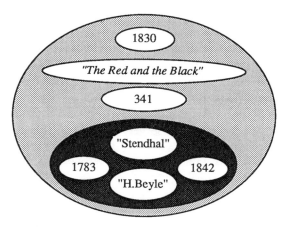

Figure 5.2   An object within an object

This technique is indeed possible with Pascal or C records, which may contain other records. But it does not permit **sharing**. Sharing is necessary when fields of different objects must refer to the same object – as opposed to distinct but identical objects. In the case of two books written by the same author, for example, the author fields of the corresponding objects should probably refer to the same author object. The reason is not only economy of space but also semantic integrity: if something in the author object changes (for example the death-year field, to record the death of an author), this change should be simultaneously reflected in all the corresponding book objects.

To allow for shared objects, fields may contain **references** to other objects. A reference may have an object as its value; two or more references may share the same object as their value. The following figure shows an example.

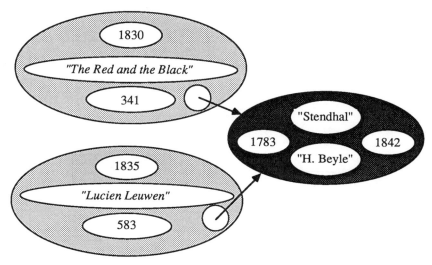

Figure 5.3   References and shared object

This technique is particularly useful for representing complex data structures such as lists, trees, queues etc. in "linked" representation. In Eiffel, all object fields are either simple (integer, boolean, character, real) or references. So an object can reference other objects (figure 5.3) but cannot contain another object (as in figure 5.2).

It was said above that a reference "may" have an object as its value. The other possibility is for a reference not to be associated with any object; if this is the case, the reference will be said to be **void**.

The notion of reference is of course very close to the concept of pointer; a void reference is similar to a null pointer. The two notions are kept separate to emphasize that references are associated with objects, whereas pointers are often seen as plain machine addresses, although typed languages such as Pascal have carefully restricted the scope of pointer manipulations.

Note that "void" is not a special *value* for references, but one of their two possible *states*. A reference is either associated with an object or void. A special void value as it exists in some languages (**nil** in Pascal, *NULL* in C) is a bizarre value which must belong to all pointer types at once.

5.1.3 Execution model

From what we have seen so far a first picture emerges, that of an object-oriented system during its execution. The system is made of a certain number of objects, with various fields, some of which may be references. Unless these references are all void, the objects refer to each other.

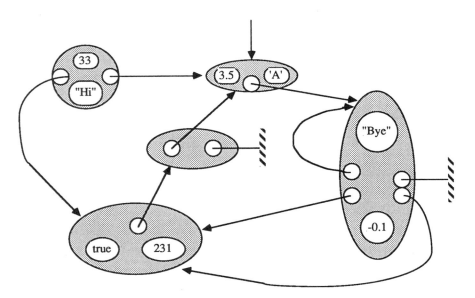

Figure 5.4 Execution model

5.1.4 Dynamic creation

What the above discussion does not show is the highly dynamic nature of a true object-oriented model. As opposed to programming in static or block-structured languages (exemplified respectively by Fortran and Algol), programming in an object-oriented language consists in dynamically creating a number of objects, according to a pattern which is usually impossible to predict at compile time. Operations performed on objects result in new objects being created, references being changed to refer to new objects or becoming void etc.

In Eiffel, execution of a system starts with the creation of an initial object, called the **root** of the system. From then on execution of the system will add new objects.

During the evolution of the system, it may well be that some objects become inaccessible, directly as well as indirectly, from the root. In figure 5.4, for example, assume the root is the object at the top right (marked by the incoming arrow): then the object containing the string "*Hi*" cannot be reached. Such objects needlessly use up memory. In implementations of object-oriented languages, where systems may create large numbers of objects and then stop using them, a fundamental problem is to reclaim the space which becomes thus wasted. This problem and the solution used in the Eiffel implementation are the subject of chapter 16.

Note that a generalization of the object-oriented paradigm to account for parallel processing gives rise to systems with more than one root.

5.2   A FIRST VIEW OF CLASSES

So we have a rough idea of what a system looks like at any stage during its execution. Now we come to the program texts that will give rise to such execution-time patterns.

5.2.1 Classes with attributes

How does one describe objects? The key is given by the abstract data type approach. Rather than describing individual objects, you should concentrate on the patterns that are common to a whole class of objects – the class of books, of authors, of points, of solids etc. As was mentioned in the previous chapter, "class" is indeed the recognized name used to describe such patterns, which are the basis of object-oriented programs.

At this stage of the discussion, a class is similar to a record type in Pascal: it describes the common structure of a group of objects. A simple class definition could be:

```
class BOOK1 feature
    title: STRING;
    publication_date: INTEGER;
    number_of_pages: INTEGER
end -- class BOOK1
```

This class describes the structure of a (potentially infinite) set of objects. All such objects will be called **instances** of the class. (Note the convention for comments, borrowed from Ada: a comment begins with two consecutive dashes -- and extends to the end of the line. The ending comment repeating the name of the class is standard coding style.)

There are no other objects than class instances: any object is an instance of some class C. C is said to be the **type** of the object.

It is important to bear in mind the distinction between objects and classes: objects are run-time elements that will be created during a system's execution; classes are a purely static description of a set of possible objects – the instances of the class. At run-time, we only have objects; in the program, we only see classes.

The **feature...** clause introduces the features of a class. The features given in this example are all **attributes**; an attribute is a component of a class that will give a field in each object of the class. (We shall soon encounter other kinds of features.)

Thus all instances of class *BOOK1* will have exactly three fields: a string field and two integer fields. Again, do not confuse the attribute (relative to the class) and the field (relative to an object):

A field in an object corresponds to an attribute in the class of which the object is an instance.

5.2.2   Types and references

Eiffel is a statically typed language: every attribute must be declared with a unique type.

The attributes of class *BOOK1* were all declared of predefined types: *INTEGER* and *STRING*. (The case of strings is special; see below.) The next step is to add attributes of class types, which represent references.

Assume there is a simple notion of person:

```
class PERSON1 feature
      first_name, last_name: STRING;
      birth_year, death_year: INTEGER;
      married: BOOLEAN
  end -- class PERSON1
```

(Note how attributes of the same type may be grouped in declarations.) Then you may want to allow a book object to include a reference to its author. This is done by simply introducing a new attribute whose type is precisely *PERSON1*:

> **class** *BOOK2* **feature**
>   *title: STRING*;
>   *publication_date, number_of_pages: INTEGER*;
>   *author: PERSON1*
> **end** -- class *BOOK2*

The Eiffel type system is quite simple (although inheritance will make it more interesting). There are two kinds of types: the four simple types, namely *INTEGER, BOOLEAN, CHARACTER* and *REAL*; any other type must be defined by a class declaration and will be called a class type.

Consider an attribute whose type is a class type. Since we do not allow objects within objects, the object fields corresponding to that attribute contain references. This explains why the language does not include a symbol meaning "reference to": when we declare *author* to be of type *PERSON 1*, we mean "reference to objects of type *PERSON1*", but there is no ambiguity since *PERSON1* is not a simple type.

Note that the above sentence stating that all the attributes of *BOOK1* are of simple types was a small lie: in contrast with *CHARACTER*, whose elements are single characters, the Eiffel type *STRING*, whose elements are character strings, is in fact a predefined class type. However for many purposes it may be treated like the simple types. Details in chapters 8 and 13.

5.3   USING CLASSES

By now you have seen how to define very simple classes. We study next how these classes may be used.

5.3.1   Clients and suppliers

There are two ways to use a class; one (inheritance) will be introduced in chapter 10; the other has already been applied in the introduction of attribute *author* and may be defined as follows:

> **Definition:** (*Clients and suppliers*): A class *A* is said to be a **client** of a class *B* , and *B* a **supplier** of class *A* , whenever *A* contains an entity declaration of the form *e: B*.

We also say that *B* **sells to** *A*, or that *A* **buys from** *B* (with apologies for this rather mercantile but convenient terminology).

The term "entity" which appears in this definition covers the object-oriented equivalent of what is known in classical approaches as a variable. So far we have seen only one kind of entity: attributes. Others will be introduced below; the full list is given in 5.4.5.

As an example of the client relation, *BOOK2* from the previous example is a client of *PERSON1* because *BOOK2* contains an attribute declaration

   author: PERSON1

A class may be its own client; for example, a simplified "bank customer" class might be of the form

   class *BANK_CUSTOMER* **feature**
       name: STRING;
       guarantor: BANK_CUSTOMER
   end

The figure below shows an instance of this class. Note that it represents a bank customer that is her own guarantor. The presence of such a cycle among instances does not necessary follow from the presence of a self-supplying class: think of a class *PERSON2* with an attribute *parent* of type *PERSON2*; clearly, the graph for the *parent* links cannot contain any cycle. (It is true, however, that an instance graph containing one or more objects from a self-supplying class must contain either a cycle or a void reference.)

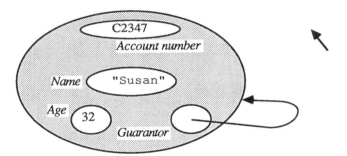

Figure 5.5   Self-reference

5.3.2   Creating objects

Assume that X is a client of *BOOK2*. For example X contains an attribute, say b, of type *BOOK2*. Then all instances of X will include a field corresponding to b; because b has been declared of a class type, these fields contain references. Any of these references may, at any time during execution, either be void or refer to an object of type *BOOK2*.

The general rule is that, unless you do something to it, a reference remains void. To change this, you must create a new object of the appropriate class type and associate it with the reference. This operation will bring the reference from the void state to its other possible state, which is called the **created** state. A reference is associated with an object if and only if it is in the created state.

The simplest operation that creates an object and associates it with a reference is written *b.Create*

Its effect, as shown by the figure below, is to create an object of the appropriate type, here assumed to be *BOOK2*, and to associate it with the reference corresponding to *b*.

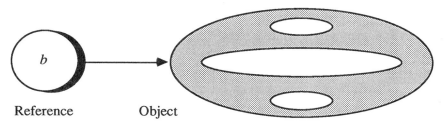

Reference   Object

Figure 5.6   Creating an object and associating it with a reference

5.3.3   Dissociating a reference from an object

It may sometimes be necessary to dissociate a reference in the created state from the associated object. This is done with another operation, written as follows:

b.Forget

Forget puts the reference back in the void state. You may think of it as an operation that cuts the link between the reference and any associated object. (More on *Forget* below.)

5.3.4   States of a reference

From the presentation of *Create* and *Forget*, the following picture emerges: a reference may be either in the void or in the created state; *Create* and *Forget* are two operations that make it possible to alternate between these two states. Others will be seen later.

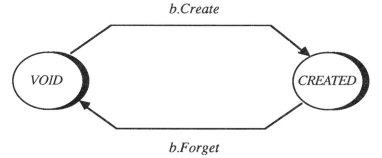

b.Create

b.Forget

Figure 5.7   States of a reference

To know the state of the reference associated with b, one may use the test $b.Void$, which returns **true** if and only if the reference is void.

The notions of object, reference and entity should not be confused:

• "Object" is a run-time notion; any object is an instance of a certain class, created at execution time and made of a number of fields.

• "Reference" is also a run-time notion: a reference is a value that either is void or denotes an object.

• In contrast, an entity has no run-time existence: an entity is simply a name (identifier) appearing in the text of a class, representing one or more references that may exist at execution time.

5.3.5 *Forget* and storage management

The *Forget* operation is sometimes misunderstood. It is an operation on the reference, **not** on the object with which the reference was associated; the operation simply suppresses the association, making the reference void again; for example, if b is the reference of figure 5.6, executing $b.Forget$ simply cuts the link between b and the object. A *Forget* operation does not affect the object itself, which may still be accessible through other references. (If the reference was void before the *Forget* operation, the operation has no effect.)

In particular, *Forget* has nothing to do with the instructions used to return space to the operating system, such as the *dispose* procedure in Pascal or *free* in C. The presence of such possibilities is one of the most dangerous aspects of these languages, as there is no guarantee that a memory cell thus reclaimed by the system is not, in fact, still accessible from other objects. Besides, the obligation to take care of memory management within application programs complicates programming by a considerable factor. In Eiffel, as in other serious object-oriented systems, memory management is automatic (although programmers may superimpose their own object management in reusable classes). These questions are discussed in more detail in chapter 16.

5.3.6 Initialization

An object creation as entailed by $b.Create$ must put some value in the fields of the object. It would not be reasonable to let the fields keep whatever values happen to be there in the corresponding memory cells. A well-defined initialization convention is thus required. (The need for initialization also has a theoretical origin, the notion of class invariant, which will be seen in chapter 7.)

The rule in Eiffel is simple: fields are initialized according to the type of the corresponding attributes, as follows:

Type	Initial value
INTEGER	0
BOOLEAN	false
CHARACTER	null character
REAL	0.0
Class types	void reference

Figure 5.8   Entity initialization by type

Unlike the initializations performed in some language systems, these rules are prescribed by the language and must be supported by all implementations; they are not implementation-dependent.

Section 5.4.7 below will explain how these default initializations may be overridden if they are not deemed appropriate for a particular class.

5.3.7   Why Create?

It is clear from the previous discussion that object creation in Eiffel is explicit. Declaring an entity, say

   b: BOOK2

does not result in an object being created at run-time: an object will only be created when some element of the system executes an operation

   b.Create

You may have wondered why this was so. Couldn't the declaration suffice to have an object created at run-time? What good is it to declare an entity if you do not create an object?

A moment's reflection, however, should convince you that the distinction between declaration and creation is actually the only reasonable solution.

As a simple argument, consider that all we are dealing with is objects. Assume that somehow we start processing the declaration of *b* and immediately create the corresponding book object. But this object is an instance of a class, *BOOK2*, which has an attribute *author* itself of class type *PERSON1*. So the book object itself has a reference field, for which we must create an object right away. Now this object itself may have reference fields which require the same treatment: we are starting on an infinite loop before we have even begun any real processing.

The actual solution is just the opposite. Objects are only created as a result of the execution of *Create* instructions (or *Clone* instructions, seen below). Furthermore, the reference fields of a newly created object are themselves initialized to void references and, in turn, will only become associated with objects through explicit *Create* operations.

5.3.8   Accessing fields; the current instance

One of the distinctive features of the object-oriented approach is that every program construct refers to some object. In contrast to classical programming, you never write a program fragment that just says "do this"; anything you write is of the form "do this *to that object*". This aspect of object-oriented programming, although sometimes difficult to grasp initially, is essential to the consistency of the approach.

How do you recognize the object to which a piece of Eiffel text applies? To answer this question, you must first note that any Eiffel text is part of a class: there is no higher-level construct in Eiffel than the class, so whatever you write is in some class. Furthermore, it is in just **one** class: classes may not be nested.

Now a class, as we have seen, describes a data type. Instances of that data type, at execution time, will be objects. The class text presents the features that are common to all such instances. It does so by actually describing a typical instance of the class, also called the **current instance**.

This gives a partial answer to the previous question: all notations in a class apply to the current instance. For example, any occurrence of *author* in class *BOOK2* means, if it is not further qualified, "the *author* field relative to the current book object". Or, within class *PERSON1*, an assignment

   birth_year := 1833

means "enter the value *1833* into the *birth_year* field of the current instance of *PERSON1*".

Often, of course, it is necessary to refer to other objects. The corresponding Eiffel notation is **dot notation**. Let *A* be a class and *e* an entity declared of type *A*. (Remember that for the moment the only entities we know are attributes, although more kinds will be introduced shortly.) assume *e* is declared of some class type *B*, and *f* is one of the attributes declared in class *B*. Then, in *A*, the notation

   e.f

denotes the *f* field of the object associated with *e* at run-time; it is called a **qualified occurrence** of *f*. Note that even qualified occurrences use the concept of current instance, as *e* itself is an entity (for example an attribute) relative to the current instance.

For example, we could find in class *BOOK2* a notation of the form

   author.birth_year

where *author* is an attribute of class *BOOK2*, declared of type *PERSON1*, and *birth_year* is one of the attributes declared in *PERSON1*. The full meaning of this notation is "the *birth_year* field of the object associated with the reference contained in the *author* field of the current instance of *BOOK2*".

This importance of the current instance explains the decentralized nature of object-oriented programming. There is no equivalent to the **main program** of classical languages, the central process from which everything else stems; instead, we have, at compile-time, a set of classes; and, at run-time, a set of objects – instances of these classes – which may access attributes from and (as we shall soon see) perform operations on each other.

Of course, to get an executable system, you must assemble a number of classes and decide where the execution process should start; but this assembly process occurs late and is described independently of the programming language itself (see 5.6 below).

In many cases, the current instance remains implicit: for example, an unqualified occurrence of attribute *author* within the text of class *BOOK2*, corresponds at run-time to the *author* field of the current *BOOK2* instance. Sometimes, however, the programmer needs a notation to explicitly name the current instance. The predefined expression *Current* is reserved for this purpose: *Current* means "the current instance of the enclosing class". (Remember that any Eiffel text is part of exactly one class.) Thus an unqualified occurrence such as *author* could also be written *Current. author*.

It is important to note that *Current* is syntactically an expression, not an entity; thus it cannot be the target of an assignment, as in

      -- NOT VALID EIFFEL
    Current := x

5.4   ROUTINES

The classes defined so far only had attributes. In other words, they were the equivalent of records, or structures; we have just seen how to access their fields.

This is not enough. We want a class to describe an abstract data type implementation. This should include not only the representation of the type's instances (as provided by the attributes), but also the operations on these instances. This is what routines are for.

5.4.1   Overview

Routines are implementations of the operations on the instances of a class. There are two kinds of routine:

- A **procedure** performs an action, that is to say may change the state of an object.
- A **function** computes some value deduced from the state of the object.

The notion of state used here is simple: every instance of a class has a certain number of fields, corresponding to the attributes of the class. The values of these fields at any point during system execution determine the state of the object. A procedure call may change this state, that is to say the values of one or more fields; a function call returns a value computed from the state (that is to say, from the attributes). Whether functions can modify the state is discussed later (7.7).

Before giving an example, let's clarify the terminology. A class is characterized by its **features**. We now know the two kinds of features: *attributes*, seen previously, and *routines*, now being introduced. Routines are further classified into *procedures* and *functions*.

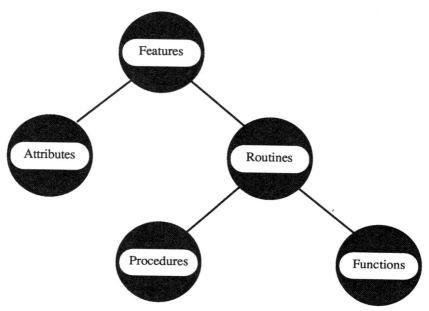

Figure 5.9   Classification of features

5.4.2   An example: use

The following is our first serious example of class, although it still remains rather limited in its application. It describes a notion of point, as could be used in, say, a graphics system. Of course, this is only a rough sketch of what a full-fledged, usable point class should be.

When introducing a new class, it is often a good idea to first show how the class is to be **used** by its clients, and only then how it is implemented. The class given below, called *POINT*, may be used in the following way. Assume a client class contains the declarations

> *p1, p2: POINT*;
> *r, s: REAL*

Then the client may create instances of *POINT* :

> *p1.Create*; ...; *p2.Create*; ...

Among the features that are available on a point are its coordinates; an example of instructions to record their values is:

> *r := p1.x*; *s := p1.y*

Here *:=* is the assignment symbol. Features *x* and *y* give the coordinates; the client does not know whether these features are implemented as attributes or functions without arguments, and does not need to know.

Operations that may be performed on a point include translation and scaling:

p2.translate (–3.5, s); ...; p2.scale (3.0)

This example shows the general syntax for executing operations, using dot notation:

entity.operation (arguments)

meaning: "apply *operation*, with *arguments*, to the object associated with *entity*". The *arguments* may be absent. Once again, note the distinctive feature of object-oriented programming: every operation applies to a specific object, which appears to the left of the dot (represented by the program name *entity*). In classical programming, the corresponding notation would be the more symmetric

operation (entity, arguments)

that is to say, *entity* would be just one among the arguments of the operation. Object-oriented programming treats arguments to operations in a very undemocratic fashion: one of them is always singled out for special treatment.

Here the first operation of the example performs on *p2* a translation by –3.5 horizontally and the value of *s* vertically; the second scales *p2* by a factor of three from the origin. Both of these operations are **procedures**, which may modify the object associated with the reference to which they apply. For example, after *p2.Create*, *p2* denotes a reference associated with a point object which, because of the default initialization rules, has both coordinates equal to zero. Then after *p2.translate (–3.5, s)*, this object will have coordinates –3.5 and *s*.

Finally, you may also apply to a point the function *distance*, which returns its distance to another point, as in

r := p1.distance (p2)

In contrast to procedures, functions normally do not modify the object associated with the reference to which they apply, but return some information about that object (here its distance to another point).

Every operation applies to a certain object, accessed through a reference denoted by an entity. For the operation to be meaningful, the object must exist. Thus if *entity.operation (arguments)* is to execute correctly, it is essential that the reference associated with *entity* be non-void. This is true not only of routine execution but also of access to attributes, as in *entity.attribute*. Attempting to access a feature of a void reference is the principal type of run-time error that may occur in Eiffel programming; the error is caught by the underlying language system, which generates an exception (see chapter 7).

5.4.3 An example: implementation

We have seen how the *POINT* class may be used by clients. Let's see now how the class itself would be written.

```
class POINT export
        x, y, translate, scale, distance
feature
        x, y: REAL;

        scale (factor: REAL) is
                -- Scale by a ratio of factor.
        do
                x := factor*x;
                y := factor*y
        end; -- scale

        translate (a, b: REAL) is
                -- Move by a horizontally, b vertically.
        do
                x := x+a;
                y := y+b
        end; -- translate

        distance (other: POINT): REAL is
                -- Distance to other.
        do
                Result := sqrt ((x – other.x) ^ 2 + (y – other.y) ^ 2)
        end -- distance
end -- class POINT
```

This class shows many of the basic properties of classes and their features.

The "export" clause lists the features that are available to clients. This clause is required to enforce a clear distinction between internal features, used only for representation purposes and public ones, offered to the outside world; the origin is the principle of information hiding. The presence in a class B of a qualified feature use, as in

```
a1: A;
...
... a1.f ...
```

is only legal if f appears in the **export** clause of class A. This applies to attributes as well as routines. In the simple class *POINT* all features are exported, but we shall encounter many classes for which this is not the case. Exportation of features and information hiding are studied in chapter 9.

Class *POINT* has two attributes: x and y, corresponding to the cartesian coordinates of a point. It also includes three routines: *scale*, *translate* and *distance*. A routine is distinguished by the presence of a clause **is...do...end** which introduces its body. (A variant, the deferred body, will be introduced in chapter 10.) A routine may have formal arguments in parentheses, as the three given here, but this is not required.

Of the three routines, *scale* and *translate* are procedures; *distance* is a function since it is declared with a result type, appearing as *: REAL* after the argument list. A function without arguments could be declared as follows (in the above class):

distance_to_origin: REAL **is**
              -- Distance to point (0, 0)
        do
              Result := sqrt (x ^ 2 + y ^ 2)
        end -- *distance_to_origin*

Note that such a declaration begins like the declaration of an attribute; it is only the **is** and what follows it that establish *distance_to_origin* as a function.

The body of a routine is a sequence of instructions, separated by semicolons if more than one, and delimited by the keywords **do** and **end**. There are few kinds of instructions in Eiffel; in this class we use only one, the assignment, already encountered above. An assignment takes the form

      entity := expression

In the body of functions, such as *distance* or *distance_to_origin*, the special entity name *Result* denotes the result of the function.

On function entry *Result* is initialized according to the standard Eiffel rules (see figure 5.8, page 77). Thus the following would be a correct implementation of a (not very interesting) routine to determine whether an integer is positive:

positive (n: INTEGER): BOOLEAN **is**
              -- Is *n* positive?
        do
            if *n > 0* **then**
                  Result := **true**
            end
        end -- *positive*

(Recall that booleans are initialized to false.)

> The presence in class *POINT* of a function *sqrt*, used to compute a square root, requires that this function be made properly accessible to the class. It may be either declared as an external routine (8.3) or inherited from a general-purpose library class (14.4.5).

5.4.4 Local variables

The implementation of *distance_to_origin* could have used the more general *distance* function:

distance_to_origin: REAL **is**
              -- Distance to point (0, 0)
        local
              origin: POINT
        do
              origin.Create;
              Result := distance (origin)
        end -- *distance_to_origin*

Note how a routine of the class (here *distance_to_origin*) may rely on another one (here *distance*) for its implementation; the call is not qualified in this case.

This version of the function introduces the notion of local variable: the optional **local** clause, at the beginning of a routine body, contains any local entities that may be useful for the computation performed by the routine. Note that *origin. Create* is enough to create an object representing the origin: because of the default initialization rules, *origin. x* and *origin. y* are zero after the *Create*.

A local variable is only available within the routine to which it belongs. It is initialized anew, according to the default initialization rules, at the beginning of each execution of the routine. Thus *origin* is initialized to a void reference whenever *distance_to_origin* is called; hence the *Create* is necessary to associate *origin* with an actual instance of *POINT*, representing (0, 0).

> This implementation is rather inefficient: a new object representing the origin will be created on each call to *distance_to_origin*. What is really needed to make this version of *distance_to_origin* practical is some way to associate *origin* with a single object, shared by all calls to the function. Chapter 13 will show how to do this.

5.4.5 A precise definition of entities

The only example of entities introduced so far is attributes. We are now in a position to see the full definition. Entities include the following:

Definition (*Entities*): An entity is one of the following:

1.   A class attribute.

2.   A local variable of a routine.

3.   A formal argument of a routine.

4.   The identifier denoting the result of a function, as expressed by the predefined entity *Result*.

5.4.6 Predefined routines

In addition to the routines defined in a class, some routines are predefined and apply to all classes. This means, of course, that the corresponding names are reserved words and may not be used for programmer-defined routines. There are five predefined routines: *Create, Forget, Void, Clone* and *Equal*.

Create, Forget and *Void* have already been mentioned. More details about *Create* are given in the next section.

The *Clone* procedure duplicates objects. The call

   a.Clone (*b*)

creates an object identical to the object attached to *b* and attaches it to *a*, or makes *a* void if *b* is void. Entities *a* and *b* must be declared with the same class type. Executing a *Clone* is the second way of creating objects; the first is by executing a *Create*, and there are no others.

Equal compares objects. If *a* and *b* are two entities of the same type, then

   a.Equal (*b*)

is true if and only if the references associated with *a* and *b* are either both void, or refer to objects that are field-by-field equal. Note that this is an equality test between objects, to be contrasted with the equality test between references, written $a = b$. If $a = b$ holds, then *a. Equal* (*b*) holds, but the reverse is not necessarily true, as shown by the following figure.

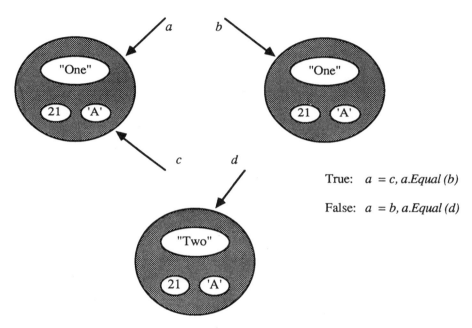

True: $a = c, a.Equal\ (b)$

False: $a = b, a.Equal\ (d)$

Figure 5.10   Reference and value equality

5.4.7   Non-default Create

In the examples seen so far, the creation operation produces an identical object each time it is called on any entity of a given class. This is ensured by the initialization rules: *p. Create*, for example, where *p* is declared of type *POINT*, will always produce a point with zero coordinates *x* and *y*.

In some cases, a more flexible initialization may be needed. For example, you may want to allow clients to specify initial coordinate values on point creation. As the class designer, you may permit such specific initializations by defining a *Create* procedure for the class. A procedure with the name *Create* is recognized as special and will be used for object initialization. You may for example add such a procedure to the *POINT* class:

class *POINT* **export**
>   *x, y, translate, scale, distance*

feature
>   *x, y: REAL*;

>   *Create (a, b: REAL)* **is**
>>   -- Initialize point with coordinates *a* and *b*
>   **do**
>>   *x := a; y := b*
>   **end**; -- *Create*
>   ... Other features as previously ...

end -- class *POINT*

If such a procedure is declared in a class, then clients will invoke it with the appropriate actual arguments, as in

>   *p: POINT*;
>   ...
>   *p.Create (34.6, −65.1)*

The effect of such a call is to perform the following three operations, in sequence:

• Create an object of the appropriate class, as given by the type with which the entity (*p* in this example) is declared.

• Initialize all fields of the objects to the default values corresponding to their declared types, according to the rules of figure 5.8 (page 77).

• Execute the procedure called *Create* in the class, with the given actual arguments.

Only the first two steps are performed if the class does not include a specific *Create* procedure.

5.5   REFERENCE AND VALUE SEMANTICS

An important notion which needs to be clarified is the difference between the "reference" and "value" semantics of such operations as assignment and equality tests.

This issue actually arises in any language which includes pointer entities (such as Pascal, Ada, Modula-2, C, Lisp etc.), but is particularly acute in an object-oriented language such as Eiffel in which all non-simple types are pointer types; in Eiffel, furthermore, the syntax does not explicitly show them to be pointers, so one needs to be particularly careful. (The detailed reasoning behind the Eiffel conventions is given in 5.8.3 below.)

5.5.1   The meaning of basic operations

The issue is apparently a simple one and may be summarized by the following remark:

> **Reference semantics rule**: An assignment of the form $a := b$ is an assignment of **values** if a and b are of simple types (integer, real, character, boolean); it is an assignment of **references**, not an assignment of objects, if they are of class types.
>
> Similarly, an equality or inequality test $a = b$ or $a /= b$ is a comparison of values for entities of simple types; it is a comparison of references to objects (not a comparison of objects) for entities of class types.

Here assignment of objects means field-by-field copy of an object to another one, as performed by *Clone*; and comparison of objects means field-by-field comparison of objects, as performed by *Equal*, which yields true if and only if each field of the first object is equal to the corresponding field of the second one. For example, in the situation of figure 5.10, the test $a = b$ yields false as a test of references but true as a test of objects (as the objects referred to by a and b are field-by-field identical).

Because of this property, the diagram showing how references may change state (page 75) must be updated to account for changes resulting from an assignment. The full diagram, also accounting for the *Clone* operation, is the following:

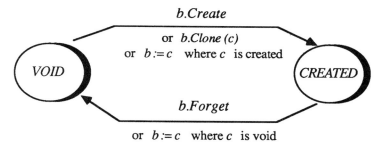

Figure 5.11   **States of a reference (revised)**

5.5.2   The consequences of sharing

The difference between the interpretations of :=, = and /= for simple and class types is important because it gives rise to different semantic properties. Consider for example the following program fragment:

```
-- Assume that here P (b) holds
a := b;
C (a)
-- Then here P (b) still holds.
```

Here we assume that $P(b)$ is a certain property of b and $C(a)$ is some action on a, not involving b. An example of this scheme using only integer entities is the following:

```
-- Assume that here b ≥ 0
a := b;
a := -1
-- Then here b ≥ 0 still holds.
```

Clearly, in such a case involving entities of simple types, the property expressed by the comments is satisfied: the assignment $a := b$ does not bind b to a, but simply changes the value of a to that of b; further operations on a do not affect b.

This property ceases to be satisfied, however, if the entities are of class types. Assume a and b are declared of a class type C and that class C has a boolean attribute x. C also has an associated routine

set_x_false **is do** $x :=$ **false end**

Then the following instance of the above scheme violates the general property:

```
-- Assume that here b is not void and b.x is true
a := b;
a.set_x_false
-- Then here b.x is false
```

The problem is that in this case the assignment $a := b$ establishes a durable binding between a and b: until further assignment, they both refer to the same object. The situation may be pictured as follows:

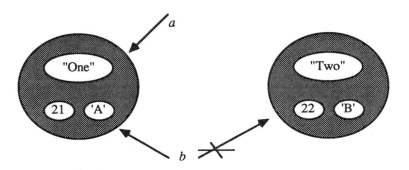

Figure 5.12   Effect of reference assignment

The properties of assignment and equality test are thus different for simple and class types:

- The interpretation for simple types is called value semantics: assignment and comparison apply to values. One might also speak, for assignment, of "copy semantics": after $a := b$, a contains a copy of the value of b, which has lost any link to b itself.

- The interpretation for class types is called reference semantics: here the operations apply to references, and may thus bind two entities. Since two equal references refer to the same object, an operation on one of the references may affect properties of the other via the object they share.

5.5.3 Aliasing and complex data structures

Reference semantics introduces what is known as **dynamic aliasing**: the possibility for a single object to be accessible through two different names; "dynamic" because aliasing occurs at run-time. (An example of static aliasing is the infamous Fortran *EQUIVALENCE* statement, which prescribes that two or more variables must share the same memory location.)

Dynamic aliasing is a dangerous facility for the reason mentioned above: after a and b have been made to refer to the same object, an operation may change the properties of the object associated with b even though the text of the operation does not involve b (but only a). This is one of the problems that make programming with references tricky in any language.

But one cannot do without references as soon as non-trivial data structures are involved. References are required for linked representations, and in particular for many of the best representations for lists, queues, trees, circular structures etc.

Object-oriented languages, which are particularly appropriate for manipulating complex data structures, must support references. The decision to use reference semantics as the basic semantics for non-simple types was taken for reasons of simplicity and uniformity.

5.5.4 Value semantics for non-simple types

Although :=, = and /= denote reference operations for entities of non-simple types, operations with value semantics are also available for these types: the instruction

> $a.Clone\ (b)$

corresponds to an assignment of values, which creates a field-by-field copy of the object referred to by b (if any), and associates a with it. Similarly, value comparison of objects (field-by-field) is available under the form

> $a.Equal\ (b)$

These operations implement what is known as **shallow copy** and **shallow equality**; this means that the operations performed on each field of the objects involved are reference assignments or comparisons, not recursive *Clone* or *Equal* operations.

As an illustration, consider the figure below. Starting from situation (1), with only the three leftmost objects in existence, the effect of $b.Clone\ (a)$ will be (2). Another interpretation, which may be called **deep copy semantics**, would be to yield (3), which may seem a more appropriate notion of copy between complex data structures.

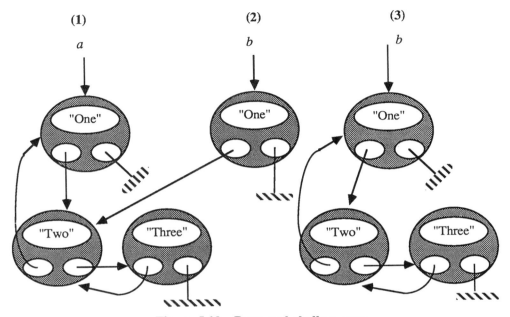

Figure 5.13   Deep and shallow copy

Similarly, *Equal* compares objects field-by-field: reference fields are compared with =, without any attempt to use *Equal* recursively. Thus *a.Equal* (*b*) will yield true if *b* is given by (2) but if it is given by (3), even though the data structure of (3) may conceptually seem a better copy of (1).

Deep assignment or comparison operations may be defined as (recursive) procedures for any given class; such operations are not defined as language primitives as it is difficult to give a single interpretation that applies to all data structures, especially circular ones.

5.6   FROM CLASSES TO SYSTEMS

The reader who is familiar with more classical programming languages may feel a bit puzzled so far: we have given the structure of individual classes but have not talked of a "main program" in the classical sense. Furthermore, we have not given any clue as to how things may ever begin at execution time.

Every object is an instance of a class; to come into being, the object needs to be associated with an entity, for example an attribute, say *a*; an instruction

    a.Create

must be executed. However *a* itself has to be declared in some class *C*; the *Create* instruction has to be executed by some routine r of C. Now a represents a field of the current instance of C, so **someone** must have created an instance of C and applied r on it; but "someone" is itself a routine relative to some object, so who created that object in the first place? As in the traditional song (the kid was eaten by the cat, the cat was bitten by the dog, the dog was beaten by the stick...), we do not see the end of the chain.

5.6.1 Systems

The absence of a notion of main program and of any structuring mechanism at a higher level than the class is an important element of the Eiffel software design philosophy. As discussed in chapter 4, it is a mistake, if one is concerned with extendibility and reusability, to organize the design of a system around its main function, as expressed by a main program. Instead, the Eiffel approach emphasizes the development of reusable software components, built as abstract data type implementations – classes.

The process of tying together a bunch of classes with a view to executing the result is called **assembly** and is the last step in the software design process. The result of such an assembly of autonomous classes is called a **system**. The concept of system is not exactly a language concept; systems are only known at the operating system level, and are associated with executable processes.

Note that one can use Eiffel without building systems. An important application is to produce **libraries** of software components (see chapter 15). In such a case there is no need for a "beginning"; programming amounts to producing collections of modules. A system is only produced when one needs a stand-alone executable process.

5.6.2 Assembling a system

A system is characterized by a **root**, which is the name of a class. Execution of the system consists in creating an instance of the root class and executing its *Create* procedure; usually this procedure will directly or indirectly create other objects and execute other procedures. Thus the *Create* procedure of a class given as root is similar to a test or demonstration driver. As all such procedures, the *Create* may have formal arguments; corresponding actual values must be provided when the system is executed. As the system will be called from outside of Eiffel (using the command language of the operating system), all the arguments of the root's *Create* must be of simple or string type.

5.6.3 The System Description File

To help picture the notion of system, it is useful to explain how a system is actually assembled and executed in the Unix implementation of Eiffel. The assembly command is called **es** for Eiffel System. This command needs a "System Description File", or SDF (which is by default the file called *.eiffel* in the current directory). When no SDF is present, the command will generate a skeleton SDF in which the programmer only has to fill in values that differ from the defaults. An SDF begins with:

ROOT: *name of the root class* (*lower case*)
SOURCE: *list of source directories*
EXTERNAL: *list of external files*
... more lines giving compilation options ...

The first line gives the name of the root class. The second gives a list of directories (a Unix directory is a node in the hierarchical file system) where the Eiffel assembly process will be able to find classes needed directly or indirectly by the root class (such as its direct and indirect suppliers but also, as will be seen in subsequent chapters, its ancestors). Similarly, the third line lists files for external (non-Eiffel) routines or libraries.

When command **es** is executed, it compiles the root and all needed classes. (Only those classes that have been significantly modified since the last **es** command are actually compiled: see chapter 15.) The results of these compilations are then linked together to produce an executable program called *root*, where *root* is the name of the root class (in lower case). This program may be executed by the command

$$root\ arg_1\ arg_2...\ arg_n$$

where the arg_i are values corresponding in number and types to the formal arguments of the root class's *Create* procedure.

It is important to note that classes remain entirely independent from the system, or more frequently the systems, in which they intervene.

5.6.4   Printing your name

Reusable software components are great, but sometimes all you want to do is just a simple task, such as printing a string. You may have been wondering how to write a "program" that will do it. Having introduced the notion of system, we can answer this burning question. (I have found that people tend to be nervous about the whole approach until they see how to do this, hence this little digression.) Consider the class

```
class SIMPLE feature
    Create is
        local
            io: STD_FILES
        do
            io.Create;
            io.output.putstring_nl ("Hello Mary!")
        end
end -- class SIMPLE
```

SIMPLE uses the library class *STD_FILES*. The entities defined in *STD_FILES* include *output*, of type *FILE*, describing the standard output file; available operations on a file include *putstring_nl* (write a string followed by a new line). *FILE* and *STD_FILES* are library classes described in appendix E. [1]

---

[1] The normal way to use *STD_FILES* is for *SIMPLE* to inherit from this class. Then the local variable *io* is not needed any more; the body of *Create* becomes just *output.putstring_nl* ("*Hello Mary!*"). Inheritance is studied in chapter 10.

To obtain a system that will print the given string, do the following:

1. • Put the above class text in a file called *simple. e* in some directory.
2. • Call **es** in this directory.
3. • You will be prompted to edit a System Description File, automatically generated from a template; just fill in the ROOT line with the name *simple* (in lower case), and check that the SOURCE line lists the directory containing the Eiffel library, so that *STD_FILES* and *FILE* will be found. This should not be a problem since the library directory is included by default in the SDF template.
4. • Exit from the editor; es will compile the system and produce an executable file called *simple*.
5. • Execute the result by simply typing *simple*. This will print on your terminal the message

> *Hello Mary!*

5.6.5   The global picture

With the above discussion of systems, we now have the full picture. In particular, we know exactly what an operation on an entity, appearing in some Eiffel text, represents.

Assume that operation *a. f* (possibly with arguments) has been executed. This call appears in routine *r* of class *C*; *a* is an attribute of this class. How does this call ever get executed? Let us play the object-oriented Sherlock Holmes and follow the trail that leads to it:

procedure of the system's root must have performed (either itself or that it calls directly or indirectly) an operation *x. Create* (...), where type *C*, and later on an operation *x. r* (...), or possibly *y. r* (...) after := *x*. The *Create* will have created an instance of *C*; then the call ed as part of the execution of *x. r* or *y. r*, will result in operation *f* he *a* field of that instance.

s a way to start the chain of events that will lead to a particular xecuted. On the other hand, the chain may not usually be deduced a single class. This is typical of the highly decentralized nature of)gramming. The primary emphasis is not on "the" execution of "the" ny) Pascal programming, but rather on services provided by a set of ed by the class features. The *order* in which services are requested ion of a particular system built from these classes is a secondary

e heart of the object-oriented method here. The method prescribes *now* the order of execution, you should not base any serious system design decision on it. The main reason, as discussed in chapter 4, is flexibility: whereas adding or changing individual services is relatively easy in a decentralized structure, a system decomposition based on the order in which operations are to be executed stands to suffer considerably from any change of external specifications.

This de-emphasis of order differentiates object-oriented design from some popular software design methods such as data-flow-oriented techniques or Jackson's JSD (see bibliographical notes to chapter 4). In contrast with these, object-oriented design implements what has been called the shopping list approach in chapter 4: a class is a bundle of features, all waiting to be picked by clients, with no constraints on the order in which they are to be used. The more order-constrained methods may sometimes yield a working program more quickly, as the initial design leaves fewer degrees of freedom. But they carry a serious risk that changes in ordering constraints will result in heavy redesign.

5.7   CLASSES VS. OBJECTS

At this point of the discussion, it is important to emphasize once again a distinction which has proved to be confusing to many novices: the distinction between class and object.

The question is actually an easy one: a class is a type; an object is an instance of the type. Furthermore, classes are a **static** concept: a class is a recognizable element of program text. In contrast, an object is a purely **dynamic** concept, which belongs not to the program text but to the memory of the computer, where objects occupy some space at run-time once they has been created as the result of *Create* or *Clone* operations. are executed, starting with the creation of the root object. Conversely, classes do not need to exist at run-time.

> Of course, classes *might* be kept at run-time, for example in an interpretive implementation. But this is only an implementation option. Classes are not conceptually needed during execution.

The distinction is just the same as that between a program and its possible executions, between a type and the values of the type, or more generally between a pattern and its instances. There shouldn't really be any risk of confusion. One of the origins of this problem is that the designers of Smalltalk, striving for generality, insisted on treating everything, including classes, as objects. The two approaches will be further compared below.

5.8   DISCUSSION

As a conclusion to this chapter, let us consider (as will be done for most of the subsequent chapters using the Eiffel notations) the rationale behind some of the decisions made in the design of the language, and explore some alternative paths. (This section may be skipped on first reading.)

5.8.1   Form of declarations

We first examine the more superficial aspect, syntax. One point worth noting is the notation for feature declarations. For routines, there is none of the keywords **procedure** or **function** such as they appear in other languages; the form of a feature determines whether it is an attribute, a procedure or a function. The beginning of a feature declaration is just the feature name, say *f* ...

When you have read this, you must still keep all possibilities open. If a list of arguments comes next, as in

   f (*a1: A*; *b1: B*; ...) ...

then you know *f* is a routine; it could still be either a function or a procedure. Next a type may come:

   f: T ...
   g (*a1: A*; *b1: B*; ...): *T* ...

The first example, *f*, can still be either an attribute or a function without arguments; in the second case, however, the suspense stops, as *g* can only be a function. Coming back to *f*, the ambiguity will be resolved by what appears after the type *T*: if nothing, *f* is an attribute; in

   f: T **is**

            -- ...
       do ... **end**

f is a function. Chapter 13 will introduce yet another variant:

   f: T **is** *value*

Here *f* is a constant attribute.

The syntax is designed to allow easy recognition of the various kinds of features, while avoiding unnecessary differences.

5.8.2   Attributes vs. functions

The grouping of attributes and routines under the same category of "features" and the similarity between their declaration forms are intentional. They are a direct application of the principle of uniform reference (2.1.4, page 16). The principle stated that clients of a module should be able to use any service provided by the module in a uniform way regardless of whether the service is implemented through storage or through computation. Here the services are the features of the class; what is meaningful for clients is the availability of certain features and their properties. Whether a given feature is implemented by storing appropriate data or by computing the result on demand is functionally irrelevant. For example, when I write

   John.age

the only important information is that *age* will return an integer, the age that is associated with the representation of a *PERSON1* accessible via reference *John*. Internally, *age* may be either an attribute, stored with each object, or a function, computed by taking the difference between the current year and a *birth_date* attribute. But the client does not need to know which of these solutions has been chosen by the designer of class *PERSON1*.

Thus the notation for *accessing* an attribute is the same as that for accessing a routine, and the notations for *declaring* these two kinds of features are as similar as conceptually possible. Then if the module programmer reverses an implementation decision (implementing as a function a feature that was initially an attribute, or conversely), clients will not be affected; their texts will not need to be changed and, in the Eiffel environment they will not be recompiled (chapter 15).

In this context, the classification given earlier for features (see figure 5.9, (page 79), distinguishing between attributes and routines, the latter being subdivided into procedures and functions, reflects the module implementor's viewpoint but is not the best from the clients' viewpoint. Here is the functional classification reflecting the clients' viewpoint:

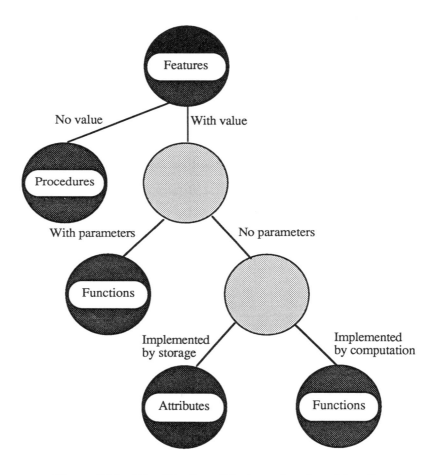

Figure 5.14   Classification of features (as viewed by clients)

As will be seen in chapter 11, the principle of uniform reference is taken further by permitting, in the inheritance mechanism, the **redefinition** of a function without arguments as an attribute.

This approach differs from the conventions that exists in many other object-oriented languages. In Smalltalk, for example, routines (called "methods") and attributes (called "instance variables") are treated differently. Only routines may be exported to clients; attributes are local to a class. To make an attribute available to clients, you must write an exported function that returns the value of that attribute.

Further discussion of these and other information hiding issues may be found in chapter 9, which also gives more details about the export clause.

5.8.3   References and simple values

Also syntactical is the issue of whether to deal differently with references and simple values. As noted above (page 86) assignment and equality test have different meanings in these two cases. Yet the same symbols are used: $:=$, $=$, $/=$, regardless of whether their operands are of simple or class types. Wouldn't it be preferable to use different sets of symbols to remind the program reader that the meanings are different?

This is indeed the solution used in Simula 67. Transposing slightly the notation and terminology of this language to Eiffel, the Simula solution is to declare an entity of a class type C as

  x: **ref** C

where the keyword **ref** reminds the reader that instances of x will be references. Assuming the declarations

  m, n: *INTEGER*
  x, y: **ref** C;

then different notations are used for operations on simple and class types, as follows:

Operation	Simple operands	Reference operands
Assignment	$m := n$	$x := y$
Equality test	$m = n$	$x == y$
Inequality test	$m /= n$	$x =/= y$

(Please note that these notations are adapted to Eiffel; the exact Simula notations are described in chapter 20.)

The decision not to include such a double set of notations in Eiffel was based on my rather negative experience with the – apparently laudable – conventions of Simula. It turns out that the distinction between the two kinds of notations is more nuisance than help. In practice, one tends to make syntactical oversights such as $:=$ instead of $:-$. Such errors will be caught by the compiler. But although compiler-checkable restrictions in programming languages are meant to help programmers, the checks are of no help here: either you know the difference between reference and value semantics, in which case the obligation to prove again, each time you write an assignment or equality, that you did understand this difference, is rather annoying; or you do not understand it, in which case the compiler message won't help you much.

The remarkable aspect of the Simula convention is that you do not in fact have a choice: for references, no predefined construct is available that would give value semantics. It might have seemed reasonable to allow both $a := b$ and $a := b$ for references, where the former operation is a reference assignment, and the latter is a field-by-field copy. Similarly, two equality tests could have been provided: reference comparison and field-by-field object comparison. This is not the case; only the reference operations are available, and any attempt to use := or = for references will produce a syntactical error.[2] Value operations (assignment, comparison), if needed, must be hand-coded specifically for each class type.

Note, by the way, that the idea of allowing both :– and :=, = and == etc. for each type, does not look so clever on closer inspection: it would mean that a trivial oversight such as typing := for :– would now go unnoticed and result in an effect quite different from the programmer's intent, for example a *Clone* where a reference assignment was intended.

As a result of this analysis, Eiffel uses a different convention from Simula's: the same symbols apply for simple and class types, with different semantics (value vs. reference). The effect of value semantics for objects of class types is achieved by predefined routines:

> *a.Clone* (*b*) for object assignment
> *a.Equal* (*b*) for object (field-by-field) comparison

These notations are sufficiently different from their reference counterparts (:= and =, respectively) to avert any risk of confusion.

Beyond the purely syntactical aspects, this issue is interesting because it typifies some of the tradeoffs that arise in language design when a balance must be found between conflicting criteria. One criterion, which won in the Simula case, may be stated as "make sure different concepts are expressed by different symbols". But the opposing forces, which dominated in Eiffel, say: "do not bother the programmer"; "weigh carefully any new restriction against the actual benefits that it will bring in terms of security and other quality factors" (here the restriction is the prohibition of := and similar operators for references); "to keep the language small and simple, do not introduce new notations unless they are absolutely necessary" (in particular, if, as in this example, existing notations will do the job and there is no danger of confusion); "if you know there is a serious risk of confusion between two facilities, make the associated notations as different as possible".

5.8.4   Result of functions

One other syntactical aspect of Eiffel is fairly independent from the object-oriented design method but worth discussing briefly as it illustrates some important issues of programming language design. This is the convention for computing the result of a function, using the *Result* predefined variable. This technique seems (strangely enough) original with Eiffel. Common techniques range between:

1.   • Using explicit return instructions.

2.   • Treating the function name as a variable.

---

[2] Simula does offer both sets of operations for one specific type: the predefined *TEXT* type, representing character strings.

Convention 1 is used in C, Ada and other languages. An instruction

> **return** *e*

terminates the function's execution, returning *e* as the value of the function. The advantage is that the returned value stands out clearly from the function text. However, the technique suffers from several drawbacks:

A. • In practice, the result must often be obtained through computation (initialization and then some operations). Thus a variable must be introduced just for the purpose of holding the intermediate results of the computation.

B. • The technique tends to promote multiple-exit modules, which are contrary to good program structuring.

C. • The language definition must specify what will happen if the last instruction executed by the function is not a **return**. The Ada result in this case is to raise ... a run-time exception! (This may be viewed as the ultimate in buck-passing: transferring the responsibility for language design flaws from the language designers not only to the programmer, but in the end to the program user.)

To solve the last two problems, it would seem preferable to treat **return** not as an instruction but as a required clause in all function bodies:

> **function** *name* (*arguments*): *type* **is**
>   **do**
>   ...
>   **return**
>   *expression*
>   **end**

However, no common language uses such a convention, which does not solve problem A.

The second common technique (2) is used in such languages as Fortran, Algol 60, Simula 67 (an Algol extension), Algol 68 and Pascal. Within a function, the function's name is treated as a variable; the value returned by a call is the final value of that variable.

The above three problems do not arise in this approach. However it raises other difficulties since the same name now ambiguously denotes both a function and a variable. This raises serious risks, especially in a language allowing recursion. There must be some convention as to when the name denotes the variable, and when it denotes a function call. Usually, a target occurrence (such as on the left of an assignment) denotes the variable, and a source occurrence (as in an expression) denotes a function call. Then the instruction

> $f := f+1$

will be either rejected by the compiler or understood as a recursive call whose result is assigned to f (the variable). The latter case is almost certainly not the intended interpretation – obviously, the programmer meant f to denote the variable in both cases – and will usually result in non-termination. Outright rejection is better but forces the programmer to introduce one more variable to stand for f, which defeats the whole purpose of the technique.

The Eiffel convention avoids the drawbacks of both techniques 1 and 2. The predefined entity name *Result* serves to denote unambiguously the result of the current function. Note that the technique would not work in a language allowing functions to be declared within functions, as the name *Result* would then be ambiguous.

This convention blends well with the initialization rules of the language: every entity, including *Result*, is initialized to a default value. Hence there is no danger of a function returning an undefined or system-dependent value. For example, a function returning a result of some class type may have a body of the form

> **if** *some_condition* **then**
>   *Result.Create* (*some_arguments*)
> **end**

with no **else** clause; if *some_condition* is not satisfied the result returned will be a *Void* reference, the default value for entities of class types.

5.8.5   The distinction between objects and classes

The difference between classes and objects has been repeatedly emphasized. In the view presented here, these concepts belong to different worlds: the program text only contains classes; at run-time, only objects exist.

This is not the only possible approach. One of the subcultures of object-oriented programming, influenced by Lisp and exemplified by Smalltalk, views classes as objects themselves, which still have an existence at run-time. Two arguments may be made for this approach:

- Keeping classes around during the execution makes it easier to change them on the spot in order to correct errors, improve the system or experiment with new facilities; there is no need to go each time through a complete edit-compile-assemble-run cycle. This is the traditional benefit of interpretive systems.

- By treating classes as objects, it is possible to define *class routines*: operations that apply to all classes, or a large set of classes, rather than to all the instances of a given class as standard features do. An example is *Create*: the default *Create* may be considered as a class procedure defined for all classes.

The view taken in the design of Eiffel is that the distinction between descriptions (of processes or classes of objects) and the corresponding executions is a fundamental one, and that any confusion should be avoided, in the same way that modern computer techniques do not encourage self-modifying programs (once thought a really clever idea).

To a certain extent, the choice depends on what you use object-oriented programming for. If you are essentially interested in quick prototyping and experimentation, the free approach – "everything is an object" – may be better adapted. If, on the other hand, you are concerned about correctness, robustness and efficiency, then a compiled approach is obviously required (correctness, for example, requires that you know what the system is before you execute it; if it can be changed during its execution, there is little hope that you can guarantee any of its properties).

My firm conviction that descriptions should not be confused with executions is reinforced by the belief that the above two arguments are not without answer:

• The problem of fast modification may be solved without melting classes and objects in the same pot, simply by advances in software technology: with separate compilation facilities and automatic configuration management as provided in Eiffel (see chapter 15), it is possible to implement changes and observe their results quickly, without impairing the orderly process of software development.

• Class routines, the object of the second argument, do exist; *Create*, *Forget* and *Clone* are examples. However in my experience there is only a small number of such cases, so that it seems better to address them through predefined language constructs than to extend the language by a facility (class routines) that considerably changes its conceptual framework although its power is usually not needed by programmers.

The Smalltalk approach is presented in more detail in chapter 20.

5.9   KEY CONCEPTS INTRODUCED IN THIS CHAPTER

• In object-oriented programming, every program construct is relative to an object. By default, this object is the "current instance", that is to say a prototypical instance of the enclosing class.

• Do not confuse objects (dynamic items) with classes (the static description of the properties common to a set of run-time objects); do not confuse objects, references to objects, and entities (program names that stand for run-time references to objects).

• In Eiffel, all entities of non-simple types have reference values. Either a reference is void or it refers to an object.

• With value (or copy) semantics, an assignment copies values, and a comparison tests values. With reference semantics, these operations act on references, not on the corresponding objects; this implies dynamic aliasing and the associated dangers (an entity being modified by an operation that apparently acts on something else). In Eiffel, interpretation of := and = is value for simple types and reference for class types. Value semantics for class types is also available via *Clone* and *Equal*.

• Classes are characterized by features, including attributes (representing fields of the corresponding objects) and routines (representing operations on these objects). Entities declared of the corresponding class types may be accessed and modified via the exported features, using dot notation. An exported attribute is accessible from the outside in read-only mode.

• Objects are created using the *Create* or *Clone* predefined features. *Create* normally assigns standard default values to all the fields of a newly created object; these values may be overridden by defining a procedure called *Create* in the class.

5.10 SYNTACTICAL SUMMARY

This section describes the syntax of the Eiffel constructs encountered in this chapter. This syntactical description and similar ones given in subsequent chapters use the notation introduced on page xvi.

Class_declaration	=	Class_header
		[Formal_generics]
		[Exports]
		[Parents]
		[Features]
		[Class_invariant]
		end ["--" class Class_name]
Class_header	=	[Deferred_mark] **class** Class_name
Deferred_mark	=	(See chapter 10)
Class_name	=	Identifier
Formal_generics	=	(See chapter 6)
Exports	=	**export** Export_list
Export_list	=	{Export_item "," ...}
Export_item	=	Feature_name [Export_restriction]
Feature_name	=	Identifier
Export_restriction	=	(See chapter 9)
Parents	=	(See chapter 10)
Features	=	**feature** {Feature_declaration ";" ...}
Feature_declaration	=	Feature_name
		[Formal_arguments]
		[Type_mark]
		[Feature_value_mark]
Formal_arguments	=	Entity_declaration_list
Entity_declaration_list	=	{Entity_declaration_group ";" ...}
Entity_declaration_group	=	{Identifier "," ...}$^+$ Type_mark
Type_mark	=	":" Type
Type	=	*INTEGER* | *BOOLEAN* | *CHARACTER* | *REAL* |
		Class_type | Formal_generic | Association
Class_type	=	Class_name [Actual_generics]
Actual_generics	=	(See chapter 6)
Formal_generic	=	(See chapter 6)
Association	=	(See chapter 11)

Feature_value_mark	=	**is** Feature_value
Feature_value	=	Constant | Routine
Constant	=	(See chapter 13)
Routine	=	[Precondition] [Externals] [Local_variables] Body [Postcondition] [Rescue] **end** ["--" Feature_name]
Precondition	=	(See chapter 7)
Externals	=	(See chapter 8)
Postcondition	=	(See chapter 7)
Rescue	=	(See chapter 7)
Local_variables	=	Entity_declaration_list
Body	=	Full_body | Deferred_body
Deferred_body	=	(See chapter 10)
Full_body	=	Normal_body | Once_body
Normal_body	=	**do** Compound
Once_body	=	(See chapter 13)
Compound	=	{Instruction ";" ...}
Instruction	=	Call | Assignment | Conditional | Loop | Check | Retry | Debug
Call	=	Qualified_call | Unqualified_call
Qualified_call	=	Expression "." Unqualified_call
Expression	=	(See chapter 8)
Unqualified_call	=	Feature_name [Actuals]
Actuals	=	"(" Expression_list ")"
Expression_list	=	{Expression Separator ...}
Separator	=	"," | ";"
Assignment	=	Entity ":=" Expression
Entity	=	Identifier | *Result*
Conditional	=	(See chapter 8)
Loop	=	(See chapter 8)
Check	=	(See chapter 7)
Retry	=	(See chapter 7)
Debug	=	(See chapter 8)
Class_invariant	=	(See chapter 7)

6

Genericity

This chapter introduces one more weapon in our arsenal of techniques for improving the flexibility and reusability of modules. By giving classes parameters representing arbitrary types, we avoid the need to write many almost identical classes, without sacrificing the safety guaranteed by static typing.

An elusive question for students of object-oriented languages is how genericity compares with another key method for improving the generality of modules: inheritance. Should inheritance and genericity be viewed as comrades or competitors in the rush towards more flexible software? This will be the subject of chapter 19.

6.1 PARAMETERIZING CLASSES

6.1.1 The issue

Genericity, as we know from the table searching example (3.6.2), is the ability to parameterize modules. The need for this facility is particularly clear for classes representing general data structures: arrays, lists, trees, matrices etc.

Assume for example you want to define a class representing stacks of integers; it will be of the form:

```
class INTSTACK export
      nb_elements, empty, full, push, pop, top
feature
      ...
end -- class INTSTACK
```

Type *INTEGER* will be used frequently in this class. For example it is the type of the result returned by *top* :

> *top: INTEGER* **is**
>   -- Top of stack
>   **do ... end**

With this approach, you must write a different class for every sort of stack: *INTSTACK* , *REALSTACK* , *POINTSTACK* etc. This does not make sense since the choice of data representations and algorithms is not affected by the type of stack elements. Instead, you should declare a **generic** stack class, parameterized by the type of the stack elements. The Eiffel syntax for declaring a generic class resembles the informal notation used in 3.6.2:

>   -- Stacks of elements of an arbitrary type *T*
> **class** *STACK [T]* **export**
>   *nb_elements, empty, full, push, pop, top*
> **feature**
>   *nb_elements: INTEGER*;
>
>   *empty: BOOLEAN* **is**
>   -- Is stack empty?
>   **do ... end**;
>
>   *full: BOOLEAN* **is**
>   -- Is stack representation full?
>   **do ... end**;
>
>   *push (x: T)* **is**
>   -- Add *x* on top
>   **do ... end**;
>
>   *pop* **is**
>   -- Remove top element
>   **do ... end**;
>
>   *top: T* **is**
>   -- Top element
>   **do ... end**;
>
> **end** -- class *STACK*

The names given in square brackets, such as *T* here, are separated by commas if more than one; they are called **formal generic parameters**.

In the class, you may use a formal generic parameter such as *T* in declarations: not only for function results (as *top*) and routine parameters (as *push*), but also for attributes and local variables.

A client may use a generic class to declare entities. In such a case, the declaration must provide types, called **actual generic parameters**, corresponding in number to the formal generic parameters, as in

> *sp: STACK [POINT]*

An actual generic parameter is one of the following:

1. • A simple type (*INTEGER*, *REAL*, *CHARACTER*, *BOOLEAN*).
2. • A class type.
3. • A formal generic parameter of the client class.[1]

In case 2, a class type is a class name, possibly followed by actual generic parameters if the class is generic. This means that an actual generic parameter may itself be parameterized, as in

> *ssp: STACK [STACK [POINT]]*

As an example of case 3, class *STACK* could contain an entity declaration of the form *implementation: ARRAY [T]* where *ARRAY* (seen below) is another generic class. *T*, formal parameter of the enclosing class *STACK*, is used as actual generic parameter to *ARRAY* in this declaration.

6.1.2   Type checking

Using genericity, you can guarantee that a data structure will only contain elements of a single type. For example, assuming class *C* contains the declarations

> *ps: STACK [POINT]*; *is: STACK [INTEGER]*; *p: POINT*

then the following are valid instructions in *C*:

> *ps.push (p)*;   -- Push a point onto a stack of points
> *is.push (45)*;   -- Push an integer onto a stack of integers
> *p := ps.top*   -- Assign to a point entity the top of a stack of points

but each of the following will be rejected by the compiler:

> *ps.push (45)*;   -- Attempt to push an integer onto a stack of points
> *is.push (p)*;   -- Attempt to push a point onto a stack of integers
> *p := is.top*   -- Attempt to access as a point the top of an integer stack

In fact, genericity is only meaningful in a typed language, where each entity is declared as being of a certain type, so that it is possible to determine whether any operation is typewise correct, either by simply looking at the program text (*static* typing) or by checking at execution time (*dynamic* typing). Eiffel is a statically typed language, where all type checking is done by the compiler. In a typeless language, there is no way to restrict the types of elements that go into a data structure such as a stack, so generic classes would not serve any purpose.

6.1.3   Operations on entities of generic types

Consider a class *C* [*U*, *V*] and an entity whose type is one of the formal generic parameters, for example *x* of type *U*. When the class is used by a client to declare entities, *U* may ultimately represent any type – simple or class. So any operation on *x* must be applicable to all types. This leaves only four kinds of operation:

---

[1] There is in fact a fourth case: types of the form **like** *something* (see chapter 11).

> **Formal generic parameter rule**: The only legal uses for an entity
> *x* whose type *U* is a formal generic parameter are the following:
>
> 1. Use of *x* as left-hand side in an assignment, *x* := *y*, where
>   the right-hand side expression *y* must also be of type *U*.
>
> 2. Use of *x* as right-hand side of an assignment *y* := *x*, where
>   the left-hand side entity *y* is also of type *U*.
>
> 3. Use of *x* as actual argument in a routine call *f* (..., *x*, ...),
>   corresponding to a formal argument declared of type *U* (which
>   implies that *f* must be a routine declared in the same class as
>   *x*).
>
> 4. Use of *x* in a boolean expression of the form *x* = *y* or *x* /= *y*,
>   where *y* is also of type *U*.

In particular, operations such as *x. Create*, *x. Forget* or any other feature
application on *x* are illegal, since there is no guarantee that the actual generic
parameter provided for *U* will be a class type.[2]

Now assume that *f* is declared in *C* as an exported attribute of type *U*, or an
exported function returning a result of type *U*, and a client has declared

   h: C [A, B]

then within the client the expression *h. f* (with parameters if needed) is considered to
be of type *A* and the compiler will check that it is used accordingly.

6.2   ARRAYS

Many of the classes of the basic Eiffel library represent general data structures and are
thus generic: stacks, queues, lists, trees, ... An important class is *ARRAY*, which
represents one-dimensional arrays. It is indeed convenient to consider arrays as a class
rather than a predefined language construct. An outline of the class (whose complete
text may be found in Appendix A) is:

```
class ARRAY [T] export
      lower, upper, size, entry, enter
feature
      lower, upper, size: INTEGER;
                  -- Minimum and maximum legal index; array size.

      Create (minb, maxb: INTEGER) is
                  -- Allocate array with bounds minb and maxb
                  -- (empty if minb > maxb)
            do ... end;
```

---

[2] Ada programmers will recognize that a formal generic parameter is treated like a "private"
type (see 18.2.4).

> entry (i: INTEGER): T **is**
>   -- Entry of index i
>   **do** ... **end**;
>
> enter (i: INTEGER; value: T) **is**
>   -- Assign value to the entry of index i
>   **do** ... **end**
> **end** -- class ARRAY

Function entry returns the value of an array element; procedure enter changes the value of an element. Create allows dynamic array allocation. The following shows how this class is typically used:

> pa: ARRAY [POINT]; p1: POINT; i, j: INTEGER
> ...
> pa.Create (–32, 101)   -- Allocate array with bounds given
> pa.enter (i, p1)   -- Assign p1 to entry of index i;
> ...
> p1 := pa.entry (j)   -- Assign to p1 the value of entry of index j

In conventional (say Pascal) notation, you would write

> pa [i] := p1   for   pa.enter (i, p1)
> p1 := pa [i]   for   p1 := pa.entry (i)

Four comments on arrays:

- Similar classes exist for arrays with more dimensions: ARRAY2 etc.

- Feature size may be implemented as either an attribute or a function, since it satisfies size = upper–lower+1. This is expressed in the actual class by an invariant, as explained in the next chapter.

- The assertion techniques introduced in the next chapter will also enable us to associate consistency conditions with enter and entry, expressing that calls are only valid if the index i is between lower and upper.

- Finally, efficient implementation of arrays requires direct access to memory. Routines Create, enter and entry are implemented through external functions (written in C in the Eiffel environment on Unix). Eiffel is easily interfaced with low-level routines of this nature; the mechanism (**external** clause) is described in chapter 8.

6.3 DISCUSSION

As has been noted, genericity is only meaningful in a typed language. The restrictions suggested may seem too harsh, however: what about declaring a stack that may contain, say, vectors as well as points? With the techniques seen so far, this is not possible, since any use of a generic class must refer to uniquely defined actual generic parameters, as in STACK [POINT] or STACK [VECTOR].

The problem will be solved by inheritance. Roughly speaking, you may declare an entity *s* to be of type *STACK [TWO_COORD]*, where *TWO_COORD* is a class general enough to encompass *POINT* and *VECTOR*. The type situation is still safe, since only entities of a type compatible with *TWO_COORD* will be accepted in operations on *s*. The techniques will be explained in chapters 10 and 11.

6.4 KEY CONCEPTS INTRODUCED IN THIS CHAPTER

- Classes may have formal generic parameters representing types.

- Generic classes serve to describe general data structures that are implemented in the same way regardless of the elements they contain.

- Genericity is only needed in a typed language, to statically ensure type consistency in data structures.

- A client of a generic class must provide actual types for the formal generic parameters.

- The only operations applicable to an entity whose type is a formal generic parameter are operations applicable to every type. The entity may serve as left- or right-hand-side of an assignment, actual routine argument, or operand of an equality or inequality test.

6.5 SYNTACTICAL SUMMARY

			Used in (chapter)
Formal_generics	=	"[" Formal_generic_list "]"	Class_header (5)
Formal_generic_list	=	{Formal_generic ","...}	
Formal_generic	=	Identifier	
Actual_generics	=	"[" Type_list "]"	Class_type (5)
Type_list	=	{Type "," ...}	

6.6 BIBLIOGRAPHICAL NOTES

A form of genericity was originally introduced by Algol 68 [van Wijngaarden 1975]. Different forms may be found in Ada (see chapters 18 and 19) and a few other programming languages such as CLU [Liskov 1981] and LPG [Bert 1983].

Genericity has also been introduced in formal specification languages: Z [Abrial 1980], Clear [Burstall 1981], OBJ2 [Futatsugi 1985] and M [Meyer 1987].

Since so many object-oriented languages are untyped, few offer genericity. One that does is Trellis/Owl [Schaffert 1986].

7

Systematic approaches to software construction

By now you can write software modules that implement classes of possibly parameterized data structures. Congratulations. This is a significant step in the quest for better software architectures.

But the techniques seen so far are not sufficient to implement the comprehensive view of quality introduced in chapter 1. The quality factors most touted in the object-oriented approach – reusability, extendibility, compatibility – must not be attained at the expense of correctness and robustness. The concern for correctness was, of course, reflected in the emphasis on strict static typing. But more is needed.

The discussion that led to the general definition of the method, in chapter 4, emphasized that classes should be implementations of abstract data types. Indeed, the classes seen so far are collections of attributes and routines, which may serve to represent the functions of an abstract data type specification. But an abstract data type is more than just a list of available operations: remember the fundamental role played by the semantic properties, as expressed by the axioms and preconditions. These are essential to capture the fundamental properties of the instances of the type.

In studying classes, we have lost sight of this fundamental aspect of the abstract data type concept. We will need to bring it back into the object-oriented method if we want our software to be not just flexible and reusable, but also correct.

Assertions and the associated concepts, explained in this chapter, provide some of the answer. Although not foolproof (see in particular the remarks in 7.11) the mechanisms presented below provide the programmer with essential tools for expressing and validating correctness arguments. The key notion here will be the concept of **programming by contract**: the relationship between a class and its clients is viewed as a formal agreement, expressing each party's rights and obligations. Only through such a precise definition of every module's claims and responsibilities can we hope to attain a significant degree of trust in large software systems.

In reviewing these concepts, we shall also encounter a key problem of software engineering: how to deal with run-time errors. A disciplined method to exception handling will be presented.

Important extensions to the notion of programming by contract will be studied in chapter 11, which presents inheritance and dynamic binding as a natural consequence of the approach: the idea of *subcontracting*.

7.1   THE NOTION OF ASSERTION

Although there is no magical recipe to ensure correctness, the general direction is clear: since correctness is the conformance of software implementations to their specifications, you should try to reduce the risk of discrepancies between the two. One way to do this is to include specification elements within the implementations themselves. More generally, you may associate with an element of executable code – instruction, routine, class – an expression of the element's purpose. Such an expression (which states what the element must do, independently of how it does it) will be called an **assertion**.

An assertion is a property of some of the values of program entities. For example, an assertion may express that a certain integer has a positive value or that a certain reference is void.

Mathematically, the closest notion is that of predicate, although the assertion language that we shall use has only part of the power of full predicate calculus.

Syntactically, assertions are simply boolean expressions, with a few extensions. The first extension is the use of the semicolon, as in

$n > 0$; **not** $x.Void$

The meaning of the semicolon is equivalent to that of an **and**; the semicolon facilitates identification of the individual components of an assertion. These components may indeed be labeled, as in

Positive: $n > 0$; Not_void: **not** $x.Void$

If present, the label is recorded by the run-time system when something goes wrong, either to produce messages or to allow handling under programmer control (see 7.10 below). Two further extensions to boolean expressions are provided in assertions: the **old** and *Nochange* notations, explained below.

In the Eiffel environment, assertions may optionally be monitored at run-time. This makes them a powerful debugging tool. They are also the basis for a disciplined exception facility, enabling systems to attempt recovery after a failure. For the time being, however, the emphasis will be on the application of assertions as a conceptual tool for increasing the correctness and robustness of software. Assertions will be studied as a technique for constructing correct systems and documenting *why* they are correct.

7.2 PRECONDITIONS AND POSTCONDITIONS

The first use of assertions is the semantic specification of routines. A routine is not just a piece of code; as the implementation of some function from an abstract data type specification, it should perform some useful task. It is essential to express this task precisely, both as an aid in design (after all, you cannot hope to check that a routine is correct unless you have specified what it is supposed to do) and, later on, as an aid to understanding its text.

The task performed by a routine may be specified by two assertions associated with the routine: a *precondition* and a *postcondition*. The precondition expresses the properties that must hold whenever the routine is called; the postcondition describes the properties that the routine guarantees when it returns.

7.2.1 A stack class

In the previous chapter, we outlined a generic stack class, under the following form:

> **class** *STACK* [*T*] **export**
>   *nb_elements, empty, full, push, pop, top*
> **feature**
>
>   ... *Declaration of the features* ...
>
> **end** -- class *STACK*

We will introduce an implementation below. Before considering implementation issues, however, it is important to note that the routines are characterized by strong semantic properties, independent of any specific representation. For example:

- Routines *pop* and *top* are only applicable if the number of elements is not zero.

- After *push*, the number of elements is increased by one; after *pop*, it is decreased by one.

Routine preconditions and postconditions are aimed precisely at making these properties explicit. They are given in clauses of routine declarations introduced by the keywords **require** and **ensure**, respectively. For example:

> **class** *STACK1* [*T*] **export**
>   *nb_elements, empty, full, push, pop, top*
> **feature**
>   *nb_elements: INTEGER*;
>
>   *empty: BOOLEAN* **is**
>   -- Is stack empty?
>   **do** ...
>   **end**; -- *empty*
>
>   *full: BOOLEAN* **is**
>   -- Is stack representation full?
>   **do** ...
>   **end**; -- *full*

```
push (x: T) is
            -- Add x on top
        require
            not full
        do ...
        ensure
            not empty;
            top = x;
            nb_elements = old nb_elements + 1
        end; -- push

pop is
            -- Remove top element
        require
            not empty
        do ...
        ensure
            not full;
            nb_elements = old nb_elements - 1
        end; -- pop

top: T is
            -- Top element
        require
            not empty
        do ...
        end; -- top
end -- class STACK1
```

Both the **require** and the **ensure** clauses are optional; when present, they appear at the places shown. The **require** appears before the **local** clause, if present. The meaning of preconditions and postconditions will now be explained in more detail.

7.2.2 Preconditions

A precondition expresses the constraints under which a routine will function properly. In the above example:

- *push* may not be called if the stack representation is full.

- *pop* and *top* may not be applied to an empty stack.

A precondition applies to all calls of the routine, both from within the same class and from clients. In a correct system, no call is ever executed in a state in which a routine precondition is not satisfied.

7.2.3 Postconditions

A postcondition expresses properties of the state resulting from a routine's execution. Here:

- After a *push*, the stack may not be empty, its top is the element just pushed, and its number of elements has been increased by one.

- After a *pop*, the stack may not be full, and its number of elements has been decreased by one.

The presence of a postcondition clause in a routine expresses a guarantee on the part of the routine's implementor that the routine will produce a result satisfying certain conditions, provided it is called with the precondition satisfied.

Two special notations are available in postconditions. One, the **old** notation, was used above to express the changes to *nb_elements*. In general, **old** *a*, where *a* is an attribute, denotes the value that the corresponding object field had on routine entry. Any occurrence of *a* not preceded by **old** in the postcondition denotes the value of the field on exit. For example the postcondition of *push* includes

$$nb\_elements = \textbf{old } nb\_elements + 1$$

expressing that *push*, when applied to any object, must increase by one the value of the *nb_elements* field of that object.

Another notation permitted only in postconditions is the boolean-valued expression *Nochange*, which yields true if and only if no attribute of the current object has changed value since the call. This expression is useful as part of larger postconditions, as in the following example. Assume we change the specification of *pop* to allow popping an empty stack, with no effect. Then the precondition on *pop* disappears, and the postcondition becomes:

> **ensure**
> ((**not old** *empty*) **and** (*nb_elements* = **old** *nb_elements* – *1*) **and not** *full*)
> **or** ((**old** *empty*) **and** *Nochange*)

(Operator precedence rules, as given in Appendix C, would allow all parentheses to be dropped here.)

7.3 CONTRACTING FOR SOFTWARE RELIABILITY

Preconditions and postconditions can play a crucial role in helping programmers write correct programs – and know why they are correct.

The presence of a precondition and postcondition in a routine should be viewed as a **contract** that binds the routine and its callers.

7.3.1 Rights and obligations

One may refer more generally to the two parties in the contract as the class and the clients. By associating clauses **require** *pre* and **ensure** *post* with a routine *r*, the class is saying to its clients:

> "If you promise to call *r* with *pre* satisfied then I, in return, promise to deliver a final state in which *post* is satisfied."

What is a contract? Perhaps the most distinctive feature of contracts as they occur in human affairs is that any good contract entails obligations as well as benefits for both parties. This is true of contracts between classes, too:

- The precondition binds clients: it defines the conditions under which a call to the routine is legitimate.

- The postcondition, in return, binds the class: it defines the conditions that must be ensured by the routine on return.

The benefits are, for the client, the guarantee that certain results will be obtained after the call; for the class, the guarantee that certain assumptions will be satisfied whenever the routine is called.

	Obligations	**Benefits**
Client Programmer	Only call *push* (*x*) on a non-full stack	Get *x* added as new stack top on return (*top* yields *x*, *nb_elements* increased by 1)
Module Implementor	Make sure that *x* is pushed on top of stack	No need to treat cases in which the stack is already full

Figure 7.1   A class contract: routine *push* from *STACK1*

7.3.2   What if the precondition is not satisfied?

The last point mentioned corresponds to the bottom right box of the table; it is worth emphasizing. If the client's part of the contract is not fulfilled, that is to say if the call does not satisfy the precondition, then the class is not bound by the postcondition. In this case the routine may do what it pleases: return any value; loop indefinitely without returning a value; or even terminate execution in some wild way.

The advantage of this convention is that it considerably simplifies the programming style. Having specified as a precondition the constraints which must be observed by calls to a routine, you, the class programmer, may assume, when writing the routine body, that the constraints are satisfied; you do not need to test for them in the body. So if a square root function begins with

sqrt (x: REAL): REAL **is**
         -- Square root of *x*
     require
         x >= 0
     do ...

then you may write the algorithm for computing the square root without any regard for the case in which *x* is negative; this is taken care of by the precondition and becomes the responsibility of your clients. (At first sight this may appear dangerous; but read on.)

The issue here is a crucial one is programming – and very practical. One of the main sources of complexity in programs is the constant need to check whether data passed to a processing element (routine) satisfy the requirements for correct processing. Where should these checks be performed: in the routine itself or in its callers? Unless module designers formally agree on a precise distribution of responsibilities, the checks end up not being done at all, a very unsafe situation or, out of concern for safety, being done several times.

Redundant checking may seem harmless, but it is not. It hampers efficiency, of course; but even more important is the conceptual pollution that it brings to software systems. Complexity is probably the single most important enemy of software quality. The distribution of redundant checks all over a software system destroys the conceptual simplicity of the system, increases the risk for errors, and hampers such qualities as extendibility, understandability and maintainability.[1]

The recommended approach is to systematically use preconditions, and then allow module authors to assume, when writing the body of a routine, that the corresponding precondition is satisfied. The aim is to permit a simple style of programming, favoring readability, maintainability and other associated qualities.

As an example, assume we want to implement the *STACK* class using the standard contiguous technique: an array of bounds 1 and *max_size*, and an integer indicator to the top of the stack, which is none other than the attribute *nb_elements*. This representation is pictured below.

---

[1] Redundant checking is a standard technique in hardware. The reason is that some object which was found to be in a correct state at some point may later have its integrity destroyed because of external events. For example the integrity of an electronic signal will be checked by both emitter and receiver. No such phenomenon occurs in software: if I can prove or check in some way that *a* is non-negative whenever *sqrt* (*a*) is called, I do not need to insert a check for $x \geq 0$, where *x* is the corresponding formal argument, in the body of *sqrt* – unless, of course, the system whose correctness I am assessing is the compiler or the linker.

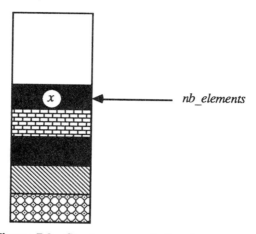

Figure 7.2   Stack representation by an array

The class may be written as follows.[2]

class *STACK2* *[T]* **export**
    push, pop, top, empty, nb_elements, empty, full
feature
    implementation: ARRAY [T];
    max_size: INTEGER;
    nb_elements: INTEGER;

    Create (n: INTEGER) **is**
            -- Allocate stack for a maximum of *n* elements
            -- (or for no elements if *n < 0*)
        do
            if *n > 0* **then** *max_size := n* **end**;
            implementation.Create (1, max_size)
        end; -- *Create*

    empty: BOOLEAN **is**
            -- Is stack empty?
        do
            Result := (nb_elements = 0)
        end; -- *empty*

---

[2] Recall that if *a* is an array, then the operation to assign value *x* to its *i*-th element is *a.enter* (*i, x*), and the value of its *i*-th element is given by *a.entry* (*i*). If, as here, the bounds of the array are 1 and *max_size*, then *i* must in both cases lie between these bounds.

```
full: BOOLEAN is
        -- Is stack full?
    do
        Result := (nb_elements = max_size)
    end; -- empty

pop is
        -- Remove top element
    require
        not empty -- i.e. nb_elements > 0
    do
        nb_elements := nb_elements - 1
    ensure
        not full;
        nb_elements = old nb_elements - 1
    end; -- pop

top: T is
        -- Top element
    require
        not empty -- i.e. nb_elements > 0
    do
        Result := implementation.entry (nb_elements)
    end; -- top

push (x: T) is
        -- Add x on top
    require
        not full
            -- i.e. nb_elements < array_size in this representation
    do
        nb_elements := nb_elements + 1;
        implementation.enter (nb_elements, x)
    ensure
        not empty;
        top = x;
        nb_elements = old nb_elements + 1
    end; -- push
end -- class STACK2
```

The code for each of these routines is simple because the bodies of *pop* and *top* do not need to test for underflow, and the body of *push* does not need to test for overflow. These constraints are taken care of in the preconditions.

You should be convinced by now that the approach advocated does not imply a lax attitude toward errors. It is actually the reverse: by forcing a clear definition of **whose responsibility** it is to check every condition required for correct operation, the method emphasizes a systematic, rigorous approach to the construction of correct programs.

One apparently surprising aspect of this implementation is that *Create* has no precondition: clients creating stacks are not required to use a positive value for the maximum size *n*! This is the way it should be. A non-negative *n* is not an error; it simply means that this particular stack will always be empty. An error would occur only if a *push* was attempted on this stack. Similarly, an array may be created, by *a.Create (low, up)*, even if *up > low*; the result is an empty array, not an error. When one defines a general data structure such as a stack or array, it is important to acknowledge that clients will, every once in a while, create empty instances, and should not be blamed for it.[3]

7.3.3 How restrictive?

The question remains, however, of how much you can trust others. Take the above implementations of *push* and *pop*. If a client does not observe the precondition, some catastrophe (out-of-bounds array reference) will occur. You do not want this to happen during the execution of an application program that happens to use stacks for its implementation.

The answer is as in real life: you trust clients to the extent that you know them. It all depends on who calls the routines. If you have direct control over the clients, then you can afford to define strict preconditions in order to keep the code simple: you take responsibility for ensuring that all calls satisfy the preconditions. If not, you should probably loosen the preconditions in order to deal explicitly with errors.

It is tempting to say "Why not loosen the preconditions anyway for added safety, and make sure that all cases are dealt with somehow?". Function *top*, for example, could produce an error message when called on an empty stack:

```
top: T is
            -- Top element
    require
        not empty -- i.e. nb_elements > 0
    do
        if empty then
            output_message ("Error: calling top on an empty stack")
        else
            Result := entry (nb_elements)
        end
    end; -- top
```

(Syntactically, *top* must always return a value of type *T*; the initialization conventions of Eiffel imply that *Result* will be the default value of type *T* in erroneous cases.)

This temptation should be resisted in the interests of simplicity and design coherence. You cannot trust that a large system will function properly unless you have

---

[3] A system that uses the inverse convention is Algol W. When a dynamically allocated array has an empty range, the program terminates in error – even if it was a perfectly valid array which simply happened to be empty on that particular run. This is too restrictive: zero should be a valid size for an array. What's wrong is any attempt to *access* elements of an array with zero size.

ensured that every component has a well-defined job, does it well, does it all and does it only. It is not the job of a stack module to deal with error messages, which are a user interface issue. Stack modules should deal with the efficient implementation of stack operations. To keep the body of *top* simple and convincing, the precondition **not** *empty* must be assumed.

So there is a strong case for defining the routines of basic modules with appropriate preconditions, without undue regard for possible usage errors.

7.3.4 Filter modules

The simple but unprotected basic modules may not be robust enough for use by arbitrary clients. The above remarks do not preclude the construction of new layers of software that will serve as filters between possibly careless clients and unprotected classes. For example, a protected version of *STACK* might be made available, as follows:

```
class STACK3 [T]          -- Protected
export
        nb_elements, empty, full, push, pop, top, error
feature
        implementation: STACK [T];

        error: INTEGER;
                -- After each operation, error
                -- will be set as follows:
                        -- error = 0: no error, operation was executed
                        -- error > 0: not executed
                                -- 1: would have provoked underflow
                                -- 2: would have provoked overflow

        Create (n: INTEGER) is
                -- Allocate stack with space for n elements

                do implementation.Create (1, n) end; -- Create

        nb_elements: INTEGER is
                -- Number of elements on stack

                do Result := implementation.nb_elements end; -- nb_elements

        -- Note that nb_elements is here a function rather than an attribute

        empty: BOOLEAN is
                -- Is stack empty?

                do Result := implementation.empty end; -- empty

        full: BOOLEAN is
                -- Is stack representation full?

                do Result := implementation.full end; -- full
```

push (*x: T*) **is**

-- Add *x* on top if possible; otherwise set error code.
-- No precondition!
do
  if *full* **then**
    error := 2
  else
    implementation.push (*x*); *error := 0*
  end
ensure
  (**old** *full* **and** *error* = 2) **or**
    (**not old** *full* **and not** *empty* **and** *top* = *x*
    and *nb_elements* = **old** *nb_elements* + *1* **and** *error* = *0*)
end; -- *push*

pop **is**

-- Remove top element if possible; otherwise set error.
-- No precondition!
do
  if *empty* **then**
    error := 1
  else
    implementation.pop; *error := 0*
  end
ensure
  (**old** *empty* **and** *error* = *1*) **or**
    (**not old** *empty* **and not** *full*
    and *nb_elements* = **old** *nb_elements–1* **and** *error* = *0*)
end; -- *pop*

top: T **is**

-- Top element if present; otherwise return 0 and set error.
-- No precondition!
do
  if *empty* **then**
    error := 1
      -- In this case result is the default value
  else
    Result := implementation.top; *error := 0*
  end
end -- *top*

end -- class *STACK3*

The operations of this class have no preconditions (or, more correctly stated, have **true** as their preconditions). For those that may result in abnormal situations, the postcondition has been refined to distinguish between correct and erroneous processing. An operation such as *s. pop* , where *s* is a *STACK3*, will set *s. error* to 0 or 1 and, in the latter case, do nothing else. Of course, it is still the caller's responsibility to check for *s. error* after the call. A general-purpose module such as *STACK3* has no way to decide what to do in the case of an erroneous popping attempt: produce an error message, take corrective action....

> The routines of the filter class may be viewed as security officers in, say, a large government laboratory. To meet experts from the laboratory and ask them technical questions, you must submit to screening procedures. But it is not the same person who checks your authorization level and answers the technical questions. The janitors are not qualified to answer the questions; and the experts, once you have been officially brought into their offices, assume you satisfy the "preconditions".

Such filter modules achieve the needed separation of concerns between algorithmic techniques to deal with normal cases and techniques for handling errors. This is the distinction between correctness and robustness explained in chapter 1: writing a module that performs correctly in legal cases is one task; making sure that other cases are also handled decently is a quite different one. Both are necessary, but they should be handled separately. Failure to do so is one of the major sources of the pollution mentioned above.

Two more remarks apply to this example:

- The particular implementation used above seems inefficient, as a *STACK3* is not an array but a structure containing a pointer (*implementation*) to a *STACK* object, itself containing a pointer to an array. These extra indirections may be avoided, however, by using inheritance. We have to wait until chapter 10 to achieve this needed simplification, which is the object of exercise 11.1.

- Rather than by literal values 0, 1 and 2, the error codes should be known to clients through symbolic names *Normal*, *Underflow*, *Overflow*; see chapter 13.

7.4   CLASS INVARIANTS AND CLASS CORRECTNESS

7.4.1   Definition and example

Preconditions and postconditions describe the properties of individual routines. There is also a need for expressing global properties of the instances of a class, which must be preserved by all routines.

As an example, consider again the implementation of stacks by arrays, but without the protections (*STACK 2*):

```
class STACK2 [T] export ... see page 118 ... feature
     implementation: ARRAY [T];
     max_size: INTEGER;
     nb_elements: INTEGER;

     ...
     Create, empty, full, push, pop, top (see page 118)
     ...
end -- class STACK2 [T]
```

The three attributes of the class – array *implementation* and integers *max_size* and *nb_elements* – constitute the stack representation. The semantic properties of stacks are given in part by the preconditions and postconditions of routines, expressed above.

However these preconditions fail to express some important consistency requirements on the representation; for example, the attributes should satisfy at all times

0 <= nb_elements; *nb_elements <= max_size*

A class invariant is such a list of assertions, expressing general consistency constraints that apply to every class instance as a whole; this is different from preconditions and postconditions, which characterize individual routines.

The above assertions involve only attributes. Invariants may also be used to express the semantic relationships between functions, or between functions and attributes. For example the invariant for *STACK 2* may include the following property describing the connection between *empty* and *nb_elements*:

empty = (nb_elements = 0)

In this example, the invariant assertion links an attribute and a function; it is not particularly interesting as it merely repeats an assertion that should appear in the postcondition of the function (here *empty*). More useful assertions are those which involve either only attributes, as above, or more than one function.

7.4.2 Form and properties of class invariants

Syntactically, a class invariant is an assertion, appearing in the **invariant** clause of the class, after the features and just before the **end**, as in

> **class** *STACK2* [*T*] **export** ... **feature**
>   *implementation: ARRAY* [*T*];
>   *max_size: INTEGER*;
>   *nb_elements: INTEGER*;
>
>   ... *Other features as before* ...
> **invariant**
>   *0 <= nb_elements*; *nb_elements <= max_size*;
>   *empty = (nb_elements = 0)*
> **end** -- class *STACK2*

An invariant for a class *C* is a set of assertions that is be satisfied by every instance of *C* at all "stable" times. Stable times are defined as those in which an instance is in a stable state, namely:

- On instance creation, that is to say after execution of a call of the form *a.Create* (...), where *a* is of type *C*.

- Before and after every remote call *a.r* (...) to a routine of the class.

It is not an error for the invariant to be temporarily violated during the execution of a remote call, provided the routine restores the invariant before exit. In particular, the routine body may include local calls (of the form *r* (...), without qualification), which are not constrained to maintain the invariant.

As a consequence, a class invariant only applies to exported routines: secret routines, which are not directly executed by clients but only serve as auxiliary tools for carrying out the functions of exported routines, are not required to maintain the invariant.

From this discussion follows the rule that precisely defines when an assertion is a correct invariant for a class:[4]

Invariant rule: An assertion I is a correct class invariant for a class C if and only if the following two conditions are met:

1. The *Create* procedure of C, when applied to arguments satisfying its precondition in a state where the attributes have their default values, yields a state satisfying I.

2. Every exported routine of the class, when applied to arguments and a state satisfying both I and the routine's precondition, yields a state satisfying I.

Note that in this rule:

- Every class is considered to have a *Create* procedure, defined as a null operation if not explicitly specified.
- The state of an object is defined by the values of all its attribute fields.
- The precondition of a routine may involve the initial state and the arguments.
- The postcondition may only involve the final state, the initial state (through the **old** and *Nochange* notations) and, in the case of a function, the returned value, given by the predefined entity *Result*.
- The invariant may only involve the state.

(The postcondition and invariant may refer to functions, but a function appearing in an assertion is an indirect way of referring to the attributes.)

It follows from the above definitions that the class invariant is implicitly added (**and**ed) to both the precondition and postcondition of every exported routine. So we could do without invariants by just extending the preconditions and postconditions of all routines in the class. This would complicate the routine texts; more importantly, we would lose the meaning of the invariant, which transcends individual routines and applies to the class as a whole. One should in fact consider that the invariant applies not only to the routines actually written in the class, but also to any ones that might be added later, thus serving as control over future evolution of the class. This will be reflected in the inheritance rules (11.1.1).

The invariant has a clear interpretation in the analogy that serves as a basis for this discussion – contracting. Human contracts often contain references to general clauses or regulations that apply to all contracts within a certain category (for example all building contracts). Invariants play a similar role for contracts between routines: the invariant of a class applies to all the contracts between a routine of the class and a client.

The invariant binds both the client programmer and the class implementor. From the latter's perspective, it makes the job of writing a class both easier and harder:

---

4 See 7.11.3 for a caveat on the use of this rule in Eiffel.

- The invariant may be added to the precondition of every routine (except *Create*), which restricts the extent of cases that must be considered in the body – making the job easier.

- But at the same time the invariant must be added to the postcondition of every routine including *Create*, which broadens the extent of properties that must be ensured by the body – making the job harder.

7.4.3 Correctness of a class

(This section may be skipped on first reading.)

With preconditions, postconditions and invariants, we can now define precisely what it means for a class to be correct.

In general, software correctness is a relative notion: saying that a program is correct or incorrect is meaningless unless you state precisely the specification against which you are assessing its correctness. With assertion techniques as they exist in Eiffel you may include this specification within the program text itself, in the form of class invariants and routine preconditions and postconditions. The class is correct if and only if its implementation, as given by the routine bodies, is consistent with this specification.

A few notations are needed to define this notion more precisely. First, the notation

$\{P\}\ A\ \{Q\}$,

where P and Q are assertions and A is an instruction or sequence of instructions, means

> The execution of A, if started in a state in which P is satisfied, terminates in a state in which Q is satisfied.

For example:

$\{x = 0\}\ x := x+5\ \{x >= 3\}$

Let C be a class, INV its class invariant. For any routine r of the class, call $pre_r\ (x_r)$ and $post_r$ its precondition and postcondition; in the precondition, x_r denotes the possible arguments of r. (If the precondition or postcondition is missing from the routine text, then pre_r or $post_r$ is just **true**.) The body of routine r is denoted by B_r.

We may assume that class C includes a *Create* procedure; if not, we just consider B_{Create} to be an empty instruction.

Finally, let $Default_C$ be the assertion expressing that the attributes of C have the default values of their types. For the above class $Default_{STACK2}$ is the assertion

implementation.Void;
max_size = 0;
nb_elements = 0

With these notations, class correctness may be defined as follows:

Definition (*Class correctness*): A class is said to be correct with respect to its assertions if and only if:

1. For every exported routine r other than *Create* and any set of valid arguments x_r:

$$\{INV \text{ and } pre_r \ (x_r)\} \ B_r \ \{INV \text{ and } post_r\}$$

2. For any valid set of arguments x_{Create} to *Create*:

$$\{Default_C \text{ and } pre_{Create} \ (x_{Create})\} \ B_{Create} \ \{INV\}$$

Condition 1 expresses that r, if called with its precondition satisfied, maintains the invariant and ensures its postcondition. Condition 2 means that *Create*, if called with its precondition satisfied, ensures its postcondition and the invariant.

Two important remarks:

- If there is no specific *Create* procedure, that is to say if B_{Create} is an empty instruction, the second condition simply amounts to saying that $Default_C$ implies INV – in other words, the default values satisfy the invariant.

- A requirement of the form $\{P\} \ A \ \{Q\}$ does not commit A in any fashion for cases in which P is not initially satisfied. The notation is thus in line with the property explained above (page 116): the contract is not binding on the routine if the client fails to observe its part of the deal. Indeed, the above definition of correctness leaves the routines of the class free to do as they please for any call that violates the precondition or the invariant.

What has just been described is how to *define* the correctness of a class. In practice, one also wants to *check* whether a given class is indeed correct. This issue will be discussed later (7.10).

7.4.4   *Create* revisited

The discussion of class invariants allows us to put the role of the *Create* procedure in proper perspective.

A class invariant expresses the set of properties that must be satisfied by objects (instances) of the class in what we have called the stable moments of their lifetime. In particular, these properties must hold upon instance creation.

The standard object allocation mechanism initializes fields to the default values of the corresponding attribute types; these values may or may not satisfy the invariant. If not, a specific *Create* procedure is required; it should set the values of the attributes so as to satisfy the invariant. So *Create* may be seen as the operation that ensures that all instances of a class start their lives in a correct mode – one in which the invariant is satisfied.

Of course, specific *Create* procedures also serve another purpose: allowing for the creation of parameterized instances of a class. However the theoretical aim – ensuring the initial validity of the invariant, in other words the initial consistency of all instances – should not be forgotten.

7.4.5 Arrays revisited

The library class *ARRAY* was sketched in the previous chapter. Its definition cannot be adequately given, however, without the proper assertions. Here is a better sketch, with preconditions, postconditions and invariant. The assertions express in particular the standard requirement on array access and modification: indices should be in the permitted range. The invariant shows the relation between *size*, *lower* and *upper*; it would allow *size* to be implemented as a function rather than an attribute.

class *ARRAY* [*T*] **export**
    lower, upper, size, entry, enter
feature
    lower: INTEGER;
        -- Minimum legal index

    upper: INTEGER;
        -- Maximum legal index

    size: INTEGER;
        -- Array size

    Create (*minb, maxb: INTEGER*) **is**
        -- Allocate array with bounds *minb* and *maxb* (empty if *minb* > *maxb*)
      do ... **end**;

    entry (*i: INTEGER*): *T* **is**
        -- Entry of index *i*
      require
      lower <= *i*; *i* <= *upper*
      do ...
      end; -- *entry*

    enter (*i: INTEGER*; *value: T*) **is**
        -- Assign *value* to the entry of index *i*
      require
      lower <= *i*; *i* <= *upper*
      do ...
      ensure
      entry (*i*) = *value*
      end -- *enter*
invariant
  size = *upper* − *lower* + *1*; *size* >= *0*
end -- class *ARRAY*

7.5   SOME THEORY

The role of assertions seen so far – routine preconditions and postconditions, class invariants – may only be properly understood in consideration of abstract data types. A class is one implementation of an abstract data type; the assertions serve to re-introduce the abstract data type into the implementation.

7.5.1   Not just a collection of functions

As described in chapter 4, an abstract data type is defined in four parts: the name of the type; the signatures of the functions; the preconditions restricting applicability of these functions; and the axioms expressing their properties. Simple-minded applications of abstract data types often overlook the last two parts. This removes much of the appeal of the approach, since preconditions and axioms express the semantic properties of the type's functions. If you omit them and simply view "stack" as encapsulating the (not specified further) operations *push*, *pop* etc., you retain the benefits of information hiding, but that's all. There is no expressed constraint on what the operations should do; "stack" becomes an empty shell, with no semantics other than suggested by the operation names.

This risk transposes to programming in an object-oriented language: the routines which are supposed to implement the operations of the corresponding abstract data types could in principle perform just about any operations. Assertions serve to avert that risk by bringing the semantics back in.

7.5.2   Classification of abstract data type functions

To show how this is done we need to recall the three kinds of function that may appear in the specification of an abstract data type (chapter 4.7.7). Let T be the type and

$$f: A \times B \times ... \longrightarrow X$$

be one of the functions in its specification. Then:

- If T appears only on the left of the arrow, f is an accessor function, which makes it possible to access properties of the type instances. In the corresponding class, f may be represented by either a function or an exported attribute.

- If T appears on both the left and the right, f is a transformer function, that yields a new object from one or more existing objects. Often f will be expressed, at the implementation stage, by a procedure which modifies an object by side-effect, rather than creating a new object as a function would do.

- If T appears on the right only, f is a constructor; in Eiffel, it corresponds to the *Create* procedure of the class. Note that there can be at most one *Create*; multiple constructors may be handled by adding arguments to the *Create* procedure (or by introducing variants of the class through inheritance; see chapter 10).

7.5.3 Expressing the axioms

This correspondence shows how the axioms of the abstract data type specifications will be transposed to the class:

- The preconditions of the specification reappear as routine preconditions.

- Axioms involving transformer functions reappear as postconditions of the corresponding procedures.

- Axioms involving only accessor functions reappear as postconditions of the corresponding functions or (especially if more than one function is involved, or if at least one of the accessors is implemented as an attribute) as clauses of the class invariant.

- Axioms involving constructor functions reappear in the postcondition of the *Create* procedure.

At this point you should go back to the axioms of abstract data type *STACK* (4.7.4) and compare them with the assertions of class *STACK* above.

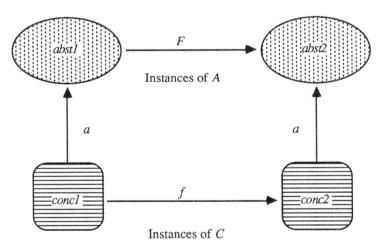

Figure 7.3 Correctness of implementations

It is instructive to think of the preceding remarks in terms of the above figure [Hoare 1972], which pictures the notion "*C* is a correct implementation of *A* ". You may view *A* as being an abstract data type, and *C* as a class implementing it (although abstract data types are defined in a purely functional way, whereas classes may involve side-effect-producing procedures). *F* is an operation on *A* and *f* is the corresponding routine on *C*. The arrows labeled *a* represent the **abstraction function** which, for any instance of *C*, or "concrete object", yields the abstract object (instance of *A*) that it represents.

The implementation is correct if (for all functions *F* and their implementations *f*) the diagram commutes, that is to say:

$$a \circ f = F \circ a$$

where $\circ$ is the composition operator. In other words, for every concrete object *c*, the abstract object *a* (*f* (*c*)), resulting from applying the concrete operation *f* to *c* and then abstracting, is the same as *F* (*a* (*c*)), obtained by applying the abstraction function first and then performing the abstract data type operation *F* on the resulting abstract object.[5]

7.6 REPRESENTATION INVARIANTS

Certain assertions appear in invariants although they have no direct counterparts in the abstract data type specifications. These assertions involve only attributes, including some secret attributes which, by definition, would be meaningless in the abstract data type. A simple example is the following property of *STACK 2*:

>   *0 <= nb_elements*; *nb_elements <= max_size*

Such assertions constitute the part of the class's invariant known as the **representation invariant**. They serve to express the consistency of the representation chosen in the class (here by attributes *nb_elements*, *max_size* and *implementation*) vis-à-vis the corresponding abstract data type.

Representation invariants should be viewed in terms of the correctness diagram (figure 7.3) and the notion of abstraction function. This function goes up in the figure: from representation to abstract data type. The inverse relation – down – is **not** a function; in other words, there may be more than one concrete object for a given abstract object.

Consider for example the abstract data type *STACK* versus its implementation by an array *implementation*, of bounds *1..max_size*, and an integer attribute *nb_elements*. To say that the abstraction function *a* is indeed a function is to express that any concrete object, as given by a pair [*implementation*, *nb_elements*] is the representation of at most one abstract stack object. This is an essential requirement: if the same pair could be interpreted as representing more than one stack, then the representation chosen would be ambiguous and hence inadequate.

Now if the inverse relation a^{-1} was a function then for any abstract stack there would be at most one [array, integer] pair representing it. This is an unjustified requirement, and is indeed violated in the example: the same abstract stack may be equally well represented by two or more implementations that only differ in the array elements for indices outside of the range *1..nb_elements*, as shown by the figure below. There is no way clients could distinguish the behaviors of these stack representations. One of the reasons is that routine *pop* executes

>   *nb_elements := nb_elements – 1*

without bothering to clear the previous top entry.

---

[5] Again, in a language allowing side-effects such as Eiffel *f* is not always a pure function, so the notation is not rigorously correct mathematically. However the underlying idea remains valid.

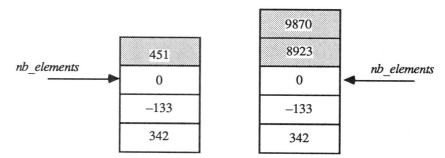

Figure 7.4   Two indistinguishable stacks

So it is proper that the arrow associated with a points up on figure 7.3; there should always be an abstraction function, but in general there is no representation function.

The abstraction function, however, is not necessarily a **total** function. In fact, it is almost always partial in interesting cases; this means that not all possible combinations of field values are valid representations of abstract objects. Here, for example, not all pairs of [*implementation*, *nb_elements*] values are valid representations of stacks; a valid representation must satisfy $nb\_elements \geq 0$ and $nb\_elements \leq max\_size$, where *implementation* has bounds 1 and *max_size*. This property is the representation invariant.

The representation invariant is the one part of the class's assertions that has no counterpart in the abstract data type specification. It relates not to the abstract data type, but to its representation; formally, it defines the **domain** of the abstraction function, when this function, as is usually the case, is partial.

7.7   SIDE-EFFECTS IN FUNCTIONS

In previous chapters, an important question was left unanswered: may functions have side-effects?   Only now, after the discussion of abstraction functions and class invariants, can we give a reasonable answer to this question. The answer is, briefly stated: side-effects are permitted in functions, but they should only affect the concrete state, not the abstract state.   This section explains the concept.

7.7.1   Side-effects in Eiffel

A side-effect on an object is an operation that may change at least one attribute of the object.   Side-effects are easy to spot in Eiffel.   Only four kinds of operation appearing in a routine may produce a side-effect on the objects to which the routine is applied:

- Assignment to an attribute x, of the form $x := y$.

- Remote call of a routine on x, of the form $x.r$, possibly with arguments, where x is an attribute of class type and r produces a side-effect.

- Local call of a routine s of the same class, where s produces a side-effect.

- Passing an attribute x as actual argument to a call (qualified or not), where the called routine produces a side-effect on the corresponding formal argument.

Note that the definition is recursive; the first case is the base case and the others involve recursive applications. In the last case, the side-effect on x in the routine may only be of the form given by the second case, since, as we shall see in the next chapter, assignments to formal arguments are not permitted.

7.7.2 Commands and queries

In principle, only procedures should have side-effects; functions should conform to what their name implies in mathematics and abstain from any side-effects on the objects to which they are applied.

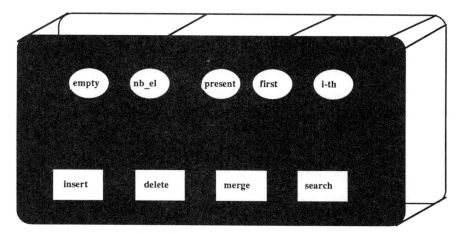

Figure 7.5   An object as machine

This approach can be illustrated as follows. An object is as a machine, to which operations may be applied by means of "buttons" (figure 7.5). There are two kinds of button: "command buttons" and "query buttons". (The machine shown on the figure represents a list object, with such commands as insertion and deletion, and such queries as the number of elements and whether a certain element occurs in the list. List classes describing such objects are studied in detail starting in chapter 9.)

If you push a query button, an indicator lights up on the button and gives you some information about the internal state of the machine. But the act of pushing the button does not change this state, so that if you push the same button ten times in a row you are guaranteed to get the same result ten times.

On the other hand, when you push a command button, you do not get any information in return, but the machine starts screeching and clicking; if, when the machine stops, you push a query button, the answer you get will usually be different from what you would have obtained before the command, since the machine has changed state.

Command buttons correspond to procedures; query buttons are either functions or attributes. Commands may change the state, but do not return a result; functions return a result, but do not change the state.

The clean separation between procedures and functions averts many of the pitfalls of traditional programming. Side-effect-producing functions, which have been elevated by some languages (C seems to be the most extreme example) to the status of an institution, conflict with the classical notion of function in mathematics. A mathematical function will always give the same result when applied to the same argument; in contrast, if *getint* () is a function (say in C) that reads an integer and returns it, then expressions

> *getint* () + *getint* ()
> and 2 * *getint* ()

will not yield the same value.

The recommended Eiffel style is to distinguish between the procedure that advances the input cursor to the next item and the function (or attribute) that yields the item last read. Assume *input* is of type *FILE* ; the sequence to read the next integer from file *input* will be something like

(IN)
> *input. advance*;
> *n := input. lastint*

Successive references to *lastint* will yield the same result in the absence of intervening calls to *advance*. In practice *lastint* may be either a function or an attribute.

An example sometimes quoted in favor of functions with side-effects is that of pseudo-random number generators, which return successive values from a sequence enjoying adequate statistical properties. The sequence is initialized by a call of the form

> *random_seed* (*seed*)

where *seed* is a seed value provided by the client. A common way to get the successive pseudo_random values is by calling a function:

> *xx := next_random* ()

But here too there is no reason to make an exception to the command/query dichotomy. In an object-oriented language, we should see a random number generator as an object with three public features: a new generator *rand* is obtained by

> *rand. Create* (*seed*);

the sequence is advanced by

> *rand. next*;

and the current value is obtained by

> *xx := rand. value*

The view of functions as side-effect-free queries is a direct consequence of the interpretation given above: functions at the Eiffel level are implementations of accessor functions at the abstract data type level.

The somewhat dogmatic distinction between commands and queries and the prohibition of side-effects (other than strictly concrete ones) in functions are essential for the proper development of large systems, where the effect of every inter-module interaction must be strictly controlled. These rules are part of the recommended Eiffel style, and are constantly observed in this book.

7.7.3   Abstract state, concrete state

From this discussion it would seem that functions should be syntactically barred from producing any side-effect. Since the operations that may produce side-effects have been precisely defined, it would not be difficult to add language rules that bar functions from containing any of these operations.

Yet this is not the case. There are no language-defined restrictions on functions. Why?

The reason is that some side-effects are harmless and, in fact, needed. They are the side-effects which only affect the concrete state of an object.

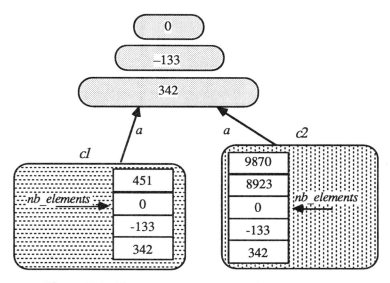

Figure 7.6   Two concrete states, one abstract object

The notion of concrete and abstract states follows from the discussion on abstraction functions. As noted, the inverse of the abstraction function a is not necessarily a function; in other words, different concrete objects c_1 and c_2 may correspond to the same abstract object a $(c_1) = a$ (c_2), as shown on the figure.

Now it may occur that the efficient computation of an accessor function (of the abstract data type) by a function of the class requires changing the state of the concrete object to which the function is applied (say going from c_1 to c_2) without changing the "abstract state" of the object, that is to say the result of a applied to the object. Side-effects of this sort are legitimate and should not be prohibited.

> In the machine analogy discussed above, such functions correspond to query buttons that may produce an internal state change having absolutely no effect on the answers given by any query button. For example, the internal circuits controlling the query buttons might be automatically switched off if nobody presses a query button for some time, and pressing a query button might switch the circuits on again. These internal state changes are unnoticeable from the outside; hence they are permitted.

The object-oriented approach is particularly favorable to clever implementations which, when computing a function, may change the concrete state behind the scenes without producing a functionally meaningful side-effect. The next section illustrates the idea.

7.7.4   Legitimate side-effects: an example

The example is an implementation of complex numbers, which alternates between representations to best accommodate the client's requests. There are two equally valid representations of complex numbers: cartesian (by axis coordinates x and y) and polar (by distance to the origin ρ and angle θ). Cartesian representation is ideal for such operations as addition or subtraction, and polar representation for multiplication or division. (Try expressing division in cartesian coordinates!)

Our class will not force its clients to choose between these representations. Rather, it will quietly alternate between them depending on the operations requested. In this process, a function call may trigger a change of representation (concrete state), which does not change the associated abstract object (a mathematical complex number).

We may assume the following public operations, among others:

class *COMPLEX* **export**
      add, subtract, multiply, divide, x, y, rho, theta, ...
feature
     ...
end

Note that x, y, *rho* and *theta* are public functions (each returning a real value). They are always defined: a client may request the abscissa of a complex number even if the number is internally represented in polar form, or its angle even if it is represented in cartesian form.

We assume that the first four operations are procedures working by side-effect; that is to say, *z.plus* (*z1*), where z and *z1* are of type *COMPLEX*, modifies z by adding *z1* to it. Alternatively, they could have been functions, called in the form *z2* := *z.plus* (*z1*); this choice does not affect the discussion.

Internally, the class includes the following secret attributes for the representation:

cartesian: BOOLEAN;
polar: BOOLEAN;
private_x, private_y, private_rho, private_theta: REAL;

Not all of the four real attributes are necessarily meaningful at all times; in fact only two need be meaningful. More precisely, the following representation invariant should be included in the class:

> **invariant**
>> *cartesian* **or** *polar*;
>> **not** *polar* **or else** (*0* <= *private_theta* **and** *private_theta* <= *Two_pi*)
>> -- **not** *cartesian* **or else** *private_x* and *private_y* are meaningful;
>> -- **not** *polar* **or else** *private_rho* and *private_theta* are meaningful

The value of *Two_pi* is assumed to be 2*π. The last two clauses may only be expressed informally, as comments. Note how a property of the form "if *P*, then *Q*" (or "*P* implies *Q*") is expressed using the **or else** operator as

> **not** *P* **or else** *Q*

The idea is that at least one of the representations is valid, although both may be. When an operation is requested, it is carried out in the representation that is best adapted to it; if the operation produces a side-effect, then the other representation ceases to be valid.

Two secret procedures are available for carrying out representation changes:

> *make_cartesian* **is**
>> -- Make cartesian representation available
>
>> **do**
>>> **if not** *cartesian* **then**
>>>> -- Here *polar* must be true
>>>> *private_x :=* *private_rho* * *cos* (*private_theta*);
>>>> *private_y :=* *private_rho* * *sin* (*private_theta*);
>>>> *cartesian :=* **true**
>>>>> -- Here both *cartesian* and *polar* are true:
>>>>> -- Both representations are available
>>> **end**
>> **ensure**
>>> *cartesian*
>> **end**; -- *make_cartesian*

> *make_polar* **is**
>> -- Make polar representation available
>
>> **do**
>>> **if not** *polar* **then**
>>>> -- Here *cartesian* must be true
>>>> *private_rho :=* *sqrt* (*private_x* ^ 2 + *private_y* ^ 2);
>>>> *private_theta :=* *atan2* (*private_y*, *private_x*);
>>>> *polar :=* **true**
>>>>> -- Here both *cartesian* and *polar* are true:
>>>>> -- Both representations are available
>>> **end**
>> **ensure**
>>> *polar*
>> **end**; -- *make_polar*

Functions *cos*, *sin*, *sqrt* and *atan2* are assumed to be taken from a standard mathematical library; *atan2* (y, x) should compute $\tan\frac{y}{x}$.

With these internal procedures, the exported procedures are easy to write; for example:

> *add* (*z: COMPLEX*) **is**
>> -- Add *z* to current
>
>> **do**
>>> *make_cartesian*;
>>> *private_x := private_x + z.x*; *private_y := private_y + z.y*;
>>> *polar :=* **false**
>
>> **ensure**
>>> $x = $ **old** $x + z.x$; $y = $ **old** $y + z.y$;
>>> *cartesian*
>
>> **end**; -- *add*

> *divide* (*z: COMPLEX*) **is**
>> -- Divide current complex by *z*
>
>> **require**
>>> *z.rho /= 0*
>>>> -- (should be replaced by
>>>> -- a numerically more realistic precondition)
>
>> **do**
>>> *make_polar*;
>>> *private_rho := private_rho / z.rho*;
>>> *private_theta := mod (private_theta − z.theta, Two_pi)*;
>>> *cartesian :=* **false**
>
>> **ensure**
>>> *rho = * **old** *rho / z.rho*; *theta = mod (***old** *theta − z.theta, Two_pi)*;
>>> *polar*
>
>> **end**; -- *divide*

Procedures *subtract* and *multiply* follow the same pattern and are left to the reader.

The technique used for these side-effect producing procedures − use whatever representation best serves the the latest client request − is also applicable to functions. For example:

> *x: REAL* **is**
>> -- Abscissa
>
>> **do**
>>> *make_cartesian*; *Result := private_x*
>
>> **end**; -- *x*

theta: REAL **is**
        -- Angle
  do
        make_polar; *Result := private_theta*
  end; -- *theta*

Functions *y* and *rho* are similar. As the procedures, all these functions may trigger a change of state (for example when *x* is called in a state where *cartesian* is false); in contrast with the procedures, however, they do not invalidate the previous representation when a new one is computed. For example, if *x* is called in a state where *cartesian* is false, both representations (all four real attributes) will be valid after the call.

This is because the functions may produce side-effects on the concrete objects only, not on the associated abstract objects. Formally, in the course of computing $z.x$ (or one of the other functions), the concrete object associated with z may be changed, say from c_1 to c_2, but only under the constraint that

$$a(c_1) = a(c_2)$$

where a is the abstraction function. The computer objects c_1 and c_2 may be different, but they represent the same mathematical object, a complex number.

Such side-effects are harmless; note in particular that they only affect secret attributes and hence cannot be detected by clients.

The object-oriented approach encourages such flexible, self-adapting representations. An example will occur in chapter 9, when we study an implementation of lists that keeps an internal cursor pointing to one of the elements; most operations apply to the cursor position, which may be moved by adequate procedures. An operation of the form "give me the value of the *i*-th element" which, abstractly, is a pure, side-effect-free function, is implemented by a sequence of side-effects: move the cursor to the requested position (to obtain the requested value), and move it back to where it was. The function leaves the list in the state in which it found it.

7.7.5 The Eiffel policy

The Eiffel rule follows from this discussion. Side-effects are prohibited in functions, except if they only affect the concrete state.

In practice, however, the restriction cannot easily be enforced by the implementation. The reason is that it is impossible for the compiler, in the absence of a completely formal specification language and theorem-proving tools, to decide whether a side-effect affects the abstract state as well as the concrete state. Note in particular that it does not suffice to check that only secret attributes may be modified: the system should also check that this modification does not affect the abstract state, which it has no way to do in its current form. (It might be a good idea, though, to produce a warning when exported attributes are modified by a function.)

The rule is a **methodological** precept and not a compiler-enforced restriction. This, however, does not diminish its importance.

7.8   OTHER CONSTRUCTS INVOLVING ASSERTIONS

Assertions may be used not only in preconditions, postconditions and class invariants, as introduced above, but also in loops and in the special **check** instruction.

7.8.1   Loop invariant and variants

The Eiffel syntax for loops also emphasizes correctness constructs. A loop may (and often should) include a **loop invariant** and a **loop variant**. These notions, although important, are independent of the object-oriented concepts and will be reviewed briefly. (This section may be skipped on first reading.)

The general form of an Eiffel loop is

> **from** *initialization_instructions*
> **invariant** *invariant*
> **variant** *variant*
> **until** *exit_condition*
> **loop** *loop_instructions*
> **end**

The **invariant** and **variant** clauses are optional. The **from** clause is required (but may be empty); it gives the loop initialization, which is considered to be part of the loop.

Executing such a loop amounts to executing the *initialization_instructions* and then, zero or more times, the *loop_instructions*; the latter are executed only as long as *exit_condition* is false. As a simple example, not yet including variant or invariant, a function to compute the greatest common divisor (gcd) of two positive integers a and b with Euclid's algorithm, using a loop, may be written as

> *gcd (a, b: INTEGER): INTEGER* **is**
>   -- Greatest common divisor of a and b
>   **require**
>   *a > 0; b > 0*
>   **local**
>   *x, y: INTEGER*
>   **do**
>   **from**
>   *x := a; y := b*
>   **until**
>   *x = y*
>   **loop**
>   **if** $x > y$ **then** $x := x - y$ **else** $y := y - x$ **end**
>   **end;**
>   *Result := x*
>   **ensure**
>   -- *Result* is the greatest common divisor of a and b
>   **end;** -- *gcd*

Note that this loop corresponds (in Pascal, C etc.) to a "while" loop, in which the loop body is executed zero or more times, not to a "repeat... until" loop in which the body is always executed at least once. In the Eiffel form, however, the test is an exit condition, not a continuation condition, and the loop syntax includes room for initialization. So the equivalent in Pascal of the above loop is

$x := a$; $y := b$;
while $x <> y$ **do**   {$<>$ is Pascal for "not equal"}
    if $x > y$ **then** $x := x - y$ **else** $y := y - x$

The invariant and variant are used to express and verify the correctness of a loop with respect to its intended specification. How do we know that function *gcd* ensures its postcondition – that it indeed computes the greatest common divisor of a and b? One way to check this is to note that the following property is true after loop initialization and preserved by every iteration:

$x > 0$; $y > 0$;
-- (x, y) have the same greatest common divisor as (a, b)

Call this property INV. INV is written as an Eiffel assertion and is only partially formal. Clearly, INV is satisfied after execution of the **from** clause. Also, if INV is satisfied before an execution of the loop body

    if $x > y$ **then** $x := x - y$ **else** $y := y - x$ **end**

under the loop continuation condition $x \neq y$, then INV will still be satisfied after execution of this instruction; this is because replacing the greater of two positive non-equal numbers by their difference leaves them positive and does not change their gcd.

We have thus shown INV to be satisfied before the first iteration and preserved by every iteration. It follows that on loop exit, when $x = y$ becomes true, INV still holds; in other words

$x = y$ **and** "(x, y) have the same greatest common divisor as (a, b)"

which implies that the gcd is x.

This proof of the correctness of function *gcd* with respect to its specification is typical of how loops may be proved using a **loop invariant**, INV in this example. More generally, a correct invariant for a loop is an assertion which is satisfied after loop initialization and preserved by every iteration of the loop body. An invariant for the loop

    from *init* **until** *exit* **loop** *body* **end**

is an assertion I satisfying the following two properties (using the notation of 7.4.3):

* $\{P\}$ *init* $\{I\}$ (where P is an assertion that holds before the loop);
* $\{$**not** *exit* **and** $I\}$ *body* $\{I\}$

The second property states that if *body* is executed in a state in which the invariant I is satisfied and the exit condition *exit* is not satisfied (so that the body will be executed at least once more), then the body will conserve the invariant.

Clearly, if these conditions are satisfied, the invariant will still be satisfied on loop exit. Since by definition the condition *exit* will be satisfied on loop exit, the loop ensures satisfaction of the output assertion *exit* **and** *I*

This approach makes it possible to write loops that must ensure a given condition *C* under the form

> **from**
> > *init*
> **invariant**
> > *C1*
> **until**
> > *exit*
> **loop**
> > *body*
> **end**

where the chosen invariant *C1* and exit condition *exit* satisfy

> *C1* **and** *exit* $\implies$ *C*

The presence of a correct invariant, as here, does not suffice to make the loop correct: one must also make sure that the loop terminates. This is obtained by exhibiting a proper loop **variant**. A variant is an integer expression whose value is non-negative after loop initialization, and is decreased by at least one by every execution of the loop body (when the exit condition is not satisfied) but never becomes negative. Clearly the variant's presence ensures that the loop terminates, as the process could not go on forever decreasing a non-negative integer expression.

In the above loop, *max* (x, y) is an appropriate variant. We may now write the loop with all of its clauses:

> **from**
> > $x := a; y := b$
> **invariant**
> > $x > 0; y > 0;$
> > -- (x, y) have the same greatest common divisor as (a, b)
> **variant**
> > *max* (x, y)
> **until**
> > $x = y$
> **loop**
> > **if** $x > y$ **then** $x := x - y$
> > **else** $y := y - x$ **end**
> **end**;

As noted, the **invariant** and **variant** clauses in loops are optional. When present, they help clarify the purpose of a loop and check its correctness. It is reasonable to say that any non-trivial loop may be characterized by an interesting invariant and variant; many of the loop examples in subsequent chapters and in the library classes of appendix A include variants and invariants, which bring useful insights into the nature and purpose of these loops.

7.8.2   The check instruction

One more construct may be used in connection with assertions. The notation

> **check**
>> *assertion 1*;
>> *assertion 2*;
>> ...
>> *assertion n*
>
> **end**

means: "at this point of the code, it is expected that the given assertions will always be satisfied".

The **check** instruction is a way of reassuring yourself that certain properties are satisfied, and (even more importantly) to make explicit for your readers the assumptions on which you are relying.

Probably the most useful application of this instruction is when calling in an unprotected fashion a routine with a precondition. Assume s is a stack and you include in your code a call

> *s.pop*

at a position where you are certain that s is not empty, for example because the call has been preceded by n "push" and m "pop" instructions, with $n > m$. Then there is no need to protect the call by an "**if not** *s.empty* **then**...". However, if the reason for the correctness of the call is not immediately obvious from the context, you may want to remind the reader that the omission of any protection was not an oversight but a conscious decision. This will be achieved by preceding the call with

> **check not** *s.empty* **end**

In normal mode, this "instruction" will have no more effect on system execution than a comment. As will be seen in the next section, there is also a debugging mode (ALL_ASSERTIONS) in which the compiler will generate an appropriate check from this instruction, so that if you did made a mistake after all it will be diagnosed clearly at run-time.

7.9   USING ASSERTIONS

What is the purpose of writing assertions? There are four main applications:

- Help in writing correct software.
- Documentation aid.
- Debugging tool.
- Support for software fault tolerance.

The first two are uses of assertions as methodological tools and will be studied first. The other two have to do with the run-time effect of assertions; they are the subject of the next section.

7.9.1   Assertions as a tool for writing correct software

The first use is perhaps the most important. Spelling out the exact requirements on each routine, and the global properties of classes and loops, helps the programmer develop software which is correct in the first place. The benefits of precise specifications and a systematic approach to program construction cannot be overemphasized. Throughout this book, whenever we encounter a program element, we shall seek to express as precisely as possible the formal properties of that element.

The key idea has already been emphasized: it is the principle of **programming by contract**. To use features from a certain module is to contract out for services. No contract agreement may be expected to cover all possible cases; good contracts are those which specify exactly the rights and obligations of each party, and the *limits* to these rights and obligations. In software design, where correctness and robustness are so important, it is surprising that with classical approaches one does not bother, most of the time, to even spell out the terms of the contracts. Assertions provide a much needed means to state precisely what is expected from and guaranteed to every party in these arrangements.

7.9.2   Using assertions for documentation

The second use is essential in the production of reusable software elements and, more generally, in organizing the interfaces of modules in large software systems. Preconditions, postconditions and class invariants provide potential clients of a module with crucial information about the services offered by the module, expressed in a concise and precise form. No amount of verbose documentation can replace a set of carefully expressed assertions.

The Eiffel automatic documentation tool **short**, introduced in chapter 9, uses assertions as an important component in extracting from a class the information that is relevant to potential clients.

7.10   COPING WITH FAILURE: DISCIPLINED EXCEPTIONS

Assertions have been presented so far as a conceptual aid to program design. You will certainly have guessed, however, that they may also have an effect on program execution – if only because it would not have been otherwise necessary to give them a precise syntactic form compatible with the rest of the language (extended boolean expressions). It is indeed possible to check assertions at run-time; this provides both a **debugging** mechanism and a mechanism for **fault tolerance** and **failure recovery**.

In a perfect world, run-time checking would not be necessary. We have seen what it means for a class to be correct; in principle, it should be possible to prove or disprove that a given system is correct (that is to say, that all its classes are correct and all calls satisfy preconditions). An ideal compiler would include a program checker that would perform this task.

Unfortunately, we are by no means close to such a goal, which would require a formal definition of the semantics of the programming language and practical tools which are beyond today's program proving technology. Although it is a worthwhile endeavor to attempt advances in these directions, we have to rely on more down-to-earth techniques for the time being. Hence the availability of mechanisms for monitoring assertions during system execution.

7.10.1   Monitoring assertions at run-time

In the Eiffel environment, compilation options make it possible to monitor assertions at run-time. You may specify separately, for each class and each type of clause involving assertions, whether the assertions are actually to be checked during execution.

Concretely, the options are selected by entering the appropriate lines in the System Description File used by the **es** compilation command (5.6.3). The lines have the following form:

NO_ASSERTION_CHECK (Y|N): *list of classes*
PRECONDITIONS (Y|N): *list of classes*
ALL_ASSERTIONS (Y|N): *list of classes*

Each of the *list of classes* may be empty; it may also consist of the keyword *ALL* to indicate that the indicated checking level should be enabled for all classes in the system. The Y or N (Yes or No) on each line makes it easier to change options without retyping the class list. These lines direct the Eiffel compiler to generate code including a specified level of run-time assertion monitoring for each class. Three levels are provided:

- No checking of assertions at all.
- Checking preconditions only (the default).
- Checking all assertions.

The default SDF generated by the compiler the first time you call **es** in a directory (see 5.6.3 and, for more details, 15.2.7) uses the following options:

NO_ASSERTION_CHECK (Y):
PRECONDITIONS (Y): ALL
ALL_ASSERTIONS (Y):

In other words, the default option is to generate checks for preconditions but no other assertions. This convention will be justified below.

The above options enable you to have the run-time system actually check that your software does not violate the assertions which it is supposed to obey. In the analogy on which this chapter is based, the assertion checking mechanisms monitors the faithfulness of clients and contractors.

Choosing the proper options is a result of a tradeoff between safety and efficiency. The checks cost execution time and also some space. If your system is correct, there is in principle no need for any check at all and you could select NO_ASSERTION_CHECK for all classes. But if one or more errors do remain after all, some execution of the system may terminate in a wild way; very unpleasant circumstances may result (such as destruction of the integrity of a data base) and you will be left in the dark as to what happened.

The default option, where only preconditions are checked, is a reasonable compromise because of the recommended programming style. As we saw at the beginning of this chapter, a precondition expresses the terms that a routine imposes on its clients, and the routine body should not test for the precondition. For example, a stack popping routine will not check for **not** *empty* if this clause is part of its precondition. This means that havoc may result if a call is incorrect, leading for example to an out-of-bounds memory reference and abnormal termination. Similarly, a real square root routine with precondition $x >= 0$ might loop forever if the actual argument is negative. So it is good practice to compile the classes with the PRECONDITIONS option on. Checking for preconditions is usually not too expensive (a 20% overhead on execution time is a good estimate on the average) and takes care of most catastrophic cases. This explains why the default option is as indicated.

7.10.2 Detecting violations

What happens when one of the checking modes is on and an assertion violation is detected at run-time?

If you have made no particular provision for this case in your classes, the run-time system will just halt the execution and print a message of the form

Class X, routine r, precondition [or postcondition, invariant etc.] i is violated.

identifying precisely the context of the violation. Since an assertion may consist of more than one clause, separated by semicolons, i serves to identify the individual clause. Remember that clauses may be labeled, as in

Positive: $n > 0$; Not_void: **not** *x.Void*

If the clause that failed was labeled, i is the label; otherwise i is the index of the clause in the assertion.

With this mechanism in place, the monitoring of assertions is a powerful debugging tool. If you attach proper assertions to your software, many errors may be found this way during testing: a call to a routine happens to violate the precondition, or fails to guarantee the postcondition on return, or violates the class invariant.

Even if you have been negligent in enriching your own classes with assertions, this mechanism may be a remarkable debugging aid because of the natural style of object-oriented programming, which relies on basic reusable classes. In Eiffel, these are the classes of the Eiffel library, which will be studied starting in chapter 9, and cover implementations of fundamental abstract data types: arrays, lists, stacks, queues, trees, files, strings etc. These classes have been carefully written and are equipped with the proper assertions. When the monitoring options are on, these assertions will be checked; many errors in application programs will result in violations of assertions of the library classes. A typical example is a call to an insertion procedure which attempts to insert an element at a position outside of the legal range for the list. Thus you may benefit from the assertion mechanism even if your own software does not include many assertions.

7.10.3 Exceptions

In some cases it may not be acceptable to know that a failure will lead to termination and a message. You may want to take control.

Such run-time recovery from failures is the aim of **exception mechanisms**. Exceptions have been built into a number of programming languages, notably PL/I, Ada and CLU. The Ada mechanism is studied in chapter 18.

As noted in the discussion of modular protection (2.1.5), exceptions are a potentially dangerous technique, which has been subjected to much misuse. Too often exceptions are simply used as a form of goto instruction, making it possible to jump out of a routine when some condition other than the standard case is encountered. In chapter 9 we shall study safer approaches to the handling of abnormal cases.

There remains a role for an exception mechanism, however, in two situations:

• When the programmer wants to take into account the possibility that errors remain in the software and to include mechanisms that will handle any resulting run-time failure, either by exiting cleanly or by attempting recovery.

• When a failure is due to some abnormal condition detected by the hardware or operating system, for example a failed attempt at input or output.

Assertion violation corresponds to the first case (the second will be examined in the next section). Despite all the efforts we make to ensure the correctness of our systems, we have to take into account human frailty and admit that errors may remain. Of course, when an error is found, the only proper action is to correct it. But this is not an excuse for not providing a mechanism which will either terminate execution in a proper way, or attempt to achieve the original goal by other means. (As we shall see below, these two possibilities are indeed the only reasonable ones; this remark is the basis for proper exception handling.)

It is important to avoid confusion in the sometimes fuzzy world of errors, failures and exceptions. We use the following terminology:

Definition (*Error, exception, failure*):

An **exception** is the occurrence of an abnormal condition during the execution of a software element.

A **failure** is the inability of a software element to satisfy its purpose.

An **error** is the presence in the software of some element not satisfying its specification.

Note that failures cause exceptions (the failure of a routine execution should trigger an exception in the routine that called it) and are in general due to errors. In Eiffel, an exception will also occur if an assertion attached to a routine is found to be violated; this assumes the proper compilation options have been selected to enable run-time monitoring of some or all assertions.

In light of the preceding discussion, only two courses of action are reasonable when an exception is detected:

• Clean up the environment, terminate and report failure to the caller. The cleaning up consists in bringing the environment to a stable state; for example, if the operation that failed was a transaction in a database, any effect that the partial execution of the operation may have had should be undone. Similarly, if the operation was execution of a process in an operating system, the process should be removed from the operating system's table of active processes. This may be termed the **organized panic** response to exceptions. It is essential in such a case to report failure to the caller (or, at the topmost level, to terminate execution with an error message).

• Attempt to change the conditions that led to the exception and try again the operation that failed. This policy may be termed **retry** (the term "resumption" is sometimes used).

Another way to express the same remark is to say that an operation may only succeed or fail; there is no middle ground. (Trivial as this comment may seem, it is not satisfied by the exceptions mechanisms of such languages as Ada, CLU or PL/I, which make it possible to exit from a routine without achieving the routine's intent, and without signaling failure to the caller. See 7.11.2 below, and 18.4 for the Ada mechanism.)

This approach fits remarkably well in the contracting metaphor developed in this chapter. An exception occurs when a contractor (a routine) detects that it is unable to fulfill its contract as planned; this may be because the client has not fulfilled its part (the routine precondition is violated), because some subcontractor (a called routine) has failed, or because the contractor itself fails to achieve its promises (the postcondition of the routine is violated at the end). But the contract with the client stipulates a certain result. So there are only two possible solutions out of the contractor's predicament: either bring back the environment to a clean state and humbly report failure to the client, which will in turn have to decide on the proper course of action for itself; or attempt again the requested operation using another approach (or the same approach after attempting to fix the reasons for the exception).

A solution which is **not** acceptable is one in which, having detected failure, the routine would quietly return control to the caller without any special notification. This would defeat the purpose of any attempt at programming for correctness and robustness.

The exception mechanism of Eiffel is based on these remarks. A routine may either succeed or fail. It succeeds only if it fulfills its contract.

Two syntactical extensions are needed to describe the details of this mechanism. The first is the optional **rescue** clause which may appear in a routine after the body and the postcondition if present:

```
routine is
      require ...
      local ...
      do
            body
      ensure ...
      rescue
            rescue_clause
      end
```

The *rescue_clause* is a sequence of instructions. Whenever an exception occurs during the execution of the normal *body*, this execution will be stopped and the *rescue_clause* will be executed instead.

The other new construct is the retry instruction, written just **retry**. This instruction may only be executed as part of a rescue clause for a routine. (It does not have to be syntactically part of the **rescue** clause, however, since it might be in a routine called by one of the rescue instructions.) Its execution consists in re-starting the routine body from the beginning.

Whenever the rescue clause executes to the end, rather than executing a **retry**, the routine execution fails; failure will be reported to the caller through an exception. A routine with no **rescue** clause will be considered to have an empty rescue clause, so that all exceptions will cause immediate failure of the routine. However a **rescue** clause may be included at the class level, just before the invariant, and will then be used by any routine of the class which does not have its own **rescue** clause.

The general definitions of "exception" and "failure" given above have a more precise version in the Eiffel context. Here is the definition for exceptions:

Definition (*Exceptions in Eiffel*): An exception may occur during the execution of a routine as a result of any of the following situations:

1. The precondition of *r* is found to be violated on entry.

2. The postcondition of *r* is found to be violated when *r* terminates.

3. The class invariant is found to be violated on entry or termination.

4. Another assertion violation (**check** violated, loop invariant not maintained by a loop iteration, variant not decreased) is found during the execution of the routine.

5. A routine called by *r* fails.

6. *r* attempts a remote feature application *a.f* in a state where *a* is a void reference.

7. An operation executed by *r* results in an abnormal condition detected by the hardware or the operating system.

Cases 1 to 4 will only occur for classes compiled with the appropriate monitoring options. Case 6 corresponds to an implicit precondition on all feature applications. Case 7 corresponds to external exceptions, resulting from such events as overflow in an arithmetic operation, and will be discussed below. As for failures:

Definition (*Failure in Eiffel*): A routine execution fails if an exception occurs during its execution and the routine terminates by executing its rescue code.

Note that the two definitions are mutually recursive.

Let us look more closely at what happens when an exception is triggered during the execution of r. The normal execution (the body) stops; the rescue clause is executed instead. Then two cases may occur:

- The first case is when the rescue clause executes a **retry**, usually after some other instructions. In this case, execution of the routine will start anew. This new attempt may succeed; in this case, the routine will terminate normally and return to its client. The call is a success; the contract has been fulfilled. Execution of the client is not affected, except of course that it will have taken longer than normal. On the other hand, an exception might occur again during the retry attempt, in which case the process of executing the rescue clause will start anew. Note in particular that if precondition checking has been enabled and the exception was due to a violated precondition, then when the execution is retried, the precondition will be checked again; this might give rise to a new exception if the instructions before the **retry** have failed to correct the cause of the violation.

- If the rescue clause does not execute a **retry**, it will execute to the end. In this case the routine fails: it returns control to its caller, signaling an exception. The same process will be applied to the client.

This mechanism strictly adheres to the rule given above: either a routine succeeds, that is to say its body executes to the end and satisfies the postcondition, or it fails. When an exception is incurred, you may either report failure or try the normal body again; but there is no way you can exit from the routine through the rescue clause and pretend to your caller that you succeeded.

The simplest form of rescue clause corresponds to the organized panic mode. For example a *pop* procedure for a stack class cannot do much when it is called on an empty stack. Perhaps it may print a message, although, as we saw, this is not really the place to worry about user interfaces. But most importantly it should leave what has been called a "clean" state. For example assume the standard implementation looks like the following:

pop **is**
>   **require**
>>   *nb_elements* >= *0*;
>   **do**
>>   *nb_elements* := *nb_elements* − *1*;
>>   "Other instructions to complete the pop operation"
>   **ensure**
>>   *nb_elements* = **old** *nb_elements* − *1*; ...
>   **end** -- *pop*

Here the operation begins by decrementing *nb_elements*. If something goes wrong, it is essential to leave the stack in a meaningful state, in particular one where *nb_elements* is not negative. The routine with its rescue clause should be of the form

pop **is**
>   **require**
>>   *nb_elements* >= *0*;
>   **do**
>>   *nb_elements* := *nb_elements* − *1*;
>>   "Other instructions to complete the pop operation"
>   **ensure**
>>   *nb_elements* = **old** *nb_elements* − *1*; ...
>   **rescue**
>>   *nb_elements* := *0*;
>>   ... Here perhaps some code to print error messages ...
>   **end** -- *pop*

The effect of the instruction *nb_elements* := *0* is to restore the class invariant, which is assumed here to include the clause *nb_elements* >= *0*. This highlights the requirements imposed on rescue clauses. The rescue clause is not bound to satisfy the postcondition of the routine: this is the role of the body (the **do** clause). If we knew how to ensure the postcondition − fulfill the contract − in the abnormal case, there would be no cause for failure. But the rescue clause must ensure the invariant of the class in cases when it does not attempt a **retry**. This is exactly the meaning of the expression "leave the environment in a stable state" used above. In an object-oriented context, the stable states are those where every object satisfy its invariant.

So the rescue clause may be viewed as a routine body whose postcondition would be the invariant of the class. To complete the picture, note that the programmer has no control over the point at which the rescue clause may be executed: an exception may occur at any point of the routine body. This means that the rescue clause should not require any special condition to execute correctly; in other words, it should accept **true** (the assertion satisfied by all states) as precondition. Hence the rule:

> **Rescue rule**: The rescue clause for a routine must be correct with respect to the precondition **true** and, except for any branch ending in a **retry**, to the postcondition given by the class invariant.

This rule is important to understand the meaning of rescue clauses. The rescue clause for a routine does not provide an alternative to the implementation given by the body; if such was the case, the rescue clause would be bound by the same postcondition. Instead, the rescue clause is only meant to "patch things up" when the routine cannot fulfill its goal; consequently, it is only constrained to ensure the invariant. This is a less strict requirement than the routine postcondition (to which the class invariant is always implicitly added).

The necessity of accepting **true** as precondition is also essential. The rescue clause must work under all circumstances. From a practical viewpoint, checking for exceptions will be disabled during the execution of a rescue clause: no assertion monitoring, no checking for void references in a qualified call, etc. (Of course, checking resumes if a **retry** is executed). So it is absolutely crucial that the rescue clause be totally safe. In practice, the rescue clause should be a short sequence of simple instructions designed to bring back the object to a stable state and to either retry the operation or terminate with failure.

7.10.4   Retrying for software fault tolerance

We have not yet seen any example of **retry**. Here is a possible case. You have written a text editor and (shame on you) you are not quite sure it is entirely bug-free. Yet you want to get some initial user feedback. Your guinea pigs are willing to tolerate a system with some remaining errors, resulting for example in the system's occasional failure to carry out a command, but they will not use it to enter serious texts (which is what you want them to do, to test your editor under realistic conditions) if they fear that a failure may result in a catastrophe, such as brutal exit and loss of the last half-hour's work. With **retry** you can provide a defense against such occurrences.

Assume the editor contains a basic command execution loop of the form

```
from ... until exit loop
      one_command
end
```

where the body of routine *one_command* is of the form

```
decode user command;
execute appropriate operation in response to command
```

The *execute...* instruction chooses among a set of available routines (for example delete a line, change a word, etc.) We shall see in 12.2 how the techniques of inheritance and dynamic binding yield simple, elegant structures for such multi-way decisions.

The assumption is that the different routines are not entirely safe; some of them may fail at unpredictable times. You may provide a primitive but safe protection against such an event by writing the routine as

one_command **is**
                    -- Get a command from the user and, if possible,
                    -- execute the corresponding operation
        do
                "Decode user command";
                "Execute appropriate operation in response to command"
        rescue
                message ("*Sorry, this command failed*");
                message ("*Please try another command*");
                message ("*Please report this failure to the author*");
                "Instructions to patch up the state of the editor"
                retry
        end; -- *one_command*

Note that some of the routines implementing individual operations might have their own **rescue** clauses, leading to failure (so that the above **rescue** clause of *one_command* takes over) but only after having printed a more informative, command-specific message.

Another example of retrying is an implementation of the "n-version programming" technique suggested by some authors as a tool for software tolerance. The idea is to offer two or more implementations for a given task, developed by different teams in environments that are as distinct as possible, in the hope that the errors, if any, will be different. This is a controversial idea, and it may be argued that the money would be better spent in improving the correctness and robustness of a single version than in financing two or more imperfect implementations. Without entering into this debate, let us see how simply the **retry** mechanism addresses this problem:

do_task **is**
        require ...
        local
                times_tried: INTEGER
        do
                if *times_tried = 0* **then**
                        implementation_1
                elsif *times_tried = 1* **then**
                        implementation_2
                end
        ensure
                . . .
        rescue
                times_tried := times_tried + 1;
                if *times_tried < 2* **then**
                        "Perhaps some instructions to reset to stable state";
                        retry
                end
        end -- *do_task*

The generalization to more than two alternative implementations is immediate.

This example is typical of the use of **retry**. The rescue clause never attempts to reach the original goal using an alternate implementation; reaching this goal, as expressed by the postcondition if there is one, is the privilege of the normal body. Note that after two attempts (or n in the general case) the routine simply executes its rescue clause to the end and thus fails.

7.10.5   Hardware and operating system exceptions

The disciplined exception mechanism of Eiffel has been described in the context of exceptions generated as a result of assertion violations. But it can also be applied to other abnormal conditions. These include attempts at object allocation (*Create* or *Clone*) that fail for lack of available memory, attempts to access inexistent objects ($x.f$ when the reference associated with x is void), and signals generated by the hardware or the operating system: arithmetic overflow or underflow, impossible I/O operation, user interrupts etc.

Such conditions may in fact be viewed formally as assertion violations. If $a + b$ provokes overflow, it means that the call has not observed the implicit precondition on + that the mathematical sum of the two arguments should be representable on the computer. A similar implicit precondition on the allocation of a new object (*Create* or *Clone*) is that enough memory is available. If a write fails, it is because the environment (files, devices, users) did not meet the conditions for applicability of the operation. But in such cases it is impractical or impossible to express the assertions, let alone check them. So the only solution is to attempt the operation and, if the hardware or operating system signals an abnormal condition, to treat it as an exception.

In the Eiffel environment, hardware and operating system exceptions may indeed be caught by the Eiffel run-time system and handled in the same way as assertion violations. As assertion checking, this processing may be enabled or disabled through a compilation option enabled or disabled through a line in the System Description File, as follows:

EXTERNAL_EXCEPTIONS (Y|N)

As an example of the use of this mechanism, consider the following problem. A real number x is given; write a routine that will return the inverse of x or, if this is impossible to compute because x is too small, will return 0.

This type of problem is essentially impossible to solve without an exception mechanism because the only really good way to know whether x has a representable inverse is to attempt the division $\dfrac{1}{x}$; but if this provokes overflow and you cannot handle exceptions, the program will crash and it will be too late to return 0 as a result.

With the **rescue/retry** mechanism the problem is easily solved:

```
quasi_inverse (x: REAL): REAL is
        -- 1/x if possible; otherwise 0
    local
        division_tried: BOOLEAN
    do
        if not division_tried then
            Result := 1/x
        else
            Result := 0
        end
    rescue
        division_tried := true;
        retry
    end
```

Note that the initialization rules ensure that *division_tried* is initialized to false. The **else** clause is not needed because the same initialization rules ensure that *Result* is 0 by default (the initializations are repeated after a **retry**), but has been included for clarity.

This example shows the need for discriminating between exceptions in a rescue clause. Here we only want to attempt the **retry** if the exception was overflow. Other exceptions, such as one generated when the interactive user presses the BREAK key, should not result in a retry. A better form for the **rescue** clause would be

```
if exception = Numerical_error then
    division_tried := true; retry
end
```

There is no **else** clause: exceptions other than *Numerical_error* will result in failure, which is the correct consequence since the routine has no provision for recovery in such cases. It is indeed possible to write the **rescue** clause in this form; a library class *EXCEPTIONS* defines the attribute *exception*, which yields the (integer) code of the last exception that occurred, and symbolic names for predefined exception codes, such as *Numerical_error*. Any class can inherit from *EXCEPTIONS* to use these facilities (see 14.4.5 for how to gain access to a library of general-purpose facilities).

7.11   DISCUSSION

7.11.1   Limitations of assertions

The approach to specification taken in Eiffel is partial: you will have noted, for example, that the assertions given for stack classes do not completely cover the axioms of the corresponding abstract data type (chapter 4). Although the characterization of *push* is complete, there is no easy way to translate the axiom for *pop*, which read

$$pop \; (push \; (x, s)) = s$$

into a postcondition for the routine *pop*.[6]

All that can be done in this case is to add an informal property to the postcondition, in the form of a comment:

pop **is**
>
>> -- Remove top element
>
> **require**
>
>> **not** *empty*
>
> **do**
>
>> . . .
>
> **ensure**
>
>> **not** *full*;
>>
>> *nb_elements* = **old** *nb_elements* − *1*
>>
>> -- *top* will return the next-to-last element *pushed*
>
> **end** -- *pop*

Bringing a full-fledged assertion language into Eiffel would have been theoretically satisfactory but totally impractical. The ability to formally express assertions of a general nature (powerful enough to describe realistic abstract data types) requires an assertion language in which one can directly manipulate sets, sequences, functions, relations and first-order predicates with quantifiers ("for all" and "there exists"). Including such concepts would have completely changed the nature and scope of the language and made it more difficult to learn – not even mentioning the problems of implementability and performance.

Executable languages including full-fledged assertion sublanguages exist, but they are experimental and not suitable for production programming. None designed so far has been based on the concepts of object-oriented programming.

The Eiffel approach is a somewhat pragmatic compromise. Assertions are offered, but they are restricted to boolean expressions, with a few extensions such as the **old** and *Nochange* notations. The form of assertions makes it possible to express formally many important properties of classes, but not all potentially interesting ones. These formal assertions may be monitored at run-time.

When an important property of a class or one of its routines may not be expressed in full formality, it is still recommended to include it informally as a comment, as was done with the invariant of *gcd* (INV, page 141). Of the four uses of assertions mentioned above, the last two obviously disappear (run-time monitoring for debugging and exception handling), one is still applicable to a large extent (help in composing correct programs) and one remains (documentation aid). Note that the automatic documentation tool **short** (chapter 9) retains comment assertions.

Since assertions are boolean expressions, they may include function calls. This possibility may be used to express conditions that would otherwise require non-formal clauses. For example, by adding a secret function *body* to the specification of *STACK*, one can indeed obtain a set of assertions that closely parallels the abstract data type specification. This is the object of exercise 7.2. This solution is not entirely

---

[6] Recall that we are distinguishing between the mathematical functions *push* and *pop* of the abstract data type specification, and their counterparts in the Eiffel text, which are procedures in the programming language sense, working by side-effects.

satisfactory since functions in the programming sense are not mathematical devices but routines, computed at run-time. In general, if a function f is used in the precondition or postcondition to a routine r, we would like f to be of a "higher quality" than r: more abstract, less operational, producing a mathematically well-defined result.

In particular, under PRECONDITIONS or ALL_ASSERTIONS, the run-time assertion checking mechanism is automatically disabled for any function call that is evaluated as part of assertion checking: since the function itself could contain preconditions and the like, we do not want the monitoring mechanism to enter into an infinite loop.

7.11.2 Disciplined exceptions

The exception mechanism described above is both powerful (because of the **retry** operation) and more restrictive than the exception mechanisms built into existing languages. Exceptions, as they have been presented, are a technique to deal with erroneous conditions that may be detected at run-time: assertion violations, hardware signals, attempts to access void references.

The approach we have explored is based on the contracting metaphor: under no circumstances should a routine pretend it has succeeded when in fact it has failed to achieve its purpose. A routine may only succeed (perhaps after experiencing some exceptions but recovering from them through one or more **retry**, unbeknownst to the client) or fail.

Exceptions in Ada, CLU or PL/I do not follow this model. Using the Ada model, and instruction

   raise *exc*

cancels the routine that executed it and returns control to its caller, which may handle the exception *exc* in a special handler clause or, if it has no such handler, will itself return control to its caller (details in 18.4). But there is no rule as to what a handler may do. Hence it is perfectly possible to ignore an exception, or to return an alternate result. This explains why the exception mechanism is often used simply to deal with cases other than the easiest case for an algorithm. Such applications of exceptions really use **raise** as a goto instruction, and a fairly dangerous one since it crosses routine boundaries. In my opinion, they are abuses of the mechanism.

There have traditionally been two viewpoints on exceptions: many practicing programmers, knowing how essential it is to remain in control at run-time whenever an abnormal condition is detected (be it due to a programming error or to an unforeseeable hardware condition such as numerical overflow or hardware failure), consider them an indispensable facility. On the other hand, computer scientists preoccupied with correctness and systematic software construction have usually viewed exceptions with suspicion, as an unclean facility used to circumvent the standard rules on control structures. The mechanism developed above will, it is hoped, appeal to both sides.

7.11.3 Class invariants and reference semantics

One more point must be included in this discussion of assertions and their practical applications. The problem has to do with class invariants; it makes checking for invariants less straightforward than in a language that would not support references.

The invariant of a class describes properties that should be satisfied by any instance of the class at all stable times of its existence; the stable times have been defined as those immediately after instance creation and immediately after any call to an exported routine. The invariant rule (page 125) and its more formal version, the definition of class correctness rule (page 127) imply that an assertion I is invariant for a class C if and only if:

1. Any legal call to *Create* produces an object that satisfies I.

2. Any legal call to any exported routine r preserves I.

Legal calls are calls satisfying the precondition, if any.

The two conditions seem sufficient to guarantee that I is indeed invariant in the sense defined above. The proof is apparently trivial: since I will be satisfied initially, and preserved by every routine call, it should by induction be satisfied at all stable times.

This informal proof, however, is not valid in the presence of reference semantics and dynamic aliasing (5.5). The problem is that attributes of an object may be modified by an operation on another object. Thus even if all $a.r$ operations preserve I on the object AO1 associated with a, there may be an operation $b.s$ (where b refers to another object) which destroys the validity of I on AO1. Whether or not the class types of a and b are the same, conditions 1 and 2 above may very well be satisfied; but I is not an invariant.

The following simple example shows the problem. Assume classes A and B, each with an attribute whose type is the other class:

> **class** A ... **feature** *forward: B* ... **end**;

> **class** B ... **feature** *backward: A* ... **end**;

We require that following the *forward* reference (if defined) from an instance of A and then the *backward* reference from the corresponding B yields the original A. This may be expressed as an invariant property of A:

INV

> *forward.Void* **or else** (*forward.backward = Current*)

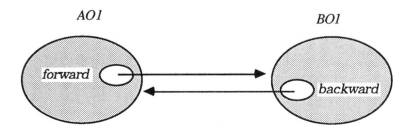

Figure 7.7   Consistency of "forward" and "backward" references

No such constraint is placed, however, on the references starting from B. The following version of A seems consistent with the invariant:

class A **export**
>> *forward, attach*

feature

>> *forward: B*;

>> *attach (b1: B)* **is**
>>> -- Chain *b1* to current instance
>> **do**
>>> *forward := b1*;
>>>> -- Update *b1*'s backward reference for consistency:
>>> **if not** *b1.Void* **then**
>>>> *b1.attach (Current)*
>>> **end**
>> **end** -- *attach*

invariant
>> INV: *forward.Void* **or else** (*forward.backward = Current*)

end -- class A;

The corresponding implementation for B is:

class B **export**
>> *backward, attach*

feature

>> *backward: B*;

>> *attach (a1: A)* **is**
>>> -- Chain *a1* to current instance
>> **do**
>>> *backward := a1*;
>> **end** -- *attach*

end -- class A;

Class A appears to be correct: its default *Create* procedure ensures the invariant INV (since it initializes *forward* to a void reference), and its sole procedure will always ensure INV.

Unfortunately INV is not necessarily satisfied at all stable times. Consider the execution of the following:

>> *a1, a2: A*; *b1: B*;
>> ...
>> *a1.Create*; *a2.Create*; *b1.Create*;
>> *a1.attach (b1)*;
>> *b1.attach (a2)*

After the last instruction, the invariant is violated on the object AO1 associated with *a1*! AO1 is chained to BO1 which is chained to the other A object, AO2, not to AO1.

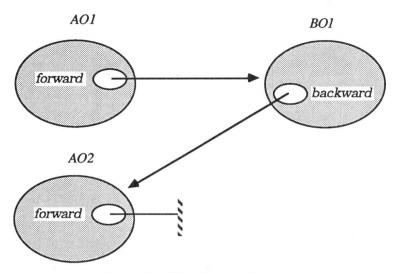

Figure 7.8   Violating the invariant

What happened? At issue is the possibility of dynamic aliasing. Every operation of the form *a1.r*, where *a1* is a reference to object AO1, preserves INV. All such operations in class *A* (here there is only one, *attach*) have been designed accordingly. But this is not sufficient to preserve the consistency of AO1, since properties of AO1 may involve other objects (such as BO1) that may be affected by operations not involving any direct reference to AO1, such as *a1*.

Whenever dynamic aliasing is permitted – and we have seen how essential it is when non-trivial data structures are needed – the problem discussed here will arise, since an operation may modify an object AO1 even though it does not explicitly involve any entity associated with AO1.

This problem is not academic. Invariants such as the one given do occur in practical cases, reflecting important properties of data structures. In the linked implementation of trees, for example (A.7), the attributes of a tree node include references to its first child and to its parent node. The following property, which is the same as INV, should be invariant:

first_child.Void **or else** (*first_child.parent = Current*)

There is no easy theoretical way to avoid the issue. In practice, however, the problem may be solved by making sure that whenever invariant monitoring is enabled (under option ALL_ASSERTIONS) checks are performed not just after the *Create* and after every routine call, but also **before** every such call. This will detect violations of the invariant due to external aliasing.

7.11.4   More to come

Before closing this chapter, we should note that assertions play an even more important role in the object-oriented approach than described here. With the introduction of inheritance (chapters 10 and 11), we shall see that assertions are essential to preserve the semantic integrity of classes and routines in the presence of the powerful mechanisms for polymorphism and redefinition.

7.12 KEY CONCEPTS INTRODUCED IN THIS CHAPTER

- Assertions are boolean expressions that serve to express the semantic properties of classes and to reintroduce the axioms and preconditions of the corresponding abstract data types.

- Assertions are used in preconditions (requirements under which routines are applicable), postconditions (properties guaranteed on routine exit) and class invariants (properties that characterize class instances over their lifetime). Other constructs that involve assertions are loop invariants and the **check** instruction.

- Routine preconditions as well as postconditions are implicitly assumed to include the class invariant.

- A precondition and a postcondition associated with a routine describe a contract between the class and its clients. The contract is only binding on the routine inasmuch as calls observe the precondition; the routine then guarantees the postcondition on return. The notion of contracting provides a powerful metaphor for the construction of correct software.

- A class describes one possible representation of an abstract data type; the correspondence between the two is expressed by the abstraction function, which is usually partial. The inverse relation is in general not a function.

- The representation invariant, which is part of the class invariant, expresses the correctness of the representation vis-à-vis the corresponding abstract data type.

- Functions should not produce any side-effect, except for side-effects that achieve an internal representation change and only involve the concrete state.

- Loops should be characterized by a loop invariant and a variant.

- Assertions serve four purposes: aid in constructing correct programs; documentation aid; debugging aid; basis for an exception mechanism.

- Exceptions are generated when an assertion is found at run-time to be violated, or when the hardware or operating system signals an abnormal condition.

- Exceptions should not be used as jumps. They are a mechanism for dealing with abnormal conditions by cleaning up the environment and either reporting failure to the caller or attempting again to achieve the aim of the operation.

- The **rescue/retry** mechanism implements this policy by guaranteeing that a routine may only terminate by either executing its body to its normal termination or signaling failure to its caller.

7.13 SYNTACTICAL SUMMARY

			Used in (chapter)
Precondition	=	**require** Assertion	Routine (5)
Postcondition	=	**ensure** Assertion	Routine (5)
Class_invariant	=	**invariant** Assertion	Class (5)
Assertion	=	{Assertion_component ";" ...}	
Assertion_component	=	[Label ":"] Boolean_expression	
Label	=	Identifier	
Boolean_expression	=	Expression	
Expression	=	(See chapter 8)	
Old_value	=	**old** Expression	Expression (8)
Nochange	=	**nochange**	Expression (8)
Loop	=	Initialization	Instruction (5)
		[Loop_invariant]	
		[Loop_variant]	
		Exit_clause	
		Loop_body	
		end	
Initialization	=	**from** Compound	
Loop_invariant	=	**invariant** Assertion	
Loop_variant	=	**variant** Integer_expression	
Integer_expression	=	Expression	
Exit_clause	=	**until** Boolean_expression	
Loop_body	=	**loop** Compound	
Check_instruction	=	**check** Assertion	Instruction (5)
Rescue	=	**rescue** Compound	Routine (5)
Retry	=	**retry**	Instruction (5)

7.14   BIBLIOGRAPHICAL NOTES

The notion of assertion comes from the work on program correctness pioneered by Floyd [Floyd 1967], Hoare [Hoare 1969] and Dijkstra [Dijkstra 1976]. Surprisingly, few programming languages have included syntactical provision for assertions; examples include Alphard [Shaw 1981] and Euclid [Lampson 1977], which were specifically designed to allow the construction of provably correct programs. Apparently, no object-oriented language has included such features before Eiffel.

The notion of class invariant comes from Hoare's work on data type invariants [Hoare 1972]. See also applications to program design in [Jones 1980] and [Jones 1986]. A formal theory of morphisms between abstract data types may be found in [Goguen 1978].

Other viewpoints on exceptions may be found in [Liskov 1979] and [Cristian 1985]. "N-version programming" (page 153) is presented in [Avižienis 1985]. Much of the work on software fault tolerance derives from the notion of "recovery block" [Randell 1975]; a recovery block for a task is used when the original algorithm for the task fails to succeed. This is different from rescue clauses which never by themselves attempt to achieve the original goal, although they may restart the execution again after patching up the environment.

EXERCISES

7.1   Completing COMPLEX

Write the abstract data type specification for class *COMPLEX* (7.7.4) and the complete class as sketched above. Assume perfect arithmetic.

7.2   Formal specification of stacks

Show that by introducing a secret function *body* which returns the body of a stack, the assertions in the *STACK* class may be made to reflect the full corresponding abstract data type specification. Discuss the theoretical and practical value of this technique.

7.3   Random number generators

Write a class implementing pseudo-random number generation, based on a sequence $n_i = f (n_{i-1})$ where f is a given function and the seed n_0 will be provided by clients of the class. Functions should have no side-effects.

7.4   Side-effect-free input functions

Design a class describing input files, with input operations, without any side-effect-producing functions. Only the class interface (without the **do...** clause describing the routine implementations, but with the routine headers and any appropriate assertions) is required.

7.5   A queue module

Write a class implementing queues (first-in, first-out policy), with appropriate assertions, in the style of the *STACK* classes of this chapter.

7.6   A set module

Write a class implementing sets of elements of an arbitrary types, with the standard set operations (membership test, addition of a new element, union, intersection etc.). Be sure to include the proper assertions. Any correct implementation, such as linked lists or arrays, is acceptable. Efficiency is not a concern for this exercise.

7.7   Dealing with incorrect user input

Write a routine that will get an integer from a user, asking the user to re-enter the input if it is not a correct integer; after five incorrect attempts by the user, however, your routine should terminate and fail. The actual reading is done through a function *get_next_integer: INTEGER* which reads an integer from the keyboard, but raises an exception if the input is not a correct integer. This function does not conform to the principles of this chapter (it uses side-effects) but is assumed to be the only one available in your environment.

7.8   Largest integer

Assume a machine that generates an exception when an integer addition overflows. Write a reasonably efficient function that will return the largest positive integer representable on the machine.

8

More aspects of Eiffel

This chapter introduces some details of Eiffel not covered by the preceding discussions. These are language aspects, not essential to the object-oriented approach – although they are of course designed to blend well with the rest of the language, and are necessary to write actual Eiffel programs.

Specifically, the following issues will be addressed: recommended style standards; lexical conventions; access to code written in languages other than Eiffel; argument passing rules; instructions; expressions; dealing with strings; input and output.

It is safe to skip this chapter on first reading if you are interested in the general properties of the object-oriented approach but willing to lose some of the finer details of the programming examples in the following chapters.

8.1 STYLE STANDARDS

Certain simple style conventions, although not part of the language proper, are recommended and are obeyed throughout this book.

8.1.1 Header comments

The most important convention is relative to comments in routines. The header comment, indented as shown below, should be present in every routine; for example:

```
distance_to_origin: REAL is
            -- Distance to point (0, 0)
    local
            origin: POINT
    do
            origin.Create;
            Result := distance (origin)
    end -- distance_to_origin
```

Such header comments should be informative, clear, and concise. In general, brevity is one of the essential qualities of comments in programs; overly long comments tend to obscure the program text rather than help the reader. The following principles should be kept in mind.

• Assume the reader is reasonably competent. There is no need to repeat in the header comment information which is obvious from the immediately adjacent program text. For example, the header comment for a routine beginning with

```
tangent_to (c: CIRCLE; p: POINT): LINE
```

should not be

```
-- Tangent to circle c through point p
```

but just

```
-- Tangent to c through p
```

as it is clear from the function header that c is a circle and p is a point.

• Avoid noise words and phrases. An example is "Return the..." in explaining the purpose of functions. In the above cases, writing "Return the distance to point (0, 0)" or "Return the tangent to..." does not bring any useful information as the reader knows a function must return something. Another example of a noise phrase is "This routine computes...", or "This routine performs...". Instead of

```
-- This routine updates the display according to the user's last input
```

write

```
-- Update display according to last user input
```

If your readers have literary inclinations, they would rather read Henry James than your comments.

• Be consistent. If a function of a class has the comment "Length of string", a routine of the same class should not say "Update width of string" if it acts on the same attribute.

• In general, comments should be of a level of abstraction higher than the code that they document. In the case of header comments, the comment should concentrate on the "what" of the routine rather than the "how" of the algorithm used.

• Finally, it is important to note that much of the important semantic information about the effect of a routine may be captured concisely in Eiffel through the **require** and **ensure** clauses introduced in the previous chapter.

8.1.2   Layout

The recommended layout of Eiffel text results from the general form of the syntax of Eiffel, which is essentially what is known as an "operator grammar", meaning that an Eiffel text is a succession of alternating "operators" and "operands". An operator is a fixed language symbol, such as a keyword (**do** etc.) or a separator (semicolon, comma etc.); an operand is a programmer-chosen symbol (identifier or constant).

Based on this property, the textual layout of Eiffel follows the "comb-like" structure introduced by Ada; the idea is that a syntactically meaningful part of a class – say an instruction, an expression etc. – should either fit on a line together with a preceding operator, or be indented just by itself on one or more lines. The picture is that of a comb, whose branches normally begin and end with operators:

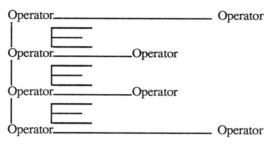

Figure 8.1   Comb-like layout

As an example, depending on the size of its constituents *a, b* and *c*, a conditional instruction (see 8.5.3 below) may be written as

    if *c* **then** *a* **else** *b* **end**

or

    if
        c
    then
        a
    else
        b
    end

or

    if *c* **then**
        a
    else *b* **end**

etc.

8.2   LEXICAL CONVENTIONS

8.2.1   Identifiers

Eiffel uses the standard ASCII character set. Identifiers are sequences of characters, all of which must be letters, digits or "underlined blank" characters (_); the first character of an identifier must be a letter.

There is no language-defined limit to the length of identifiers (Of course, overly long identifiers are unreasonable for readability.) However only the first 12 characters of a **class name** are significant. This is because a class must be stored in a file and many operating systems limit the length of a file name. Longer class names are accepted (with a warning from the compiler), but you will run into trouble if two classes of a given system begin with the same 12 characters.

8.2.2   Letter case in identifiers

Both lower-case and upper-case letters are allowed in identifiers. However, **letter case is not significant in identifiers**: thus *Hi*, *hi*, *HI* and *hI* will be understood as the same identifier. The rationale for this convention is that it is dangerous to allow two identifiers that differ from each other by just one character, say *Structure* and *structure*, to denote different program elements. Better force the programmer to use some imagination than risk serious mistakes.

In spite of this rule, certain standard conventions are recommended for enhancing program readability, although they are not enforced by the compiler or other tools in the Eiffel environment (chapter 15). They are the following:

   • Names of types, such as simple types (*INTEGER* etc.), class names (such as *POINT*) and formal generic parameters to classes (such as *T* in *STACK* [*T*]) are written in upper case.

   • Names of predefined features (*Create, Void, Clone, Forget,* etc.), predefined entities and expressions (*Result* and *Current*) and programmer-defined symbolic constants (such as *Pi*, see chapter 13) start with an upper-case letter.

   • All other identifiers are written in lower case: non-constant attributes, formal routine arguments, local variables.

These rules are consistently observed in this book and the Eiffel library.

8.2.3   Choice of names

Eiffel has a set of **reserved words**, or identifiers pre-empted by the language definition, such as **class**, *Current* etc., which cannot be used to name other language elements (classes, attributes etc.). The list of these is given in appendix D.

The choice of names in a class is not constrained by choices made in other classes (except for the class names themselves, of course, as it must be possible to distinguish classes from each other). Thus common feature names such as *value* may be used in as many classes as wished.

Within a class, the rules are designed to avoid any confusion: Consider the following lists of names within a given class containing *n* routines among its features:

> **Naming rule**: Consider the following lists of names within a given class containing n routines among its features:
>
> 1. The list F of feature names.
>
> 2. The list C of class names used in the class, including the name of the class itself and other class names used to declare types of entities.
>
> 3. For the i-th routine ($i = 1, 2, \ldots n$), the list F_i containing the names of formal arguments, external routines and local variables of the routine.
>
> Then:
>
> - Neither F nor any F_i may contain any duplicate elements.
>
> - F must be disjoint from every F_i.

However, F_i need not be disjoint from F_j for $i \neq j$ (the same local names may be used in different routines).

8.3   EXTERNAL ROUTINES

Any software design method emphasizing reusability must recognize the need for accessing code written in other languages. It is hard to convince potential users that reusability begins today and that all existing software must be discarded.

In general, openness to the rest of the world is an important requirement in new software tools. This might be termed the "principle of modesty": authors of new tools should make sure that users can still access previously available tools.

But, modesty is not an excuse for "upward compatibility", which means carrying over all the mistakes of past systems. It is essential to preserve the consistency and integrity of the new tools. They should be *interfaced with*, not embedded in, previous achievements.

These ideas have been applied to Eiffel: provision has been made to use routines written in other languages; however such routines remain external to the Eiffel text itself. Thus the limit is clearly drawn.

An example of a class largely implemented through external routines is *ARRAY*, which relies on C routines: *Create* uses the C routine *allocate* which dynamically allocates a memory area; *entry* uses *dynget*, which accesses elements in a dynamically allocated area; and *enter* uses *dynput*, which modifies elements. The text of the class is given in Appendix A.

An Eiffel routine that needs one or more routines written in other languages must list them in an **external** clause. For example, an Eiffel function for computing square roots might rely on a library function written, say, in C or Fortran. The Eiffel function may be declared as

```
sqrt (x: REAL): REAL is
        -- Square root of x
    require
        x >= 0
    external
        c_sqrt (x: REAL): REAL name "c_sqrt" language "C";
        abs (x: REAL): REAL name "abs" language "C";
    do
        Result := c_sqrt (x)
    ensure
        abs (Result ^ 2 – x) <= 10 ^ (–8)
    end -- sqrt
```

For each external routine, the **external** clause lists the types of its arguments and, if the routine is a function, the type of its result. The language name is also indicated; the range of languages known by Eiffel depends on the implementation. The **name** subclause serves to declare the name by which the routine is known externally. This clause may be omitted if (as here) the external name is identical to the local name; it is useful, however, for languages which have identifier naming conventions different from those of Eiffel (for example, a C function name may begin with an underscore _, not allowed as first character of an Eiffel identifier).

This technique ensures a clean interface between the Eiffel world and other languages. An external routine is encapsulated in an Eiffel routine; client code will see the Eiffel version. For example, the C routine *c_sqrt* above has been elevated to the (more dignified) status of Eiffel routine, complete with precondition and postcondition; other Eiffel code will access it through the Eiffel version *sqrt*.

One extreme but not altogether absurd way to use Eiffel would indeed be to rely solely on external routines, written in some other language, for all actual computation. Eiffel would then serve as a pure packaging tool, using the powerful encapsulation mechanisms of object-oriented design: classes, information hiding, the client relation and inheritance.

8.4 ARGUMENT PASSING

The problem of argument passing is what happens to $a_1, a_2, ..., a_n$ in a routine call

$$p (a_1, a_2, ..., a_n)$$

corresponding to a routine

$$p (x_1: T_1, x_2: T_2, ..., x_n: T_n) \text{ is } ...$$

where the routine could be a function as well as a procedure, and the call could be qualified, as in $b. p$ (...). The a_i are called actual arguments, and the x_i are called formal arguments. (Although "parameter" is often used as a synonym for "argument", we reserve the former term for generic type parameters, and for global system parameters in chapter 13.)

The most important aspect of argument passing is the question of what operations are permitted on formal arguments, and what effect they have on the corresponding actual arguments.

The Eiffel approach is simple. A routine call amounts to executing the routine body, where formal arguments are considered to stand for the corresponding actual arguments in the given call. Within the routine body, formal arguments are "protected": no direct modification is permitted on them. A direct modification on x is one of the following operations:

- An assignment with x as target, of the form $x := ....$

- If x is of a class type, any operation that may modify the reference associated with x: $x.Create (...)$, $x.Forget$, $x.Clone (y)$ for some y.

The set of operations that a routine may perform on its arguments is thus highly restricted. The restriction is harsher than in the passing mechanism known as call by value, where formals are initialized to actuals but may then be the object of arbitrary operations. Here direct modifications are simply not permitted on the arguments.

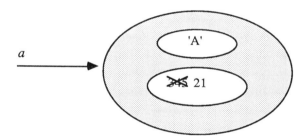

Figure 8.2   Modifying an object without modifying a reference

Note that the prohibition only applies to direct modifications. For arguments of class types, this means that the **references** may not be modified; but, if the references are not void, the associated **objects** may be modified through appropriate procedures, as shown on the figure. For example, if x_i is one of the formal arguments to routine p, the body of the routine could contain a call of the form

     $x_i.r (...)$

where r is a routine declared in the class T_i (the type of x_i). This routine may modify the fields of the object associated with x_i at execution time, which is the object associated with the corresponding actual argument a_i.

Thus a call $q (a)$ cannot change a itself; that is to say, it cannot change the value of a if a is of a simple type, and if a is of a class type it cannot associate a with a new object or make it void if it was not. On the other hand, the call may result in changes to the object with which a is associated, if any.

Since no direct modification may be performed by a routine on its formal arguments, the actual arguments to any routine may be arbitrary expressions. (If direct modifications were permitted and had an effect on the corresponding actuals, the actuals would have to be restricted to program elements that may change their values;

in other words only entities could be permitted.)

Because of these conventions, the only way a routine may return a value to its caller is through its result, if the routine is a function. This implies in particular that at most one result may be returned. The effect of multiple results may be achieved by returning a result of a certain class type, with more than one attribute. For example, a function may not return two values corresponding to the title and publication year of a book, but may return a single value of type *BOOK*, with attributes *title* and *publication_year*.

As we just saw, routines may produce side-effects on the objects referenced by their actual arguments (if not on the references themselves). In the case of functions, this possibility is restricted as described in the previous chapter (7.7).

8.5 INSTRUCTIONS

Eiffel is a procedural language, in which computation is expressed through commands, or instructions. (The word "statement" is commonly used but is misleading: a statement is an expression of facts, not a command.) Eiffel instructions are not particularly original; only loops have some non-standard features. The instructions include:

- procedure call
- assignment
- conditional
- loop
- check
- debug

8.5.1 Procedure call

A procedure call instruction is either local or remote. It involves a routine, possibly with actual arguments. In a call instruction, the routine must be a procedure; if it is a function, the call is syntactically an expression. The rules presented here apply to both cases.

A local call is a call to a routine applied to the current instance, and appears under the form:

p	(without arguments), or
$p\ (x, y, ...)$	(with arguments)

A remote call is applied to an object, represented by an expression: assuming that a is an expression of type C, where C is a class, and q is one of the procedures in class C, then a remote call is of the form $a.q$. Again, q may be followed by a list of actual arguments; a may be a local function call with arguments, as in $a(m).q(n)$.

Multidot remote calls, of the form $a.q_1.q_2...q_n$ are also permitted. (a as well as the q_i may be followed by a list of actual arguments.)

Export controls apply to remote calls, as follows. We say that a feature f declared in a class B is **available** to a class A if f is listed in the export clause of B. As will be seen in the next chapter, a feature may be exported to a number of specified classes only; if this is the case A should be one of them. Then:

Remote call rule: A remote call of the form $b.q_1.q_2....q_n$ appearing in a class C is correct only if the following conditions are satisfied:

1. The feature appearing after the first dot, q_1, must be available to C, or must be one of the predefined features *Create, Clone, Forget, Equal, Void*.

2. In a multidot call, every feature after the second dot, that is to say every q_i for $i > 1$, must be available to C; the last feature may also be *Equal* or *Void*. It may not be *Create, Clone* or *Forget*.

The second rule is easily understandable if you realize that $u.\, v.\, w$ is a shorthand for

$$x := u.v;\ x.w$$

which is only valid if w is available to C, the class where this code appears. Whether or not it is available to D, the class type of u, is irrelevant.

This also rules out the case in which w is an operation that may perform a direct modification on u, such as *Create*, *Clone* or *Forget*. If you could write

$$u:\, D;\ \ldots$$
$$u.v.Create$$

where v is an exported attribute of D, it would mean that D has granted its clients the right to allocate or re-allocate v, a quite significant privilege. If this is indeed the intent of D's designer, a special procedure, say *allocate_v*, should be added to the features of D and exported. The same applies to *Clone* and *Forget*.

8.5.2 Assignment

The assignment instruction is written

$$x := e$$

where x is an entity and e an expression. Recall that an entity is either:

- A class attribute.
- A local variable of a routine.
- A formal argument.
- The predefined entity *Result*, standing for the result of the enclosing function.

As we just saw, a formal argument may not be the target of an assignment. Eiffel expressions are studied below.

8.5.3   Conditional

The basic form of conditional instruction is written

> **if** *boolean_expression* **then**
> > *instruction*; *instruction*; ...
>
> **else**
> > *instruction*; *instruction*; ...
>
> **end**

This will execute the first sequence of instructions if the *boolean_expression* evaluates to true, and the second otherwise. The **else** part may be omitted if the second instruction list is empty:

> **if** *boolean_expression* **then**
> > *instruction*; *instruction*; ...
>
> **end**

When there are more than two interesting cases, you can avoid nesting conditional instructions in **else** parts by using one or more **elsif** branches, as in

> **if** c_1 **then**
> > *instruction*; *instruction*; ...
>
> **elsif** c_2 **then**
> > *instruction*; *instruction*; ...
>
> **elsif** c_3 **then**
> > *instruction*; *instruction*; ...
>
> ...
>
> **else**
> > *instruction*; *instruction*; ...
>
> **end**

which does not have the unnecessary nesting of

> **if** c_1 **then**
> > *instruction*; *instruction*; ...
>
> **else**
> > **if** c_2 **then**
> > > *instruction*; *instruction*; ...
> >
> > **else**
> > > **if** c_3 **then**
> > > > *instruction*; *instruction*; ...
> > > >
> > > > ...
> > >
> > > **else**
> > > > *instruction*; *instruction*; ...
> > >
> > > **end**
> >
> > **end**
>
> **end**

The **else** part remains optional when there are one or more **elsif** clauses.

8.5.4　Loop

The syntax of loops was introduced in the previous chapter (7.8.1):

> **from** *initialization_instructions*
> **invariant** *invariant*
> **variant** *variant*
> **until** *exit_condition*
> **loop** *loop_instructions*
> **end**

The **invariant** and **variant** clauses are optional. The **from** clause is required (but may be empty); it gives the loop initialization, which is considered to be part of the loop.

Leaving aside the optional clauses, the execution of such a loop consists of executing the *initialization_instructions* followed by the loop process. The loop process is defined as follows: if the *exit_condition* is true, the loop process is a null instruction; if it is false, the loop process is the execution of the *loop_instructions* followed by a new loop process.

8.5.5　Check

The **check** instruction was introduced in the previous chapter (7.8.2). It serves to express that certain assertions must be satisfied at certain points:

> **check**
> 　　　*assertion; assertion; ...; assertion*
> **end**

8.5.6　Debug

The **debug** instruction is a facility for conditional compilation. It is written

> **debug** *instruction; instruction; ...* **end**

For every class, the DEBUG compilation option may be turned on or off. If on, any debug instruction in the class is equivalent to the instructions it contains; if off, it has no effect on the execution of the routine in which it appears.

This instruction may be used to include special actions that should only be executed in debugging mode, for example instructions to print out the values of some entities. Other facilities for debugging Eiffel systems are described in chapter 15.

8.5.7　Retry

The last instruction is **retry** (7.10.3). It may be executed as part of a rescue clause to restart a routine that was interrupted by an exception. Any attempt to execute this instruction other than during the processing of a rescue clause triggers an exception.

8.6 EXPRESSIONS

Expressions include the following varieties:

- constants
- entities (attributes, local variables, formal routine arguments)
- function calls
- *Current*
- expressions with operators.

8.6.1 Constants

There are two boolean constants, written **true** and **false**.

Integer constants follow the usual form and may be preceded by a sign. Examples are

453   –678   +66623

Real constants use a decimal point. Either the integer part or the fractional part may be absent. A sign may be given. An integer power of 10 is specified by *e* followed by the exponent value. Examples are

52.5   –54.44   +45.01   .983   –897.   999.e12

Character constants consist of a single character written in quotes, as in *'A'*. Special characters are entered as shown below. (A "bit pattern" is a machine-dependent code encoded as three octal digits *ddd*.)

Name	Character	Coded as
newline	NL(LF)	\n
horizontal tab	HT	\t
backspace	BS	\b
carriage return	CR	\r
form feed	FF	\f
backslash	\	\\
single quote	'	\'
null character	NULL	\0
bit pattern	*ddd*	\ddd

Figure 8.3   Escape sequences for special characters

Character constants describe single characters. Strings of more than one character will be handled by the library class *STRING* (see 8.7 below).

8.6.2   Function calls

Function calls follow the same syntax as procedure calls (page 172). They may be local or remote; in the latter case, multidot notation is available. Assuming the proper class and function declarations, examples are:

> *b.f*
> *b.g (x, y, ...)*
> *b.h(u, v).i.j (x, y, ...)*

The remote call rule introduced for procedures applies to function calls as well.

8.6.3   "Current" expression

The reserved word *Current* denotes the current instance of the class and may be used in an expression. Note that *Current* itself is an expression, not an entity; thus an assignment to *Current*, of the form

> *Current := value*

is syntactically illegal.

When referring to a feature (attribute or routine) of the current instance, it is not necessary to write *Current.f*; just *f* suffices. Because of this rule, *Current* is less frequently used in Eiffel than in object-oriented languages where every feature reference must be explicitly qualified. (In Smalltalk, for example, there is no such convention; a feature is always qualified, even when it applies to the current instance, written *self*.) Example uses of *Current* include:

- Creating a copy of the current instance, as in *x. Clone (Current)*.

- Testing whether a reference is to the current instance, as in the test *x = Current*.

- Passing a reference to the current instance as argument to a routine, as in *x. f (Current)*.

- Using *Current* as "anchor" in a "declaration by association" of the form **like** *Current* (see 11.4).

8.6.4   Expressions with operators

Operators are available to construct composite expressions.

Unary operators are + and –, applicable to integer and real expressions, and **not**, applicable to boolean expressions.

Binary operators, which take exactly two operands, are the exponentiation operator $\hat{\ }$ ($a \hat{\ } 2$ is the square of a) and the relational operators

> $=$ $/=$ $<$ $>$ $<=$ $>=$

where $/=$ is the not equal operator. The relational operators yield boolean results. Their operands may be of type integer or real; comparison of character values is also permitted, using the order of the ASCII character set.

Multiary expressions involve one or more operands, combined with operators. Numerical operands may be combined using the following operators:

    + – * /

Boolean operands may be combined with the operators **and, or, and then** and **or else.** (The last two are explained in the next section.)

The precedence of operators is given in appendix C.

8.6.5   Non-commutative boolean operators

The non-commutative boolean operators, patterned after their Ada counterparts, are **and then** and **or else.** They have the following meaning: a **and then** b has value false if a has value false, and otherwise has the value of b; a **or else** b has value true if a has value true, and otherwise has the value of b.[1]

The difference with the standard **and** and **or** operators is that the above operators may be defined when the first operand has enough information to determine the result (false for **and,** true for **or**), but the second is undefined. A simple example is the boolean expression

    $i \neq 0$ **and then** $j / i = k$

which, according to the above definition, has value false if i is equal to zero (as the first operand is false). If the expression had been written using **and** rather than **and then,** then its second operand would be undefined when i is zero, so that the status of the whole expression is unclear in this case. This uncertainty is reflected in what may happen at run-time:

- If the compiler generates code that evaluates both operands and then takes the boolean "and" of the result, a division by zero will result at run-time.

- If, on the other hand, the generated code only evaluates the second operand when the first is true, otherwise returning false as the value of the expression, then the expression will indeed evaluate to false.

By using **and then,** the programmer ensures the second case. Similarly,

    $i = 0$ **or else** $j / i \neq k$

will evaluate to true if i is zero, whereas the **or** form may either evaluate to true or result in a run-time error.

Note that an expression using **and then** always yields the same value as the corresponding expression written using **and** if both are defined. But the **and then** form may yield a value (false) in cases when the **and** form does not. The same holds with **or else** (and true) with respect to **or.** In this sense, the non-commutative operators may be said to be "more defined than or equal to" their respective counterparts.

One might wonder why two new operators are needed; would it not be simpler and safer to just keep the standard operators **and** and **or** and take them to mean **and then** and **or else**? This would not change the value of any boolean expression when

---

[1] A note on the conventions of this book: the boolean values are written in normal font, as true and false; boldface is reserved for the language keywords **true** and **false.**

both operands are defined, but would extend the set of cases in which expressions may be given a consistent value. This interpretation of boolean operators is indeed used in some programming languages, notably ALGOL W or C. There are, however, both theoretical and practical reasons for keeping two sets of distinct operators:

- On the theoretical side, the standard mathematical boolean operators are commutative: *a* **and** *b* always has the same value as *b* **and** *a*, whereas *a* **and then** *b* may be defined when *b* **and then** *a* is not.

- In practice, some compiler optimizations become impossible if the compiler is required to evaluate the operands in a given sequence, as is the case with the non-commutative operators. Thus it is preferable to use the standard operators if both operands are known to be defined.

Note that the non-commutative operators may be simulated by conditional instructions in a language that does not include such operators. For example, instead of

$b := i \mathrel{/=} 0$ **and then** $j / i = k$

one may write

if $i = 0$ **then** $b := $ **false** **else** $b := (j / i = k)$ **end**

The **and then** form is of course simpler.

The non-commutative operators are especially useful in assertions. In particular, **or else** serves to express properties of the form "*a* implies *b*", or "If *a*, then *b*". It is well known that "*a* implies *b*" may be written as "**not** *a* **or** *b*". Often, however, property *b* is meaningless if *a* is false, so that the proper formulation uses **or else** rather than **or**.

As an example, assume that an assertion (for example in a class invariant) expresses that the first value of a certain list l of integers is non-negative – provided, of course, that the list is not empty. This may be expressed as

$l.empty$ **or else** $l.first >= 0$

Using **or** would have been incorrect here as $l.first$ is not defined for an empty list. The example classes from the library in appendix A contain many such examples. (See for example the invariant for class *LINKED_LIST*.)

8.7   STRINGS

Class *STRING* describes character strings. This class is treated somewhat specially: the identifier *STRING* is recognized as a reserved word, and string constants are also part of the predefined language syntax.

A string constant is written enclosed in double quotes, as in

$"ABcd\ Ef\~*\_\ 01"$

The double quote character must be preceded by a backslash \ if it appears as one of the characters of the string. For non-printable characters, the conventions introduced on figure 8.6.1 (page 176) for constants of type *CHARACTER* apply.

It is possible to write a string constant over more than one line; each incomplete line should end with a backslash, immediately followed by the line feed character; the string resumes after the first backslash on the next line. Any characters before the first backslash on the continuation line are ignored. For example:

> "*ABCDEFGHIJKLM*
> *NOPQRSTUVWXYZ*" ;

More details on constant strings are given in chapter 13.

Non-constant character strings are also instances of class *STRING*, whose *Create* procedure takes as argument the expected initial length of the string, so that

> *text1, text2: STRING*; *n: INTEGER*;
>
> . . .
>
> *text1.Create* (*n*)

will dynamically allocate a string *text1*, reserving the space for *n* characters. Numerous operations are available on objects of this class, such as concatenation, character or substring extraction, comparison etc. (They may change the length of the string, automatically triggering re-allocation if it becomes greater than the initial estimate *n*.) Appendix E, which shows the summary version of this class as produced by **short** (chapter 9), may be used as a reference.

Note that assignment of a *STRING* to another implies sharing: after *text2 := text1*, any modification to the contents of *text2* will also affect the contents of *text2* and conversely. Duplication, as opposed to sharing, is achieved by *text2 := text1.duplicate*.

8.8 INPUT AND OUTPUT

Two classes provide the basic input and output facilities of Eiffel: *FILE* and *STD_FILE*.

Among the operations defined on an object *f* declared of type *FILE* are the following:

> *f.Create* ("*name*") --Associate *f* with a file of name *name*
> *f.open_write* -- Open *f* for writing
> *f.open_read* -- Open *f* for reading
> *f.putstring_nl* ("*A_STRING*") --Write the given string on *f*, followed by a new line

Appendix E shows the summary version of these classes and will serve as a reference.

For I/O operations on the standard input, standard output and standard error files, it is sufficient to inherit from *STD_FILE*, which defines three attributes, *input*, *output* and *error*. The summary version of this class is also included in appendix E.

8.9   KEY CONCEPTS INTRODUCED IN THIS CHAPTER

• The syntactical structure of Eiffel is comb-like (operator operand operator ... operand operator).

• Letter case is not significant in identifiers, although standard conventions are recommended.

• Proper routine header comments, concise and to the point, are an essential component of well-documented systems.

• External routines are accessible through a well-defined interface.

• Routines may not directly modify their arguments, although they may change the *objects* associated with arguments.

• Eiffel includes a small set of instructions: assignment, conditional, loop, call, debug, check.

• Expressions follow common usage in programming languages. *Current* is an expression denoting the current instance. Not being an entity, *Current* may not be the target of an assignment.

• Non-commutative boolean operators yield the same values as the standard boolean operators when both operands are defined, but are defined in some cases when the standard operators are not.

• Strings, input and output are treated using library classes.

8.10   SYNTACTICAL SUMMARY

			Used in (chapter)
Externals	=	**external** External_list	Routine (5)
External_list	=	{External ";" ...}	
External	=	Feature_name	
		[Formal_arguments]	
		[Type_mark]	
		[External_name]	
		Language	
Language	=	**language** String_constant	
External_name	=	**name** String_constant	
Expression	=	{Unqualified_expression "." ...}	Assignment, Call etc. (5)
Unqualified_expression	=	Constant | Entity |	
		Unqualified_call | *Current* |	
		Old_value | Nochange |	
		Operator_expression	

Used in (chapter)

Constant	=	(See chapter 13)	
Entity	=	(See chapter 5)	
Unqualified_call	=	(See chapter 5)	
Old_value	=	(See chapter 7)	
Nochange	=	(See chapter 7)	
Operator_expression	=	Unary_expression |	
		Binary_expression |	
		Multiary_expression |	
		Parenthesized	
Unary_expression	=	Unary Expression	
Unary	=	**not** | "+" | "–"	
Binary_expression	=	Expression Binary Expression	
Binary	=	^ | = | /= | < | > | <= | >=	
Multiary_expression	=	{Expression Multiary ...}⁺	
Multiary	=	"+" | "–" | "*" | "/" |	
		and | **and then** | **or** | **or else**	
Parenthesized	=	"(" Expression ")"	
Conditional	=	**if** Then_part_list	Instruction (5)
		[Else_part] **end**	
Then_part_list	=	{Then_part **elsif** ...}⁺	
Then_part	=	Boolean_expression	
		then Compound	
Else_part	=	**else** Compound	
Loop	=	(See chapter 7)	Instruction (5)
Check	=	(See chapter 7)	Instruction (5)
Debug	=	**debug** Compound **end**	Instruction (5)

9

Designing class interfaces

Few issues are more important in software development than the proper design of module interfaces. Anybody who has participated in a multi-person, or just multi-week software project knows that, beyond a certain step, many if not most of the decisions, discussions, disputes and confusions tend to revolve around matters of module interface specification: "Who takes care of making sure that...?", "But I thought you only passed me normalized user input...", "Why are you processing this since I already took care of it?" and so on.

If there was just one issue on which to expect significant advances from object-oriented methods, then it would have to be this one. From the outset of this presentation, object-oriented design has been presented as an architectural technique, whose aim is to produce software systems made of coherent, properly interfaced modules. Although our view of the object-oriented approach will only be partial until we have encountered inheritance, we have by now accumulated enough techniques to explore the actual impact of object-oriented techniques on the design of effective module interfaces.

Design is not a science but a skill. It can be taught in part, but not through absolute rules or theorems. Although general principles do exist, the best advice is often given through examples. This chapter and the following ones review a number of examples based on the **Eiffel library**, a repository of classes covering many of the basic data structures and algorithms of everyday programming. The ability to reuse libraries of "canned" software components is indeed one of the major benefits of the object-oriented approach. Because the quality requirements are highest on a reusable module (since repeated usage will quickly and pitilessly bring out any flaw in its design or implementation), their design demands the utmost attention and craftsmanship, and provides a magnifying glass over almost all of the problems of interface design.

We shall indeed begin our review of a few important interface techniques by considering issues raised by the implementation of a library class which may at first appear deceptively simple – a class implementing linked lists. First we shall need to look at some technical details of list implementation (in the next section). Then we shall make a first, simple-minded attempt and analyze why its result is inadequate. The remedy will illustrate some general design principles. Next we shall study (9.3) the crucial problem of how to handle abnormal cases, and refine the principle of information hiding by introducing (9.4) the notion of selective exports. Finally section 9.5 will explain how to document a class interface, and the last section will discuss some of the language issues involved.

9.1 LISTS AND LIST ELEMENTS

9.1.1 Linked list representation

A good example of interface issues is provided by linked lists, a commonly used data structure which is clearly a prime candidate for inclusion in a library of general-purpose modules.[1]

Linked lists are representations of sequences which make it easy to perform the operations of *insertion* and *deletion*. The elements of the sequence are cells, which will be called "linkables"; every linkable contains a value and a pointer to another element, as shown by the following picture:

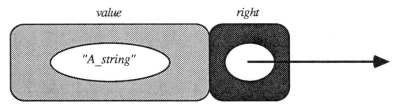

Figure 9.1   Linkable cell

Let us call T the type of the values. Clearly, as we want a structure that may be used for any T, the classes considered should be generic with T as their generic parameter.

The list itself is represented by a separate cell, the header. At the least, a header cell contains a reference to the first linkable cell (this reference is void if the list is empty); depending on the actual implementation chosen, it is often convenient to add other items to the header, such as a count of the number of elements. Figure 9.2 shows an example list of characters.

---

[1] Since the classes of the actual Eiffel library rely on aspects of the language introduced later, the descriptions given in this chapter are in some cases more primitive or less elegant. Appendix A describes some of the classes as they appear in the library.

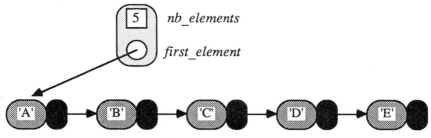

Figure 9.2   Linked list

The advantage of this representation is that an insertion or deletion is fast if you have a reference to the linkable immediately to the left of the insertion or deletion point: a simple pointer manipulation will do, as shown below for the deletion case.

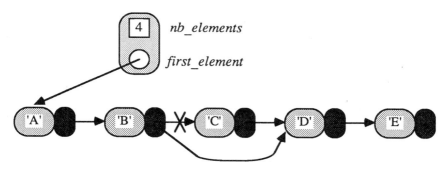

Figure 9.3   Deletion in a linked list

On the other hand, this representation is not very good for finding an element known by its value or its position: these operations require sequential list traversal. Array representations, in contrast, are good for accessing by position, but poor for insertions and deletions. Of course, many other representations exist; the linked list is an important one, which serves as a starting point for many others. In the next chapter, we will see how to define many possible implementations of lists (linked, contiguous etc.) as incremental variations on the same basic theme rather than as independent efforts.

9.1.2   Two simple classes

We clearly need two classes: one for lists (headers), the other for list elements (linkables). Let us call them *LINKED_LIST* and *LINKABLE*. Both are generic.

Note that the notion of *LINKABLE* is essential for the implementation, but not relevant to most clients. We should strive towards an interface which provides client modules with list manipulation primitives, without forcing them to worry about implementation details such as the presence of linkable elements.

The attributes of this class, corresponding to figure 9.1, may be given as

> **class** *LINKABLE1* [*T*]
> -- Linkable cells, for use in connection with linked lists
> **export** ... *see below* ... **feature**
> *value: T*;
> *right: LINKABLE1* [*T*]
> **end**

To yield a true class rather than just a record definition, operations must be added. What should a client be allowed to do on a linkable? Access to the *value* and *right* fields must be possible, but these are available as attributes and only need to be included in the **export** clause. If clients are to modify these fields as well, specific procedures are needed. Also, it does not make much sense to create a list element without giving its initial value, so the class should have its own *Create* procedure. This yields a usable version:

> **class** *LINKABLE* [*T*]
> -- Linkable cells, for use in connection with linked lists
> **export**
> ... *see below* ...
> **feature**
> *value: T*;
> *right: LINKABLE* [*T*];
>
> *Create* (*initial: T*) **is**
> -- Initialize with value *initial*
> **do** *value := initial* **end**;
>
> *change_value* (*new: T*) **is**
> -- Replace value with *new*
> **do** *value := new* **end**;
>
> *change_right* (*other: LINKABLE* [*T*]) **is**
> -- Put *other* to the right of current cell
> **do** *right := other* **end**
> **end** -- class *LINKABLE*

Now consider the linked lists themselves, to be accessed internally through their headers. It appears worthwhile to include the following features, among others:

- The number of elements.
- A test of whether the list is empty.
- A reference to the first element (void if the list is empty).
- The value of the i-th element, for any legal index i.
- A routine to change the value of the i-th element.
- Routines to insert or delete an element at position i.
- A routine to search for an element of a certain value.

etc.

Here is a sketch of a first version; full routine bodies are only given for *value* and *insert*.

class *LINKED_LIST1* [*T*]
                    -- One-way linked lists
export
          nb_elements, empty, value, change_value, insert, delete, search...
feature

          first_element: LINKABLE [*T*];
          nb_elements: T;

          empty: BOOLEAN **is**
                    -- Is list empty?
               do *Result := (nb_elements = 0)* **end**; -- *empty*

          value (i: INTEGER): T **is**
                    -- Value of *i*-th list element
               require
                    1 <= i ; i <= nb_elements
               local
                    elem: LINKABLE [*T*]; *j: INTEGER*
               do
                    from
                         j := 1; elem := first_element
                    invariant *j <= i* **variant** *i − j*
                    until
                         j = i
                    loop
                         j := j + 1; elem := elem.right
                    end;

                    Result := elem.value
               end; -- *value*

          change_value (i: INTEGER; v: T) **is**
                    -- Replace by *v* the value of *i*-th list element
               require
                    1 <= i ; i <= nb_elements
               do
                    ...
               ensure
                    value (i) = v
               end; -- *change_value*

```
insert (i: INTEGER; v: T) is
            -- Insert a new element of value v
            -- so that it becomes the i-th element
    require
            1 <= i ; i <= nb_elements + 1
    local
            previous, new: LINKABLE [T]; j: INTEGER
    do
                    -- Create new cell
            new.Create (v);

            if i = 1 then
                            -- Insert at head of list
                    new.change_right (first_element); first_element := new
            else
                    from
                            j := 1; previous := first_element
                    invariant
                            j >= 1; j <= i - 1; not previous.Void
                            -- previous is the j-th list element
                    variant
                            i - j - 1
                    until j = i - 1 loop
                            j := j + 1; previous := previous.right
                    end ;

                            -- Insert after previous
                    previous.change_right (new);
                    new.change_right (previous.right)
            end;

            nb_elements := nb_elements + 1
    ensure
            nb_elements = old nb_elements + 1; not empty
    end; -- insert

delete (i: INTEGER) is
            -- Remove i-th list element
    require
            1 <= i ; i <= nb_elements
    do
            ...
    ensure
            nb_elements = old nb_elements - 1
    end; -- delete

search (v: T): INTEGER is
            -- Position of first element of value v in list (0 if none)
    do ... end
```

... Other features ...

invariant
>   *empty* = (*nb_elements* = *0*);
>   *empty* = *first.element.Void*
end; -- *class LINKED_LIST1*

It is a good idea to try to complete *change_value*, *delete* and *search* for yourself in this first version (make sure the class invariant is maintained).

9.1.3   Encapsulation and assertions

Before we consider better versions, a few comments are in order on our first attempt.

Class *LINKED_LIST1* certainly shows that even on fairly simple structures pointer manipulations are tricky, especially when combined with loops. The use of assertions helps get them right (see procedure *insert* and the invariant); but the sheer difficulty of this type of programming is a strong argument for encapsulating such operations once and for all in reusable modules, as promoted by the object-oriented approach.

Also, note the application of the principle of uniform reference (2.1.4): although *nb_elements* is an attribute and *empty* a function, clients do not need to know these details. They are protected against any later reversal of these implementation decisions.

Finally, the semantics might have been expressed more precisely using assertions. For example *insert* should be given as:

insert (*i: INTEGER*; *v: T*) **is**
>   -- Insert at position *i* a new element of value *v*
>   **require**
>   *1* <= *i* ; *i* <= *nb_elements* + *1*
>   **local**
>   *elem, new: LINKABLE* [*T*]
>   **do**
>   ... As above ...
>   **ensure**
>   *nb_elements* = **old** *nb_elements* + *1*;
>   **not** *empty*
>   -- The element of index *i* has value *v*
>   -- For *1* <= *j* < *i*, the element of index *j* has not changed its value
>   -- For *i* < *j* <= *nb_elements*,
>   -- the element of index *j* has the value
>   -- that the element of index *j* – *1* had before the call
>   **end**; -- *insert*

Note that these assertions are only partially formal. The preconditions and postconditions of other routines should be completed in a similar fashion.

9.1.4 A critique of the class interface

How usable are these simple classes? Let us evaluate their design.

A worrying aspect of *LINKED_LIST1* is the presence of significant redundancies: *value* and *insert* contain almost identical loops, and similar ones will need to be included in the routines whose code has been left to the reader (*change_value*, *search*, *delete*). Yet it does not seem possible to factor out the common part. For an approach that emphasizes reusability, this is not a promising start.

This problem is one of implementation, internal to the class: lack of reuse of internal code. But it is in fact representative of a problem of a more serious nature – a poorly designed class interface.

Consider routine *search*. As it stands, it returns the index at which a given element has been found in the list, or *nb_elements* + *1* if the element is not present. How does a client use this result? Typically, the client may want to perform an insertion or deletion at the position found. But both insertion and deletion require traversing the list again! For example, *insert* (i, v) goes through the first i elements, even if i is the result of *search* – obtained by this same traversal.

In the design of a general-purpose module that will get used over and over again, one cannot treat such inefficiencies lightly. Although programmers may be prepared to pay a small performance price for a high level of reusability, this price must remain negligible. Here it is unacceptable.

9.1.5 Simple-minded solutions

How can we remove this blatant inefficiency? Two apparent solutions spring to mind:

- We could rewrite *search* so that it returns not an integer but an actual *LINKABLE* reference to the cell where the requested value is found (or a void reference if the search is unsuccessful). Then the client has a direct handle on the actual linkable cell and may perform the needed operations (insert, delete etc.) without retraversal.

- We could try to provide enough primitives to deal with various combinations of operations (search and then insert, search and then delete etc.).

However the first solution defeats the whole idea of encapsulating data structures in classes: clients would directly manipulate the representations, with all the dangers involved. As noted above, the notion of linkable is internal; we want client programmers to think in terms of lists and list values, not of list cells and pointers. Otherwise it does not make sense to use classes for data abstraction.

The second solution was attempted in an early version of the Eiffel library. An attempt was made to provide routines that would cover common combinations of operations. For example, insertion before the occurrence of a known value would be achieved not by a call to *search* followed by a call to *insert* but by a single call to

> *insert_before_by_value* (*v*: *T*; *v1*: *T*) **is**
>   -- Insert a new element of value *v* in front of first occurrence
>   -- of *v1* in list, or at end of list if no such occurrence
>   **do** ... **end**

This solution was indeed keeping the internal representation hidden from clients, while avoiding the inefficiencies of the initial version.

But we soon realized we were in for a long journey. Consider how many variants need to be provided:

insert_before_by_value
insert_after_by_value
insert_after_by_position
insert_after_by_position
delete_before_by_value

…

insert_at_end_if_absent

…

Writing general-purpose reusable software components is a difficult task, and there is no guarantee that you will get every module right the first time. So you should be prepared to update the components as they become applied more widely. However the process must converge: after an initial tune-up period, each component should stabilize. If not – that is to say, if almost every new use brings in the need for extension or modification – your approach to reusability is obviously flawed. This appeared to be the case with the list class we had at that point: it looked like every new client of lists needed a special variant of the basic operations, warranting the introduction of a new primitive.

To make matters worse, all basic list routines are rather complex, with loops similar to the one for *insert*; they have much in common but all differ from each other by small details. The prospect of a robust, reusable linked list class seems to be eluding us.

9.2 OBJECTS AS MACHINES

Fortunately, there is a way out of this predicament. The solution lies in taking a different view of the underlying abstract data type.

9.2.1 Introducing a state

The mistake made so far has been to treat a list as a passive repository of information. To provide clients with a better service, the list should become more active by "remembering" where the last operation was performed.

The idea has already been encountered in the discussion of side-effect in functions (7.7.2, "Commands and queries"; see figure 7.5, page 133). We should not hesitate to look at objects as machines with an internal state, and introduce both procedures, or commands that change the state, and functions, or queries on the state. This approach will yield an interface which is both simpler and more efficient than what we have considered so far.

A list will be a machine, then, with a state that may be explicitly changed. The state of a list should include not just the contents of the list but also a currently active position, or **cursor**, as illustrated below. We should not hesitate to provide clients with commands that officially move the cursor.

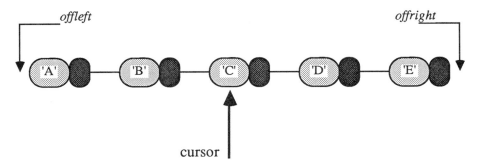

Figure 9.4   List with cursor

Examples of commands that may move the cursor will include such traversal operations as *search*, which is not a function any more but a procedure. This procedure does not return a result (this will be the privilege of a query function) but simply moves the cursor to a position where the sought element appears. More precisely, *l.search* (x, i) should move the cursor to the i-th occurrence of x in list l. A convention will be introduced below for the case in which x has fewer than i occurrences in the list.

Other commands may be defined to act on the cursor:

• Procedure *start* moves the cursor to the first position; a precondition is that the list be non-empty.

• Procedure *finish* has the same precondition and moves the cursor to the last position.

• Procedure *back* and *forth* move the cursor to the next or previous position.

• *go* (i) moves the cursor to a specific position.

The cursor position will be given by a query function *position*, which may in practice be implemented as an attribute. Other useful query functions on the cursor, returning boolean values, are *isfirst* and *islast*, with obvious meaning.

The procedures that build and modify a list – insertion, deletion, changing a value – may be simplified because they do not have to worry about positions: they will simply act on elements at the current cursor position. For example, *delete* will not be called as *l.delete* (i) any more, but simply as *l.delete*, which deletes the element at the current cursor position. In each case we need to establish precise conventions about what happens to the cursor after an operation. The following is a set of consistent conventions:

• Procedure *delete*, with no argument, deletes the element at cursor position and positions the cursor under its left neighbor (so that attribute *position* is decreased by 1).

- Procedure *insert_right* (*v* : *T*) inserts an element of value *v* to the right of the cursor and does not move the cursor (*position* is unchanged).

- Procedure *insert_left* (*v* : *T*) inserts an element of value *v* to the left of the cursor and does not move the cursor (so that the value of *position* must be increased by 1).

- Procedure *change_value* (*v* : *T*) changes the value of the element at cursor position. The value of this element is given by the query function *value*, which now has no argument and could be implemented as an attribute.

9.2.2   Maintaining consistency: the representation invariant

In defining such interfaces based on a strong notion of state, it is essential to introduce the appropriate assumptions ensuring that the state is always well-defined. For example, what happens to the cursor if it was on the first element of the list and a *delete* is executed? The general convention defined above is to move the cursor to the left neighbor, but here there is none. A moment's reflection on this and other cases will lead to a consistent convention: allow the cursor to go beyond the list limits by at most one position, left or right. Then the effect of all list operations will always be uniquely defined.

This property is a typical **representation invariant**. Recall (7.6) that a representation invariant expresses the consistency of a representation, given by a class, vis-à-vis the underlying abstract data type, even when this abstract data type is not explicitly specified. Here the class invariant will include the property

    0 <= position ; position <= nb_elements + 1

The boolean-valued query functions *offleft* and *offright* will allow clients to determine whether the cursor is off limits.

What about an empty list? Again, consistency suggests that it should be treated as being *both* offleft and offright, and that this should be the only case where both functions return true. This yields another pleasant clause for the class invariant:

    empty = (*offleft* **and** *offright*)

As this is an equality of boolean values, the = sign may be read as "if and only if". This is an important type of clause for invariants, involving functions rather than attributes, to express a consistency constraint on the results returned by various possible queries on the state of an object. Note that such clauses would be meaningless for functions producing side-effects.

Note that functions *offleft* and *offright* may have initially seemed superfluous, since the queries *position* = *0* and *position* = *nb_elements* + *1* appear to do the job for clients. But giving these queries an autonomous status naturally leads to above convention on the empty list, and to the realization that *offright* is more appropriately defined as

    empty **or** *position* = *nb_elements* + *1*

More invariant clauses are given in the class text as presented below.

9.2.3 The client's view

The above provides the basis for a simple an elegant interface to the implementation of linked lists. Operations such as "search and then insert" are obtained through two successive calls, but with no significant loss of efficiency. For example, if *LINKED_LIST* is the name of the revised class, a client may perform a search-and-insert by:

> *l: LINKED_LIST [INTEGER]*; *m, n: INTEGER*;
>
> ...
>
> *l.search (m, l)*;
> **if not** *offright* **then** *l.insert_right (n)* **end**

Recall that *search* (x, i) moves the cursor to the i-th occurrence of x in the list if it exists. In line with the above conventions, it seems appropriate to specify that the result when x has fewer than i occurrences will be to put the list in the *offright* state; note that this choice is not entirely satisfactory, since *offleft* would seem just as justified. This is an example of over-specification, although a tolerable one.

To delete the third occurrence of a certain value, a client will execute:

> *l.search (m, 3)*;
> **if not** *offright* **then** *delete* **end**

To insert a value at position i:

> *l.go (i)*; *l.insert_left (i)*

and so on. A clear and easy to use interface has been obtained by making the internal state explicit, and providing clients with the appropriate commands and queries on this state.

9.2.4 The internals

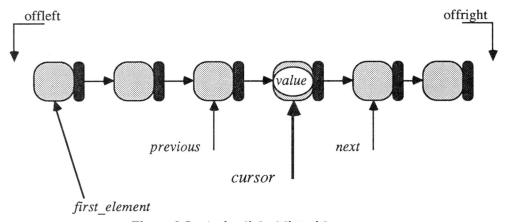

Figure 9.5   Active linked list with cursor

Not only does the new solution yield a good interface, it also simplifies the implementation considerably. The unneeded redundancies between the various routines are removed; this is because each routine now has a more restricted specification, concentrating on just one task. For example, insertion and deletion procedures no longer have to traverse the list; they just carry out a local modification. Other routines (*back*, *forth*, *go*, *search*) are charged with positioning the cursor at the right place. The redundant traversal loops that plagued the previous version are not needed.

Below are some examples of the class's internals, designed accordingly. Figure 9.5 shows an instantaneous list state.

Class *LINKED_LIST* contains the following secret attributes:

> *first_element, active, previous, next: LINKABLE [T]*

Attribute *first_element* is a reference to the first element (or void if the list is empty). Attributes *previous*, *active* and *next* refer to the elements before, at and after the cursor; keeping both the previous and the next elements is needed to handle insertions and deletions efficiently.

Clients may know the state of the list by accessing the public attributes

> *nb_elements, position: INTEGER*

and the boolean-valued functions *empty, isfirst, islast, offleft* and *offright*. Function *isfirst*, for example, returns true if and only if the cursor is on the first element (which implies that the list is not empty). Regarding the last two functions, recall that we allow the cursor to move at most one position off the left or right edge of a list.

The allowable states and the properties of these features are characterized by the following class invariant:

invariant

    -- The first set of assertions is independent of the linked representation:
        nb_elements >= *0*;
        position >= *0*; *position* <= *nb_elements* + *1*;
        (**not** *empty*) **or** (*position* = *0*);

        empty = (*nb_elements* = *0*);
        offright = (*empty* **or** (*position* = *nb_elements* + *1*));
        offleft = (*position* = *0*);
        isfirst = (*position* = *1*);
        islast = (**not** *empty* **and** (*position* = *nb_elements*));

    -- The next two assertions are theorems (deducible from the previous ones):
        empty = (*offleft* **and** *offright*);
        not *empty* **or** (**not** *isfirst* **or** **not** *islast*);

    -- The next assertions describe the linked list representation:
        empty = *first_element.Void*;
        empty **or else** (*first_element.value* = *first*);

        active.Void = (*offleft* **or** *offright*);
        previous.Void = (*offleft* **or** *isfirst*);
        next.Void = (*offright* **or** *islast*);

(*offleft* **or** *isfirst*) **or else** (*previous.right* = *active*);
(*offleft* **or** *offright*) **or else** (*active.right* = *next*);

This invariant shows once again the power of assertions, in particular class invariants, in expressing the most important properties of data structures.

The functions themselves are easy to write. For example:

offright: BOOLEAN **is**
        -- Is cursor position off right edge?
    do
        Result := empty **or** (*position* = *nb_elements* + *1*)
    end; -- offright

The value of the element at cursor position is given by the *value* function, which may be implemented as follows:

    value: T **is**
            -- Value of element at cursor position
        require
            not *offleft*;
            not *offright*
        do
            Result := active.value
        end; -- value

In this function definition, *T* is the generic type parameter to the class. The precondition expresses that *value* is only defined if the cursor points to a valid list element; you should check the invariant to see that this precondition excludes the case in which the list is empty. Finally, *value* in *active.value* refers not to the *value* function in class *LINKED_LIST* but, since *active* is of type *LINKABLE* [*T*], to the *value* feature of that class (also a function). Different classes may, of course, use the same feature names, as there is never any ambiguity.

Another category of features of class *LINKED_LIST* includes procedures for moving around: *start*, *finish*, *forth*, *back*, *go*, *search*. Here for example is *go* :

    go (*i: INTEGER*) **is**
            -- Move cursor to position *i*
        require
            i >= *0*; *i* <= *nb_elements* + *1*;
            not *empty* **or** *i=0*;
        do
            if *i* = *0* **then**
                go_offleft
            else
                        check not *empty* **end**;

```
from
      if offleft or i < position then start end
invariant
      position <= i
variant
      i - position
until
      position = i
loop
      if position = 1 then previous := active
      else previous := previous.right end;

      position := position + 1;
                  check not previous.Void end
end; --loop

if position > 1 then active := previous.right end;

if position >= nb_elements then next.Forget
else next := active.right end
end -- if
ensure
position = i
end; -- go
```

Procedure *go_offleft* (secret, since clients will simply use *go* (0)) must be written separately. Procedure *go* has been written so as to perform the optimal traversal in all cases; in highly reusable components, it pays off to optimize every operation. Such components are worth careful individual crafting.

Procedure *search* is left to the reader (exercise 9.2). Note that it will also contain a loop; however this loop is significantly different from *go*'s loop. In contrast with the previous solution, these are the only two loops in the basic routines of *LINKED_LIST*.

Because of the way *go* has been written, the bodies of procedure *forth* and *back* may simply be written as *go* (*position* + *1*) and *go* (*position* - *1*).

Sometimes you may want to remember a position and return to it later. Procedures *mark* and *return* (left to the reader) may be used for that purpose. If two or more *mark* commands are successively executed, the corresponding *return* commands will retrieve marked positions in last-in, first-out order.

Procedures *go*, *mark* and *return* may be used to implement the function *i_th* (*i*: *INTEGER*) which returns the value of the *i*-th element of the list, for legal *i*. The body of this function may be written as:

   mark; *go* (*i*); *Result := value*; *return*

Although a function, *i_th* produces side-effects by calling cursor-moving procedures. But these side-effects are acceptable because they are only temporary: *i_th* leaves the list in the exact state in which it found it, although no compiler could possibly deduce this. This is an acceptable case of side-effect in a function, as discussed in 7.7.4: the abstract state is not affected; only a concrete (and in this case temporary) side-effect is produced. Such side-effects are harmless, and quite convenient.

The last category of features includes procedures for insertion and deletion. For example, the basic deletion operation (illustrated below) may be written as:

delete **is**

  -- Delete element at cursor position
  -- and move cursor to its right neighbor.
  -- (If no right neighbor, list becomes offright).
 require
  not offleft; *not offright*;
 do
  active := *next*;
  if not *previous.Void* **then**
   previous.change_right (*active*)
  end;
  if not *active.Void* **then**
   next := *active.right*
  end;
  nb_elements := *nb_elements* − *1*;
   -- Update *first_element* if needed
  if *nb_elements* = *0* **then**
   first_element.Forget;
   position := *0*
  elsif *position* = *1* **then**
   first_element := *active*;
  end
 end; -- *delete*

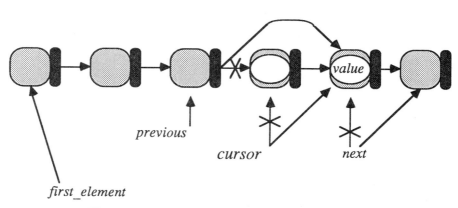

first_element

Figure 9.6   Deletion in a linked list with cursor

Again, this routine shows the trickiness of data structure operations even for such fundamental structures as linked lists, and the benefits of encapsulating them in carefully verified reusable modules – once the interface is right.

Other operations are left to the reader.

9.2.5 Data structures as machines

The notion of active data structure is widely applicable. Giving data structures an explicit state often yields simple, easy to document interfaces. Examples sketched in 7.7.2 showed that such abstractions as files or random number generators may be similarly treated. Most common data structures may be characterized by an internal state and a current position.

This approach might, at first sight, appear to contradict the "abstractness" of the abstract data type approach, on which object-oriented programming is based. But this is not the case. The theory of abstract data types suggests that data structures should be given an abstract description based on applicable operations and the formal properties of these operations. This by no means implies that the data structures should be passive repositories of data. It is actually quite the opposite: by introducing a state and operations on this state, we make the abstract data type specification richer as it has more functions and more properties. (Note, by the way, that the state is a pure abstraction, never accessed directly but only manipulated through commands and queries.) In the end the view of objects as state machines reflects abstract data types which are more *operational*, but this in no way makes them any less abstract.

9.3 DEALING WITH ABNORMAL CASES

Special cases are the scourge of programmers. The necessity to account for all possible situations, erroneous user input, failures of the hardware or of the operating system is a powerful impediment in the constant battle against software complexity.

This problem strongly affects the design of module interfaces, as it is much more difficult to deal with abnormal situations when they may be due to some processing performed in another module. Many a software designer has wished that the problem would simply go away; it would be so nice to write clear, elegant algorithms for normal cases, and rely on external mechanisms to take care of all the others. Much of the hope placed in exception mechanisms results from this dream. In Ada, for example, you may deal with an abnormal case by writing something like

> **if** *abnormal_situation_detected* **then**
>> **raise** *an_exception*;
> **end**;
> "Go on with normal processing"

where execution of the **raise** instruction stops the execution of the current routine or block and transfers control to an "exception handler" written in one of the direct or indirect callers. But this is a control structure, not a method for dealing with abnormal cases. In the end you still have to decide what to do in these cases: Can the situation be corrected? If so, how can this be achieved and what should be done next? If not, how quickly and gracefully can you terminate the execution?

There is room, as we saw in chapter 7, for a disciplined exception mechanism. But in most cases exceptions do not help solve the basic issues that arise when programmers are dealing with abnormal cases. In the rest of this section, we shall look at some simple yet powerful methods which are applicable in a wide variety of cases. Then we shall examine the remaining cases in which exceptions, at least under the restricted form studied in chapter 7, remain indispensable.

9.3.1   The a priori scheme

Perhaps the most important criterion in dealing with abnormal cases at the module interface level is specification. If you know exactly what inputs each software element is prepared to accept, and what guarantees it ensures in return, half the battle is won.

Assertion techniques are particularly useful here. In particular, preconditions are essential to express the applicability of an operation. Ideally, every externally available operation should be equipped with a precondition which fully describes the conditions under which the operation is valid:

> *operation* (*x:* ...) **is**
> > **require**
> > > *precondition* (*x*)
> >
> > **do**
> > > ... Code that will only work if *precondition* is met ...
> >
> > **end**

If this precondition is indeed complete, in the sense that any call satisfying it is guaranteed to succeed, then client code may be written in a simple form:

> **if** *precondition* (*y*) **then**
> > *operation* (*y*)
>
> **else**
> > ... Appropriate alternate action ...
>
> **end**

This is what may be called the a priori scheme: check applicability before use.

Note that in some cases the context of the call implies that the precondition is satisfied, and consequently the **if...then...else** structure is not needed. In such cases it is good practice to precede the call with an instruction

> **check** (*precondition* (*y*))

to remind the reader that the verification was not omitted by mistake. In debugging mode (ALL_ASSERTIONS, see 7.10.1), the **check** instruction will trigger a run-time check.

In such an ideal context, execution-time violations of the rules may only result from design errors: a client not abiding by the rules. The only long-term solution in this case is to correct the errors. We have seen, however, how fault-tolerance techniques based on exceptions (triggered by assertion violations or other events) may to a certain extent allow partial recovery through the **retry** mechanism; for example an interactive system may let its users try a new command when the one initially requested has failed to execute correctly.

9.3.2   Obstacles to the a priori scheme

There are three limitations to the a priori scheme:

- Sometimes, it is not practical to test the precondition before a call for efficiency reasons.

- Because of the limitations of assertion languages (such as the assertion language embedded in Eiffel), certain assertions may not fit in the available formalism.

- Finally, some applicability conditions depend on external events and are not assertions at all.

An example of the first case is a linear equation solver. A function for solving an equation of the form $ax = b$, where a is a matrix, and x (the unknown) and b are vectors, might take the following form in an appropriately designed *MATRIX* class:

> *inverse (b: VECTOR): VECTOR*

so that a particular equation will be solved by $x := a.\ inverse\ (b)$.

A unique solution only exists, however, if the matrix is not "singular" (a singular matrix has a zero determinant or, equivalently, has a row which is a linear combination of others). We could add this requirement as a precondition to *inverse* and shift the responsibility to clients, which would contain calls of the form

> **if** *a.singular* **then**
>   ... Appropriate error action ...
> **else**
> $x := a.inverse\ (b)$
> **end**

This technique works but is very inefficient: determining whether a matrix is singular is essentially the same operation as solving the associated linear equation. Standard algorithms for solving the equation (Gaussian elimination) will at each step compute a divisor, called the pivot; if the pivot found at some step is zero or below a certain threshold, this shows that the matrix was singular. This result is obtained as a byproduct of the attempt to solve the equation; obtaining it separately does not cost significantly less. Doing the job in two steps – first to find out whether the matrix is singular, and then, if it is not, to solve the equation – is a waste of effort.

Examples of the second above case include those in which the precondition is a global property of a data structure and would need to be expressed with quantifiers, for example the fact that a graph is not cyclic or that a list is sorted. Note that we could in practice express most such assertions using functions; but then we would be back in the first case, as the precondition would be too costly to check before every call.

Finally, the third limitation arises in cases where it is impossible to test the applicability of the operation without attempting to execute it, because interaction with the outside world – a human user, a communication line, a file system – is involved.

9.3.3   The a posteriori scheme

In some cases where the a priori scheme does not work, a simple-minded solution is still possible. The idea is to check after the fact rather than before. This **a posteriori** scheme will work if a failed attempt has no irrecoverable consequences. Then one may try the operation and then determine whether it succeeded.

The matrix equation problem provides a good example. With an a posteriori scheme, client code will now be of the form

```
a.solve (b);
if a.solution_found then
        x := a.solution
else
        ... appropriate error action ...
end
```

In other words, function *inverse* has been replaced by a procedure *solve*, which could more appropriately be called *attempt_to_solve*. A call to this procedure sets the attribute *solution_found* to true or false depending a solution was found or not; if it was, the procedure makes the solution itself available through attribute *solution*.

With this method, any function that may produce an error condition is transformed into a procedure, the result being made available, if it exists, through an attribute set by the procedure.

This works also for input-output operations. For example a "read" function that may fail is better expressed as a procedure that attempts to read, and two attributes, one (boolean) which says whether the operation succeeded, and another which yields the value read in the successful case.

Note that these techniques are one more variation on the command/query theme. A function that may raise an exceptional condition while computing a certain value is not side-effect-free, and it is better decomposed into a procedure that attempts to compute the value, and two queries (functions or attributes), one which determines success and the other which yields the value in case of success.

The read example is particularly interesting in this respect (exercise 9.5). Very often, read functions as they are provided by programming languages or the associated libraries force the client to state in advance the type of the element to be read: the primitives are of the form "read integer", "read string" etc. Then inevitably exceptions occur when the actual input does not match its expected form. A good read procedure should attempt to read the next input item without any preconception of what it will be, and then **return** the information about the type of this item in the form of an attribute available to clients through queries.

This example highlights one of the important principles of dealing with failures: whenever applicable, methods for **engineering out** failures are preferable to methods for dealing with failures once they have occurred.

9.3.4   The role of an exception mechanism

The previous discussion has shown that in most cases methods based on standard control structures – essentially conditional instructions – are adequate for dealing with abnormal cases. Although the a priori scheme is not always practical, it is often possible to check success after attempting an operation. The operational (state machine) approach to objects provides the appropriate background.

There remain, however, cases in which both a priori and a posteriori techniques are inadequate. The above discussion leaves only three categories of such cases:

- In some cases, abnormal events such as numerical failure or memory exhaustion would lead to preemptive action by the hardware or operating system, such as raising an exception and, if the exception is not caught, terminating execution abruptly. This is often intolerable, especially in systems with continuous availability requirements such as telephone exchanges.

- There are also cases in which abnormal situations, although not detectable through a precondition, must be diagnosed at the earliest possible time; the operation must not be allowed to run to completion (for a posteriori checking) because it could lead to disastrous consequences, such as destroying the integrity of a database or even endanger human lives (as in a robot control system).

- Finally, the programmer may wish to include some form of protection against the most catastrophic consequences of any remaining errors in the software; this is the use of exceptions for software fault tolerance, as described in 7.10.4.

In such cases, exception-based techniques appear necessary. The orderly exception mechanism presented in 7.10 provides the appropriate tools.

9.4 SELECTIVE EXPORTS

The principle of information hiding (2.2.5) plays a central role in the construction of modules with adequate interfaces. The basic application of this mechanism in object-oriented languages is the presence of an export restriction mechanism, as offered in Eiffel by the **export** clause.

One aspect of the export mechanism has not been presented yet: the usefulness, in certain cases, of exporting a feature to some classes only.

A typical example is provided by class *LINKABLE*, whose export clause was intentionally left blank (page 186). The features of this class, namely *value*, *right*, *Create*, *change_value* and *change_right*, are needed by *LINKED_LIST*. However information hiding dictates that we should not allow arbitrary classes to access these features; the notion of linkable cell is used only for the implementation of linked lists, and it would be dangerous to let arbitrary modules manipulate linkable cells directly. The features of *LINKABLE* should be available to *LINKED_LIST* and no other class.

To express that a feature is exported to selected classes only, the class implementor will list these classes, enclosed in braces and separated by commas, after the name of the feature in the export clause. For example:

```
class LINKABLE [T]
            -- Linkable cells, for use in connection with linked lists
export
      value {LINKED_LIST}, change_value {LINKED_LIST},
      right {LINKED_LIST}, change_right {LINKED_LIST}
feature
      ... as above ...
end -- class LINKABLE
```

As a special case, if a class *C* contains elements of the form *a: C;*

  ...

  ... a.f

then *f* must be available to *C* itself. This implies that *f* appears in the export clause of the class: either *f* is exported without restriction, or *C* is one of the selected classes for *f*. For example, the actual library version of *LINKABLE* (see appendix A) uses an expression of the form

  before.right

where *before* is of type *LINKABLE* [*T*]. To enable this, the subclause for *right* in the export clause of *LINKABLE* must be

  right {*LINKED_LIST, LINKABLE*}

  Selective export clauses are useful when a group of related classes, as *LINKABLE* and *LINKED_LIST* here, need some of each other's features for their implementations, although these features remain private to the group and should not be made available to other classes.

9.5 DOCUMENTING A CLASS

Assume you have implemented a class with a well-designed interface. You want to enable other classes – clients – to use it. How will their implementors know what services it offers?

9.5.1 Showing the interface: the *short* class abstracter

According to the principle of information hiding, not all information contained in a class is relevant to its clients. The structure of Eiffel makes it clear what information is secret:

  • Any non-exported feature and anything having to do with it (for example, a clause of an assertion which refers to the feature).

  • Any routine implementation, as given by the **do**... clause.

  Client programmers, and prospective client programmers, should be able to use the class through an abstract description from which all this secret information has been removed.

> It is worth recalling (see 2.2.5) that the purpose of information hiding is abstraction, not protection. We do not necessarily wish to prevent client programmers from accessing secret class elements, but rather to *relieve* them from having to do so. In a software project, programmers are faced with too much information, and need abstraction facilities to concentrate on the essentials. Information hiding makes this possible by separating function from implementation, and should be viewed by client programmers as help rather than hindrance.

How do we make the public information available to client programmers? One approach is to require the class implementor to provide a separate description of the class, containing only the interface information. (This is essentially what is done in Ada and Modula-2.) But here it would be foolish, since this information is a subset of the class as written. Why not use a computer tool to extract it?

In the Eiffel environment, this task is performed by the "class abstracter", the **short** command. If c is the name of an Eiffel class, executing

> **short** c

will produce an abbreviated version of c, containing the public information only. The output is exactly what a client needs to know about the class, no more and no less.

This command provides an excellent documentation tool. The quality of the documentation produced is due in part to the the presence of assertions, which are retained by the command (except for clauses involving secret features). Judiciously chosen preconditions and postconditions, in particular, will explain the purpose of a routine much better than long-winded comments. As a typical example, procedure *forth* in *LINKED_LIST* is characterized by the following assertions, retained by **short**:

> **require**
> > **not** *offright*
> **ensure**
> > *position* = **old** *position* + *1*

This says simply and precisely what the routine does. In more difficult cases, the assertions will only express some of the properties of the routine; but they are a useful complement to the routine header and header comment, both of which are retained by **short**.

9.5.2   The meaning of short

Underlying the **short** class abstracter is a principle of software engineering: **avoid documentation**. Although all software engineering textbooks recommend writing good documentation, any approach that treats code and documentation as separate products is bound to suffer from the consistency problem. Incorrect documentation is often worse than no documentation. How can we be sure that the software and its documentation agree? With some effort, this can be achieved initially; but it is very hard to guarantee throughout a software project that every change to the code will be reflected in the documentation, and conversely. Furthermore, since documentation is usually non-formal, it is impossible to write software tools that verify the consistency.

Ideally, we should be able to circumvent the issue altogether by enabling software to be self-documenting: the documentation would then be viewed as a subset of the code, with appropriate tools to extract the relevant information at various levels of abstraction. Command **short** is a step in this direction.

The above principle is not fully applicable in the current state of software engineering. At the global system level, in particular, there remains a need for high-level documentation, expressing system architecture and fundamental design decisions, which is not easily obtained from the code. (This documentation is often best given in graphical form.) But the goal of making documentation a product that is *extracted* by computer tools rather than prepared separately by human beings is an ideal worth pursuing. Command **short** partly achieves it in the Eiffel context.

9.5.3 A complete class interface

An example of **short**'s output is given below. It is the interface of the *LINKED_LIST* class from the Eiffel basic library. To give the reader some appreciation for what is involved in a realistic, full-fledged reusable software component, the command has been applied to the complete class as present in the library, including a number of features not mentioned in the above discussion. The only simplifications made relate to uses of inheritance and associated language constructs, not yet studied.

The keywords used in the output (**class interface, exported features** etc.) differ from their Eiffel counterparts to avoid any confusion with an actual Eiffel class. Optionally, **short** may also generate a correct Eiffel "deferred" class (10.3).[2]

class interface *LINKED_LIST* [T]
exported features

  nb_elements, empty, position,
  offright, offleft, islast,
  isfirst, value, i_th, first,
  last, change_value, change_i_th,
  swap, start, finish, forth, back,
  go, search, mark, return,
  index_of, present, duplicate,
  wipe_out, delete,
  delete_all_occurrences, delete_right,
  delete_left, insert_right,
  insert_left, merge_right, merge_left,
  sublist, split

feature specification

  nb_elements: INTEGER

  empty: BOOLEAN
    -- Is list empty?

  position: INTEGER

  offright: BOOLEAN
    -- Is cursor off right edge?

  offleft: BOOLEAN
    -- Is cursor off left edge?

isfirst: BOOLEAN
    -- Is cursor on first element?
  ensure
    not *Result*
    or else not *empty*

islast: BOOLEAN
    -- Is cursor on last element?
  ensure
    not *Result*
    or else not *empty*

value: T
    -- Value of element
    -- at cursor position
  require
    not *offleft*;
    not *offright*

i_th (i: INTEGER): T
    -- Value of *i*-th element
  require
    $i >= 1$;
    $i <= nb\_elements$;

first: T
    -- Value of first element
  require
    not *empty*

---

[2] On option, **short** will generate output suitable for typesetting (by the troff formater under Unix). This option was used to produce the result shown.

last: T
> -- Value of last element
> **require**
> **not** *empty*

change_i_th (i: INTEGER; v: T)
> -- Assign *v* to value
> -- of *i*-th element
> **require**
> $i >= 1$;
> $i <= nb\_elements$;
> **ensure**
> *i_th (i) = v*

swap (i: INTEGER)
> -- Exchange value of *i*-th element
> -- with value of element
> -- at cursor position
> **require**
> **not** *offleft*;
> **not** *offright*;
> $i >= 1$;
> $i <= nb\_elements$
> **ensure**
> *i_th (i)* = **old** *value*;
> *value* = **old** *(i_th (i))*

start
> -- Move cursor
> -- to first position
> **ensure**
> (**old** *empty* **and nochange**)
>   **or else** *isfirst*

finish
> -- Move cursor to last position
> **ensure**
> (**old** *empty* **and nochange**)
>   **or else** *islast*

forth
> -- Move cursor
> -- to next position
> **require**
> **not** *offright*
> **ensure**
> *position* = **old** *position + 1*

back
> -- Move cursor
> -- to previous position
> **require**
> **not** *offleft*
> **ensure**
> *position* = **old** *position – 1*

go (i: INTEGER)
> -- Move cursor to *i*-th position
> **require**
> $i >= 0$;
> $i <= nb\_elements + 1$
> **ensure**
> *position = i*

search (v: T; i: INTEGER)
> -- Move cursor to *i*-th element
> -- of value *v*; if none, go offright.
> **require**
> $i > 0$
> **ensure**
> *offright*
> **or else** *(value = v)*

mark
> -- Save cursor position

return
> -- Move cursor
> -- to last saved position

index_of (v: T; i: INTEGER):
>   *INTEGER*
> -- Index of *i*-th element
> -- of value *v*, 0 if none
> **require**
> $i > 0$
> **ensure**
> *Result* $>= 0$;
> *Result* $<= nb\_elements$
> -- If *Result* = 0, there are less
> -- than *i* elements of value *v*;
> -- if Result > 0, *Result* is
> -- the position of the *i*-th
> -- element of value *v*

present (v: T): BOOLEAN
    -- Does *v* appear in list?

duplicate (n: INTEGER):
  LINKED_LIST [T]
    -- Complete clone of sublist
    -- beginning at cursor position,
    -- and containing
    -- *min (n, nb_elements − position)*
    -- elements
  require
    not *offleft*;
    not *offright*;
    n >= 0

wipe_out
    -- Make list empty
  ensure
    empty

insert_right (v: **like** *first)*
    -- Insert an element of value *v*
    -- to the right of cursor position
    -- Do not move cursor
  require
    empty **or not** *offright*
  ensure
    nb_elements = **old** *nb_elements + 1*;
    position = **old** *position*

insert_left (v: **like** *first)*
    -- Insert an element of value *v*
    -- to the left of cursor position
    -- Do not move cursor
  require
    empty **or not** *offleft*
  ensure
    nb_elements = **old** *nb_elements + 1*;
    position = 2
      or else *position =* **old** *position + 1*

delete
    -- Delete cursor element; move
    -- cursor to its right neighbor
    -- (If no right neighbor,
    -- list becomes offright)
  require
    not *offleft*;
    not *offright*;

delete_right (n: INTEGER)
    -- Delete
    -- *min (n, nb_elements - position)*
    -- elements to the right
    -- of cursor position
    -- Do not move cursor
  require
    not *offright*;
    n >= 0

delete_left (n: INTEGER)
    -- Delete
    -- *min (n, position-1, 0)*
    -- elements to the right
    -- of cursor position
    -- Do not move cursor
  require
    not *offleft*;
    n >= 0

delete_all_occurrences (v: **like** *first)*
    -- Delete all elements of
    -- value *v*; go offright
  ensure
    offright

merge_right (l: LINKED_LIST [T])
    -- Merge l into list after cursor.
    -- Do not move cursor
  require
    empty **or not** *offright*;
    not *l.Void*
  ensure
    nb_elements >= **old** *nb_elements*;
    l.empty

merge_left (l: LINKED_LIST [T])
> -- Merge l into list after cursor.
> -- Do not move cursor

> **require**
>> *empty* **or not** *offleft*;
>> **not** *l.Void*

> **ensure**
>> *nb_elements* >= **old** *nb_elements*;
>> *l. empty*

sublist: LINKED_LIST [T]

split (n: INTEGER)
> -- Remove from list -- *min (n, position-nb_elements)*
> -- elements starting at cursor position
> -- Make extracted sublist accessible through attribute *sublist*

> **require**
>> **not** *offleft*;
>> **not** *offright*;
>> *n* >= *0*;

> **ensure**
>> -- *nb_elements* = **old** *nb_elements* − *min (n, nb_elements* − **old** *position* + *1)*

invariant

> *empty* = (*nb_elements* = *0*);
> *offright* = (*empty* **or** (*position* = *nb_elements* + *1*));
> *offleft* = (*position* = *0*);
> *isfirst* = (*position* = *1*);
> *islast* = (**not** *empty* **and** (*position* = *nb_elements*));
> *nb_elements* >= *0*;
> *position* >= *0*;
> *position* <= *nb_elements* + *1*;
> (**not** *empty*) **or** (*position* = *0*);
> (*offleft* **or** *offright*) **or else** (*value* = *i_th* (*position*));

end interface -- class *LINKED_LIST*

9.6 DISCUSSION

A number of issues pertaining to information hiding and interfaces could have been resolved differently. The following paragraphs examine the choices and explain the Eiffel solutions.

9.6.1 Export or hidden clause

First, one has a choice between listing the public (exported) features or the secret ones. In Simula 67, for example, some features are explicitly declared as "hidden". Similarly, the Eiffel export clause could have been replaced by, say, a **secret** clause. But it seems a bit silly to draw the client programmer's attention to precisely those features that he cannot use directly.

9.6.2 Listing complete interfaces

The export clause only lists feature names. This does not provide clients with enough information to use the class; complete information would describe the whole class interface, that is to say the headers of all exported routines, complemented by the routine pre- and postconditions. Application of this idea has led the designers of Ada to introduce a double declaration for each module of the language, called a package. The so-called "specification" part only lists routine headers; the "body" lists the headers plus the routine bodies.

The main drawback of this technique is that it forces programmers to write things twice. In Eiffel, the task of separating the interface from the implementation is performed by a tool, **short**, as described above; the programmer provides the information only once. As opposed to an Ada package specification part, the export clause contains no redundant information, as the presence of a feature in this list is in itself a useful piece of information ("the feature declared with this name in the feature clause is public"), whereas repeating the routine's header would be redundant. Programming language designers should not victimize programmers by forcing them to write elements that do not bring new information and may be readily produced by a software tool.

Let us introduce (and refute!) three objections to this argument:

- First, the argument could be abused to the point of removing *any* sort of redundancy from programming languages. Many type declarations, for example, could be made optional; a reasonably smart compiler could find out that an entity which only participates in integer operations must be of integer type. Even so, typed languages force programmers to declare the types of all entities; this enables compilers to perform consistency checks that often result in the detection of errors. However the above discussion does not argue against all redundancy, only against languages which force tedious repetitions of sometimes large program elements.

- Another objection is that some of the tediousness could be removed by using program composition tools (structure editors). But if the job can be done by tools, why force it into the language? Leave it to the programming environment, as with **short** for Eiffel.

• The most serious objection is methodological: in some cases, it may be a good idea to first declare the interface, making it available to the outside world even before an implementation has been written. An Ada package specification may indeed be compiled separately from the corresponding body, and other packages may be compiled with reference to the specification only (although they obviously cannot be executed until an implementation has been provided). This is a sensible way to work in some cases; however Eiffel offers a much more general mechanism, **deferred routines** (see chapter 11), which goes beyond the Ada mechanism by allowing a given specification part to have not just one but several implementations within the same Eiffel system. However this mechanism is independent from export controls, which play a simpler role: informing a client programmer about what is available and what is not.

9.6.3   Listing imports

The export clause of every class lists the features made available to other classes. Why, one may ask, isn't there also an "import" clause which lists features obtained from other classes?

An import clause is indeed present in the modular language Modula-2. In a typed object-oriented language like Eiffel, it would not serve any purpose other than documentation. To use a feature f from another class C, you must be a client or a "descendant" of that class. In the former case (the only one seen so far), this means that every use of f is of the form

$a.f$

where, since Eiffel is typed, a must have been declared:

$a: C$

Hence there cannot be any ambiguity as to where f came from. The same is true of the "descendant" case.

Requiring imports to be declared explicitly would again be forcing the programmer to write redundant information. Instead, we consider the listing of imports to be a documentation facility and leave this task to appropriate software tools in the programming environment.

9.6.4   Selective exports

Selective export clauses (as for exporting the features of *LINKABLE* to *LINKED_LIST* only) are useful to share features between a set of related classes. The need for this facility may be traced to a precise reason: the lack of a higher-level structuring module than the class.

The only structuring mechanism at a higher lever than the class is the system (5.6.1). A system is simply a set of classes, assembled for the sole purpose of obtaining an executable program; it is not a module. A class remains independent from any systems to which it may belong.

If classes could be grouped into higher-level modules, then *LINKED_LIST* and *LINKABLE* could be declared together so as to make some features of *LINKABLE* accessible to *LINKED_LIST* only. One may imagine either Ada-style packages of classes (a purely syntactical grouping mechanism), or the possibility for classes to contain other classes (using the conventions of block structure to prevent access to inner classes from the outside). The second solution is available in Simula.

Either solution would mean that program units could be nested. This would immediately raise issues of scope, nesting conventions and visibility rules, as they exist in block-structured languages (Algol, Pascal, Ada, Simula). Much complexity would be added for little practical benefit. Furthermore, nesting is in part redundant and in part incompatible with inheritance (chapters 10 and 11), a much more fundamental component of the object-oriented method, and a much more effective facility for structuring large software systems.

In contrast, selective exports are just a modest extension to the basic export mechanism. They address the need for special relationships between certain classes but do not affect the status of classes as free-standing software components.

9.6.5 Exporting attributes

In Eiffel, any feature may be exported: routine or attribute. Exporting a routine entitles clients to execute it; exporting an attribute entitles clients to access its value (in read mode), but not to modify (write onto) it. This is made quite clear by the syntax of the language, under which a qualified attribute application, of the form

>   *x.attrib*

(with possibly more levels of qualification) is an expression, not an entity. Thus the notation

>   *x.attrib := a*

is syntactically erroneous. To make *attrib* accessible in modification mode, one must write and export an appropriate procedure, of the form:

```
set_attrib (v: T) is
            -- Set to v the value of attrib
    do
        attrib := v
    end -- set_attrib
```

One could imagine a syntax for specifying access rights in the export list, for example as

>   **class** *C* **export**
>   *attrib1* [*A*], *attrib2* [*AM*], ...

where *A* would mean access and *M* modification. (Specifying *A* could have been optional: if you export something you must at least allow clients to access it in read mode). This would have avoided the need for writing procedures similar to *set_attrib*, which do occur fairly frequently in Eiffel applications.

However the benefit is not worth the extra complication brought into the language. Besides, this solution is not flexible enough: in many cases, one wants to export specific ways of modifying an attribute. For example, the following class exports a counter and the right to modify it not arbitrarily but only by increments of +1 or –1:

```
class COUNTING export
        counter, increment, decrement
feature
        counter: INTEGER;
        increment is
                    -- Increment counter
            do
                    count := count + 1
            end; -- increment
        decrement is
                    -- Decrement counter
            do
                    count := count - 1
            end; -- decrement
    end -- class COUNTING
```

A similar case occurs in the *LINKED_LIST* class developed in this chapter: the *position* attribute is accessible to clients; as far as modifying it, there is no *set_position* (*p*) procedure that would just do *position := p*, but the attribute is available for controlled modification through the traversal routines *start, finish, go, back, forth, search* etc.

In summary, there are really four possible kinds of rights you may want to grant clients on an attribute:

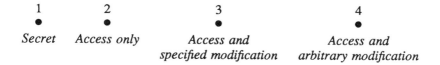

1	2	3	4
●	●	●	●
Secret	*Access only*	*Access and*	*Access and*
		specified modification	*arbitrary modification*

Figure 9.7　Possible client privileges on an attribute

The solution retained is a consequence of this discussion. Exporting an attribute only gives clients access permission (case 2); permission to modify is specified by writing and exporting appropriate procedures, which give clients either full rights in the *set_attrib* style (4) or restricted rights (3).

In many object-oriented languages such as Smalltalk, attributes cannot be exported at all; the interface only contains routines. This means that to export an attribute in access mode (cases 2, 3 and 4), one must write a function of the form

```
get_attrib: T is
            -- Value of the attrib attribute
    do
            Result := attrib
    end -- set_attrib
```

Such functions do not appear very useful. They imply run-time overhead (a problem that might be removed by making the compiler detect special cases), and they tend to clutter the code. It seems better to export the attributes themselves, in access mode.

This discussion on a fairly specific language trait is typical of the principles and tradeoffs involved in language design: do not needlessly bother the programmer; do not base decisions on the often elusive prospect of an optimizing compiler; know when to stop introducing new language constructs at the point of diminishing returns.

9.7 KEY CONCEPTS INTRODUCED IN THIS CHAPTER

- A class should be known by its interface, which specifies the services offered independently of their implementation.

- Class designers should strive for simple, coherent interfaces.

- One of the key issues in designing modules is which features should be exported, and which should remain secret.

- The design of reusable modules is not necessarily right the first time, but the interface should stabilize after some use. If not, there is a flaw in the way the interface was designed.

- Good interfaces are often obtained by considering data structures as active machines, with an internal state that is remembered from one feature call to the next.

- Abnormal situations are best dealt with through standard control structures, either through the a priori scheme, which checks applicability before calling an operation, or through the a posteriori scheme, which attempts the operation and then examines whether it has succeeded. A disciplined exception mechanism remains necessary in cases when abnormal operations must be canceled immediately, or would be pre-empted by the environment.

- To implement groups of related classes, selective exports are needed.

- Software documentation should, as much as possible, be a part of the software itself rather than a separate product. Appropriate tools should be available to extract the documentation automatically. Command **short** is one of the tools available in the Eiffel environment for this purpose.

- Proper use of assertions (preconditions, postconditions, invariants) is essential for documenting interfaces.

- When exported, a feature is made available to clients for execution if it is a routine and for read access if it is an attribute. In the latter case, it is not necessary to provide a specific function. To enable attribute modification by clients, however, appropriate procedures must be written and exported.

9.8   SYNTACTICAL SUMMARY

			Used in (chapter)
Export_restriction	=	"{" *Class_list* "}"	*Export_list* (5)
Class_list	=	{*Class_name* "," ...}	

9.9   BIBLIOGRAPHICAL NOTES

The work of Parnas [Parnas 1972] introduced many seminal ideas on the design of interfaces.

The notion of "active data structure" (page 191) is supported in some programming languages by control abstractions called iterators. An iterator is a mechanism defined together with a data structure, which describes how to apply an arbitrary operation to every element of an instance of the data structure. For example, an iterator associated with a list describes a looping mechanism for traversing the list, applying a given operation to every list element; a tree iterator specifies a tree traversal strategy. Iterators are available in the programming language CLU [Liskov 1981]; [Liskov 1986] contains a detailed discussion of the concept.

The idea of self-documenting software (page 205) is treated differently (and more thoroughly) in [Knuth 1984]; see exercise 9.7.

EXERCISES

9.1   Number of elements as function
Adapt the definition of class *LINKED_LIST* [*T*] so that *nb_elements* is a function rather than an attribute, the interface of the class being unchanged.

9.2   Searching in a linked list
Write the procedure *search* (*x*, *i*) (searching for the *i*-th occurrence of *x*) for *LINKED_LIST*.

9.3   Two-way lists
Write a class describing two-way linked lists, with the same interface as *LINKED_LIST*, but more efficient implementations of some operations such as *back*, *go* and *finish*.

9.4   Circular lists
Explain why the *LINKED_LIST* class may not be used for circular lists. (Hint: show what assertions would be violated). Write a class *CIRCULAR_LINKED* that implements circular lists.

9.5   Input files

Define the interface for a class *FILE* implementing input operations in the style recommended on page 202. (See also 7.7.2.)

9.6   Documentation

The (somewhat extreme) principle stated on page 205 says: "avoid documentation". Expand and refine this principle, considering various kinds of documentation in software, and discuss what styles of documentation are appropriate in various circumstances and at various levels of abstraction.

9.7   Self-documenting software

The approach to self-documenting software advocated in this chapter emphasizes terseness and does not readily support long explanations of design decisions. "Literate programming", a style of program design described in [Knuth 1984], elegantly combines techniques from programming, writing and text processing to integrate a program, its complete design documentation and its design history within a single document. Knuth's method relies on a classical paradigm: top-down development of a single program. Starting from Knuth's paper, discuss the transposition of this method to the object-oriented development of reusable software components.

10

Introduction to inheritance

Systems are not born into an empty world.

Almost always, new software expands on previous developments; the best way to create it would seem to be by imitation, refinement and combination. But most design methods ignore this aspect of system development. In the object-oriented approach, it is an essential concern.

Classes, as seen so far, are not sufficient. They do provide a good modular decomposition technique. They also possess many of the qualities expected of reusable software components: they are homogeneous, coherent modules, their interface may be clearly separated from their implementation according to the principle of information hiding, and they may be precisely specified thanks to assertions. But more is needed to fully achieve the goals of reusability and extendibility.

For reusability, any comprehensive approach must face the problem of repetition and variation, analyzed in chapter 3. To avoid rewriting the same code over and over again, wasting time, introducing inconsistencies and risking errors, we must find techniques to capture the striking commonalities that exist within groups of similar structures – all implementations of lists, all text editors, all file handlers, and so on – while accounting for all the differences that arise in individual cases.

For extendibility, the type system described so far has the advantage of guaranteeing type consistency at compile time, but prohibits combination of elements of diverse forms even in legitimate cases. For example, we cannot yet define an array containing geometrical objects of different types: *POINT*, *VECTOR*, *SEGMENT* etc.

Progress in either reusability or extendibility demands that we take advantage of the strong conceptual relations that hold between classes: a class may be an extension, specialization or combination of others. We need support from the method and the language to record and use these relations. Inheritance provides this support.

10.1   POLYGONS AND RECTANGLES

Inheritance will first be presented through a simple example. The example is sketched rather than complete, but it shows the essential ideas well.

10.1.1   Polygons

Assume we want to build a graphics library. Classes in this library will describe geometrical abstractions: points, segments, vectors, circles, ellipses, general polygons, triangles, rectangles, squares and so on.

Consider the class describing general polygons. Operations will include computation of the perimeter, translation, rotation etc. The class will look like:

class *POLYGON* **export**
    vertices, translate, rotate, perimeter, ...
feature
    ...

    vertices: LINKED_LIST [POINT];
        -- The use of a linked list is only one possible implementation

    translate (a, b: REAL) **is**
        -- Move by *a* horizontally, *b* vertically
    do ... end;

    rotate (center: POINT; angle: REAL) **is**
        -- Rotate by *angle* around *center*
    do ... end;

    display **is**
        -- Display polygon on screen
    do ... end;

    perimeter: REAL **is**
        -- Length of the perimeter
    do ... end;
invariant

    vertices.nb_elements >= 3
        -- A polygon has at least three vertices
        -- (See exercise 10.2)
end -- class *POLYGON*

The attribute *vertices* refers to a list of the vertices of a polygon. A typical procedure is *translate* : to translate a polygon, it suffices to translate every vertex in turn.

```
translate (a, b: REAL) is
        -- Move by a horizontally, b vertically
   do
        from
              vertices.start
        until
              vertices.offright
        loop
              vertices.value.translate (a, b);
              vertices.forth
        end
   end -- translate
```

To understand this procedure, remember that in class *LINKED_LIST* feature *value* yields the value attached to the currently active list element (where the cursor is). Since *vertices* is of type *LINKED_LIST* [*POINT*], *vertices.value* is a point, to which we may apply procedure *translate* defined on objects of type *POINT* (5.4.3). There is no problem in giving the same name, *translate*, to routines in different classes, as the target of any routine always has a clearly defined type (this is the Eiffel form of overloading).

Another routine, more important for the rest of this discussion, is the function to compute the perimeter of a polygon. Since our polygons have no special properties, the only way to compute their perimeter is to loop through their vertices and sum the edge lengths. Here is an implementation of *perimeter*:

```
perimeter: REAL is
        -- Length of the perimeter
   local
        this, previous: POINT
   do
        from
              vertices.start; this := vertices.value
        until
              vertices.islast
        loop
              previous := this;
              vertices.forth;
              this := vertices.value;
              Result := Result + this.distance (previous)
        end;
        Result := Result + this.distance (vertices.first)
   end -- perimeter
```

The loop simply sums the successive distances between adjacent vertices. Function *distance* was defined in class *POINT* (5.4.3). Entity *Result*, representing the value to be returned by the function, is automatically initialized to 0 on routine entry. Finally, recall that in class *LINKED_LIST* feature *first* yields the value of the first list element.

10.1.2   Rectangles

Now assume we need a new class representing rectangles. We could of course start from scratch. But a rectangle is a special class of polygon; many of the features are the same. For example, a rectangle will probably be translated, rotated or displayed in the same way as a general polygon. On the other hand, a rectangle has special features (such as a diagonal), special properties (the number of vertices is four, the angles are right angles), and special versions of some operations (for example, there is a better way to compute the perimeter than the general algorithm used above).

We can take advantage of this commonality by defining class *RECTANGLE* as an **heir** to class *POLYGON*. This means that all the features of *POLYGON* – called a **parent** of *RECTANGLE* – are applicable to the heir class as well. This effect is achieved by giving *RECTANGLE* an **inheritance clause,** as follows:

> **class** *RECTANGLE* **export**
>   *vertices, translate, rotate, perimeter, diagonal, side1, side2, ...*
> **inherit**
>   *POLYGON*
> **feature**
>   *... features specific to rectangles ...*
> **end**

The **feature** clause of the heir class normally does not repeat the features of the parent: they are automatically available because of the inheritance clause. Only the features which are specific to the heir are given there.

There may be an exception, however: some features of the parent may be redefined to have a different implementation. An example here is *perimeter*, which has a more appropriate implementation for rectangles: no need to compute four edges – the result is simply twice the sum of the two side lengths. An heir that redefines a feature for the parent must announce it in the inheritance clause, as follows:

> **class** *RECTANGLE* **export**
>   ...
> **inherit**
>   *POLYGON* **redefine** *perimeter*
> **feature**
>   ...
> **end**

This allows the **feature** clause of *RECTANGLE* to contain a new version of *perimeter*, which will supersede the *POLYGON* version for rectangles. If the **redefine** subclause was not present, then a new declaration of *perimeter* among the features of *RECTANGLE* would be an error: since *RECTANGLE* already has a *perimeter* feature inherited from *POLYGON*, this would amount to a feature defined twice.

The redefined version of a routine has arguments which match those of the original in number and, usually, in type (although the exact rule, which will be seen in 11.3.2, is more general).

The *RECTANGLE* class looks like the following:

class *RECTANGLE* **export**
>   *vertices, translate, rotate, perimeter, diagonal, side1, side2, ...*

inherit
>   *POLYGON* **redefine** *perimeter*

feature
>   *side1, side2: REAL*;   -- The two side lengths
>
>   *diagonal: REAL*;   -- Length of the diagonal
>
>   *Create (center: POINT; s1, s2, angle: REAL)* **is**
>   -- Create rectangle centered at *center*, with side lengths
>   -- *s1* and *s2* and orientation *angle*
>   **do** ... **end**; -- *Create*
>
>   *perimeter: REAL* **is**
>   -- Length of the perimeter;
>   -- redefinition of the *POLYGON* version
>   **do**
>   *Result := 2 ∗ (side1 + side2)*
>   **end** -- *perimeter*

invariant
>   *vertices.nb_elements = 4*;   -- A rectangle has four sides
>   *vertices.i_th(1).distance (vertices.i_th(2)) = side1*;
>   *vertices.i_th(2).distance (vertices.i_th(3)) = side2*;
>   *vertices.i_th(3).distance (vertices.i_th(4)) = side4*;
>   *vertices.i_th(4).distance (vertices.i_th(1)) = side1*;
>   -- Assertions expressing that the angles are right angles
>   -- are left to the reader.

end -- class *RECTANGLE*

Because *RECTANGLE* is an heir of *POLYGON*, all features of the parent class are still applicable to the new class: *vertices*, *rotate*, *translate*, *perimeter* (in redefined form) and any others. They do not need to be repeated in the new class.

This process is transitive: any class that inherits from *RECTANGLE*, say *SQUARE*, also has the *POLYGON* features. The following terminology is appropriate:

> **Definition** (*Descendant*): A class that inherits directly or indirectly from *A* is said to be a **descendant** of *A*. A class is considered to be one of its own descendants. Descendants of *A* other than *A* itself are called its **proper descendants**.

> **Definition 2**: If *B* is a descendant (proper descendant) of *A*, *A* is said to be an **ancestor** (proper ancestor) of *B*.

Pictorially, we shall always represent inheritance by an arrow pointing upward; the convention is that the arrow represents the relation "inherits from":

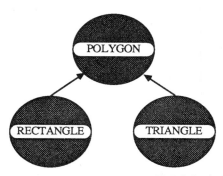

Figure 10.1   *RECTANGLE* and *TRIANGLE* inherit from *POLYGON*

10.1.3   The case of *Create*

There is one exception to the rule that all features from the parent are automatically available to the descendants: *Create*.

> **Create rule**: The *Create* procedure is never inherited directly. It is the only feature with this property.

This rule has a clear motive: because heirs normally have more features and more specific properties than their parents, instance creation often requires different arguments. For example, a reasonable way to create a rectangle has been suggested in the above *Create* procedure: give a point to serve as center, the two side lengths, and an orientation. For general polygons, however, such a technique would be inappropriate. The *Create* of class *POLYGON*, which was omitted above, could take a list of points as argument:

> *Create (lp: LINKED_LIST [POINT])* **is**
>   -- Create polygon with vertices given by *lp*
> **do ... end**

This method, in turn, would be awkward for rectangles, since only lists of four elements satisfying the invariant of class *RECTANGLE* would be acceptable.

Note that feature *vertices* is still applicable to rectangles. As a consequence, the *Create* procedure of *RECTANGLE* should set up the *vertices* list with the appropriate point values (the four corners, to be computed from the center, side lengths and orientation given as arguments).

The Create rule means that a class that does not define any *Create* procedure will be considered to have the standard *Create*, initializing all attributes to their default values; it never inherits a parent's *Create*.

Since *Create* is never inherited, it may not be "redefined" in the manner of a normal routine such as *perimeter*. It simply has to be defined by each class in the form that best suits the class – including the default form if no specific *Create* procedure is declared. The *Create* of a class has no relation whatsoever to the *Create* of its ancestors; in particular, its arguments may be different in number and types.

The Create rule says "... never inherited *directly*". The reason for this qualification is the fairly frequent case in which the *Create* of a class needs to rely internally on the algorithm of a parent's *Create*. To facilitate the process, the original procedure may be obtained from the parent under a different name. This renaming technique will be explained below (10.4.8).

10.1.4   Type consistency

Inheritance is consistent with the Eiffel type system. The rules, given formally in the next chapter, are easy to explain on the above example. Assume the following declarations:

> *p: POLYGON*;
> *r: RECTANGLE*

Then the following are legal:

- *p.perimeter*: no problem, since *perimeter* is defined on polygons.

- *p.vertices, p.translate* (...), *p.rotate* (...), with correct arguments.

- *r.diagonal, r.side1, r.side2*: the three features considered are declared at the *RECTANGLE* level.

- *r.vertices, r.translate* (...), *r.rotate* (...): the features considered are declared at the *POLYGON* level, and so are applicable to rectangles, which inherit all polygon features except *Create*.

- *r.perimeter*: same case as the previous one. The version of the function to be called here is the redefinition given in *RECTANGLE*, not the original in *POLYGON*.

The following feature applications, however, are illegal: *p.side1, p.side2, p.diagonal*. The features considered are not available at the polygon level.

More generally, this property may be described as the first fundamental typing rule:

> **Feature application rule**: In a feature application *x.f*, where the type of *x* is obtained from a class *A*, feature *f* must be defined in one of the ancestors of *A*.

Recall that the ancestors of *A* include *A* itself. The formula "where the type of *x* is obtained from a class *A* " is a reminder that a class type involves more than just a class name if the class is generic: *LINKED_LIST [INTEGER]* is a class type "obtained from" the class name *LINKED_LIST*. However the generic parameters play no part in the above rule.

In Eiffel, all type rules, including the feature application rule, are static; this means that all checking may be performed on the sole basis of the text of a system, without any need for run-time controls. The compiler will reject any class containing incorrect feature applications. Once a system has been compiled, there is no risk that a feature will ever be applied at run-time to an object that is not equipped to handle it.

10.1.5   Polymorphism

The properties of inheritance sketched so far address reusability: building modules as extensions of existing ones. There is another, equally important aspect, more directed towards extendibility: the concept of polymorphism, and its natural complement, dynamic binding.

"Polymorphism" means the ability to take several forms. In object-oriented programming, this refers to the ability of an entity to refer at run-time to instances of various classes. In a typed environment such as Eiffel, this is constrained by inheritance: for example, we want to allow an entity of type *POLYGON* to refer to a *RECTANGLE* object; but an entity declared of type *RECTANGLE* may not refer to a *POLYGON* object.

Assuming the above declarations (*p* of type *POLYGON*, *r* of type *RECTANGLE*), the following assignment is correct:

$$p := r$$

Do not forget that entities of class types denote references to objects, not the objects themselves. The above assignment is a mere reference assignment. If *r* was not void before the assignment, it referred to a *RECTANGLE* object; after the assignment, *p* will refer to that same object. This kind of polymorphism does not involve objects changing their form at run-time, or being converted from one format to another; it simply means that a given entity may refer to objects of various kinds.

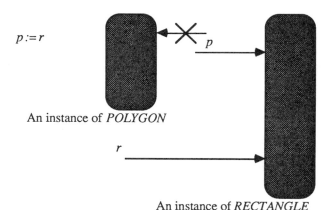

An instance of *POLYGON*

An instance of *RECTANGLE*

Figure 10.2   Polymorphic assignment

It is on purpose that the *RECTANGLE* object has been drawn bigger on the figure: since a proper descendant inherits all the features of its ancestors, it will always have at least as many attributes, and instances will consequently have at least as many fields (although not necessarily more).

Polymorphism is the key to making the type system more flexible. For example, it yields an answer to the question asked in the introduction to this chapter: how to gather in the same array references to objects of different types, for example points, vectors and complex numbers. If all these types are represented as heirs to a class

TWO_COORD, then the array may be declared as

> *a: ARRAY [TWO_COORD]*

so that the elements entered into *a* may be references to instances of any of the heir classes, as shown on the figure (exercise 10.3).

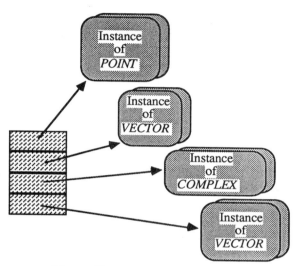

Figure 10.3   A polymorphic array

10.1.6   Limits to polymorphism

Unrestrained polymorphism would be incompatible with the notion of type. In the Eiffel type system, polymorphism is controlled by inheritance. The principle is illustrated by the polygons and rectangles example: in contrast to *p := r*, the assignment

> *r := p*

is illegal. This is the second fundamental typing rule:

> **Type compatibility rule:** The assignment *x := y*, where the type of *x* is given by a class *A* and the type of *y* is given by a class *B*, is only legal if *B* is a descendant of *A*. The same rule applies if *x* is a formal routine argument and *y* is the corresponding actual argument in a call to the routine.

Again, remember that a class is its own descendant. The rule as given says nothing about the case in which *A* or *B* have generic parameters; the complete rule will be given in the next chapter. Roughly speaking, the same constraint applies to the actual generic parameters: those used in the type of *y* must be descendants of the corresponding ones for x.

Like the previous rule, the type compatibility rule is purely static and may be checked at compile-time, without need for run-time checks. No class that violates the rule will be accepted by the compiler.

> The rule may be illustrated like this. Assume I am absent-minded enough to write just "Animal" in the order form I send to the Mail-A-Pet company. Then, whether I receive a dog, a ladybug or a gray whale, I have no right to complain. (The hypothesis is that classes *DOG* etc. are all descendants of *ANIMAL*.) If, on the other hand, I specifically request a dog, and the mailman brings me one morning a box with a label that reads *ANIMAL*, or perhaps *MAMMAL* (an intermediate ancestor), I am entitled to return it to the sender – even if from the box come unmistakable sounds of yelping and barking. Since my order was not fulfilled as specified, I shall owe nothing to Mail-A-Pet.

10.1.7 Static type, dynamic type

It is sometimes useful to use the terms "static type" and "dynamic type" of a reference. The type with which an entity is declared is called the static type of the corresponding reference. If, at run-time, the reference becomes associated with an object of a certain type, this type becomes the dynamic type of the reference. The type compatibility rule says that the dynamic type is always a descendant of the static type.

Note that the distinction is only applicable to references and would be meaningless for entities or objects. (Recall the three levels defined in 5.3.4: an entity is an identifier in the class text; at run-time its value is a reference; the reference may be associated with an object.) An entity is declared with a certain type. An object is created at run-time as an instance of a certain class. In both cases, there is no way the type of the entity or object can ever change. Only a reference may be polymorphic: it is a run-time representation of an entity, which determines its static type, and may refer to objects, which determine its dynamic types.

10.1.8 Are the restrictions justified?

The two typing rules may sometimes appear too restrictive. For example, both of the following will be statically rejected:

1. $p := r; r := p$
2. $p := r; x := p.diagonal$

In 1, we refuse to assign a polygon to a rectangle even though that polygon happens at run-time to be a rectangle (like refusing to accept a dog because it comes in a box marked "animal"). In 2, we decide that *diagonal* is not applicable to p even though at run-time it would in fact be – as it were by accident.

But a careful look at the problem reveals that the retained solution is the most reasonable one. If you attach a reference to an object, better avoid later problems by making sure that they are of compatible types. And if you want to apply a rectangle operation, why not declare the target as a rectangle?

In practice, cases of the form 1 and 2 are highly unlikely. Assignments such as $p := r$ will be executed as part of some control structure that may depend on run-time conditions, such as user input. A realistic application of polymorphism is

```
r.Create (...); ...
screen.display_icons;          -- Display icons representing various polygons
screen.wait_for_mouse_click;  -- Wait for the user to click the mouse button
x := screen.mouse_position;   -- Find out at what position the mouse was clicked
chosen_icon := screen.icon_where_is (x); -- Find out what icon
                                         -- is associated with mouse position
if chosen_icon = rectangle_icon then
      p := r
elsif ...
      p := "some other type of polygon" ...
   ...
end;
```

... Uses of *p*, for example *p. display*, *p. rotate*, ...

It is in this kind of situation that polymorphic entities such as *p* are needed. Clearly, operations valid for rectangles only, such as *diagonal*, should be applied to *r* only (for example in the first clause of the **if**). Where *p* as such is going to be used, in the instructions following the **if** instruction, only operations defined for all variants of polygons are applicable to it.

10.1.9   Dynamic binding

Operations defined for all variants of polygons need not be *implemented* identically for all variants. For example, *perimeter* has different versions for general polygons and for rectangles; let us call them $perimeter_{POL}$ and $perimeter_{RECT}$. You may imagine further variants for other special kinds of polygons. This immediately raises a fundamental question: what happens to a polymorphic entity when a routine with more than one version is applied to it?

In a fragment such as

```
p.Create (...); x := p.perimeter
```

it is clear that $perimeter_{POL}$ will be applied. It is just as clear that in

```
r.Create (...); x := r.perimeter
```

$perimeter_{RECT}$ will be applied. But what if the polymorphic entity *p*, statically declared as a polygon, dynamically refers to a rectangle? Assume you have executed

```
r.Create (...);
p := r;
x := p.perimeter
```

The rule known as **dynamic binding** implies that **the dynamic form of the object** determines which version of the operation is applied. Here $perimeter_{RECT}$ will be applied.

This ability of operations to automatically adapt to the objects to which they are applied is one of the most important properties of object-oriented systems. We will examine its implications in 10.2.2 below.

10.1.10   Redefinition and assertions

Dynamic binding is a powerful facility, but it obviously carries risks. If a client of *POLYGON* calls *p.perimeter*, it expects to get the value of *p*'s perimeter. But now because of dynamic binding, the client may well be calling another routine, as redefined in some descendant. In *RECTANGLE*, the redefinition was for better efficiency; but in principle you could redefine *perimeter* to compute, say, the area.

This is contrary to the spirit of redefinition. Redefinition should change the implementation of a routine, not its semantics. Fortunately, in Eiffel, we have a way to constrain the semantics of a routine – assertions. The basic rule for controlling the power of redefinition and dynamic binding is simple: the precondition and postcondition of a routine apply to any redefinition in a descendant class. Furthermore, the invariant of a class also applies to descendants.

The exact formulation of these rules will be given in the next chapter. But you may note from now on that redefinition is not completely free: only semantics-preserving redefinitions are permitted. It is up to the routine writer to express the semantics in a sufficiently precise way. Subsequent redefinitions are constrained by this specification.

10.1.11   Implementation of redefinition

One further remark on redefinition is appropriate here, in anticipation of chapter 15 on implementation issues. One might fear that dynamic binding would be an overly costly mechanism; it seems to require a run-time search of the inheritance graph, implying that the overhead grows with the depth of the inheritance graph, and becomes unacceptable with multiple inheritance (see below).

Fortunately it is not so in Eiffel. There is no serious penalty to pay for this facility, as the time needed to find the appropriate variant of an operation during execution is constant (independent of the inheritance graph structure and the number of redefinitions), and small. More on this question in 15.4.2.

10.2   THE MEANING OF INHERITANCE

The following sections will look at natural extensions of the basic concepts seen so far: deferred classes, which contain partially defined routines, and multiple inheritance, whereby classes may inherit from more than one parent. Before introducing these techniques, it is important to explain why inheritance is such a revolution for the software designer preoccupied with reusability and extendibility.

Classes, it was said, are both modules and types. The introduction of inheritance brings a new light to both viewpoints, which we shall consider in turn.

10.2.1   The module perspective

From the module viewpoint, inheritance is a key reusability technique.

A module is a set of services offered to the outside world. Without inheritance, every new module must itself define all the services it offers. Of course, the *implementations* of these services may rely on services provided by other modules: this is the purpose of the client relation. But there is no way to define a new module as simply adding new services to previously defined modules.

Inheritance provides precisely this possibility. If B inherits from A, all the services (features) of A are automatically available in B, without any need to further define them. B is free to add new features for its own specific purposes. An extra degree of flexibility is provided by redefinition, which allows B to take its pick in the implementations offered by A: some may be kept as they are, others may be overridden by locally more appropriate ones.

This favors a style of software development completely different from traditional approaches. Instead of trying to solve every new problem from scratch, the idea is to build on previous accomplishments and extend their results. The spirit is one of both economy – why redo what has already been done? – and humility, in line with Newton's famous remark that he could reach so high only because he stood on the shoulders of giants.

The full benefit of this approach is best understood in terms of the **open-closed principle** introduced in section 2.3. (You may wish to reread that section now in the light of the concepts just introduced.) The principle stated that a good module structure should be both open and closed:

- Closed, because clients need the module's services to proceed with their own development, and once they have settled on a version of the module should not be affected by the introduction of new services they do not need.

- Open, because there is no guarantee that we will include right from the start every service potentially useful to some client.

This double requirement looks like a dilemma, and classical module structures offer no clue. But inheritance solves it. A class is closed, since it may be compiled, stored in a library, baselined, and used by client classes. But it is also open, since any new class may use it as parent, adding new features. When a descendant class is defined, there is no need to change the original or to disturb its clients. This property is fundamental in applying inheritance to the construction of reusable software.

If the idea were driven to the extreme, every class would add just one feature to those of its parents! This, of course, is not recommended. The decision to close a class should not be taken lightly; it should be based on a conscious judgment that the class as it stands already provides a coherent set of services to potential clients.

Note also that the open-closed principle applies to new services rather than changes in the specification of previously defined services. If bad judgment resulted in a feature being poorly defined, there is no way we can update the class without impacting its clients. Thanks to redefinition, however, the open-closed principle remains applicable if the change is only in the *implementation* of the service, not affecting the specification.

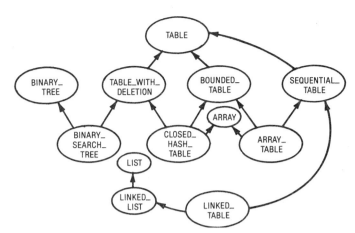

Figure 10.4   Table classes

Among one of the toughest issues in designing reusable module structures (3.3.5) was the necessity to take into account commonalities that may exist between groups of related data abstractions – all hash tables, all sequential tables etc. Here at last we have a way to do so: by using class networks connected by inheritance, we can take advantage of the logical relationships that exist between these implementations. The diagram above is a rough and partial sketch of a possible structure for a table management library (see exercise 10.10). Arrows represent inheritance. The scheme naturally uses multiple inheritance, discussed in more detail below.

In this context the reusability requirement may be expressed quite concretely: the idea is to move the definition of every feature **as far up** in the diagram as possible, so that it may be shared (without need to repeat its definition) by the greatest possible number of descendant classes.

10.2.2   The type perspective

From the type perspective, inheritance addresses both reusability and flexibility. The key here is dynamic binding.

A type is a set of values characterized (as we know from the theory of abstract data types) by certain operations. *INTEGER* describes a set of numbers with arithmetic operations; *POLYGON*, a set of objects with operations *vertices*, *perimeter* etc.

From this viewpoint, inheritance represents what is often called the *is-a* relation, as in "every dog is a mammal", "every mammal is an animal" and so on. Similarly, every rectangle *is-a* polygon.

What does this relation mean?

• If we consider the values in each type, the relation is simply set inclusion: dogs are a subset of animals; similarly, although instances of *RECTANGLE* are not a subset of *POLYGON* instances, objects that may be referenced by entities of type *RECTANGLE* are a subset of objects that may be referenced by entities of type *POLYGON*. (The former are instances of *RECTANGLE* and its descendants; the latter, instances of *POLYGON* and its descendants.)

• If we consider the operations applicable to each type, saying that every *B* is an *A* means that every operation applicable to instances of *A* is also applicable to instances of *B*. (With redefinition, however, *B* may provide its own implementation, which for instances of *B* overrides the implementation given in *A*.)

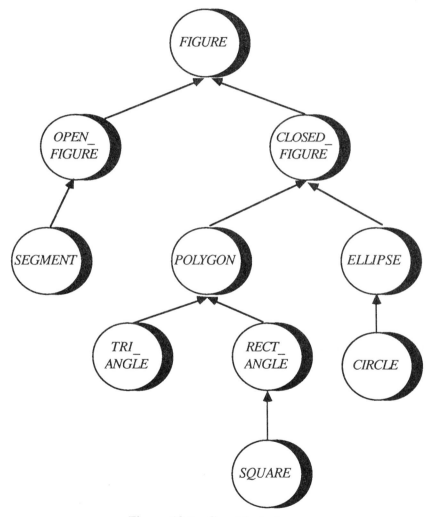

Figure 10.5   Graphical classes

Redefinition and dynamic binding play a basic role here. With inheritance, you can describe *is-a* hierarchies representing many possible type variants. An example is the above hierarchy of classes representing geometrical figures, of which our *POLYGON* and *RECTANGLE* classes were just two elements. Each new version of a routine such as *translate*, *rotate*, *display* etc. is defined in the module that describes the corresponding data structure variant. The same is true of the inheritance graph for tables (page 230): each class in the graph will provide its own implementation of *search*, *insert*, *delete* etc., unless this implementation is inherited.

What is crucial is the **decentralized software architectures** permitted by this approach. Every operation variant is defined within the module that defines the corresponding type variant. Contrast this with classical approaches. In Pascal or Ada, you may use a type *FIGURE* with variants to define the various forms of figures. But this means that every routine that does something to figures (*translate* and the like) must discriminate between possibilities:

```
case f.figuretype of
    polygon: (...);
    circle: (...);
    ...
end
```

The same is true of the routines *search* and others in the table case. The trouble is that all these routines possess far too much **knowledge** about the overall system: each must know exactly what types of figures are allowed in the system. Any addition of a new type, or change in an existing one, will impact every routine.

Ne sutor ultra crepidam, the shoemaker should not look beyond the sandal, is a software design principle: a rotation routine has no business knowing what are all classes of figures.

This distribution of knowledge among too many routines is a major source of inflexibility in classical approaches to software design. Much of the difficulty in modifying software may be traced to it; it also explains in part why software projects are so difficult to keep under control, as apparently small changes will impact many modules and force developers to reopen modules that were thought to be closed for good.

You can remedy this problem with object-oriented design. A change in a particular implementation of an operation will only affect the class to which the implementation applies. Addition of a new type variant will in many cases leave the others completely unaffected. Again, decentralization is the key: classes manage their own implementations and do not meddle in each other's affairs. Applied to humans, this would sound like a very selfish philosophy, Voltaire's *Cultivez votre jardin*, tend your own garden. Applied to modules, it is an essential requirement for obtaining decentralized structures that will yield gracefully to requests for extension, modification, combination and reuse.

Note finally the role of dynamic binding with respect to the last of the reusability issues that we have not tackled yet. This is the requirement of "representation independence" (3.3.4): the ability to request an operation with more than one variant, without having to know which variant will be applied. The example used in chapter 3 was a call

present := search (x, t)

which would use the appropriate search algorithm depending on the run-time form of *t*. With dynamic binding, we have exactly that: if *t* is declared as a table, but may be instantiated as any of binary search tree, closed hash table etc. (assuming all needed classes are available), then the call

> *present := t.search (x)*

will find, at run-time, the appropriate version of *search*. What was shown in chapter 3 to be impossible with overloading and genericity is attained here: a client may request an operation, and let the underlying language system automatically find the appropriate implementation.

Thus classes, inheritance, redefinition, polymorphism and dynamic binding, taken together, provide a remarkable set of answers to the set of reusability requirements raised in chapter 3, and satisfy all the criteria and principles of modularity developed in chapter 2.

10.2.3 Extension and specialization

Inheritance is sometimes viewed as extension and sometimes as specialization. Although these two interpretations appear contradictory, there is truth in both – but not from the same viewpoint.

It all depends, again, on whether you look at a class as a type or a module. In the first case, inheritance, or *is-a*, is clearly specialization; "dog" is a more specialized notion than "animal", and "rectangle" than "polygon". This corresponds to the subsetting relation already noted: if B is heir to A, the objects that may be associated at run-time with an entity of type B (instances of B and its descendants) form a subset of the set of objects that may be associated with an entity of type A (instances of A and its descendants).

From the module perspective, though, where a class is viewed as a provider of services, B implements the services (features) of A plus its own. So with respect to features implemented the subsetting goes the other way: the features applicable to instances of A are a subset of those for instances of B.[1]

So inheritance is specialization from the type viewpoint and extension from the module viewpoint.

This double interpretation explains why this presentation avoids the term "subclass", and prefers "heir" and "descendant" (and similarly parent and ancestor rather than "superclass"). "Subclass" naturally connotes "subset" but, from what we just saw, this term may cause confusion.

---

[1] We say services *implemented* rather than services offered (to clients) because of the way information hiding combines with inheritance: as explained in 11.5, B may hide from its clients some of the features exported by A to its own.

10.3 DEFERRED CLASSES

We now proceed to study more techniques associated with inheritance.

As noted, routines may be redefined in descendant classes. In some cases you may want to force redefinition. This is the reason for a very important design tool: deferred classes.

10.3.1 Moving arbitrary figures

To understand the need for deferred routines and classes, consider again the *FIGURE* hierarchy (page 231).

The most general notion is that of *FIGURE*. Applying the mechanisms of polymorphism and dynamic binding, you may want to write code such as the following:

(AA)

```
f: FIGURE; c: CIRCLE; r: RECTANGLE;
...
c.Create (...); r.Create (...);
...
"Get the user to choose an icon" (see page 227)
if chosen_icon = circle_icon then
        f := c
elsif chosen_icon = rectangle_icon then
        f := r
elsif ...
        ...
end;
```

f.translate (a, b)

In other words, you want to apply *translate* to a figure f, and let the underlying dynamic binding mechanism pick the appropriate version, depending on the actual form of f, which is only known at run-time (to emphasize this, we have assumed that it depends on the user's interactive choice). The hypothesis is that each one of the classes *RECTANGLE* and *CIRCLE* has its own version of *translate*; the version for *RECTANGLE* comes from *POLYGON*, and the one for *CIRCLE* is easy to write.

With the redefinition mechanism, this would work just fine. But here's the rub: there is nothing to redefine! *FIGURE* is a very general notion, covering all kinds of two-dimensional figures. There is no way you can write a general-purpose version of *translate* without more information on the figures involved.

So here is a situation where the code, (AA), would execute correctly thanks to dynamic binding, but is statically incorrect since *translate* is not a valid feature of *FIGURE*. The type checking mechanism will catch *f. translate* as an invalid operation.

You could, of course, introduce a *translate* procedure at the *FIGURE* level, which would do nothing. But this is a dangerous road to follow; *translate* (a , b) has a well-defined intuitive semantics, and "do nothing" is not a proper implementation of it.

10.3.2   Deferring a routine

What you need is a way to specify *translate* at the *FIGURE* level, while making it incumbent on descendants to provide actual implementations. This is achieved by declaring the routine as "deferred". The instruction part of the body (**do** *Instructions*) is replaced by the keyword **deferred**. For example, in *FIGURE*, you may declare

> *translate* (*a, b: REAL*) **is**
>   -- Move by *a* horizontally, *b* vertically
>   **deferred**
>   **end** -- *translate*

This means that the routine is known in the class where it is defined, but implemented in descendants only. This way the class extract (AA) is correct.

FIGURE itself is called a "deferred" class; it defines a group of related data type implementations, rather than a single one. The precise definition is the following:

> **Definition**: A deferred class is a class *C* that contains a deferred routine. This routine may either be introduced in *C* as deferred, or inherited from a parent and not effectively redefined in *C*.

In this definition, we say that a routine definition is effective if it is not deferred. A non-deferred class will also be called an effective class.

FIGURE is an example of the first case of the definition. As an example of the second, we can assume that class *OPEN_FIGURE* on figure 10.5 does not provide an effective definition of *translate*; so *OPEN_FIGURE* is a deferred class even if it introduces no deferred routine of its own.

A deferred class must begin with the two keywords **deferred class**, rather than just **class**, to remind the reader that one or more routines are deferred.

A descendant of a deferred class will be an effective class if it provides effective definitions for all routines deferred in its ancestors, and does not introduce any deferred routine of its own. In our example, effective classes like *POLYGON* and *ELLIPSE* must provide implementations of *translate*, *rotate* and any other routines that are deferred in their ancestors. They do not need to list these routines in their **redefine...** subclause, as they were not effectively defined in the first place.

10.3.3   What to do with deferred classes

The natural question to ask is "what happens if a deferred routine is applied to an instance of a deferred class?" The Eiffel answer is drastic: there is no such thing as an instance of a deferred class.

> **Deferred class no-instantiation rule**: *Create* may not be applied to an entity whose type is given by a deferred class.

This rule removes any danger of writing meaningless feature applications. But it may appear to limit the usefulness of deferred classes to little more than a syntactic device to fool the type checking system.

This would be true but for polymorphism and dynamic binding. You cannot create **objects** of type *FIGURE*, but you can declare polymorphic **entities** of this type as *f* above, which play an essential role in object-oriented programming.

10.3.4   Specifying the semantics of deferred routines

Deferred routines are made even more useful by the assertion mechanism. Syntactically, it was said that the keyword **deferred** replaces the **do** *Instructions* part. This leaves room for the other components: the routine header, the precondition and the postcondition. Hence the function of a deferred routine may be precisely specified even though its implementation is entrusted to descendants.

Consider the example of lists, as introduced in the previous chapter. Actually, chapter 9 only dealt with a specific implementation, *LINKED_LIST*. A more general deferred class, *LIST*, is also available in the library; it describes sequential lists independently of any particular implementation, and serves as parent of both *LINKED_LIST* and other implementations such as *FIXED_LIST* (lists implemented by arrays). One of the routines in *LIST* is *forth* (advance cursor by one position), described by

> *back* **is**
>   -- Move cursor left by one position
>   **require**
>   **not** *offleft*;
>   **deferred**
>   **ensure**
>   *position* = **old** *position* - *1*
>   **end** -- *forth*

Recall that **old**, in postconditions, refers to the value of the following element before the routine call. Another example, also from in the basic library, is the class *STACK* [*T*] describing stacks independently of any particular representation; it has *FIXED_STACK LINKED_STACK* etc. as descendants. One of the routines is *push* which, at the *STACK* level, can only be deferred:

> *push* (*x: T*) **is**
>   -- Add *x* on top of stack
>   **require**
>   **not** *full*
>   **deferred**
>   **ensure**
>   **not** *empty*;
>   *top* = *x*
>   **end** -- *push*

The boolean functions *empty* and *full* (also deferred at the general *STACK* level) express whether the stack is empty, and whether its representation is full.

Only with assertions do deferred classes attain their full power. Remember that preconditions and postconditions apply to all redefinitions of a routine. This is especially important for a deferred routine: its precondition and postcondition, if present, apply to all effective definitions of the routine in descendants. For example, all variants of *push* in descendants of *STACK* are constrained by the above specification. Because of this property, a deferred definition can in fact be quite informative even though it does not prescribe any specific implementation.

10.3.5   Back to abstract data types

Loaded with assertions, deferred classes come very close to representing abstract data types. A typical example is provided by the *STACK* class, given in full below. Note how routines which are themselves non-deferred may be expressed in terms of deferred ones: for example, *change_top* may be implemented as a *pop* followed by a *push*. (This implementation may be inefficient in some representations, for example with arrays, but effective descendants of *STACK* may redefine the routine.)

Class *STACK* should be compared with the abstract data type specification of 4.7.5 (page 55). The similarities are striking. Note in particular how the functions of the abstract data type specification map to features of the class, and the PRECONDITIONS paragraph maps to routine preconditions. Axioms are reflected in routine postconditions and in the class invariant.

> **deferred class** *STACK* [*T*] **export**
>
> > *nb_elements, empty, full, top, push, pop, change_top, wipe_out*
>
> **feature**
>
> > *nb_elements: INTEGER* **is**
> > > -- Number of elements inserted.
> > > **deferred**
> > > **end**; -- *nb_elements*
> >
> > *empty: BOOLEAN* **is**
> > > -- Is stack empty?
> > > **do**
> > > > *Result := (nb_elements = 0)*
> > > **ensure**
> > > > *Result = (nb_elements = 0)*
> > > **end**; -- *empty*
> >
> > *full: BOOLEAN* **is**
> > > -- Is stack full?
> > > **deferred**
> > > **end**; -- *full*
> >
> > *top: T* **is**
> > > -- Last element pushed.
> > > **require**
> > > > **not** *empty*
> > > **deferred**
> > > **end**; -- *top*

push (*x: T*) **is**
            -- Push *x* onto stack.
        require
                not *full*
        deferred
        ensure
                not *empty*; *top* = *x*; *nb_elements* = **old** *nb_elements* + *1*
        end; -- *push*

pop **is**
            -- Remove top element.
        require
                not *empty*
        deferred
        ensure
                not *full*; *nb_elements* = **old** *nb_elements* − *1*
        end; -- *pop*

change_top (*x: T*) **is**
            -- Replace top element by *x*
        require
                not *empty*
        do
                pop; *push* (*x*)
        ensure
                not *empty*; *top* = *x*; *nb_elements* = **old** *nb_elements*
        end; -- *change_top*

wipe_out **is**
            -- Remove all elements.
        deferred
        ensure
                empty
        end; -- *wipe_out*

invariant

        nb_elements >= *0*
end -- class *STACK*

The addition of operations *change_top*, *nb_elements* and *wipe_out* is not an important difference since they could be specified as part of the abstract data type (exercise 4.3). Another minor difference is the absence of an explicit equivalent of the abstract data type function *new*, since in Eiffel the predefined *Create* takes care of object creation. There remain three significant differences.

The first is the presence in the class of a function *full*, needed to account for implementations that will only accept a limited number of successive insertions, for example array implementations. This is typical of constraints that are irrelevant at the specification level but must be taken into account in designing actual systems. Note, however, that this is not an intrinsic difference between abstract data types and deferred classes, since the function could also be added to the formal specification, yielding a "less abstract" abstract data type. Also, no generality is lost since we may conceive an implementation in which *full* always returns false.

The second difference is that an abstract data type specification is purely functional, in the mathematical sense: it comprises only functions, without side-effects. A deferred class, on the other hand, is procedural in spite of its abstractness; *push*, for example, is specified as a procedure that will modify a stack, not as a function that takes a stack and returns a new stack.

Finally, the assertion mechanism of Eiffel is only partially formal, which means that some abstract data type axioms may not be fully expressed. Here, of the four stack axioms

1.	*empty* (*new* ())
2.	**not** *empty* (*push* (x, s))
3.	*top* (*push* (x, s)) = x
4.	*pop* (*push* (x, s)) = s

all but the last have a direct equivalent in the class's assertions. Ways may be found to "cheat" and express 4 in the class, but they fall beyond the scope of this discussion.

10.3.6   Deferred classes as partial implementations

Not all deferred classes are as close as *STACK* to an abstract data type. In fact, deferred classes cover the whole spectrum between a fully abstract class like *STACK*, where all the fundamental features are deferred, and an effective class such as *FIXED_STACK*, describing just one implementation of an abstract data type. Deferred classes in-between describe partially implemented abstract data types or, said differently, groups of possible implementations.

Typical examples may be found in the inheritance diagrams for tables (page 230) and figures (page 231). Such intermediate classes as *SEQUENTIAL_TABLE* or *OPEN_FIGURE* are deferred classes, describing groups of related implementations.

Until now, we have considered that a class described one implementation of an abstract data type. This view must now be expanded: a class describes an implementation or (in the case of a deferred class) a group of related implementations of an abstract data type.

10.3.7   Deferred classes for high-level design

Deferred classes are essential if you want to use object-oriented methods not just for implementation, but starting at the global design stage. At this stage, the aim is to produce a system architecture and a functional description of each module, leaving implementation details to later refinements.

The advice commonly given is to use for design a formalism of higher level than programming languages: a PDL (Program Design Language). But this approach has several flaws.

- By introducing a gap between design and implementation, it poses a grave threat to software quality. The necessity of translating from one formalism to another may bring in errors and endangers the integrity of the system.

- The two-tiered approach is particularly detrimental to maintenance and evolution. It is very hard, if not impossible, to guarantee that design and implementation will remain consistent throughout the system's evolution.

- Finally, most existing PDLs offer no support for the formal specification of functional properties of modules independently of their implementation, in the form of assertions or a similar technique.

In contrast, using deferred classes for design means that the same language is applied over the design, implementation and evolution stages. The conceptual gap is removed, as transition from high-level module descriptions to implementations can now proceed smoothly, within one formalism. But even unimplemented operations of design modules, now represented by deferred routines, may be characterized quite precisely by preconditions and postconditions.

Eiffel is both a design and an implementation language. The same concepts and constructs are applied at both stages; only the level of abstraction and detail differs.

10.3.8 Factoring out common behaviors

What is particularly useful with deferred classes is the possibility for an effective routine to rely on deferred routines for its implementation. In *SEQUENTIAL_TABLE*, for example, it is possible to write the routine *search* fully, with a body of the general form

       from *start* **until** *over* **or else** *found* **loop** *next* **end**

where routines *start, over, found* and *next* are deferred: they will be implemented by descendant classes such as *ARRAY_TABLE, LINKED_TABLE, FILE_TABLE* (see the discussion in 3.3.5).

This example illustrates a major benefit of object-oriented design. You may use deferred classes to **capture common behaviors** in a set of problems. Only what is common is described in the deferred class; variations are left to descendants.

Several of the design examples of chapter 12 rely on this technique, which is the reason for the central role of deferred classes in the object-oriented approach to reusability. The technique is particularly useful in writing application-specific libraries and has been used in many different contexts. A typical example from the Basic Eiffel Library is a general-purpose object-oriented parser.

This factoring out of common behaviors in partially deferred classes may be a multi-level process and is one of the essential contributions of the object-oriented approach to reusability.

10.4 MULTIPLE INHERITANCE

In the examples seen so far, heirs only had one parent. This is known as **single** inheritance. Multiple inheritance is also extremely useful.

10.4.1 The marriage of convenience

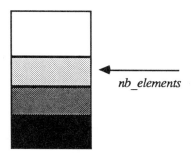

Figure 10.6   Fixed stack

One of the important applications of multiple inheritance is to provide an implementation of an abstraction defined by a deferred class, using facilities provided by an effective class. For example, stacks may be implemented by arrays. Since both stacks and arrays are described by classes (abstract in the former case), the best way to implement class *FIXED_STACK*, describing stacks implemented as arrays, is to define it as an heir to both *STACK* and *ARRAY*. The general form is:

                    -- Stacks implemented by arrays
class *FIXED_STACK* [*T*] **feature**
                    ... Same exported features as in *STACK* ...
inherit
        STACK [*T*];
        ARRAY [*T*]
feature
        ... Implementation of the deferred routines of *STACK* ...
        ... in terms of *ARRAY* operations ...
end -- class *FIXED_STACK*

FIXED_STACK offers the same functionality as *STACK*. It gives effective versions of the routines deferred in *STACK*, implemented here in terms of array operations. Three examples will be shown: *full*, *nb_elements* and *push*.

The condition under which a stack is full is given by

full: BOOLEAN **is**
        -- Is stack representation full?
    do
        Result = (nb_elements = size)
    end -- *full*

where *size* is an attribute inherited from arrays.

The case of *nb_elements* is interesting because it shows how a function may be redefined as an attribute. In class *STACK*, *nb_elements* is a deferred function. For fixed stacks, however, *nb_elements* is best implemented as an integer attribute, representing the pointer to the current top position (see the arrow on figure 10.6). It is indeed permitted to use an attribute rather than an effective routine as implementation of a previously deferred routine. This is obtained by giving the effective definition of the feature in *FIXED_STACK* as simply

   nb_elements: INTEGER

This possibility to redefine a function without arguments (deferred or not) as an attribute is a direct application of the principle of **uniform reference** (2.1.4): when a given service may be offered either through computation or through storage, the clients should not have to know which solution is chosen. We have seen the application of this principle to basic Eiffel: the notation, *a. service*, is the same in both cases. With inheritance, the property goes further: it means that a descendant may decide to reimplement a function with no arguments as an attribute.

The last feature to be shown from *FIXED_STACK* is the effective definition of *push*, using the properties of arrays. The body of this procedure is:

   nb_elements := nb_elements + 1;
   enter (nb_elements, x)

Recall that *enter* is the primitive for modifying array elements: *enter (i, v)* assigns value *v* to the *i*-th element.

Besides providing effective implementations of routines deferred in *STACK*, class *FIXED_STACK* may also redefine some which were not deferred. In particular, with an array representation, *change_top (x: T)* may be implemented more efficiently than by a *pop* followed by a *push*. It is enough to execute

   enter (nb_elements, x)

Do not forget, if this redefinition is to be correct, to announce it in the inheritance clause:

   class *FIXED_STACK* [*T*] **export** ... **inherit**
      STACK [*T*]
         redefine *change_top*;
      ARRAY [*T*]
   feature ... **end**

(Notice how there may be a redefine subclause for each parent listed.)

The *FIXED_STACK* example is representative of a common kind of multiple inheritance, which may be called the **marriage of convenience**. It is like a marriage uniting a rich family and a noble family. The bride, a deferred class, belongs to the aristocratic family of stacks: it brings prestigious functionality but no practical wealth – no implementation. The groom comes from a well-to-do bourgeois family, arrays, but needs some luster to match the efficiency of its implementation. The two make a perfect match.

It is interesting to compare *FIXED_STACK*, as sketched here, with class *STACK2* of 7.3.2, which gave an array implementation of stacks without any use of inheritance.

Note in particular how avoiding the need for the class to be a client of *ARRAY* simplifies the notation (the previous version had to use *implementation. enter* where we can now just write *enter*).

10.4.2 Forms of multiple inheritance

Marriages of convenience are not the only interesting applications of multiple inheritance. Often, the relationship between the parents is more balanced; each brings some functionality and some implementation. In many cases, none is a deferred class. A typical example is a class describing windows in a multi-windowing system supporting hierarchical nesting: a window may contain subwindows, which themselves may contain more subwindows, and so on. This notion is best described by having *WINDOW* inherit from three parents:

* The first parent, say *SCREEN_OBJECT*, perhaps a descendant of *FIGURE*, embodies the geometrical properties of windows, with features such as height, width, procedures to move the object on the screen etc.

* The second, say *TEXT*, contains the textual properties of windows, viewed as sequences of characters or lines, with primitives for manipulating the textual contents.

* The last should be the library class *TREE* which accounts for the hierarchical structure: subwindow, sibling window, parent window, procedures for adding a subwindow, removing one etc.

This example shows how essential multiple inheritance is for obtaining the full benefits of the object-oriented method. Without the *TREE* parent, the developer of *WINDOW* would have to write specific routines for manipulating the hierarchical window structure, which would be a stupid waste of effort. Trees are so general a structure that we can expect a general library class *TREE* to contain all the necessary features: *right_sibling, insert_child, is_leaf, parent* etc. Without the *SCREEN_OBJECT* parent, *WINDOW* would need to contain its own screen handling primitives. Having to choose between them is like having to choose between one's mother and father.

10.4.3 Trees are lists and list elements

Class *TREE* itself, as implemented in the Eiffel library, provides a particularly striking example of the power of multiple inheritance. A tree is a hierarchical structure made of nodes, each containing some information. In fact there is no significant distinction between the notion of tree and that of node, as a node may be identified with the subtree of which it is the root. Hence we should aim for a class *TREE* [*T*] that describes both trees and nodes. The formal generic parameter *T* represents the type of information attached to every node; the tree below, for example, is an instance of *TREE* [*INTEGER*].

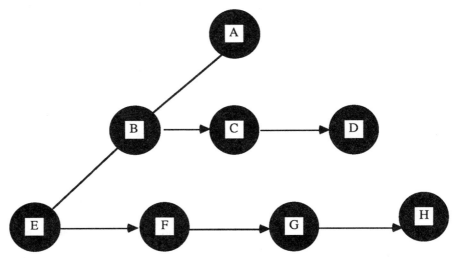

Figure 10.7 Tree as list

What are the operations on a tree or node? A node has a set of children, other nodes. We need to access these children; we also need routines to change a child, insert a child, delete a child etc. All this looks suspiciously similar to what was obtained in the previous chapter for lists; we obtained an implementation, *LINKED_LIST*, providing exactly those features.

Rather than writing routines for insertion, deletion etc. that will needlessly repeat the work done for lists, better inherit from *LINKED_LIST*. We are justified in doing so, as this is an instance of the *is-a* relation: a tree may be viewed as a list of its subtrees. (By inheriting from *LINKED_LIST* rather than a more abstract notion of list, we commit ourselves to a linked representation; this is not the only possible choice, but suffices for the present discussion.)

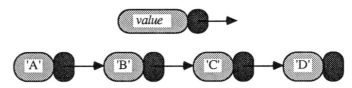

Figure 10.8 List and list elements

Only a face-lift is needed to use list operations for trees: they should now apply to nodes (subtrees) rather than list elements. This leads to another key observation: a node is not only a list, but also a list element itself, since it may have siblings. List elements were described in chapter 9 by a special class, *LINKABLE*. Hence the solution: make *TREE* an heir not only to *LINKED_LIST* but to *LINKABLE* as well!

The general structure is

      class *TREE [T]* **export... inherit**
         LINKED_LIST [T];

         LINKABLE [T]
     feature ...

Of course, this is not quite enough: one must add the specific features of trees, and the little mutual compromises which, as in any marriage, are necessary to ensure that life together is harmonious and prolific. (For example, trees have the notion of "parent" of a node, and the corresponding features may not be obtained from either list or list elements.) But it is significant that the features specific to class *TREE* fit on little more than a page (see A.7 in Appendix A, which lists the complete class). Yet this *TREE* class is quite powerful (I have used it for such applications as a hierarchical windowing system and a language-independent structural editor); it is remarkable that, for the most part, it is simply engendered as the legitimate fruit of the union between lists and list elements.

This process is exactly that used in mathematics to combine theories: a *topological vector space*, for example, is a *vector space* that also is a *topological space*; here too, some connecting axioms need to be added to finish up the merger.

10.4.4   Other uses

Further common uses of multiple inheritance include the following.

- Testing a class involves general mechanisms for getting and storing user input, outputting results etc. These mechanisms may be encapsulated in a class *TEST*. One way to test a class *X* is to define a new class *X_TEST*, as heir to *X* and *TEST*. Without multiple inheritance, this would be impossible, as *X_TEST* would have to choose between inheriting from *TEST* and from *X*'s own ancestor if it has one.

- A basic problem in programming with complex data structures is how to store such structures in long-term memory (files). In object-oriented programming, this is known as the problem of persistent objects. In the Eiffel environment, a class *STORABLE* is defined, with routines *store* and *retrieve*; a whole data structure may be stored and retrieved using these routines if the root of the structure is an object whose type is a descendant of *STORABLE*.

- Multiple inheritance is also convenient when a set of facilities, for example routines from a mathematical library, may be needed by various classes. You can encapsulate a group of related routines in a class *R* and add *R* to the list of parents of any class that needs the facilities. This is a slightly different use of classes from what has been seen so far (*R* is not really an abstract data type implementation), yet it is quite useful in practice. Chapter 13 will introduce a related technique: encapsulating a set of constants in a class, to be used as parent by any class that needs the constants.

10.4.5   Multiple inheritance in the basic library

Below is the inheritance graph for some of the classes in the Eiffel library.

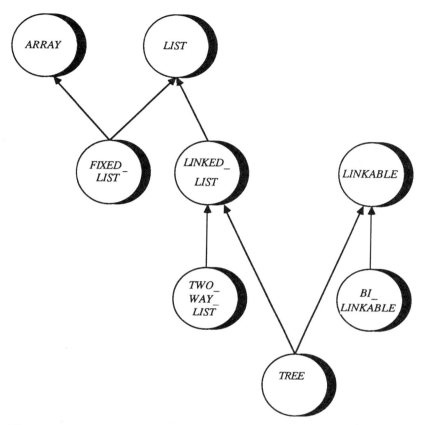

Figure 10.9   Inheritance in a library of reusable software components

10.4.6   Name clashes and renaming

Heirs to more than one class have direct access to the features of all their parents, without any need for qualification. This raises the problem of name clashes: what happens in

    class C **export** ... **inherit**
        A;
        B
    feature ... **end**

if both A and B have a feature named the same, say f?

    The Eiffel rule is simple: such clashes are prohibited. Class C as given is incorrect and the compiler must reject it. [2]

---

[2] The complete form of the rule prohibiting name clashes includes the possibility of "repeated inheritance" and will be given in the next chapter (11.6.5).

The rule is rather harsh on programmers in the absence of further mechanisms. In an approach emphasizing construction-box-like combination of modules from several sources, we may expect attempts to combine separately developed classes that contain identically named features. Going back to these classes to remove the clashes would be a catastrophe – the very opposite of the open-closed principle, which says one should leave modules undisturbed when reusing them for new extensions.

> If you look back at the definitions of *LINKED_LIST* and *LINKABLE* in chapter 9, you will find that the above construction of *TREE* raises a name clash: both classes have a feature called *value*. For lists, *value* is the value associated with the element at cursor position; for list elements, it is the value stored in the element. (Both classes also have an associated procedure *change_value*.) In both cases the choice of name seems reasonable, and we would not like to have to go back and change it simply because someone just got a clever idea for defining trees by combination of these two classes.

It is a mistake to blame the parents for a name clash occurring in inheritance: the problem is in the heir. There too should the solution be. Name clashes may be removed by introducing one or more **rename** subclauses in the inheritance clause.

For each parent listed, this optional subclause, which comes before the redefine subclause if any, indicates which of the parent's features should be known under a different name in the new class. Renaming may be used to remove name clashes in heirs. If, for example, both *A* and *B* contain a feature *f*, then *C* may still inherit from both as follows:

> **class** *C* **export** ... **inherit**
>   *A* **rename** *f* **as** *A_f*;
>   *B*
> **feature**
>   ...
> **end**

Both within *C* and in clients of *C*, the *f* feature from *A* will be referred to as *A_f*, and the one from *B* as *f*. Clients of *A*, on the other hand, will still know the feature as *f*.

Of course, we could have chosen instead to rename the *B* feature, or both.

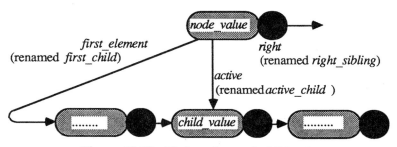

Figure 10.10 **Node value and child value**

For example, *TREE* renames the *value* feature from *LINKABLE* as *node_value* since this feature denotes the value attached to the current node. The name clash disappears; the *value* feature from *LINKED_LIST*, which denotes the node value of the child at cursor position, may keep its name.

10.4.7   Further uses of renaming

Renaming has applications other than name clash removal. The name under which a class inherits a facility from its ancestors is not necessarily the most telling one for its clients. Indeed, in most cases, clients of a class should not need to know the inheritance structure that led to its implementation. What counts is the services it offers, and these should have the most expressive names possible. For example, a client of *TREE* needs tree manipulation services, and usually does not care how clever the derivation of *TREE* from *LINKED_LIST* and *LINKABLE* may be. Through renaming, a class may offer its clients a consistent set of names for the services it offers, regardless of how these services were built from facilities provided by ancestors.

In the *TREE* case, features of *LINKED_LIST* include *empty*, a boolean function, and *nb_elements*. To say that a node, viewed as a list of subtrees, is empty, is to say that it is a leaf; and the number of subtrees of a node is commonly called its "arity". Renaming serves to offer clients of *TREE* the proper tree terminology: *empty* is renamed as *is_leaf* and *nb_elements* as *arity*.

The full inheritance clause of *TREE* is given below to illustrate this important technique.

> **class** *TREE* [*T*] **export** ... **inherit**
>
> > *LINKABLE* [*T*]
> >
> > > **rename**
> > >
> > > > *value* **as** *node_value*, *change_value* **as** *change_node_value*,
> > > > *right* **as** *right_sibling*, *left* **as** *left_sibling*,
> > > > *put_between* **as** *bi_linkable_put_between*
> > >
> > > **redefine**
> > >
> > > > *put_between*, *right_sibling*, *left_sibling*;
> >
> > *LINKED_LIST* [*T*]
> >
> > > **rename**
> > >
> > > > *first_element* **as** *first_child*, *last_element* **as** *last_child*,
> > > > *active* **as** *child*,
> > > > *insert_linkable_right* **as** *insert_child_right*,
> > > > *insert_linkable_left* **as** *insert_child_left*,
> > > > *delete* **as** *delete_child*, *delete_right* **as** *delete_child_right*,
> > > > *delete_left* **as** *delete_child_left*,
> > > > *nb_elements* **as** *arity*, *empty* **as** *is_leaf*
> > >
> > > **redefine**
> > >
> > > > *first_child*, *duplicate*
>
> ...

10.4.8 Accessing a parent's *Create*

One more application of renaming has to do with the Create rule (page 222). As noted, *Create* is never inherited; however it may be useful to reuse the algorithm used in a parent's *Create*. This is achieved by renaming it, as in

> **inherit**
> *C* **rename** *Create* **as** *C_Create*

making the *Create* procedure of *C* available within the new class under its new name.

> Recall that the instruction *x.Create* (...), where *x* is of type *C*, executes three operations: allocating memory for a new object to be associated with *x*; performing the default initializations on the fields of this object; and applying to it the body of the *Create* procedure of *C*, if it exists. Clearly, when *Create* is inherited under a new name, as above, the name *C_Create* only refers to the procedure itself, excluding the first two operations. *C_Create* is a normal procedure, which may be used within the new class and, if appropriate, exported.

A typical example is found in *FIXED_STACK*, obtained above by inheritance from *STACK* and *ARRAY*. To create a stack, you must allocate the appropriate array. The *Create* procedure of *ARRAY* allocates an array with given bounds:

> *Create* (*minb, maxb: INTEGER*) **is**
>   -- Allocate array with bounds *minb* and *maxb*
>   -- (empty if *minb* > *maxb*)
> **do** ... **end**;

This procedure is needed for the *Create* of *FIXED_STACK*, which will implement a stack as an array of given size:

> **class** *FIXED_STACK* [*T*] **export** ... *see above* ... **inherit**
>   *ARRAY* [*T*]
>   **rename**
>   *Create* **as** *array_Create*, *size* **as** *max_size*;
>   *STACK* [*T*]
>   **redefine** *change_top*
> **feature**
>   *Create* (*n: INTEGER*) **is**
>   -- Allocate stack for at most *n* elements
>   **do**
>   *array_Create* (*1, n*)
>   **ensure**
>   *max_size* = *n*
>   **end**; -- *Create*
>
>   ... *Other features* ...
> **invariant**
>   *nb_elements* >= *0*; *nb_elements* < *max_size*;
> **end** -- class *FIXED_STACK*

This extract shows that the class also renames *size* from *ARRAY* as *max_size*; this is to avoid any confusion on the part of client programmers, as the "size" of a stack could mistakenly be thought to denote its current dynamic size (given by *nb_elements*).

Also noteworthy is the difference between the two clauses of the invariant. The first clause was already present in the parent class *STACK* and expresses a property of the abstract data type. (As we shall see in the next chapter, parent's invariants are automatically inherited, so that the explicit inclusion of this clause in *FIXED_STACK* was not necessary). In contrast, the second clause involves *max_size*, that is to say the array representation: it is a **representation invariant**.

10.5   DISCUSSION

This chapter has introduced the basic concepts of inheritance. We now briefly discuss some of the conventions introduced. Further details are found in the next chapter.

10.5.1   Renaming

Any language that has multiple inheritance must deal with the problem of name clashes. Apart from the solution described above, there are two possible conventions:

- Require clients to remove any ambiguity.
- Choose a default interpretation.

With the first convention, a class C inheriting two features called f, one from A and one from B, would be accepted by the compiler, possibly with a warning message. Nothing bad would happen unless a client of C, contains something like

> $x: C$;
>
> ... $x.f$ ...

which would be illegal. The client would be required to qualify the reference to f, perhaps with a notation such as $x.f|A$ or $x.f|B$, to specify which variant is requested.

However this solution runs contrary to one of the principles emphasized above: that the inheritance structure leading to a class is a private affair between the class and its ancestors, and in most cases is not relevant for clients. When I use service f from C, I do not want to know whether C introduced it itself or got it from A or B.

With the second convention, $x.f$ is legal and the underlying language mechanisms select one of the variants, based on some criterion, like the order in which the parents of C are listed. This may be combined with the first convention to allow the user to request explicitly another variant. This approach has been implemented in several languages supporting multiple inheritance (such as Loops and Flavors, see chapter 20). But it seems dangerous to let some underlying system choose for the programmer. Besides, the approach is incompatible with type checking: there is no reason why two features with the same name in different parents should be typewise compatible.

The Eiffel policy solves these problems; it also brings some side benefits, such as the ability to rename inherited features with names that are meaningful to clients.

10.5.2   Explicit redefinition

The **redefine** subclause was introduced into the language to enhance readability and safety. The compiler does not need such a subclause: since a feature may be defined only once in a class, a feature declared in a class with the same name as an ancestor's feature can only be a redefinition of that feature – or a mistake. The possibility of a mistake should not be taken lightly, as a programmer may be inheriting from a class without being aware of all the features declared in that class's ancestors. To avoid this dangerous case, any redefinition must be explicitly requested. This is the aim of the **redefine** subclause, which is also helpful to a reader of the class. This subclause is retained in the output of **short**, the command for extracting class interfaces.

10.5.3   Selective inheritance

When you inherit from a class, you inherit all its features. One might wonder whether in some cases part of the heritage might be rejected. The answer in Eiffel as in most object-oriented languages intended for actual software development is that it may not.

Examples of situations where selective inheritance might be needed are easy to conceive if, rather than software development, one considers artificial intelligence, especially the area of knowledge representation, to which inheritance concepts may also be fruitfully applied. When it comes to representing knowledge about models of the physical world, some flexibility may be required. For example, you may want a "bird" class to have *fly* as one of its features; all the same, you may like to introduce "ostrich" as a descendant of "bird", even though one of the features will be inapplicable – ostriches do not fly.

The choice here is between an extra level of flexibility which, in my experience, is not indispensable in normal software development, and safety, which *is* needed. The restrictive interpretation of *is-a*, according to which every feature of the parent class is applicable to the heir as well, is simple, easy to explain and safe.

Recall that the solution still retains considerable flexibility thanks to redefinition: even though an heir may not reject a parent's feature, it may use redefinition to override its implementation or, as we shall see in the next chapter, change its type.

10.6   KEY CONCEPTS INTRODUCED IN THIS CHAPTER

- With inheritance, new classes may be defined by extension, specialization and combination of previously defined ones.

- A class inheriting from another is said to be its heir; the original is the parent. Taken to an arbitrary number of levels (including zero), these relations yield the notion of descendant and ancestor.

- Inheritance is a key technique for both reusability and extendibility.

- The full use of inheritance requires redefinition (the possibility for a class to override the implementation of some of its proper ancestors' features), polymorphism (the ability for a reference to become associated at run-time with instances of different classes), dynamic binding (the dynamic selection of the appropriate variant of a redefined feature), type consistency (the requirement that an entity of a class type be only associated with instances of descendants of its classes), multiple inheritance (the ability to define classes with two or more parents) and renaming (the possibility to change the name of an inherited feature, both to avoid name clashes and to provide locally better terminology).

• From the module perspective, an heir extends the services of its parents. This serves reusability.

• From the type perspective, the relation between and heir and a parent of the original class is the *is-a* relation. Associated with dynamic binding, this serves both reusability and flexibility.

• Inheritance techniques, especially dynamic binding, permit highly decentralized software architectures where every variant of a polymorphic operation is declared within the module that describes the corresponding data structure variant.

• Dynamic binding is achieved in Eiffel at a marginal run-time cost.

• Deferred classes contain one or more deferred (non-implemented) routines. These classes describe partial implementations, or groups of implementations, of abstract data types.

• Deferred classes are essential in the use of object-oriented methods at the design stage.

• Assertions are applicable to deferred routines, allowing deferred classes to be precisely specified.

• Selective inheritance is not supported in Eiffel: you inherit all or nothing.

10.7 SYNTACTICAL SUMMARY

			Used in (chapter)
Parents	=	**inherit** Parent_list	Class_declaration (5)
Parent_list	=	{Parent ";" ...}	
Parent	=	Class_type	
		[Rename_clause]	
		[Redefine_clause]	
Class_type	=	(See chapter 5)	
Rename_clause	=	**rename** Rename_list	
Rename_list	=	{Rename_pair "," ...}	
Rename_pair	=	Feature_name **as** Feature_name	
Redefine_clause	=	**redefine** Feature_list	
Feature_list	=	{Feature_name "," ...}	
Deferred_body	=	**deferred**	Body (5)

10.8   BIBLIOGRAPHICAL NOTES

The concepts of (single) inheritance and dynamic binding were introduced by Simula 67, on which references may be found in chapter 20. Deferred routines are also a Simula invention, under a different name (virtual procedures) and different conventions.

The *is-a* relation is studied, more with a view towards artificial intelligence applications, in [Brachman 1983].

A formal study of inheritance and its semantics is given in [Cardelli 1984].

EXERCISES

10.1   Polygons and rectangles

Complete the versions of *POLYGON* and *RECTANGLE* sketched at the beginning of this chapter. Include the appropriate *Create* procedures.

10.2   How few vertices for a polygon?

Polygons as defined have at least three vertices (see invariant page 218); note that function *perimeter* (page 219) would not work for an empty polygon. Update the definition of the class so that it will apply to degenerate cases of polygons with fewer than three vertices.

10.3   Geometrical objects with two coordinates

Write the class *TWO_COORD* mentioned on page 224 and its heirs *POINT*, *COMPLEX* and *VECTOR*. Be careful to attach each feature to its proper level in the hierarchy.

10.4   Inheritance without classes

In 10.2, two interpretations were given of inheritance: as a module, an heir class offers the services of its parent plus some; as a type, it embodies the *is-a* relation (every instance of the heir is also an instance of each of the parents). The "packages" of modular but not object-oriented languages such as Ada or Modula-2 are modules but not types; inheritance in its first interpretation might still be applicable to them. Discuss how such a form of inheritance could be introduced in a modular language. Be sure to consider the "open-closed principle" in your discussion.

10.5   Circular lists and chains

Explain why the *LIST* class may not be used for circular lists. (Hint: show what assertions would be violated; a similar question was posed in exercise 9.4). Define a class *CHAIN* that can be used as parent both to *LIST* and to a new class *CIRCULAR* describing circular lists. Update *LIST* and if necessary its descendants accordingly. Complete the class network to provide for various implementations of circular lists.

10.6   Deferred classes and rapid prototyping

Deferred classes may not be instantiated, for reasons explained in 10.3. On the other hand, it was argued that a first version of a class design might have all routines deferred. It may be tempting to attempt the "execution" of such a design: in software development, one often wishes, for rapid prototyping purposes, to execute incomplete implementations; the idea is to get an early hands-on experience of some aspects of the system even though other aspects have not been finalized. Discuss the pros and cons of having a "prototype" option in the Eiffel compiler, which would allow instantiation of a deferred class and execution of a deferred routine (amounting to a null operation). Discuss the details of such an option.

10.7   Linked stacks

Write the class *LINKED_STACK* which describes a linked list implementation of stacks, as an heir to both *STACK* and *LINKED_LIST*. The description of *LINKED_LIST* may be found in appendix A.

10.8   Trees

One way to look at a tree is to see it as a recursive structure: a list of trees. Instead of the technique employed in 10.4.3, where *TREE* is defined as heir to both *LINKED_LIST* and *LINKABLE*, an attractive solution seems to define

    class *TREE* [*T*] **export** ... **inherit**
        LINKED_LIST [*TREE* [*T*]]
    feature ... **end**

Can you expand this definition into a usable class? Compare it with the method used in the text.

10.9   Complex numbers

The example discussed in 7.7.4 used complex numbers with two possible representations, cartesian and polar; changes in representations were carried out behind the scenes in response to user-requested operations. Study whether equivalent results may be obtained with inheritance, by writing a class *COMPLEX* and its heirs *CARTESIAN_COMPLEX* and *POLAR_COMPLEX* .

10.10   Table searching library (term project)

Using figure 10.4 and the discussion in chapter 3 (see in particular 3.3.5), design a library of table management routines covering two or more broad categories of table representations, such as hash tables, sequential tables, tree tables etc. You may rely on the basic library classes of Appendix A. See also 10.3.8.

11

More about inheritance

The previous chapter introduced inheritance as a fundamental ingredient in the object-oriented approach to reusability and extendibility. Some important technical details were left out for the sake of simplicity. This chapter takes a closer look at some of the more delicate yet important aspects of inheritance, by examining how inheritance combines with other concepts introduced in previous chapters: assertions, the type system, and information hiding. It also discusses the problem of shared ancestors, raised by multiple inheritance, and introduces the solution: repeated inheritance.

11.1 INHERITANCE AND ASSERTIONS

It was pointed out in the previous chapter that the inheritance mechanism, while extremely powerful, is also dangerous if misused. Were it not for the assertion mechanism, redefinition and dynamic binding could be used to treacherously change the semantics of operations without much possible client control.

The basic rule for avoiding this has already been sketched: in a descendant class, all ancestors' assertions (routine preconditions and postconditions, class invariants) still apply. This section examines the issue more closely, expresses the rule in a more precise form, and uses the results obtained to take a new look at inheritance, viewed as subcontracting.

11.1.1 Invariants

The rule for class invariants is simple:

> **Parents' invariant rule**: The invariants of all the parents of a class apply to the class itself.

The parents' invariants are considered to be added to the class's own invariant, "addition" being here a logical **and**. (If no invariant is given in a class, it is considered to have **true** as invariant.) Note that by induction the invariants of all proper ancestors, direct or indirect, apply.

It is not necessary to repeat the parents' invariants in the invariant clause of a class; they are considered to be automatically included.

11.1.2 Preconditions and postconditions

The case of routine preconditions and postconditions is slightly more delicate. The idea is that these assertions apply to any redefinition of the routine, but may be changed to yield a more restrictive specification.

More precisely, we say that an assertion is **stronger** than another if it logically implies it, and is different; for example, $x \geq 5$ is stronger than $x \geq 0$. If A is stronger than B, B is predictably said to be **weaker** than A. Also, the notations pre_r and $post_r$ are used to denote the precondition and postcondition of a routine r. Then:

> **Assertion redefinition rule**: Let r be a routine in class A and s a redefinition of r in a descendant of A, or an effective definition of r if r was deferred. Then pre_s must be weaker than or equal to pre_r, and $post_s$ must be stronger than or equal to $post_r$.

In other words, when redefining a routine, you may only replace its precondition by a weaker one, and its postcondition by a stronger one.

Because of this rule, it is not possible to reconstruct a routine's precondition and postcondition from those of its previous incarnations in ancestors; we cannot just "and" a set of assertions as in the case of class invariants. So the **require** and **ensure** clause must always be given for a routine, even if it is a redefinition, and even if these clauses are identical to their antecedents in the original. The reason is that they could be different, under the constraints of the assertion redefinition rule.

The rule that preconditions may be weakened may appear strange at first. It should be understood in the context of redefinition and dynamic binding.

The point to remember is that if s redefines r then because of the dynamic binding mechanism a client of A may issue a call to r which is in fact handled by s. (For example, when requesting $p.perimeter$ where p is declared of type $POLYGON$, you will actually execute the version redefined in $RECTANGLE$ if p dynamically refers to a rectangle object.) Thus any condition that is incumbent on r must also apply to s. This means that s:

- must accept all calls that were acceptable to r: thus its precondition may not be stronger (although it could be weaker);

- must guarantee the output condition that was guaranteed by r: thus its postcondition may not be weaker (although it could be stronger).

Consider the following example. I am writing a class *MATRIX* which implements linear algebra operations. Among the features I am offering to my clients is a matrix inversion routine. Following the precepts of the preceding chapters, it is actually a combination of a procedure and an attribute: procedure *invert* inverts the matrix, and sets attribute *inverse* to the value of the inverse matrix. As we saw in the last chapter, *invert* should also set a boolean attribute *inverse_valid*, so that *inverse* is only meaningful if this attribute has value true; otherwise the inversion has failed because the matrix was singular. However for the purpose of the discussion we shall ignore the singularity case.

Of course I can only compute an approximation of the inverse of a matrix. I am prepared to guarantee a certain precision of the result, but since since I am not very good at numerical analysis, I shall only accept requests for a precision not better than 10^{-6} (say). The resulting routine will look like this:

invert (epsilon: REAL) **is**
        -- Inverse of current matrix, with precision *epsilon*
    require
        epsilon >= 10 ^ (–6)
    do
        "Computation of inverse"
    ensure
        product(inverse).distance(identity) <= epsilon
    end *sqrt*

The postcondition is written under the assumption that the class contains a function *distance*, so that *m1.distance (m2)* is $|m1 - m2|$, the norm of the matrix difference of *m1* and *m2*, and a function *product* (here applied to the current matrix) which yields the product of two matrices; *identity* is assumed to denote the identity matrix.

Now a bright young programmer-numerician is hired for the summer and rewrites my *invert* routine using a much better algorithm, which approximates the result more closely and accepts a smaller *epsilon*:

    require
        epsilon >= 10 ^ (–20)
    . . .
    ensure
        product(inverse).distance(identity) <= epsilon / 2

The author of this routine is far too clever to rewrite a full *MATRIX* class; only a few routines need to be adapted. They will be included in a descendant of *MATRIX*, say *NEW_MATRIX*.

The above change of assertions is compatible with the assertion redefinition rule, since the new precondition is weaker than the original ($\varepsilon \geq 10^{-20}$ is implied by $\varepsilon \geq 10^{-6}$) and the new postcondition is stronger than the original.

This is how it should be. A client of the original class *MATRIX* may be requesting a square root but, through dynamic binding, actually calling the version redefined in *NEW_MATRIX*:

> *m1: MATRIX*; *m2: NEW_MATRIX*; *x: REAL*;
> *m1.Create* (...); *m2.Create* (...);
> ...
> **if** *condition* **then** *m1* := *m2* **end**;
> *m1.invert* (*precision*)
>   -- May use either the *MATRIX* or the *NEW_MATRIX* version

It is essential that any call that is acceptable from *MATRIX*'s standpoint and would be correctly treated by *MATRIX* be also accepted and correctly treated by *NEW_MATRIX*. For example it would be a serious mistake to make the precondition of the new *invert* stronger than the original (as in *epsilon* $\geq 10^{-5}$), or its postcondition weaker. In the first case, calls which are correct from *MATRIX*'s standpoint would be rejected; in the second, the result returned would not be as good as guaranteed by *MATRIX*.

There is no reason, on the other hand, why *NEW_MATRIX* should not accept calls with weaker preconditions, or return a stronger postcondition. Only *NEW_MATRIX*'s direct clients will really be in a position to benefit from this more powerful specification; clients of *MATRIX* can only rely on the properties of *invert* as specified in *MATRIX*.

11.1.3 Implementation of the rules

You will recall that Eiffel is not a fully formal language and its environment does not include mechanisms for proving the validity of classes according to their assertions. The rules given are thus methodological and not statically enforced.

When run-time checking of assertions is invoked (option ALL_ASSERTIONS), the parents' invariant rule is applied: after *every* execution of the *Create* or any exported routine, the run-time system will check not only the current class's invariant but also the invariants of all ancestors. But no such policy is possible for routines, at least for preconditions: since preconditions may be weakened in a descendant, the precondition of the original routine is not required to hold on entry to the redefined version. Because of this the assertions associated with the version actually called are checked. (Note that the *postconditions* of the ancestors must still hold, since they may only be strengthened. However it seems inappropriate to treat preconditions and postconditions differently.)

11.1.4 Subcontracting

The assertion redefinition rule should be interpreted in view of the "contracting" metaphor introduced in chapter 7. Remember that a routine call was presented as a contract: the client is bound by the precondition and entitled to the postcondition, and conversely for the class implementor.

Now it becomes clear what inheritance, with redefinition and dynamic binding, really is about: subcontracting. When you have accepted a contract, you do not necessarily want to carry it out yourself. Sometimes you know of somebody else who can do it cheaper and perhaps better. This is exactly what happens when a client requests a routine from *MATRIX* but, through dynamic binding, may actually call at run-time a version redefined in a descendant of *MATRIX*. Here "cheaper" refers to routine redefinition for more efficiency, as in the rectangle perimeter example of the previous chapter, and "better" to improved assertions in the sense that we just saw.

In this context the assertion redefinition rule simply says that if you are an honest subcontractor and accept a contract, you must be willing to do the job originally requested, or more than the requested job, but not less. There are two ways you could do less:

- By requesting a stronger precondition.
- By ensuring a weaker postcondition.

Conversely, you may do more than expected by either

- Accepting weaker preconditions.
- Guaranteeing stronger postconditions.

Remember that the stronger the precondition, the easier the contractor's work: the best possible precondition for a contractor is "false", for which any routine body will do, as no client will ever be able to satisfy its part of the requirements. This is also, of course, the worst possible precondition for a client: it means the routine cannot possibly do anything useful for you, even if the postcondition looks great. Conversely, false is the hardest possible postcondition for a contractor – one that no contractor can ever ensure – and the best possible one for clients, as anything else could be deduced from it. Real situations, of course, lie in-between these extremes.

In this *"Programming is Contracting"* paradigm, class invariants are general constraints that apply to both contractors and clients. The parents' invariant rule expresses that all such constraints are transmitted to subcontractors.

It is only with assertions, and with the two rules of this section, that inheritance takes on its full meaning for object-oriented design. The contracting/subcontracting metaphor is a powerful analogy to guide the development of correct object-oriented software.

11.2 REDEFINITION VS. RENAMING

For each parent listed in the inheritance clause of a class, every routine inherited from the parent may be renamed, or redefined, or even both. It is important not to confuse the two facilities. The following discussion should dispel any misunderstanding.

Redefinition is applied to ensure that the *same* feature name refers to *different* actual features depending on the type of the object to which it is applied (that is to say, the dynamic type of the corresponding entity). It is thus an important **semantic** mechanism for providing the object-oriented brand of polymorphism.

Renaming, on the other hand, is a syntactic mechanism, making it possible to refer to the *same* feature under *different* names in different classes.

Either or both techniques may be applied (in a descendant B of a class A) to a feature of A, say f. They address different questions:

- For redefinition: "Can I have a different implementation for f when it is applied to entities of dynamic type B?";
- For renaming: "Can I change the name under which the original (A) implementation of f may be applied to entities of static type B?".

The effect of combining these two mechanisms in various ways is summarized in the table below. We assume that entities $a1$ and $b1$ are declared of types A and B respectively. It is important to distinguish between the name of a feature, f in our example, and the feature itself (represented for example by the body of a routine), which we call ϕ. By renaming the feature in B we associate with ϕ a new name f'; by redefining it we associate with f a new feature ϕ'.

When $a1$ is of dynamic type A, $a1.f$ will always refer to feature f, and the notation $a1.f'$ will always be illegal. Thus the only interesting cases are the interpretation of $a1.f$ when the dynamic type of $a1$ is B and the interpretations of $b1.f$ and $b1.f'$. The table shows what actual feature is associated with each of these notations in each legal case. Note that "illegal" combinations are statically so and must be caught by the compiler.

#		$a1.f$	$b1.f$	$b1.f'$
1	f not redefined f not renamed	ϕ	ϕ	illegal
2	f not redefined f renamed f'	ϕ	illegal	ϕ
3	f redefined ϕ' f not renamed	ϕ'	ϕ'	illegal
4	f redefined ϕ' f renamed f'	ϕ'	ϕ'	ϕ
5	f not redefined f renamed f' f' redefined ϕ''	ϕ''	illegal	ϕ''
6	f redefined ϕ' f renamed f' f' redefined ϕ''	ϕ''	ϕ'	ϕ''

Figure 11.1   Combining redefinition and renaming

All cases, with the exception of case 6, occur in the library extracts given in appendix A.

Case 2 is standard renaming: we prefer to call the feature f' rather than f when applied to entities of type B. The reason may be to avoid a name clash in multiple inheritance, or simply to provide a terminology better adapted to the B context. But the actual implementation is the same in both classes: $b1.f'$ for $b1$ of type B denotes the same feature as $a1.f$ for $a1$ of type A.

Case 3 is the standard redefinition: there is a special implementation of *f* for objects of type *B*, namely ɸ'; this implementation completely overrides the original, ɸ, for any entity whose type is *B*, be it the static type (as with *b1*) or the dynamic type (as with *a1*).

Case 4 is like case 3; but here the original implementation ɸ, defined in *A*, is still needed in *B*. This often occurs because the algorithm for ɸ' internally calls the algorithm for ɸ. Without renaming, there would be no way to refer to ɸ within *B*, as the name *f* now denotes ɸ'. Renaming makes it possible to keep the old version available under a different name.

In case 5, it is appropriate both to give a new name to *f* in *B*, and to change the implementation. The original implementation is not needed. This case is a combination of 2 and 3.

Finally, in case 6, everything is combined: we need a specific *B* implementation of the feature, we want to refer to it locally under a new name, but we still need access to the original version.

11.3   THE EIFFEL TYPE SYSTEM

With inheritance, the type system of a language such as Eiffel is both safe, in the Algol-Pascal-Ada tradition, but also more flexible, as you can mix entities of various types in a data structure (for example, an array of type *FIGURE* may contain elements of types *POLYGON*, *CIRCLE* etc.). The basic typing rule was seen in the last chapter; here we shall see it in more detail and complement it by the important rules governing redefinition. The discussion leads to a new and interesting concept: declaration by association.

11.3.1   Type compatibility rule; the notion of conformance

The type compatibility rule as given in 10.1.6 did not take all possible cases into account; in particular, genericity was not clearly addressed. Types are used to define entities; recall (5.10) how types are constructed:

> **Definition** (*Types in Eiffel*): An Eiffel type is one of the following:
> 1.   A simple type (*INTEGER, BOOLEAN, REAL, CHARACTER*).
> 2.   A formal generic parameter of the enclosing class.
> 3.   A class type, that is to say a class name, possibly followed by actual generic parameters in square brackets, as in *TREE* [*REAL*].
> 4.   **like** *anchor*, a form which will be explained below (11.4).

In case 3, an actual generic parameter is itself a type, of any of the four given forms.

The full type compatibility rule is the following:

> **Type compatibility rule**: An assignment $x := y$ or a call r (..., y, ...) where the formal argument corresponding to y is x, are correct if and only if one of the following holds of the respective types X and Y of x and y:
>
> 1. X and Y are identical.
> 2. X is *REAL*, and Y is *INTEGER*.
> 3. Y conforms to X (defined next).

Case 3 uses the notion of **conformance** of a type to another. In the previous chapter, we used the terminology "Y is a descendant of X" rather than "Y conforms to X". However this was a simplification since the notion of descendant applies to classes, whereas here we are talking of class *types*, which are classes possibly qualified by actual generic parameters. (*TREE* is a class; *TREE* [*POINT*] is a class type.) Also, class types include the **like** *anchor* form not yet introduced. The notion of conformance is needed for a correct definition.

> **Definition** (*Conformance*): A type Y is said to conform to a type X if and only if one of the following applies:
>
> 1. X and Y are identical.
> 2. X and Y are class types, X has no generic parameters, and Y lists X in its inheritance clause.
> 3. X and Y are class types, X is of the form P [$U_1, U_2, ... , U_n$], and the inheritance clause of Y lists P [$V_1, V_2, ... , V_n$] as parent, where every V_i conforms to the corresponding U_i.
> 4. Y is of the form **like** *anchor*, and the type of *anchor* conforms to X.
> 5.   There is a type Z such that Y conforms to Z and Z conforms to X.

Case 5 is there to allow indirect conformance. Case 4 will be explained below (11.4.3).

According to this definition, for example, if class *TREE* is a descendant of *LIST* (both having a generic parameter) and *POINT* is a descendant of *FIGURE*, then

- *TREE* [*INTEGER*] conforms to *LIST* [*INTEGER*].

- *TREE* [*POINT*] conforms to *LIST* [*POINT*].

- *TREE* [*POINT*] conforms to *LIST* [*FIGURE*].

In each case, this corresponds to the fact that an expression of the first type listed is assignable to an entity of the second — a desirable property indeed.

The rule as given is fully recursive, so that for example *TREE* [*TREE* [*POINT*]] conforms to *LIST* [*LIST* [*FIGURE*]], although such nested examples rarely occur.

11.3.2 The redefinition rule

We have seen redefinition as a mechanism for substituting an algorithm for another – or, in the case of effective definitions of previously deferred routines, providing an algorithm where only a specification was previously given. Redefinition also has an important type aspect, which we have not encountered yet.

Consider any element declared with a type. Excluding local routine variables, the element could be an attribute, a formal routine argument or a function result. Then redefinition may be used to change its type, as follows:

Type redefinition rule: An attribute, a function result or a formal routine argument declared in a class may be redeclared with a new type in a descendant class, provided the new type conforms to the original one.

The attribute, function or routine is considered to be redefined. Unless it was originally deferred, it must be listed in the **redefine** subclause of the descendant class.

In this definition, "conforms to" refers to type conformance as defined above. Note that in the case of a routine argument, the whole routine is considered to be redefined.

The idea here is that a class may provide a more specialized version of an element declared in an ancestor. Consider for example class *LINKABLE* from the Eiffel library, introduced in chapter 9 to describe the linked list elements used in *LINKED_LIST*, one of the implementations of lists. A partial view of the class is:

```
class LINKABLE [T] export
    ...
feature
    value: T;
    right: LINKABLE [T];

    change_right (other: LINKABLE [T]) is
            -- Put other to the right of current cell
        do right := other end

    ... Other features ...
end -- class LINKABLE
```

The next section will introduce a variant *TWO_WAY_LIST* of *LINKED_LIST*, describing lists whose elements are chained to their predecessors as well as to their successors. The implementation of this class must rely on two-way list elements, say "bi-linkables", which are like "linkables" with one more field, *left*. Class *BI_LINKABLE* should be an heir of *LINKABLE*. However we must be careful: we certainly do not want to mix up linkables and bi-linkables in a two-way list (although it would do no harm to introduce bi-linkables in a one-way list: this is polymorphism). So we should redefine *right* and *change_right* to guarantee that two-way lists remain homogeneous.

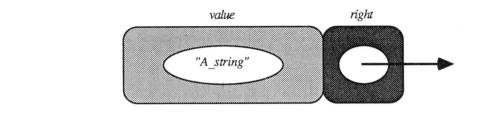

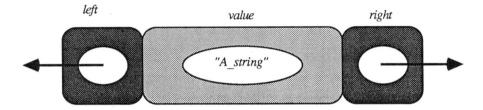

Figure 11.2   Linkable and bi-linkable

```
class BI_LINKABLE [T] export
        ...
inherit
        LINKABLE [T]
                redefine right, change_right
feature
        left, right: BI_LINKABLE [T];

        change_right (other: BI_LINKABLE [T]) is
                -- Put other to the right of current element
            do
                    right := other;
                    if not other.Void then
                            other.change_left (Current)
                    end
            end; -- change_right;

        change_left (other: BI_LINKABLE [T]) is
                -- Put other to the left of current element
                ... Left to the reader ...

        ... Other features ...
invariant
        right.Void or else right.left = Current;
        left.Void or else left.right = Current;
end -- class BI_LINKABLE [T]
```

(Note: try writing change_left. There's a pitfall! Solution in appendix A.)

11.3.3   More about redefinition

One more use of redefinition was mentioned in 10.4.1 and deserves further discussion: redefining a function without arguments as an attribute. We saw this possibility applied to a deferred function, *nb_elements* from *STACK*, redefined as an attribute in *FIXED_STACK*. Here is an example with an effective routine, again using linked lists.

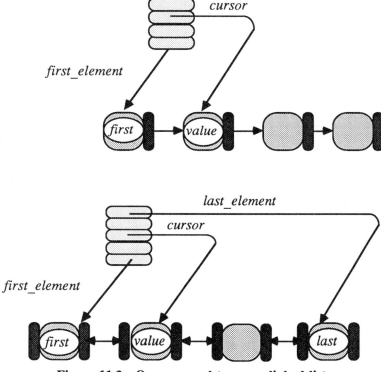

Figure 11.3   One-way and two-way linked lists

Class *LINKED_LIST* describes one-way lists. Its feature *last*, which yields the last element of the list, is naturally implemented as a function; for a one-way list, there is no simpler way to get the value of the last element than to traverse the list and find that element. A possible implementation is

    mark; *go* (*nb_elements*); *Result* := *value*; *return*

(Recall that *mark* and *return* make it possible to mark the current cursor position and return to it. This is necessary to avoid an unwanted side-effect from the function.)

    An heir of *LINKED_LIST* in the library (appendix A) is *TWO_WAY_LIST* which, as its name indicates, keeps links both ways. A two-way list structure is fully symmetric with respect to left and right, and keeps a reference to the last element, whereas a one-way list only includes a reference to the first element. So no computation is needed in the two-way case to obtain the last element; *last* may be redefined as an attribute.

One might expect the reverse to be also acceptable: redefine an attribute as an argumentless function. Unfortunately, this is not possible because assignment, an operation applicable to attributes, makes no sense for functions. Assume a routine *r* of a class *A* contains the instruction

   a := expression

where *a* is an attribute. Were *a* to be redefined as a function in a descendant of *A*, then *r* (assumed not redefined itself) would be unapplicable to an instance of the descendant; one cannot assign to a function.

In the legal case, redefining a function as an attribute, an interesting question arises: what happens to the assertions? The original function may have been characterized by a precondition and a postcondition. The rule follows from the discussion at the beginning of this chapter:

- An attribute is always defined, and hence may be considered to have precondition **true**. But this does not raise any problem since a precondition may be weakened in a redefinition.

- For the postcondition, there is no provision for syntactically attaching an assertion to an attribute. However any property ensured by the initial function should also be satisfied by the attribute. Such a property should be included in the **invariant** of the class, which is the proper place to express constraints on the attribute. Note that in accordance with the rules given earlier the constraint may be stronger than the initial postcondition.

As before, these rules are methodological guidelines, not enforced by the current Eiffel implementation.

11.4 DECLARATION BY ASSOCIATION

The type redefinition rule could make life quite unpleasant in some cases, and even cancel some of the benefits of inheritance. Let us see how and explain the solution – declaration by association.

11.4.1 Type inconsistencies

As an example of the problems that may arise with the type redefinition rule, consider the following example from *LINKED_LIST*. Here is the procedure for inserting a new element with a given value at the right of the current cursor position:

insert_right (*v: T*) **is**
>   -- Insert an element of value *v* to the right of cursor position.
>   -- Do not move cursor.
> **require**
>>   *empty* **or not** *offright*
> **local**
>>   *new: LINKABLE* [*T*]
> **do**
>>   *new.Create* (*v*);
>>   *insert_linkable_right* (*new*)
> **ensure**
>>   ... (See appendix A, A.6 for postcondition) ...
>   **end**; -- *insert_right*

To insert a new element of value *v*, we must create this element, of type *LINKABLE* [*T*]; the actual insertion is carried out by the secret procedure *insert_linkable_right*, which takes a *LINKABLE* as argument. This procedure performs the appropriate pointer manipulations.

In the descendants of *LINKED_LIST*, such as *TWO_WAY_LIST* or *TREE*, procedure *insert_right* should still be applicable. Unfortunately, it will not work as given: although the algorithm is still correct, the local variable *new* should be declared and created as a *BI_LINKABLE* or a *TREE* rather than a *LINKABLE*. Thus the whole procedure must be redefined and rewritten for two-way lists – a particularly wasteful task since the new body will be identical to what it was for one-way lists, with the exception of a single declaration (*new*). For an approach that purports to solve the reusability issue, there is nothing to be proud of!

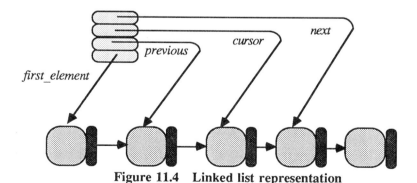

Figure 11.4   Linked list representation

11.4.2   A serious problem

If you look more closely at the class, you will realize that the problem is of even greater scope. *LINKED_LIST* contains more than a few declarations referring to type *LINKABLE* [*T*], and most will need to be redefined for two-way lists. Remember for example that the representation of a list keeps four references to linkable elements:

first_element, previous, active, next: LINKABLE [T]

All of these must be redefined as *BI_LINKABLE [T]* in *TWO_WAY_LIST*. Internal procedures such as *insert_linkable_right*, mentioned above, take linkables as arguments, and must also be redefined. It seems that we shall end up repeating in *TWO_WAY_LIST*, for purposes of declaration only, most of the code that was written for *LINKED_LIST*.

11.4.3   Introducing an anchor

Declaration by association will correct this sad state of affairs. A type defined by association has the form

like *anchor*

where *anchor* (the source, or "anchor" of the association) is either a feature of the current class or the predefined expression *Current*.

A declaration of the form *elem:* **like** *anchor* in a class *A* has the following meaning. Assume *anchor* is declared of some type *X*; *X* must be a class type, and may not itself be of the form **like** *other_anchor*. Then within class *A*, *elem* will be treated as if it itself had been declared of type *X*; there is no difference between the two declarations

- .I elem: **like** *anchor*
- .I elem: X

The difference only comes up in descendant classes of *A*. Being declared "like" *anchor*, *elem* will automatically follow any redefinition of the type of *anchor*, without the need for explicit redefinition by the programmer.

The advantage of this technique is that when there exists a bunch of elements in a class (attributes, function results, formal routine arguments, local variables) whose types must be identically redefined in descendant classes, then we can dispense with all but one of the redefinitions: it is enough to declare all elements as **like** the first one, and redefine only the first. All others will automatically follow suit. This mechanism is called declaration by association; the element that serves to declare the others is called the anchor of the association.

Let's apply this technique to *LINKED_LIST*. We can choose one of the attributes of type *LINKABLE [T]* as anchor, for example *first_element*. The attribute declarations become:

first_element: LINKABLE [T];
previous, active, next: **like** *first_element*

Procedure *insert_right* may now (and should) be written as follows:

insert_right (v: T) **is**
            -- Insert an element of value *v* to the right of cursor position.
            -- Do not move cursor.
    require
            empty **or not** *offright*
    local
            new: **like** *first_element*
    do
            new.Create (v);
            insert_linkable_right (new)
    ensure
            . . .
    end; -- *insert_right*

With this form, it is enough to redefine *first_element* as a *BI_LINKABLE* in class *TWO_WAY_LIST*, as a *TREE* in class *TREE* etc.; all entities declared "like" it follow automatically and do not need to be listed in the redefine clause. Neither is redefinition necessary now for function *insert_right*.

Declaration by association is essential to reconcile the type system of object-oriented programming with reusability. A quick look at appendix A will show that **like**... declarations are used extensively.

11.4.4 *Current* **as anchor**

As was mentioned above, the anchor may be *Current*, denoting the current instance. An entity declared **like** *Current* in a class *A* will be treated within the class as being of type *A* and, in any descendant *B* of *A*, as being of type *B* — without any need for redefinition.

This facility is particularly useful for functions returning a value of the same type as their argument. As an example, assume we add to class *POINT* a function yielding the conjugate of a point, that is to say its mirror image along the horizontal axis:

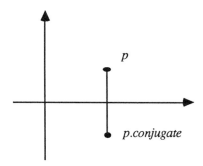

Figure 11.5 Conjugate of a point

The function can be written as follows in *POINT*:

```
conjugate: POINT is
        -- Conjugate of current point
    do
        Result.Clone (Current);        -- Get a copy of current point
        Result.translate (0, –2*y)     -- Translate result vertically
    end -- conjugate
```

Now consider a descendant of *POINT*, perhaps *PARTICLE*, where particles have attributes other than x and y: perhaps a mass and a speed. Conceptually, *conjugate* is still applicable to particles; it should yield a particle result when applied to a particle argument. The conjugate of a particle is identical to this particle except for the y coordinate. But if we leave the function as it stands, it will not work for particles, as code of the following form violates the basic type compatibility rule:

p1, p2: PARTICLE; *p1.Create* (…); …
p2 := p1.conjugate

In the underlined assignment, the right-hand side is of type *POINT*, but the left-hand side is of type *PARTICLE*; the type compatibility rule would require the reverse.

To correct the problem without having to redefine *conjugate* in *PARTICLE* and every other descendant of *POINT*, it suffices to amend the declaration of the function so that it reads

conjugate: **like** *Current* **is**
        … *The rest exactly as before* …

Then the result type of *conjugate* gets automatically redefined in every descendant.

Another example of this facility occurs in class *LINKABLE*. By now, you have probably guessed that in the declarations given so far,

right: LINKABLE [*T*];
change_right (*other: LINKABLE* [*T*]) **is**…

LINKABLE [*T*] should be replaced by **like** *Current*. Similarly, *left* in *BI_LINKABLE* should be declared as **like** *Current*.

11.4.5   When not to use declaration by association

Not every declaration of the form *x: A* within a class *A* should be replaced by *x:* **like** *Current*.

Consider for example the feature *first_child* of trees, which describes the first child of a given tree node. This feature is actually a rename of the feature *first_element* of *LINKED_LIST*; in *LINKED_LIST*, the feature was declared of type *LINKABLE* [*T*]. In *TREE*, we need to redefine it so that it now denotes a tree, rather than a general linkable. It may seem appropriate to use an association for the redefinition:

first_child: **like** *Current*

This is not incorrect, but may be too restrictive in practice. Class *TREE* may itself have descendants, representing various kinds of trees (or tree nodes). Examples might include *UNARY* (nodes with just one child), *BINARY* (nodes with two children),

BOUNDED_ARITY (nodes with a bounded number of children) etc. If *first_child* is anchored to *Current*, every node must have children of the same type: unary if it is unary, and so on.

This may be the desired effect. Often, however, you will want more flexible structures, permitting for example a binary node to have a unary child. This is obtained by redefining the feature not by association but simply as

    first_child: TREE [*T*]

This solution is not restrictive: if you change your mind and decide we need trees with nodes that are all of the same type, you may leave *TREE* as it is and write a small class, say *HOMOGENEOUS_TREE*, which inherits from *TREE* and redefines *first_child* as

    first_child: **like** *Current*

ensuring consistency of all the nodes in a tree. To facilitate such a redefinition, the other features of *TREE* representing nodes, such as *parent* or some function results, are declared as **like** *first_child*; but *first_child* itself is not declared by association in *TREE*.

11.4.6   The type compatibility rule for entities declared by association

Recall that Y must conform to X in any assignment $y := x$, for x of type X and y of type Y, and whenever an entity initially declared of type X is redefined to be of type Y.

Conformance of Y to X when at least one of these types is defined by association was expressed above as part of the definition of conformance (page 262), but we can only understand it now. Two cases of that definition apply: case 1, in which Y and X are identical (both of the form **like** *anchor*, for the same *anchor*); and case 4, given as follows:

> Y is of the form **like** *anchor*, and the type of *anchor* conforms to X.

In case 4, consider the assignment $x := y$ with x of type X and y of type **like** *anchor*. In any descendant class, y will have the same type as *anchor*. If the original type of *anchor* is U, descendants may only redefine *anchor* to types that conform to U. Thus for all such assignments to be correct it suffices that U should conform to X.

When X itself is of the form **like** *left_anchor*, only case 1 applies: Y must be identical to X. Just having Y conform to U, the type of *anchor*, would not be sufficient: *left_anchor* could be redefined in a descendant to any type conforming to U, even one that does not conform to Y.

11.4.7   A static mechanism

One last remark on declaration by association, to dispel any possible misunderstanding that might remain about this mechanism: it is a purely static rule; no change of object forms is entailed at run-time. The constraints may be checked at compile-time.

Declaration by association may be viewed as a syntactic device, avoiding many spurious redeclarations by having the compiler insert them. As it stands, it is an essential language tool for reconciling reusability and type-checking in an object-oriented language.

11.5   INHERITANCE AND INFORMATION HIDING

Another important question that may be asked in connection with inheritance is how this mechanism combines with another fundamental aspect, information hiding and, in Eiffel, the **export** clause.

The Eiffel answer is quite simple: except for a rule regarding selective exports (given below), the two mechanisms are completely orthogonal. A class D is free to export or not any feature f that it inherits from an ancestor D. All four possibilities are open:

- f exported in both A and B.
- f secret in both A and B.
- f secret in A, but exported in B.
- f exported in A, but secret in B.

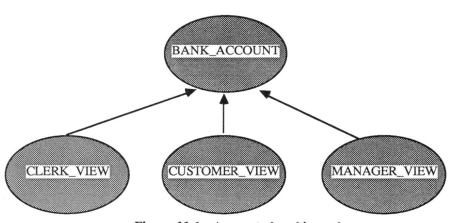

Figure 11.6   Account class hierarchy

This solution has several interesting applications. One is to use inheritance to provide different views of a data structure. Imagine a class *BANK_ACCOUNT* that contains all the necessary tools for dealing with bank accounts, with procedures such as *open*, *withdraw*, *deposit*, *secret_code* (for withdrawal from an automatic teller machine), *change_secret_code* etc.; but this class is not meant to be used directly by clients and it has no export clause. Various heirs to *BANK_ACCOUNT* provide different views: they do not add any feature, but simply differ in their export clauses. One will export *open* and *deposit* only, another will also include *deposit* and *secret_code*, and so on.

The notion of view is a classical one in databases, where it is often necessary to provide different users with different abstract notions of an underlying set of data.

Another application occurs in the Eiffel library. Feature *right* of class *LINKABLE* is secret in this class or, more precisely, is exported only to *LINKED_LIST*; this is in fact true of all the features of *LINKABLE*, since this class was initially designed only for the purpose of internally implementing linked lists. But in class *TREE*, implemented as heir to *LINKABLE* as well as *LINKED_LIST*, *right* now denotes access to the right sibling of a node, a quite respectable public feature which should be exported.

Along with the flexibility evidenced by the above examples, the main reason for making the mechanisms of inheritance and information hiding independent is simplicity. As it stands, the convention is easy to explain. Assume it is extended to allow the hiding of features from descendants. The examples make it clear that export restrictions in a class should not always apply to descendants. So a mechanism distinct from export restrictions would be needed for descendants: every feature would have to be specified as available to clients (exported) or not, and as available to descendants or not. Simula has such a possibility (chapter 20). But the benefits of adding the second facility do not seem worth the extra complexity; it seems in fact that few Simula programmers ever bother to use both mechanisms.

A further argument in favor of the approach used here is that any restrictions on descendants would directly contradict the open-closed principle, which we have studied as one of the primary concepts behind inheritance. The advantage of inheritance is that it enables you to take any existing class, written by you or somebody else, yesterday or 20 years ago, and extend it in ways that were not necessarily foreseen by its original designer.

LINKABLE and *TREE* are a case in point: when the former was designed in chapter 9, we had no reason to make its features public to any class other than *LINKED_LIST*. It is only later that we found a new public application for them in a descendant, *TREE*.

Without this openness, inheritance would lose much of its appeal. Thus it is not clear whether we want to allow a class designer to restrict descendants as to what features they may or may not export to their own clients.

In the picture that emerges from this discussion, the two ways of using a class – as client or as descendant – are seen as quite different. A class *A* is an abstract data type implementation (a partial implementation in the case of a deferred class); this means that the class internally contains both the interface, as expressed in an abstract data type specification (the tip of the iceberg) and the implementation part. The above conventions are the simplest possible: they mean that if you are a client of the class, you access it through its interface only; and that if you are a descendant you have access to its implementation.

Objections sometimes heard to this policy seem to be based on the premise that reusing an implementation is bad. But this is not the case: both kinds of reuse – reuse of an implemented abstraction through its specification, reuse of an implementation – are legitimate. There is nothing wrong with reusing an implementation if this is what you need – a good implementation for a certain abstraction. In such cases information hiding is simply not relevant. Reusing an implementation is, of course, a more committing decision than just reusing an interface: you cannot reasonably expect, as in the other case, to be protected against changes in implementation! In general, inheriting is indeed a more committing decision than just being a client. But in some cases it is the proper decision.

More discussions of when to "buy" and when to inherit will be found in 14.5.

To be true to this view, we must introduce a rule regarding selective exports. When A is exporting f to B only, as in

> **class** A **export**
> $\qquad ..., f \{B\}, ...$
> $\quad ...$

f is available to B for the implementation of B's own features. With the above view of inheritance, the descendants of B have access to B's implementation; so they should be able to access whatever is accessible to B – like f. This is not so much a theoretical principle as an experimental observation: what is needed by a class tends to be needed by its descendants too. But we do not want to have to come back and modify A (to extend its export clause) whenever a new descendant is added to B.

Here the principle of information hiding should be combined with the open-closed principle. The designer of A is entitled to decide whether or not to make f available to B; but he has no right to limit the freedom of the designers of the B line of classes to provide new extensions and implementation variants. In fact, what descendants B has, if any, is not his business.

This discussion explains the following rule:

> **Selective export inheritance rule**: A feature selectively exported to a class is available to every descendant of that class.

11.6 REPEATED INHERITANCE

11.6.1 Sharing ancestors

One of the delicate problems raised by the presence of multiple inheritance is what happens when a class is an ancestor of another in more than one way. If you allow multiple inheritance into a language, then sooner or later someone is going to write a class D with two parents B and C, each of which has a class A as a parent – or some other situation in which D inherits twice (or more) from A. This situation is called repeated inheritance and must be dealt with properly.

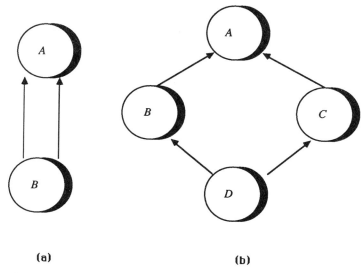

(a)   **(b)**

Figure 11.7   Repeated inheritance – direct (a) or indirect (b)

There is no restriction to repeated inheritance in Eiffel; it may even be direct, with a class listing another more than once among its parents, as in

class *B* **export** ... **inherit**
    A **rename** ... **redefine** ...;
    A **rename** ... **redefine** ...;

   ...

11.6.2   Transcontinental drivers

Repeated inheritance is not an anomaly, but a real and potentially useful occurrence. The following example provides an illustration. Assume a class *DRIVER* with attributes such as

    age: INTEGER;
    address: STRING;
    number_of_traffic_violations: INTEGER;

and routines such as

    birthday **is do** *age := age+1* **end**;
    pay_yearly_fee **is** ... ;

etc.

An heir of *DRIVER*, taking into account the specific characteristics of US tax rules, may be *US_DRIVER*. Another may be *FRENCH_DRIVER* (with reference to places where cars are driven, not citizenship).

Now (as you will have guessed) we may want to consider people who drive in both France and the US, perhaps because they reside in each country for some part of the year. The natural way to express this is to use multiple inheritance: class

FRENCH_US_DRIVER will be declared as heir to both *US_DRIVER* and *FRENCH_DRIVER*.

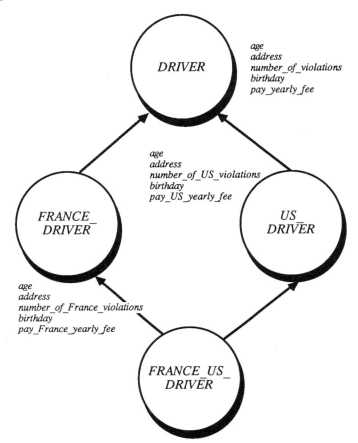

Figure 11.8   Driving cars in two countries

What happens with the features which are inherited twice from the common ancestor *DRIVER* such as *address*, *age*, *number_of_traffic_violations* etc.? Applied strictly, the prohibition against name clashes (page 247) appears to imply that renaming is needed.

But this solution seems too extreme here as the name clashes are only apparent: the conflicting features are in fact the same feature, coming from the common ancestor *DRIVER*. The two versions of *age*, for example, are really the same (unless one is trying to hide something, one should declare the same age to both the US and French authorities). On the other hand, the *number_of_traffic_violations* attributes inherited from both parents should remain distinct. This will be achieved simply by renaming them at the inheritance point, as *number_of_us_traffic_violations* and *number_of_french_traffic_violations*.

11.6.3   The repeated inheritance rule

The Eiffel convention for repeated inheritance follows from this discussion:

> **Repeated inheritance rule**: In repeated inheritance, any feature from the common parent is considered shared if it has not been renamed along any of the inheritance paths. Any feature which has been renamed at least once along any of the inheritance paths is considered replicated.

This rule applies to attributes as well as routines; a consequence is that it is an error for the body of a non-renamed routine (which would be shared) to contain references to one or more renamed attributes or routines (which would be duplicated, leaving the meaning of the shared routine ambiguous).

This rule yields the desired flexibility in combining classes. For example the **inherit** clause of class *FRENCH_US_DRIVER* might look like:

> **inherit**
>   *FRENCH_DRIVER*
>   **rename**
>   *address* **as** *french_address,*
>   *number_of_traffic_violations* **as**
>   *number_of_french_traffic_violations,*
>   *pay_yearly_fee* **as** *pay_french_yearly_fee,*
>   . . .
>   *US_DRIVER*
>   **rename**
>   *address* **as** *us_address,*
>   *number_of_traffic_violations* **as**
>   *number_of_us_traffic_violations,*
>   *pay_yearly_fee* **as** *pay_us_yearly_fee,*
>   . . .

Note that features *age* and *birthday*, which have not been renamed along any of the inheritance paths, will be shared, which is indeed the desired effect.

The Eiffel implementation (chapter 15) achieves sharing or duplication of attributes according to the above rule; no space is lost (that is to say, no space needs to be reserved in class instances for inaccessible attributes). The same effect is achieved for routines. For shared routines, no code is duplicated; for routines which must be replicated according to the above rules, code must be duplicated. This is the only case in the Eiffel implementation in which code is ever duplicated.

11.6.4   Repeated inheritance and genericity

As given, the repeated inheritance rule raises a problem for features involving formal generic parameters. Consider the following scheme (which could also arise with indirect repeated inheritance):

```
class A [T] feature
    f: T; ...;
end

class B inherit
    A [INTEGER]; A [REAL]
end
```

In class *B*, the repeated inheritance rule would imply that *f* is shared. But this leaves an ambiguity on its type: does it return an integer or a real? The same problem would occur if *f* was a routine with an argument of type *T*.

Such an ambiguity is not acceptable. Hence the rule:

> **Genericity in repeated inheritance rule**: The type of any feature that would be shared under the repeated inheritance rule, and the type of any of its arguments if it is a routine, may not be a generic parameter of the class from which the feature is inherited.

The ambiguity will be removed by renaming the offending feature at the point of inheritance, resulting in duplication rather than renaming.

11.6.5   The renaming rule, revisited

To take repeated inheritance into account, the rule prohibiting name clashes (10.4.6) may be precisely expressed as follows:

> **Renaming rule**: A name clash is said to occur in a class *D* when two parents *B* and *C* of *D* both include a feature with the same name *f*.
>
> Such a name clash is only permitted if *f* was defined in an ancestor *A* of both *B* and *C*, has not been renamed along any of the inheritance paths from *A* to *B* and to *C*, and does not involve any generic parameter of *A* as either its type or the type of any of its arguments (if it is a routine). Any other name clash must be removed by renaming.

11.6.6   Repeated inheritance in practice

Instances of repeated inheritance similar to the "transcontinental driver" case, with duplicated features as well as shared ones, do occur in practice, but not frequently. You must have reached a certain level of sophistication in object-oriented programming before you need this facility. If you are writing a straightforward application and end up using repeated inheritance, the chances are you are making things more complicated than you need to.

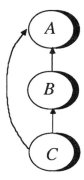

Figure 11.9   Unneeded repeated inheritance

A typical beginner's mistake is illustrated in this inheritance diagram: C inherits from B, and also needs facilities from A; but B itself inherits from A. Forgetting that inheritance is transitive, the programmer wrote

class C ... **inherit**
$\quad$ B;
$\quad$ A
...

This happens in particular when A is a class implementing general purpose facilities like input or output (such as the class *STD_FILES* from the basic Eiffel library), needed by B as well as C. But it is enough for C to inherit from B: this makes C a descendant of A.

In the absence of renaming, no harm will result thanks to the above rule: inherited features will be shared. The rule is also essential to ensure that other, legitimate cases of repeated inheritance will be treated correctly.

11.7   KEY CONCEPTS INTRODUCED IN THIS CHAPTER

- Invariants of parents are automatically added to a class's invariant.

- In a routine redefinition, or effective definition if it was deferred, the precondition may be kept or weakened and the postcondition may be kept or strengthened. Both must be written explicitly.

- Inheritance and dynamic binding introduce a style of programming by subcontracting.

- Redefinition and renaming may be combined for the same feature. The former ensures that the same feature name refers to different implementations of a features, or to features with different types; the latter, a syntactic facility, changes the name under which a class's clients refer to a feature.

- Type conformance governs assignment, argument passing and type redefinition. Generally speaking, a class type conforms to another if its class is a descendant of the other's class, and every generic parameter conforms to the other's corresponding generic parameter.

- An argumentless function may be redefined as an attribute, but not the other way around.

- Declaration by association is an important part of the type system; it avoids many redundant redefinitions.

- The mechanisms of inheritance and information hiding are orthogonal. Descendants can hide features that were exported by their ancestors, or export features that were secret.

- Repeated inheritance occurs whenever a class is descendant of another in more than one way. Non-renamed features are shared; renamed features are duplicated.

11.8   SYNTACTICAL SUMMARY

			Used in (chapter)
Association	=	**like** Anchor	Type (5)
Anchor	=	Feature_name | *Current*	

11.9   BIBLIOGRAPHICAL NOTE

See [Snyder 1986] for a different viewpoint on the relationship between inheritance and information hiding.

EXERCISES

11.1   Inheriting for simplicity and efficiency

Rewrite and simplify the protected stack example of 7.3.4, making class *STACK3* a descendant rather than a client of *STACK* to avoid unneeded indirections. (Use the rules governing the relationship between inheritance and information hiding.)

11.2   Extract?

The assignment $y1 := x1$ is not permitted if $x1$ is of a class type X, $y1$ of a class type Y, and X is a proper ancestor of Y. It might seem useful, however, to include a predefined primitive *Extract* such that the instruction $y1.Extract (x1)$ copies the values of the fields of the object associated with $x1$ to the corresponding fields in the object associated with $y1$, assuming neither reference is void. Explain why the *Extract* primitive, although once considered for inclusion into Eiffel, is **not** part of the language. (**Hint:** examine correctness issues, in particular the notion of invariant.)

12

Object-oriented design: case studies

We have by now seen many individual software components, either in detailed form or sketched. This chapter discusses the application of the object-oriented method to more complete examples.

12.1 OUTLINE OF A WINDOW SYSTEM

The first example will only be sketched. It shows how the object-oriented approach influences the architecture of a routine package.

Assume we want to make multiple windowing facilities available to various application programs. An object-oriented design for a windowing package should concentrate on the types of objects involved. Finding the basic classes is not difficult since they will directly reflect the physical objects of the problem: screen, window, mouse, keyboard...

> It was said in 4.6, with respect to the often heard question "how do you find the objects?" (whose proper formulation, of course, should refer to *classes* rather than objects), that in many cases the most important classes of a system are simply obtained by looking at the classes of physical objects in the external reality handled by the system. The present case is a typical example.

The window package should provide a set of facilities for writers of interactive applications. To avoid any confusion, let us call "application programmer" the writer of any interactive system using the package (for example, the author of a screen-oriented editor) and reserve the term "user" for the person working with such an interactive system (for example, a person composing a document with the text editor).

12.1.1 Properties of windows

Consider class *WINDOW*. A design for such a class should account for the properties of windows, described by attributes and procedures for modifying these attributes. For example a window has a height and a width, which yield the following features:

> *height, width: INTEGER*; -- Expressed in number of lines, columns

> *set_height (h: INTEGER)* **is**
> -- Set height to *h*
> **do**
>   *height := h*
> **end**; *set_height*

> *set_width (w: INTEGER)* **is** ...

At a given state of execution, a window may be in normal mode or inverse video; hence the following features of the class:

> *inverse: BOOLEAN*;
> *set_inverse* **is do** *inverse :=* **true end**;
> *set_direct* **is do** *inverse :=* **false end**;

The user may or may not be permitted to use the keyboard when the cursor is in the window:

> *write_ignored: BOOLEAN*;
> *enable_write* **is do** *write_ignored :=* **true end**;
> *disable_write* **is do** *write_ignored :=* **false end**;

Disabling write means that any characters typed in the window will be ignored.

There are two ways to define a boolean attribute: here *direct* and *write_enabled* could have been chosen rather than *inverse* and *write_ignored*. The standard convention is to always use the form that describes a situation departing from default mode, so that the default *Create*, which initializes boolean attributes to **false**, will automatically put objects in the appropriate initial mode.

Another attribute governing what happens to the user's input in the window is *echo*, which expresses whether input is actually shown on the screen:

> *no_echo: BOOLEAN*;
> *set_echo* **is do** *no_echo :=* **false end**;
> *set_no_echo* **is do** *no_echo :=* **true end**;

The notion of *echo* is not redundant with *write_ignored*; in fact, all four combinations of the values of these attributes are meaningful. For example, when a password is being typed, write is enabled but input is not echoed (this is also what happens with some editors, such as Vi under Unix, which accept commands in the form of characters that are not echoed on the screen). When write is disabled, input is ignored, and the application programmer may choose to echo it or not to echo it.

More properties are amenable to similar descriptions: brightness, color etc. One of the nicest aspects of object-oriented design is that you do not have to grasp the full picture immediately: if you forget some attributes and the associated routines, you may add them later without much fuss. This is the shopping list approach (4.3.2).

12.1.2 Associated text, input, output

A window is used to show some associated text (or graphics, but we shall limit ourselves to text for this discussion). Rather than add text manipulation facilities to windows, it is better to declare an attribute

>   *text: STRING*

which describes the associated text. The corresponding routines are

>   *associate_text* (*t: STRING*) **is do** *text := t* **end**;
>   *dissociate_text* **is do** *text.Forget* **end**

All string operations will be performed on *text*, rather than directly on the window. The text shown in a window may be modified in two ways:

- Output: the application may change the *text* field; the result will be reflected in the window's space on the screen.

- Input: characters entered by the user in write-enabled and echo mode will update the corresponding characters in the *text* field.

Both operations should be controlled by the application. We may look at an interactive session as maintaining two images of the screen: the **internal image**, or view of the windows maintained by the application; and the **external image**, or view seen by the user.

The two views are not necessarily identical at all times: the operations seen above, changing window attributes and the characters in *text*, affect the internal image only; user input acts on the external image only. The two views are reconciled by either of the following two routines:

- *write* changes the external image (screen) to reflect the changes made by the application to the internal image;

- *read* looks at all user input since the last read or write operation, to make the internal image conform to the external image.

The text shown in the window reflects the value of the *text* attribute; *text*, which may contain new line characters, is interpreted as a two-dimensional text (sequence of lines) for display purposes. Any part of this two-dimensional structure which is beyond the window's limits is clipped off from the window display. The characters shown are those beginning at index *cursor* in *text*; *cursor* is an attribute of the class, 1 by default (start at first character), which may be changed by the routine

>   *move_text* (*n: INTEGER*) **is** ...

The way *text* is reflected in the window may be changed. For example, rather than clip off out-of-bounds text, you may want it to wrap around either continuously or at word boundaries (blank or new line). These options are described by attributes and changed by appropriate routines, whose specification is left to the reader. You may also want the text in the window to appear justified:

>   *justified: BOOLEAN*;
>   *justify_text* **is do** ... **end**;
>   *dont_justify_text* **is do** ... **end**;

12.1.3   Hierarchies of windows

Again, the shopping list approach allows us to add further facilities as needed. So far, *WINDOW* is like a record type (Pascal, Ada) or structure type (C), to which we would have attached not only the description of fields in the type instances but also the routines to change these fields. An important property of windows that cannot be expressed in this first step is their ability to be nested: windows should be permitted to contain subwindows. We could introduce a class *SUBWINDOW* to account for this possibility. It is better, however, to strive at more generality and remove any difference between windows and subwindows. This will allow windows to be nested to an arbitrary degree.

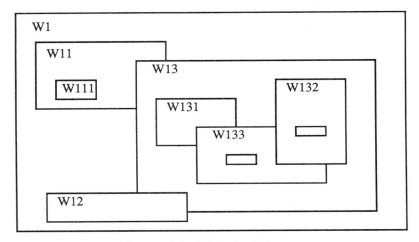

Figure 12.1   Nested windows

Subwindows of a window could be described by an attribute

subwindows: LIST [WINDOW]

and the associated routines. But this would lead to unnecessary work. If we give windows a fully hierarchical structure, it means they are organized as trees. To take care of this aspect of windows, it suffices to make *WINDOW* an heir of *TREE* (10.4.3): then there is no need to write specific routines for inserting or deleting subwindows, changing a subwindow, accessing the parent window etc. All these operations are obtained "for free" by using inheritance. To ensure proper terminology, we should use renaming:

> **class** *WINDOW* **export** ... **inherit**
> > *TREE*
> > > **rename**
> > > > *child* **as** *subwindow,*
> > > > *parent* **as** *superwindow,*
> > > > *insert_child* **as** *insert_subwindow,* etc.
>
> ...

As is sometimes the case, a good implementation technique suggests some interface improvements. So far, an attribute of a window, such as brightness, color etc., was set to a standard default value unless explicitly changed by the application. With hierarchical subwindows, it is better to specify that, by default, the value of each attribute of a subwindow is set to the corresponding value for its superwindow; the standard defaults are only used for windows without superwindows.

This also applies to the *text* attribute: in this case, a subwindow gets from its superwindow's text the substring corresponding to the subwindow's relative position in the superwindow.[1]

These ideas may be generalized, putting subwindows to very general use. If all attribute values are obtained from the superwindow, screen updates may be produced by simply creating an appropriate subwindow and changing only those characteristics that differ from the parents'. For example:

- If one word in a window w, or even just one character, is to be shown in, say, inverse video, we create a new window w', make it a subwindow of the first ($w'.attach\ (w)$), give it the appropriate size ($w'.set\_height\ (1)$, $w'.set\_width\ (...)$), move it to the appropriate position ($w'.move\ (..., ...)$) and change its attribute ($w'.set\_inverse$).

- If, on the other hand, the text appearing at a certain position of w must be temporarily overridden with some other text, we create w', make it a subwindow of w, attach to it a text t different from the text obtained by default from w ($w'.associate\_text\ (t)$), but do not change any other attribute.

We leave the design at this stage. Of course, many problems still have to be resolved; in particular, good algorithms are needed to ensure fast redisplay of the screen when only part of the hierarchical window structure has been changed. A proper interface must also be found with the underlying terminal handling system.

This example shows how an object-oriented design leads to a simple structure organized around the key object classes. The classes do not need to be complete the first time, but may be progressively extended. Inheritance makes it possible to reuse ready-made implementations of fundamental software concepts (here trees) in various contexts (here windows). The simplicity of the implementation suggests interesting module specification ideas.

12.2   UNDOING AND REDOING

Our second example addresses a problem that is faced by the designers of all interactive systems, such as text editors: undoing and redoing. It will show how inheritance and dynamic binding provide a fully general and regular solution to an apparently intricate and many-faceted problem.

---

[1] It is tempting to say that the subwindow "inherits" its attribute values from its superwindow. But better stay away from any potential confusion with inheritance as applied to classes.

12.2.1 The importance of redoing

Regardless of any other functions, any good interactive system must allow its users to cancel the effect of a command. The primary aim is to allow users to recover from typing mistakes that may be damaging. But a good undo facility goes further. It frees users from having to concentrate nervously on every key they type. Beyond this, it encourages a "What if...?" style of interaction in which users try out various sorts of input, knowing that they can back up easily if the result is not what they expect.

To enable the full application of these ideas, the undo facility should make it possible to back up more than one level by executing successive UNDO commands. The maximum number of levels should be bounded only by memory limitations. This implies a companion "redo" facility, which will re-execute an undone command. (In a system with just one-level undo, REDO is just UNDO performed immediately after another UNDO.)

When both UNDO and REDO are present, a "skip" facility may be useful, allowing the user after n UNDO commands to skip m commands before redoing p commands $(0 \le p+m \le n)$. If, however, we know how to implement UNDO and REDO, SKIP only raises user interface problems, which fall beyond the scope of this discussion.

12.2.2 Requirements

A good undo-redo mechanism should satisfy the following properties.

1. • The mechanism should not require redesign for each new command.
2. • It should make reasonable use of storage.
3. • It should be applicable to both one-level and arbitrary level UNDO.

The first requirement excludes the case in which UNDO and REDO would be treated as just any other command in the system (the editor in our example). Were UNDO a command, it would need a structure of the form

> **if** "last command was INSERT" **then**
> "undo the effect of INSERT"
> **elsif** "last command was DELETE" **then**
> "undo the effect of DELETE"
> etc.

We know how bad such structures are for extendibility. They have to be changed with the addition of every new command; furthermore, the code in each branch will mirror the code for the corresponding command (the first branch, for example, has to know a lot about what *INSERT* does), which points to a flawed design.

The second requirement excludes the obvious solution of saving the whole system state before every command execution; UNDO would just restore the saved image. This would work but is terribly wasteful of space, and in practice incompatible with the third requirement. Of course, something has to be saved if we want to enable later cancellation of a command; for example, we cannot undo a line delete operation unless we have stored somewhere the index of the deleted line and its text. But we want a solution in which the amount of information stored before each command execution is little more than the strict minimum logically required to undo the command, for example the line index and its text in the deletion example.

You may wish to ponder this problem by yourself before reading the following solution.

12.2.3 Command as a class

The suggested solution is almost disappointing in its simplicity. The key remark is that the problem is characterized by a fundamental data abstraction: *COMMAND*, representing any editor command other than UNDO and REDO. The only way to miss the solution is to forget that execution is only one of the operations that may be applied to a command: the command might be stored, tested – or undone. Thus we should include a class of the form

>**deferred class** *COMMAND* **export**
>>*execute, undo*
>
>**feature**
>>*execute* **is deferred end**; -- "do" is a reserved word in Eiffel
>>*undo* **is deferred end**;
>
>**end** -- class *COMMAND*

COMMAND describes the abstract notion of command and is naturally a deferred class. Command types are represented by descendants of this class, such as

>**class** *LINE_DELETION* **export**
>>*execute, undo*
>
>**inherit**
>>*COMMAND*
>
>**feature**
>>*index_of_deleted_line: INTEGER*; *last_deleted_line: STRING*;
>>
>>*set_deleted_line* (*n: INTEGER*) **is**
>>>-- Set to *n* the number of next line to be deleted
>>>
>>>**do**
>>>>*index_of_deleted_line := n*
>>>
>>>**end**; -- *set_line_number*
>>
>>*execute* **is**
>>>-- Delete line
>>>
>>>**do**
>>>>"Delete line number *index_of_deleted_line*";
>>>>"Store text of deleted line in *last_deleted_line*"
>>>
>>>**end**; -- *execute*
>>
>>*undo* **is**
>>>-- Restore last deleted line
>>>
>>>**do**
>>>>"Put back line given by *last_deleted_line*
>>>>at line number *index_of_deleted_line*"
>>>
>>>**end**; -- *undo*
>
>**end** -- class *LINE_DELETION*

And similarly for each command class. Commands are viewed as full-fledged objects, which carry along (in attributes such as *index_of_deleted_line* and *last_deleted_line*) the information necessary to execute or undo themselves.

This gives a simple structure for the editor's basic execution loop:

```
current_command: COMMAND

from
    ...
until
    over
loop
    "decode user's request";
    if "request is QUIT" then
        over := true
    elsif "request is normal command (not UNDO)" then
        "Create appropriate command object current_command";
            -- current_command is created as an instance of some
            -- descendant of COMMAND, such as LINE_DELETION
        current_command.execute
    elsif "request is UNDO" then
        if not current_command.Void then
            current_command.undo
        else
            message ("Nothing to undo")
        end
    end
end -- loop
```

Note that the information stored before each command execution is an instance of some descendant of *COMMAND* such as *LINE_DELETION*. The second above requirement is satisfied since this information only describes the difference between each state and the previous one, not the state itself.

12.2.4 Multi-level undo

The preceding scheme assumes a single level of undo. The generalization to an arbitrary level of undo-redo is immediate: replace attribute *current_command* by a circular list

```
history: CIRCULAR_LIST [COMMAND]
```

keeping references to the last n commands. Circular lists may be represented, for example, by arrays (exercise 10.5). The branch for UNDO becomes:

```
if not history.empty then
    history.value.undo;
    history.back
else
    message ("Nothing to undo")
end
```

and the branch for REDO is

> **if not** *history.full* **then**
>   *history.forth*;
>   *history.value.execute*
> **else**
>   *message* ("*Nothing to redo*")
> **end**

    The appropriate primitives have been assumed on class *CIRCULAR_LIST* (exercise 10.5).

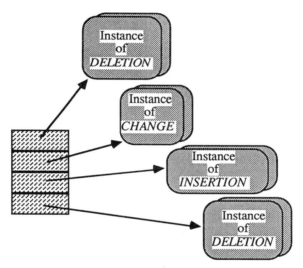

Figure 12.2   A polymorphic array of "undoable" commands

    Note the fundamental role of polymorphism and dynamic binding in this solution. The entity *current_command*, in the one-level version, and the circular list *history*, in the undo-redo version, contain references to objects that are instances of arbitrary descendants of *COMMAND*. The simplicity and generality of the above solution are due to its use of calls of the form

> *current_command.execute*
> *current_command.undo*
> *history.value.execute*
> *history.value.undo*

where the procedures are applied to entities of type *COMMAND*, and automatic run-time mechanisms (dynamic binding) are responsible for finding the appropriate version to apply in each case.

12.2.5 Pre-computing command objects

An interesting question is how to implement the operation written as

"Create appropriate command object *current_command*"

in the basic loop of the editor as given above. The most obvious solution is of the form

> **if** "request is LINE DELETION" **then**
>   *ld. Create*; *current_command := ld*
> **elsif** "request is LINE INSERTION" **then**
>   *li. Create*; *current_command := li*
> etc.

where *ld* is declared of type *LINE_DELETION*, *li* of type *LINE_INSERTION*, and so on. This conditional instruction discriminates among all possible user commands. The disadvantages of such multi-branch decision structures have been repeatedly emphasized in previous discussions. Here, however, one may point out that the conditional instruction is the only one of this kind that will remain in the entire editor structure; surely some component of the editor must discriminate between user commands.

Still, it is possible to do away with the multi-branch conditional through the following scheme, which is applicable to many similar situations. Let us associate an integer code between 1 and *n* to each possible command. Then during editor initialization we may create an array

command_template: ARRAY [COMMAND]

and initialize its elements in such a way that the *i*-th element ($1 \leq i \leq n$) refers to an instance of the heir class of *COMMAND* corresponding to code *i*; for example, we create an instance of *LINE_DELETION* and associate it with the first element of the array (assuming line deletion has code 1), and so on. In other words, we pre-compute *n* command objects, one for each type of command, and make them accessible through array *command_template*, each at the index given by the corresponding command code.

Then there is no more need for any conditional instruction. The operation "Create appropriate command object *current_command*" is simply written as

current_command. Clone (command_template. entry (code))

where *code* is the code of the current user command. This obtains from the array a command object corresponding to the current command, makes a fresh copy of it through the *Clone*, and associates it to *current_command*. Note that the *Clone* is essential in the multi-level undo case, since array *history* may contain more than one instance of a given command class; on figure 12.2, for example, the array contains two instances of *DELETION*.

Array *command_template* is another example of a data structure which must be polymorphic.

12.3 FULL-SCREEN ENTRY SYSTEMS

Our last example will serve to contrast the object-oriented approach with classical functional decomposition.

The problem – panel-driven entry systems – is a common one in data processing. An interactive application is to be written, whose users are guided by full-screen panels at each stage in a session.

Interactive sessions for such systems have a well-defined general pattern. A session goes through a certain number of *states*. In each state, a certain panel is displayed, showing questions to the user. The user will fill in the required answer; this answer will be checked for consistency (and questions asked again until an acceptable answer is found); then the answer will be processed in some fashion (for example the system will update a data base). As part of the user's answer will be a choice for the next step to perform, which the system will translate into a transition to another state, where the same process will be applied.

An example entry panel for an imaginary airline reservation system is given below, with no claim to realism or good ergonomic design. The screen is shown towards the end of a step; items in italics are the user's answers.

```
                      - Enquiry on Flights -

Flight sought from: Santa Barbara     to: Paris
Departure on or after: Nov 21         on or before: Nov 21

Preferred airline (s):
Special requirements:

AVAILABLE FLIGHTS: 1
Flt# AA 42      Dep 8:25    Arr 7:45      Thru Chicago

Choose next action:
        0 – Exit
        1 – Help
        2 – Further enquiry
        3 – Reserve a seat
```

Figure 12.3   A panel in an interactive application

The process begins in an initial state, and ends whenever a final state is reached. The overall structure of a session is conveniently represented by a transition graph which shows the possible states and the transitions between them. The edges of the graph are labeled by integers corresponding to the possible user's choices for the next step when leaving a state. Below is a graph representing a simple airline reservation application.

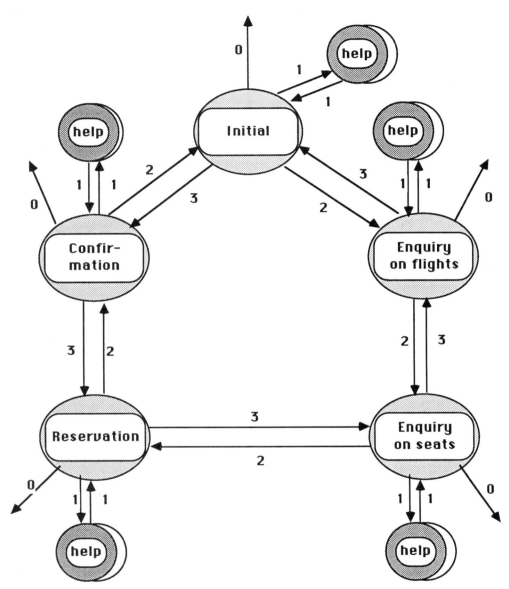

Figure 12.4   Transition graph for an interactive application

The problem is to come up with a design and implementation for such applications, achieving as much generality and flexibility as possible.

12.3.1   A simple-minded attempt

Let us begin with a straightforward, unsophisticated program scheme. This version is made of a number of blocks, one for each state of the system: $B_{Enquiry}$, $B_{Reservation}$, $B_{Cancellation}$ etc. A typical block (expressed in an ad hoc programming notation, not Eiffel) looks like the following:

> $B_{Enquiry}$:
>
> > output "enquiry on flights" panel;
> > **repeat**
> > > read user's answers and choice C for the next step;
> > > **if** error in answer **then** output appropriate message **end**
> > **until not** error in answer **end**;
> > process answer;
> > **case** C **in**
> > > C_0: **goto** Exit,
> > > C_1: **goto** B_{Help},
> > > C_2: **goto** $B_{Reservation}$,
> > > ...
> >
> > **end**

and similarly for each state.

This structure has something to speak for it: it will do the job. But there is much to criticize. One may immediately point to the numerous **goto** instructions, which give it that famous "spaghetti bowl" look. But this is not just a control structure issue. Beyond the presence of explicit branch instructions, the above scheme is flawed because the physical form of the problem has been wired into the algorithm. The branching structure of the program is an exact reflection of the transition structure of the transition graph.

From the standpoint of reusability and extendibility this is terrible. In actual data entry systems, the graph of figure 12.4 may be quite complex. Examples with 300 states are not uncommon. The transition structure of such a system is unlikely to be right the first time; even after a first version of the system is working, users will inevitably come up with requests for new transitions, shortcuts, new "help" states etc. The prospect of having to modify the whole structure (not just program elements, but the overall organization) for any such change is not enticing.

To improve the solution we must separate the graph structure from the traversal algorithm; this seems appropriate as the structure depends on the application (such as airline reservation) whereas its traversal may be described generically. The functional decomposition obtained below will also remove the heretic gotos.

12.3.2   A functional, top-down solution

The structure of the graph should be encapsulated in a two-argument function, say *transition*, such that *transition* (s, c) is the state obtained when the user chooses c when leaving state s. The word "function" is used in its mathematical sense; *transition* may be represented either by a function in the programming sense, that is to say a routine returning a value, or by a data structure such as an array. We can afford to postpone the choice between these solutions and just rely on *transition* without committing ourselves as to how it is implemented.

Function *transition* is not sufficient to describe the transition graph: we also need to define the state, say *initial*, which is used to begin the traversal, and a boolean-valued function *is_final* (*s*) that determines whether a state is final. (The initial state is assumed to be unique, whereas there may be more than one final state.)

Given this representation, the following orthodox-looking functional architecture may be proposed. In the top-down method, any system must have a "top", or main program; here it should clearly be the routine that describes how to execute a complete interactive session.

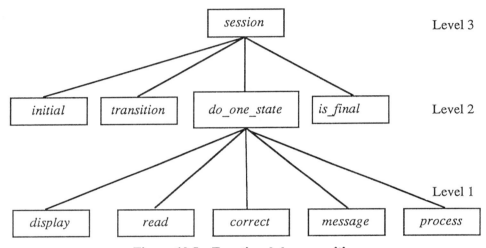

Figure 12.5   Functional decomposition

This routine may be written so as to emphasize its application-independence. (The language used in the presentation of the functional top-down solution is again an ad hoc programming notation and bears no connection to Eiffel.) We assume that an adequate representation is found for states (type *STATE*) and for the user's choice after each state (*CHOICE*).

> *session* **is** -- Execute a complete session of the interactive system
>
>   *current: STATE*; *next: CHOICE*
> **begin**
>   *current := initial*;
>   **repeat**
>   *do_one_state* (*current, next*);
>   -- The value of *next* is returned
>   -- by routine *do_one_state*
>   *current := transition* (*current, next*)
>   **until** *is_final* (*current*) **end**
> **end** -- *session*

Procedure *session* does not show direct dependency on any interactive application. To describe such an application, one must provide three of the elements on level 2 in figure 12.5: *transition* function (routine or data structure); *initial* state; *is_final* predicate.

To complete the design, we need to refine the *do_one_state* routine which describes the actions to be performed in each state. The body of this routine is essentially an abstracted form of the contents of the successive blocks in our initial spaghetti version:

> *do_one_state* (**in** *s: STATE*; **out** *c: CHOICE*) **is**
>   -- Execute the actions associated with state *s*,
>   -- returning into *c* the user's choice for the next state
>
>   *a: ANSWER*; *ok: BOOLEAN*;
> **begin**
>   **repeat**
>   *display* (*s*); *read* (*s, a*); *ok* := *correct* (*s, a*);
>   **if not** *ok* **then** *message* (*s, a*) **end**
>   **until** *ok* **end**;
>
>   *process* (*s, a*); *c* := *next_choice* (*a*)
> **end** -- *do_one_state*

Fully writing the remaining routines would require entering into the details of the application; at this point only specifications may be given:

- *display* (*s*) outputs the panel associated with state *s* .

- *read* (*s* , *a*) reads into *a* the user's answer to the display panel of state *s*.

- *correct* (*s* , *a*) returns true if and only if *a* is an acceptable answer to the question displayed in state *s*; if so, *process* (*s* , *a*) processes answer *a*; if not, *message* (*s* , *a*) outputs the relevant error message.

Note that the type *ANSWER* has been left unspecified. A value of this type, say *a*, globally represents the input entered by the user in a given state; it is assumed to include the user's choice for the next step, written *next_choice* (*a*). (*ANSWER* is in fact already very much like a class, even though the rest of the system architecture is not object-oriented at all.)

12.3.3 Data transmission

Have we now a satisfactory solution? Not from the standpoint of reusability.

True, some separation has been achieved between what is generic and what is specific to a given application. But this does not bring much in terms of flexibility. The main problem is the data transmission structure of the system. Consider the signatures (argument and result types) of the routines:

do_one_state	(**in** *s: STATE*; **out** *c: CHOICE*)
display	(**in** *s: STATE*);
read	(**in** *s: STATE*; **out** *a: ANSWER*)
correct	(**in** *s: STATE*; *a: ANSWER*): *BOOLEAN*
message	(**in** *s: STATE*, *a: ANSWER*)
process	(**in** *s: STATE*, *a: ANSWER*)

All these routines share the state s as parameter, coming from the top module *session* (where it is known as *current*). The flow of data, pictured below, shows that the state's presence is far too pervasive. As a result, all the above routines must perform some form of case discrimination on s, as in

       case s **of**
            $State_1:$ ...,
            ...,
            $State_n:$ ...
      end

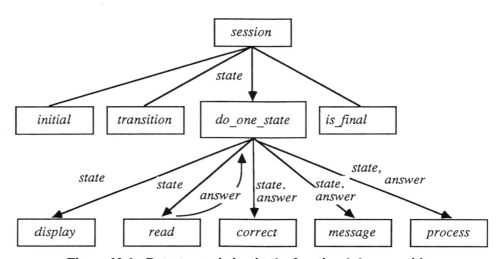

Figure 12.6   Data transmission in the functional decomposition

So here again is a long and complex control structure, with too much knowledge distribution all over the system. Every routine knows about all states in the application. This will make extensions very hard to implement, as adding a new state, for example, will entail modifications throughout the software.

The situation is in fact even worse than it appears. It would seem desirable to profit from the similarity that exists between all interactive applications of the general class studied here by storing the common parts as routines in a library. But this is impossible in practice: all the above routines depend on the particular application (such as airline reservation), which should be added as explicit parameter if the routines were to be made fully general. This means that a general-purpose version of *display*, for example, should know about all states of all possible applications in a given environment! Function *transition* should contain the transition graph for all applications. This would be unmanageable.

12.3.4   The law of inversion

What went wrong? In general, too much data transmission in a software architecture, as evidenced here by figure 12.6, points to a flaw in the design. The remedy, which leads directly to object-oriented design, may be expressed by the following rule:

> **The law of inversion**: If there is too much data transmission in your routines, then put your routines into your data.

Instead of building modules around operations (as *session*, *do_one_state* etc.) and distributing the data structures between the resulting routines, with the effects seen above, object-oriented design does the reverse: it uses the most important data structures as the basis for modularization, attaching each routine to the data structure to which it applies most closely.

This law is the key to obtaining an object-oriented design from a classical functional decomposition: reverse the viewpoint and attach the routines to the data structures.

It is of course best to design in an object-oriented fashion from the beginning; then no "inversion" is needed. However the process of moving from a functional decomposition to an object-oriented structure is interesting in itself, if only because most people have been originally exposed to functional methods and will often come up initially with architectures that are too functional. After such a false start, one must isolate the most important data abstractions, which will serve as basis for the modules in an object-oriented architecture. How can they be found?

Data transmission provides a good clue to answer this question. The data structures that get constantly transmitted back and forth between routines are obviously important. Here the first candidate is obvious: the state (*current*, *s*). Our object-oriented solution will thus include a class *STATE* implementing the corresponding abstract data type. Among the features of a state are the five routines of level 1 on figure 12.5, describing the operations that are performed in a state (*display*, *read*, *message*, *correct* and *process*), and the routine *do_one_state*, as seen above, but without the state parameter. In Eiffel notation, the class has the following general form:

class *STATE* **export**

    next_choice, display, read, correct,
    message, process, do_one_state

feature

    user_answer: ANSWER;
    next_choice: INTEGER;

    do_one_state **is**
        do
            ... Body of the routine ...
        end;

display **is** ...;

read **is** ...;

correct: BOOLEAN **is** ...;

message **is** ...;

process **is** ...;

    end -- class *STATE*

The features of the class include two attributes: *next_choice* and *user_answer*; the other six are routines. Each routine, as compared to its counterpart in the functional decomposition, has lost its explicit *STATE* parameter, which of course reappears in calls made by clients:

s: STATE; *b: BOOLEAN*; *choicecode: INTEGER*; ...
s.do_one_state; *s. read*;
b := s.correct; *choicecode := s.next_choice*;
etc.

In the previous approach, *do_one_state* returned as result the user's choice for the next step. However this this is not in line with the principle of separation between commands and queries (7.7.2). It is preferable to treat *do_one_state* as a command, whose execution may change the answer to the query "what choice did the user make in the last state?", itself available through attribute *next_choice*.

Similarly, the *ANSWER* parameter to the level 1 routines is now replaced by the secret attribute *user_answer*. The reason is information hiding: client code does not need to look at answers except through the interface provided by the exported features.

12.3.5 Inheritance and deferred features

Not all the routines of *STATE* may be given in full detail. Routine *do_one_state* and attribute *next_choice* are common to all states; but the others are state-specific.

Inheritance and deferred classes provide the solution. At the *STATE* level, we know the following: routine *do_one_state* in all detail; attribute *next_choice*; the existence of the level 1 routines (*display* etc.) and their specifications, but not their implementations. These routines should be deferred; class *STATE*, which describes a set of abstractions, the set of possible states, rather than a single abstraction, is a deferred class. This gives:

deferred class *STATE* **export**

    next_choice, display, read, correct,
    message, process, do_one_state

feature

    user_answer: ANSWER; -- Secret attribute

    next_choice: INTEGER;

```
do_one_state is
            -- Execute the actions associated with the current state
            -- and assign to next_choice
            -- the user's choice for the next state.
      local
            ok: BOOLEAN
      do
            from
                  ok := false
            until
                  ok
            loop
                  display; read; ok := correct;
                  if not ok then
                        message
                  end
            end; -- loop
            process;
      end -- do_one_state

display is
            -- Display the panel associated with current state
      deferred
      end; -- display;

read is
            -- Return the user's answer into user_answer
            -- and the user's next choice into next_choice
      deferred
      end; -- read;

correct: BOOLEAN is
            -- Return true if and only if user_answer is a correct answer
      deferred
      end; -- correct

message is
            -- Output the error message associated with user_answer
      require
            not correct
      deferred
      end; -- message;
```

> *process* **is**
>   -- Process user's answer
>   **require**
>   *correct*
>   **deferred**
>   **end**; -- *process*
>   **end** -- class *STATE*

Specific states will be defined by descendants of *STATE*, providing implementations of the deferred routines. An example would look like:

> **class** *ENQUIRY_ON_FLIGHTS* **export** ...
> **inherit**
>
>   *STATE*
>
> **feature**
>
>   *display* **is**
>   **do**
>   ... specific display procedure ...
>   **end**;
>
>   ... and similarly for *read, correct, message* and *process* ...
>
> **end** -- class *ENQUIRY_ON_FLIGHTS*

This architecture separates, at the exact grain of detail required, the elements that are common to all states and those that are specific to individual states. Common elements are concentrated in *STATE* and do not need to be redeclared in descendants of *STATE* such as *ENQUIRY_ON_FLIGHTS*. The open-closed principle is satisfied: *STATE* is closed in that it is a well-defined, compilable unit; but it is also open, since any number of descendants may be added at any time.

STATE is typical of classes that embody the common behavior of a large number of possible objects. Inheritance and the deferred mechanism are essential to capture such behavior in a self-contained reusable component. Other typical examples include a class that embodies the facilities needed to test any class (exercise 12.6) and one that provides a general "history facility" and other facilities commonly needed by interactive systems (exercise 12.5).

12.3.6   Describing a complete system

To complete the example, we must also adapt the routine that was the top (main program) of the functional decomposition: *session*. But now we now better. As discussed in chapter 4, the "top" of the top-down method is mythical: most real systems have no such thing – at least if the top is meant to be a routine ("*the* function of the system"). With few exceptions, large software systems perform a number of functions, each of which is equally important. Here again, the abstract data type approach is more appropriate; it considers the system, taken as a whole, as an abstract entity capable of rendering a certain number of services.

Here the obvious candidate is the notion of **application**, describing a specific interactive system such as the airline reservation system. It makes sense to associate with this concept a full-fledged abstract data type, which will yield a class, say *APPLICATION*, at the design and implementation stages. For although *APPLICATION* will clearly have among its features the routine *session* describing the execution of an application, there are many more things we may want to do on an application – each of which will naturally be turned into a feature of the class. Examples come immediately to mind:

- Add a new state.
- Add a new transition.
- Build an application (by repeated application of the preceding two operations).
- Remove a state, a transition.
- Store the complete application, its states and transitions, into a database.
- Simulate the application (for example on a line-oriented display, or with stubs replacing the routines of class *STATE*, to check the transitions only).
- Monitor usage of the application.

and so on.

Renouncing the notion of "main program" and seeing *session* as just one feature of class *APPLICATION*, adds considerable flexibility.

The features of the class will include the remaining elements at levels 2 and 3 on figure 12.5. The following implementation decisions appear appropriate.

- The transition function is represented by a two-dimensional array *transition* of size $n \times m$, where n is the number of states and m the number of possible exit choices.

- States are numbered 1 to n. A one-dimensional array *associated_state* yields the state corresponding to any integer in the interval $1..n$. Note, however, that numbers are associated with states with respect to a given application only; there is no "state number" attribute permanently associated with a state.

- The number of the initial state is kept in the attribute *initial_number* and set by the routine *choose_initial*. For final states, the convention is that a transition to pseudo-state number 0 denotes session termination; normal states have positive numbers.

- The *Create* procedure of *APPLICATION* uses the *Create* procedures of the library classes *ARRAY* and *ARRAY2*. The latter describes two-dimensional classes and is patterned after *ARRAY*; its *Create* takes four parameters, as in *a.Create (1, 25, 1, 10)*, and its *entry* and *enter* routines use two indices, as in *a.enter (1, 2, x)*. The bounds of a two-dimensional array a are *a.lower1* etc.

Here is the class describing applications:

```
class APPLICATION export
      session, first_number, enter_state,
      choose_initial, enter_transition, ...
feature
      transition: ARRAY2 [STATE]; associated_state: ARRAY [STATE];
            -- (Secret attributes)

      first_number: INTEGER;

      Create (n, m: INTEGER) is
            -- Allocate application with n states and m possible choices
      do
            transition.Create (1, n, 1, m);

            associated_state.Create (1, n)
      end; -- Create

      session is -- Execute application
      local
            st: STATE; st_number: INTEGER;
      do
            from
                  st_number := first_number;
            invariant
                  0 ≤ st_number; st_number ≤ n ;

            until st_number = 0 loop
                  st := associated_state.entry (st_number);
                  st.do_one_state;
                  st_number :=
                        transition.entry (st_number, st.next_choice)

            end -- loop
      end; -- session

      enter_state (st: STATE; number: INTEGER) is
            -- Enter state st with index number
      require
            1 ≤ number;
            number ≤ associated_state.upper
      do
            associated_state.enter (number, st)
      end; -- enter_state
```

choose_initial (*number: INTEGER*) **is**
      -- Define state number *number* as the initial state
  require
      1 ≤ *number*;
      number ≤ *associated_state.upper*
  do
      first_number := *number*
  end; -- *choose_initial*

enter_transition (*source, target, label: INTEGER*) **is**
      -- Enter transition labeled *label*
      -- from state number *source* to state number *target*
  require
      1 ≤ *source*; *source* ≤ *associated_state.upper*;
      0 ≤ *target*; *target* ≤ *associated_state.upper*;
      1 ≤ *label*; *label* ≤ *transition.upper2*;
  do
      transition.enter (*source, label, target*)
  end -- *enter_transition*

... *Other features* ...

invariant

      transition.upper1 = *associated_state.upper*
end -- class *APPLICATION*

An interactive application will be represented by an entity, say *air_reservation*, declared of type *APPLICATION* and handled as follows. The application is created by

    air_reservation.Create (*number_of_states, number_of_possible_choices*).

The states of the application must be defined separately as entities declared of descendant types of *STATE* and created. Each state, say *s*, is assigned a number *i* with respect to the application:

    air_reservation.enter_state (*s, i*).

One state, say the state numbered i_0, is chosen as initial:

    air_reservation.choose_initial (i_0)

Each transition (from state number *sn* to state number *tn*, with label *l*) is entered by

    air_reservation.enter_transition (*sn, tn, l*)

This includes exit transitions, for which *tn* is 0.

The application may now be executed by *air_reservation.session*.

During system evolution one may at any time use the same routines to add a new state, a new transition etc. The class may of course be extended, either by itself, or through the addition of descendants, to accommodate more features such as the ones mentioned earlier: deletion, simulation etc.

EXERCISES

12.1 Windows as trees

Class *WINDOW* (12.1) inherits from *TREE* [*WINDOW*]. Explain the generic parameter. Show that it yields an interesting clause in the class invariant.

12.2 Is a window a string?

A window has an associated text, described (page 273) by an attribute *text* of type *STRING*. Rather than having this attribute, should *WINDOW* be declared as an heir to *STRING*?

12.3 Doing windows fully

Complete the design of the *WINDOW* class, showing exactly what is needed from the underlying terminal handling mechanism.

12.4 Undo-redo in Pascal

Explain how a solution imitating the undo-redo technique of 12.2 may be implemented in Pascal, Ada (using record types with variants) or C (using structure and union types). Compare with the object-oriented solution.

12.5 A history mechanism

A useful feature to include in a command-oriented interactive tool is a history mechanism which remembers the last commands executed, and allows the user to re-execute a previous command, possibly modified, using simple mnemonics. Under Unix, for example, you may direct the C-shell (a command language), to remember the last few executed commands; then you may type *!–2* to mean "re-execute the next-to-last command", or *ˆyesˆnoˆ* to mean "re-execute the last command, replacing the characters *yes* in the command text by *no* ".

   History mechanisms, when they exist, are built in an ad hoc fashion. On Unix, for example, many interactive tools running under the C-shell, such as the Vi editor or the dbx debugger, would greatly benefit from such a mechanism but do not offer one. This is all the more regrettable that the same concept of command history and the same associated facilities are useful for any interactive tool independently of the functions it performs – command language, editor, debugger.

   Design a class implementing a general-purpose historic mechanism, in such a way that any interactive tool needing such a mechanism will obtain it by simply inheriting from that class. (Note that multiple inheritance is essential here.)

   Discuss the extension of this mechanism to a general *USER_INTERFACE* class that can be used to quickly produce interactive tools.

12.6 Testing environment

Proper testing of a software component, for example a class, requires a number of facilities to prepare the test, input test data, run the test, record the results, compare them to expected results etc. Define a general *TEST* class that defines an appropriate testing environment and may be inherited by any class in need of being tested. (Note again the importance of multiple inheritance.)

13

Constants and shared objects

Often, components of a software system will need to access constant or shared information.

An example of constant information is the value of a global system parameter (such as the size of the available memory), which is determined during initialization and then used by several modules. An example of shared information is, in an interactive system, an object representing a message window on the screen: various modules of the system may need to send output to this window, and hence need to access the same associated object.

A solution is to pass the common value or object as a routine argument; but this soon becomes clumsy if too many components need it. Besides, argument passing assumes that one module owns the value and then passes it on to others; in the case of truly shared values, this is inadequate.

In classical programming, it is not difficult to provide for shared objects: just declare them as global variables, owned by the main program. But in the decentralized style of design made possible by object-oriented techniques, there is neither a main program nor global variables. How do we allow components to share data in a simple way, without jeopardizing their autonomy, flexibility and reusability?

This chapter presents a set of solutions. It begins with the straightforward case of symbolic constants of simple types and continues with shared instances of class types. The device introduced to handle the latter case, "once functions", will prove to have a wider range of applications, in particular for strings. The chapter ends with a discussion of the decisions that led to the design of the language features presented.

13.1   CONSTANTS OF SIMPLE TYPES

Symbolic constants of simple types (integer, boolean, character, real) are treated in Eiffel as class attributes, which simply happen to have fixed values for all instances of the class. The syntax, straightforward, is illustrated by the following examples:

> *Zero: INTEGER* **is** *0*;
> *Ok: BOOLEAN* **is true**;
> *Pi: REAL* **is** *3.1415926524*;
> *Percent: CHARACTER* **is** *'%'*;

As these examples indicate, the recommended convention for names of constant attributes is to start with a capital letter.

The value of a constant attribute may not be redefined in a descendant class.

Like other attributes, constant attributes are either exported or secret; if exported, they may be accessed by clients of the class through dot notation. If C is the class containing the above declarations and x is declared of type C, then $x.Percent$ denotes the percent character (if x is not *Void*).

In contrast with other attributes, constant attributes do not occupy any space at run-time in instances of the class. Thus there is no run-time penalty for adding as many constant attributes as needed. In this respect, constant attributes are similar to macros.

Recall that values of *CHARACTER* type are single characters. Constants of string type, denoting character strings of arbitrary length, will be discussed below.

13.2   USE OF CONSTANTS

Constants defined in a class may be used in client classes as suggested above. An example is the use of constants as error codes, as in the following extract from a class describing files:

> **class** *FILE* **export**
>   *open, ...* (*other I/O primitives*) *...*
>   *error_code,*
>   *Ok, Open_error, ...* (*other I/O error codes*) *...*
>
> **feature**
>   *error_code: INTEGER*;   -- Normal (non constant) attribute
>   *Ok: INTEGER* **is** *0*;
>   *Open_error: INTEGER* **is** *1*;
>   *...*;

```
open (file_name: STRING) is
        -- Open file with name file_name
        -- and associate it with current file object
    do
        error_code := Ok;
        ...
        if "something went wrong" then
            error_code := Open_error
        end
    end; -- open
    ...
end -- class FILE
```

A client may call *open* and compare the resulting error code to any of the constants to test how the operation went:

```
f: FILE; ...
f.open;
if f.error_code = f.Open_error then
    "Appropriate action"
else
    ...
```

Often, however, a group of constants is needed without being attached to any particular object. For example, a system performing physics computations may use some numerical constants; or a text editor may need character constants describing the character keys associated with various commands. In such a case, the constants will still be grouped in a class (where else could they be?), but there will not be any instances of that class; it is simply used as parent for the classes that need to access the constants. The scheme is the following:

```
class EDITOR_CONSTANTS feature -- No export clause needed

    Insert: CHARACTER is 'i';

    Delete: CHARACTER is 'd'; -- etc.

    ...
end -- class EDITOR_CONSTANTS

class SOME_CLASS_FOR_THE_EDITOR export ... inherit

    EDITOR_CONSTANTS;
    ... Other possible parents ...
feature ...

    ... Routines of the class have access to the constants
    ... declared in EDITOR_CONSTANTS ...
end -- class SOME_CLASS_FOR_THE_EDITOR
```

A class of this sort is used only to introduce constants that other classes will access through inheritance, and does not at first sight appear as an "abstract data type implementation" (our working definition of the notion of class). But it definitely serves a useful purpose.

Note that in practice a class such as *SOME_CLASS_FOR_THE_EDITOR* may also use inheritance in the standard way, requiring one or more "true" parents. So the technique used here for introducing constants would not work without multiple inheritance; in a single-inheritance environment, constant definition classes such as *EDITOR_CONSTANTS* would fight with the main "true" parent over parental rights.

13.3 CONSTANTS OF CLASS TYPES

The need to refer to fixed values through identifiers arises not only for values of simple types, but for objects of class types as well. However the case of constants of class types is slightly more delicate.

13.3.1 Manifest constants are inappropriate for class types

As typical example, assume a class describing complex numbers, such as

> **class** *COMPLEX* **export** ... **feature**
>
>> *x, y: REAL*; -- Real and imaginary parts
>>
>> *Create* (*a, b: REAL*) **is**
>>> **do**
>>>> *x := a*; *y := b*
>>>
>>> **end**; -- *Create*
>>
>> ... Other features ...
>
> **end** -- class *COMPLEX*

Then class *COMPLEX* or one of its clients or descendants may need to use the complex number i, with real part 0 and imaginary part 1.

It may seem necessary to have a notation similar to what was shown above for simple types: a declaration of the form

> *i: COMPLEX* **is** "Expression specifying the complex number (0, 1)"

It is not clear, however, how the expression after the **is** should be written. Constants of simple types use what is called a **manifest constant**: a notation that unambiguously denotes a value of a type obvious from the context. For example, *345* is a manifest constant of type integer, *'A'* is a manifest constant of type character etc. But there are no manifest constants of class types.

We could devise a notation for manifest constants of class types; perhaps something like *COMPLEX* (*0, 1*). However such a possibility would defeat the principles of modularity which serve as the basis for the whole object-oriented method. Were it available, the clients of *COMPLEX* which need constants of this type would have to know exactly what the attributes of *COMPLEX* are. Then the designer of *COMPLEX* could not add a secret attribute, or re-implement an attribute such as *x* as a function (a real possibility if one decides to switch internally to a polar representation), without rendering invalid all the clients that have declared such constants. This runs contrary to every principle that we have seen.

Besides, how can we make sure that such manifest constants will satisfy the class invariant if there is one?

This last remark opens the way to a correct solution. As pointed out in chapter 7, ensuring that objects conform to the class invariants as soon as they are created is the role of procedure *Create*. It would thus be unreasonable to allow creation of objects other than through *Create* (or the other safe primitive, *Clone*). This leads us to reject the whole idea of manifest constants of class types, and to treat constants of class types more as functions of a special form.

13.3.2 Once functions

Constants of class types may indeed be viewed as functions. For example *i* could be defined within class *COMPLEX* itself as

> *i: COMPLEX* **is**
> > -- Complex number with real part 0 and imaginary part 1
> **do**
> > *Result.Create (0, 1)*;
> **end** -- *i*

This works, since the function will always return a reference to an appropriate object. But it is a waste of time and space: each use of *i* in the client will result in the creation of a new object, although all such objects are identical.

To deal with such cases, Eiffel provides the notion of a **once function**. A once function is identical to a standard function, except that its body will only be executed the first time the function is called in the system that includes it (at most once, hence the name); subsequent calls will not execute the body any more, but simply return the same value as the first call.

A once function is declared in exactly the same way as a normal function, except that the keyword **do** introducing the body is replaced by **once**. So *i* may be declared as

> *i: COMPLEX* **is**
> > -- Complex number with real part 0 and imaginary part 1
> **once**
> > *Result.Create (0, 1)*;
> **end** -- *i*

This declaration yields the desired effect. The first time function *i* is called in a system's execution, its body will be executed: an appropriate object will be created and the function will return a reference to that object. This reference will be remembered by the Eiffel run-time system, so that subsequent calls will return the same reference without allocating a new object.

From an efficiency viewpoint, accessing *i*, beyond the first access, is only marginally slower than accessing an attribute.

13.3.3 Shared objects

For class types, as you may have noted, the "once" mechanism actually offers constant *references*, not necessarily constant *objects*. The mechanism guarantees that the body of the function is executed only once, and that the result computed by this first call is repeatedly returned by subsequent ones without further execution of the body.

If the function returns a value of a class type, its body will usually contain a *Create*, as in the example of *i*. All calls will return a reference to the object created by the first. Although the *Create* will never be executed again, nothing prevents callers from modifying the object through the reference. Therefore the mechanism provides **shared** objects rather than constant ones.

An example of a shared object is a window used to show error messages in an interactive system. Assume the interactive system includes a class *WINDOW* of the following form, used to manipulate areas on the screen:

```
class WINDOW export
        set_text, ...

feature

        Create (...) is
                ... Arguments to Create indicate the size and position
                        of the window on the screen ...
                do ... end -- Create;

        text: STRING;      -- Text to be displayed in window

        put_text (s: STRING) is
                        -- Put text s in window
                do
                        ...;
                        text := s
                end; -- put_text

        ...
```

In case a component of the system detects a user error, it outputs a message in a certain window reserved for that purpose. This will be done by

message_window.put_text ("Appropriate error message")

The same *message_window* is used by all components of the system. It is appropriately described by a once function:

```
message_window: WINDOW is
                -- Window where error messages will be output
        once
                Result.Create ("size and position arguments")
        end; -- message_window
```

Here the message window object must be shared by all its users, but it is not a constant object: each call to *put_text* changes the object by putting its own chosen text in it. (Exercise 13.1 discusses where attribute *message_window* should be declared).

Thus once functions provide a mechanism for constant references and shared objects.

13.3.4   Once functions returning results of simple types

Once functions have further applications. One of these applications is to represent global system parameters, used by several classes in a system. These parameters will usually be constant over a given system execution; they are initially computed from user input, or from some other parameter obtained from the environment. For example:

- The components of a low-level system may need to know the available memory space, obtained from the environment at initialization time.

- A terminal handler may start by querying the environment about the number of terminal ports: once obtained, these data elements are then used by several modules in the application.

Such global parameters are similar to shared objects as seen above; but in general they are values of simple types rather than class instances. They may be represented by once functions returning results of simple types. The scheme is the following:

```
const_param: T is
        -- A parameter computed only once
    local
        envir_param: T'        -- Any type (T or another)
    once
        "Get the value of envir_param from the environment";
        Result := "some value computed from envir_param"
    end -- const_param
```

As with class types, the body of a once function returning a result of a simple type is only executed the first time the function is called. Subsequent calls will always return the same value, without further computation. Thus once functions of simple types describe dynamically computed constants.

Assume the above code is in some class *ENVIRONMENT*. Any class that needs to access the value of *const_param* will get it by simply listing *ENVIRONMENT* among its parents. There is no need here for an initialization routine as might be used in classical approaches to compute *const_param*, along with all other global parameters, at the beginning of system execution. As was seen in chapter 2, such a routine would have to access the internal details of many other modules, and hence would violate the criteria and principles of modularity: decomposability, few interfaces, information hiding etc. In contrast, classes such as *ENVIRONMENT* may be designed as coherent modules, each of which describes a set of logically related global parameters. The first component that requests the value of a global parameter such as *const_param* at execution time will trigger its computation from the environment.

> The introduction to this chapter mentioned that argument passing is inappropriate for a truly shared value, because none of the modules that use the value have more claim to own it than any of the others. This is especially true in the cases just seen: if, depending on the order of events in each execution of the system, any one among a set of modules may trigger the computation of the value, it would be improper to designate any single one among them as the owner.

13.3.5   Once procedures

The "once" mechanism is useful not just for functions but for procedures as well.

A once procedure may be useful when some facility used on a systemwide basis must be initialized, but it is not known in advance which system component will be the first to use the facility. It is like having a rule that whoever comes in first in the morning should turn on the heating.

A simple example is a graphics library containing a certain number of display routines. The first display routine to be called in a given system execution must set up the terminal. Of course, this can be enforced by requiring clients of the library to perform an initialization call before the first display call. However this is a nuisance for clients and does not really solve the problem anyway: to deal properly with errors, any routine should be able to detect that it has been called without proper initialization; but if it is smart enough to detect this case, the routine might just as well do the initialization and avoid bothering the client with need to take care of it in the first place! This may be done in a simple fashion through a once procedure:

```
check_setup is
        -- Perform terminal set-up if not done yet
    once
        terminal_setup -- Actual set-up action
    end --
```

Then every display routine in the library should begin with a call to *check_setup*.

13.3.6   Arguments

Once routines – procedures and functions – are syntactically identical to normal routines, with the exception of the keyword **once** replacing **do**. In particular, they can have arguments. But because of the way the mechanism is defined, these arguments are only useful in the call that gets executed first; because subsequent calls have no effect, their arguments are useless.

In terms of the above analogy, imagine a thermostat dial which anyone coming into the building may turn to any marking, but such that only the first person to do so will set the temperature: subsequent attempts have no effect.

13.3.7   Once functions and redefinition

Once functions of class types carry a serious potential risk in a strongly typed language with inheritance like Eiffel. If not dealt with carefully, they could result in violations of the type system. The problem arises in connection with redefinition and declaration by association.

Assume a class *A* with just one attribute, and a descendant *B* that adds one attribute:

class *A* **feature**
    x: INTEGER
end

class *B* **inherit** *A* **feature**
    y: CHARACTER
end

Assume now that *A* also includes a once function *f*, returning a result of type *A*:

f: A **is do** *Result.Create* **end**;

and that *B* redefines *f* as returning a value of type *B*:

f: B **is do** *Result.Create* **end**;

This is permitted by the fundamental typing rule, since *B* is a descendant of *A*.

Let us see what may happen at run-time. Assume that the first evaluation of *f* appears in

a1.Create;
a2 := a1.f

where *a1* and *a2* are declared of type *A*. The evaluation of *f* creates an object of type *A*, and associates it with entity *a2*, also of type *A*. Fine. But assume now that a subsequent use of *f* is

b2 := b1.f

where *b1* and *b2* are of type *B*.

According to the standard typing rules, if *f* were a normal function, this would be perfectly legal: since the result type of *f* is redefined to *B* in class *B*, *b1.f* is of type *B* and may be assigned to *b2*. But this does not work with once functions! The result of *f* has already been evaluated, so this new call will return a reference to the object created by the first call – an object of type *A*, not of type *B* as the client is entitled to expect.

A reference to an object of type *A* has been assigned to an entity of type *B*, a proper ancestor of *A*. That's the wrong way around! Any subsequent attempt to access *b2.y* will wreak havoc, even though *y* is a valid attribute of class *B*. We have violated the golden rule of the Eiffel type system: that a set of classes accepted by the compiler will never attempt at run-time to apply a feature to an object for which the feature is not defined.

The problem is easy to spot: a once function declared in a class is conceptually like an attribute whose value in all instances of the class and its descendants is a reference to a single shared object. Thus the class and its descendants must have a compatible view of the attribute's type. This precludes any redefinition of this type.

Once the problem has been recognized, the solution is straightforward: disallow redefining the result type of a once function. This also implies that the result of a once function may not be declared by association (**like** *anchor*, see 11.4), which implies automatic redefinition in every descendant. In fact, *f* could have been declared by association in *A* in the above example:

f: **like** *Current* **is do** *Result.Create* **end**;

avoiding the explicit redefinition in *B*, but with the same risk of inconsistency at run-time.

This gives rise to a rule restricting the use of once functions. Besides prohibiting redefinition, the rule also takes into account another potential danger, which would arise if the result type were allowed to refer to a formal generic parameter of the class in which a once function is declared. In

    class *C* [*T*] ... **feature**
        f: T **is once** ... **end**
    end

the instances of *C* may involve various actual types for *T*; the same inconsistency might arise as with redefinition. The problem also arises if the type of *f* is not directly *T* but refers to *T*, as in *D* [*T*].

The rule for once functions follows from these remarks:

> **Once function rule**: The result type of a once function may not be redefined in a descendant class; it may not be of the form **like** *something*; it may not refer to a formal generic parameter.

In the Eiffel system, violating the third part of this rule (generic parameters) produces a warning message, but does not prevent compilation of the class. This is because some violations may be harmless. An example having to do with memory management is discussed in 16.5.3 (see exercise 16.5). Violation of the first or second part is a fatal compilation error.

Note that the first prohibition of the rule applies to redefining the *type* of a once function, not its body. A once function may be redefined in descendants, provided its type remains the same. The version used is the one that gets computed first. Although an appropriate convention could be devised to allow the redefinition of a once function into a normal function or conversely, such manipulations appear more confusing than useful and are prohibited.

13.4   CONSTANTS OF STRING TYPE

At the beginning of this chapter, character constants, with single character values, were introduced. The syntax was illustrated by

    Percent: CHARACTER **is** *'%'*;

Often, classes will also need symbolic constants representing multi-character strings. As stated in 8.7, there is a notation for manifest string constants, using double quotes. For example:

(S1)

> *Message: STRING* **is** *"Syntax error"*

Recall that *STRING* is a class of the Eiffel library, not a simple type. So the value associated with an entity such as *Message* at run-time is an object (an instance of *STRING*). As you may have guessed, the above declaration is a shorthand for the declaration of a once function, here of the form:

(S2)

> *Message: STRING* **is**
>> -- String of length 12, with successive characters
>> -- *'S', 'y', 'n', 't', 'a', 'x', ' ', 'e', 'r', 'r', 'o', 'r'*
>
> **once**
>> *Result.Create (12)*;
>> *Result.enter (1, 'S')*;
>> *Result.enter (2, 'y')*;
>>
>> ...
>> *Result.enter (12, 'r')*;
>
> **end**

(The *Create* procedure for strings takes as argument the expected length of the string; *enter* (i, c) replaces the i-th character with c.)

Such string entities are therefore not constants but references to shared objects. Any part of the system that has access to *Message* may change the value of one or more of its characters.

In principle, the notation for manifest string constants, "...", is syntactically not an expression, but an abbreviation for a **once...end** function body, as in (S2). This would imply that a manifest constant cannot be passed as actual argument to a routine; rather than

(S3)

> *message_window.display ("CLICK LEFT BUTTON TO CONFIRM EXIT")*;

the correct form would be

(S4)

> *Message: STRING* **is** *"CLICK LEFT BUTTON TO CONFIRM EXIT"*;
>
> ...
> *message_window.display (Message)*

For obvious reasons of convenience, however, form (S3) is permitted and interpreted as equivalent to (S4). Similarly, the following is accepted and correctly handled:

> *greeting := "Hello!"*

Thus a manifest string constant is in fact treated as an expression; its evaluation will produce the same result as if it had been defined as a once function.

13.5 DISCUSSION

In this discussion, the term "global parameters" refers to both global constants and shared objects; "initialization" of a dynamic constant includes object creation in the latter case.

13.5.1 Initializing globals and shared objects: language approaches

One of the problems addressed by this chapter is an instance of a quite general programming issue: how to deal with global constant and shared objects, and particularly their initialization in libraries of software components.

Since the initialization of a global parameter should be done just once, the more general question is how to enable a library component to determine whether it is the first to request a certain service.

The issue may be reduced to an apparently simple one: how to share a boolean variable and initialize it consistently. We can associate with a global parameter p, or any group of global parameters that need to be initialized at the same time, a boolean indicator, say *ready*, which has value true if and only if initialization has been performed. Then any access to p in the library will be preceded by

> **if not** *ready* **then**
>   "*create or compute p*";
>   *ready* := **true**
> **end**

But of course this only moves the problem further, as *ready* itself is a global parameter that must somehow be initialized to false before the first attempt to access it.

A common solution in block-structured languages such as Algol or Pascal is to use for *ready* a global variable, that is to say a variable declared at the highest syntactical level. The main program will do the initialization. But this does not work in the case of a library of autonomous modules which, by definition, is not connected to any specific main program.

In Fortran, a language designed to allow routines to be compiled separately (and thus to enjoy a certain degree of autonomy), the corresponding solution is to include all global parameters, and in particular *ready* indicators, in a shared data area called a common block, identified by its name; every subroutine accessing a common block must include a directive of the form

> *COMMON /common_block_name/ data_item_names*

But there are two problems with this approach:

• First, the names of common blocks used by designers of two different sets of routines may conflict when the routines are combined. Changing one of the names is dangerous as, by nature, common block names will be shared by several routines, to which the change must be propagated; errors resulting from incomplete propagation will be hard to spot.

• The other problem is initialization of entities in a common block, such as our *ready* indicators. Because there is no default initialization rule, any data in a common block must be initialized in a special module called a "block data" unit.

Before Fortran 77, there was just one block data unit, which made it very hard to combine routines depending on global data. In Fortran 77, block data units may be named; this means that routines using global data may be combined in various contexts – provided programmers do not forget to include all the relevant block data units. A serious risk of accidental inconsistency exists.

The C solution is conceptually almost identical to the Fortran 77 technique. The *ready* indicator should be declared in C as an "external" variable, common to more than one "file" (the C compilation unit). Only one file may contain the actual definition and initial value of the variable (false in our case); others will state that they need this variable by including an **extern** declaration, which corresponds to the Fortran COMMON directive. The usual practice is to group such definitions in special "header" files, with names conventionally ending with **.h** under Unix; they correspond exactly to the block data units of Fortran. Not surprisingly, the same problems arise. Under Unix, however, the second problem (maintaining consistency by not forgetting to include necessary definitions with a module) is alleviated by the presence of the "Make" tool, which helps programmers keep track of file dependencies.

A solution would appear to be at hand with modular languages such as Ada or Modula 2 (chapter 18) where routines may be gathered in a higher-level module, or "package" in Ada terms: if all the variables, constants and routines used by a group of related global parameters are in the same package, the associated *ready* indicators may be declared as boolean variables in the same package, which will also contain the initialization. This solution is also applicable in the last two languages considered, Fortran 77 and C, if one uses multiple-entry subroutines in the former or, in the latter, files containing more than one routine (see chapter 17).

But this technique does not address the problem of initialization in autonomous library components. Its equivalent in Eiffel is trivial: when several routines of the same class need to share a parameter, it may be represented as an attribute of the class and initialized by the *Create*. The serious question discussed in this chapter is what to do when objects or parameters must be shared between routines in **different** modules. Ada, Modula, C and Fortran provide no new answer in this case. In C and Fortran, the techniques seen above (common blocks, shared definition files) will be required; in Ada, packages may be nested in bigger ones, hampering the autonomy and reusability of components.

In contrast, the "once" mechanism preserves the independence of classes, but allows context-dependent initializations.

13.5.2   Manifest string constants

Eiffel allows string constants (or more properly, as we have seen, shared objects) to be declared in manifest form, using double quotes: "..." (S1). A consequence of this policy is that the Eiffel language definition, and any Eiffel compiler, must rely on the presence of class *STRING* in the Eiffel library. This is slightly annoying, as it is desirable to make the language and its compiler as independent as possible from the availability of any particular library classes. But the technique chosen is a compromise between two extreme solutions:

- *STRING* could have been a simple type. This, however, would have meant adding all string operations (concatenation, substring extraction, comparison etc.)

as language constructs, making the language considerably more complex, even though only few applications require all these operations. Some applications do not even need strings at all. Furthermore, the applications using strings may need operations that the designer of Eiffel, despite his great wisdom, will have overlooked; or they may want to substitute special implementations for some of the available operations. All this suggests that *STRING* should be a class, with all the associated mechanisms. In particular, arbitrary classes should be permitted to inherit from *STRING* .

• On the other hand, treating *STRING* as just any other class precludes manifest constants: this means that the "..." notation (S1) is not available, and that the characters may always be entered one by one through successive applications of *enter*, as was shown in (S2). This would be rather harsh on the poor programmers, and not very elegant.

As a result, *STRING* is treated as a class – the only class with manifest constants. The compiler must know about this class to process such constants correctly.

In the current implementation of Eiffel, there is only one other class known to the compiler: *ARRAY* . In this case, the reason is not a conceptual requirement but just efficiency: although *enter* and *entry* are conceptually routines, access to and modification of array elements should not imply the overhead of routine calls.

13.5.3 Enumerated types

In the first example of this chapter, showing the use of integer constants, you may have noted the absence of enumerated types in the Pascal style. Pascal allows the declaration of a variable

>   *code: ERROR*

with a type definition of the form

>   **type** *ERROR* = (*Normal, Open_error, Read_error*)

Being declared of type *ERROR* , *code* may only take the values of this type: the three symbolic codes given.

The equivalent effect may be obtained in Eiffel by defining the symbolic codes as integer constants, and *code* as an integer attribute:

(A)

>   *Normal: INTEGER is 0*;
>   *Open_error: INTEGER is 1*;
>   *Read_error: INTEGER is 2*;
>   *code: INTEGER*

It is appropriate here to constrain the value of *code* by an invariant in the class:

(A')

>   *Normal <= code*; *code <= Read_error*

Normal, Open_error and *Read_error* are standard integer constants. Since invariants can only be strengthened in descendants, the possible values of *code* could be further constrained in a descendant class (to just two possible values, for example), but not extended.

Inheritance notwithstanding, the run-time effect of the above construction is the same as with the Pascal version; any reasonable Pascal compiler will represent values of an enumerated type by integers. (A good compiler may take advantage of the small number of possible values to represent entities such as *code* by short integers.) The only significant difference is that Eiffel programmers have to come up with the integer values (here 0, 1, 2), whereas in Pascal the compiler concocts them itself.

Another technique for representing enumerated types in Eiffel, using once functions, is the object of exercise 13.2. This technique does not require an explicit choice of integer values.

Introducing Pascal-like enumeration types would be a conceptual disaster in Eiffel: they would conflict with the type system of the language, which is otherwise simple (the four simple types on the one hand, and class types on the other). It does not seem feasible to combine this notion elegantly with inheritance.

Note that enumerated types raise some semantic problems even in non-object-oriented languages. In particular, the status of the symbolic names is not clear. Should they be considered reserved words? Can two enumerated types share one or more symbolic names (as *Orange* both in type *FRUIT* and in type *COLOR*)? Are they exportable and subject to the same visibility rules as variables?

A further argument against enumeration types is that they would be difficult to pass to and from routines written in other languages, such as C or Fortran, impairing the openness of the Eiffel environment.

We could allow *entities*, not types, declared by enumeration. This would mean permitting

(B)
> *code:* (*Normal, Open_error, Read_error*)

as a mere abbreviation for (A) and (A') above. As the three symbolic codes are now considered to be normal constants, they are subject to the standard language rules with respect to exportation, inheritance and other issues.

Such a convention would simply be a syntactical facility and would not be difficult to implement. But since the benefit gained – relieving programmers from the need to assign integer values to possible symbolic codes – did not seem to justify the addition of a new language feature, useful only in specific cases, the feature was kept out of the language.

In general, Eiffel is a somewhat ascetic language. The emphasis in its design has been on devising powerful notations for the most advanced and the most common constructs, rather than shorthands for all possible cases. The aim was to make Eiffel a member of the class (including Pascal and, before the 1977 standard, Fortran) of languages that serious programmers usually master entirely, as opposed to those of which most programmers know only a subset (the examples of PL/I and Ada spring to mind). The size of Eiffel, measured by such criteria as the number of keywords or the number of syntactical constructs, is comparable to that of Pascal. The benefits of such economy of design in terms of ease of learning, ease of use, ease of debugging, decreased error rates and more generally programmer's self-confidence, should offset such annoyances as the need to choose integer values once in a while.

Why this conviction that enumerated constants, coded in Eiffel as (A) and (A'), will only be needed occasionally? True, enumerated types are commonly used in Pascal or Ada. But if you look at their legitimate uses in these languages, you will note that most of them are of a form similar to

type *FIGURE_SORT* = (*Circle, Rectangle, Square, ...*)

to be used as discriminants in a record type with variants:

> *FIGURE* =
> > **record**
> > > *perimeter: INTEGER*;
> > > *... Other attributes common to figures of all types ...*
> > > **case** *fs: FIGURE_SORT* **of**
> > > > *Circle:* (*radius: REAL*; *center: POINT*);
> > > > *Rectangle: ... attributes specific to rectangles ...*;
> > > > *Square: ...*
> > > > ...
> > > **end**
> > **end**

Entities of a record type with variants are usually processed by case instructions discriminating on the different variants, as in

> **var** *f: FIGURE*;
> ...
> **procedure** *rotate* (*f*);
> > ...
> **begin**
> > **case** *f* **of**
> > > *Circle: ... appropriate actions to rotate a circle ...*;
> > > *Rectangle: ...*;
> > > *Square: ...*
> > > ...

But of course we know better. In an object-oriented language this is not how we should tackle problems of this sort. Rather than a type with a fixed set of alternatives, we should define a deferred class *FIGURE*, with a deferred version of procedures such as *rotate*, and descendant classes declaring specialized versions of these procedures. We have seen the advantages of this technique in terms of flexibility and reusability.

Since this most important application of enumeration types (in languages such as Pascal or Ada) is superseded in object-oriented programming by a judicious use of inheritance and dynamic binding, it seems reasonable, in the few remaining cases of declaration by enumeration, to pass on to the programmers the small burden of assigning integer values to the elements of the enumeration.

13.6   KEY CONCEPTS INTRODUCED IN THIS CHAPTER

- A challenging problem in any programming language is how to allow for parameters or objects that must be shared by various modular components, and initialized at run-time by whatever component happens to need them first.

- Manifest constants of simple types are declared in Eiffel as attributes, occupying no space in objects.

- Eiffel has neither enumerated types nor case instruction.

- Except for strings, there are no manifest constants of class types.

- A once routine, which differs from a normal function by one keyword, **once** instead of **do,** is evaluated only once during a system's execution: the first time it is called by any component of the system. In the case of a function, subsequent calls return the same value as the first (a simple value, or a reference to an object); in the case of a procedure, subsequent calls have no effect.

- Constants of class types and shared objects may be implemented as once functions. The two cases are actually identical: only references are constant; the objects they refer to are shared.

- Once procedures are used for operations that should be performed only once over the execution of a system.

- The type of a once function may not be redefined, and it may not be declared by association.

- Constants of string types are treated internally as once functions, although they appear to the user as manifest constants written in double quotes.

13.7   SYNTACTICAL SUMMARY

			Used in (chapter)
Constant	=	Integer_constant |	Feature_value (5)
		Character_constant |	Expression (8)
		Boolean_constant |	
		Real_constant |	
		String_constant	
Integer_constant	=	[Sign] Integer	
Sign	=	'+' | '–'	
Character_constant	=	"'" Character "'"	
Boolean_constant	=	**true** | **false**	
Real_constant	=	[Sign] Real	
String_constant	=	'"' String '"'	
Once_body	=	**once** Compound	Full_body (8)

13.8   BIBLIOGRAPHICAL NOTES

The difficulties raised by enumerated types in programming languages (cf. page 318) are studied in [Welsh 1977] and [Moffat 1981].

EXERCISES

13.1   Sharing a message window

In the message window example (page 310), various components of an interactive system share an object representing a window, accessible through the feature *message_window*, implemented as a once function. In what class should *message_window* be declared?

13.2   Emulating enumerated types with once functions

Show that a Pascal enumerated type of the form

type *ERROR* = (*Normal, Open_error, Read_error*)

may be represented by a class with a once function for each value of the type, alleviating the need to invent explicit integer codes.

13.3   Once functions in generic classes

Give an example of a once function whose result involves a generic parameter (page 314), and, if not corrected, would yield a run-time error.

14

Techniques of object-oriented design

The object-oriented style of design is characterized by a set of distinctive techniques. Many of them have already been mentioned in passing, but a group portrait, as given in this chapter, should help you confirm your mastery of the method.

14.1 DESIGN PHILOSOPHY

Let us first review some basic features of the object-oriented approach to system design.

14.1.1 The structure of systems

In a pure object-oriented approach, classes provide the only system structuring mechanism. Classes should be considered as autonomous entities; although they may be connected by strong relations – client and inheritance – they are all at the same level from the language point of view. As opposed to procedures (in Algol 60, Pascal etc.) or packages (in Ada), classes may not be nested within each other. (This is true of Eiffel. Some languages, notably Simula 67, do permit class nesting; experience shows, however, that this facility is not commonly used, as it yields overly complex structures. In particular, nesting tends to be either in conflict or redundant with inheritance.)

This autonomy of software components is essential for reusability. With textual nesting as available in block-structured languages, it is difficult to construct libraries of components that may be freely reused and combined.

14.1.2 The shopping list approach

A class is a repository of services (exported features) available on the instances of an abstract data type. A key aspect of the method is what has been called the shopping list approach (4.3.2), meaning that these services are made equally available to clients: there is no notion of relative importance or merit; neither is there any constraint on the order in which services may be called. Both of these properties are important.

The first was emphasized in the discussion classes *WINDOW* and *APPLICATION* in chapter 12: what in a functional approach would be considered "the" main function of a system is demoted in an object-oriented architecture to the status of one among equals.

The second aspect has to do with the order in which various facilities offered by some system or subsystem are called. It is often a mistake to freeze this order too early, as sequencing of actions is one of the aspects of system architecture that tends to change most often during development and evolution. In object-oriented design, the facilities of a module are just there for other modules to use in the order they desire.

This refusal to concentrate too early on sequential constraints is, in my view, one of the key differences between object-oriented design and techniques like data-directed design or JSD, Jackson's System Design method (see the bibliographical notes to chapter 4). In these methods, the order in which transformations are applied to items of data is viewed as an important factor in system design. The risk is that any change in the order requirements will imply painful redesign if they were used as primary criteria for devising the architecture.

Note that order constraints on the use of facilities from a module may often be described more abstractly through assertions. For example, an order constraint might specify that, in a stack module, any sequence of *pop* calls must have been preceded by at least the same number of *push* calls. However the assertions on *pop* and *push*, deduced from the abstract data type axioms of stacks, express the same property more abstractly, without reference to order of calls.

14.1.3 Add as many facilities as needed

A consequence of the shopping list principle is the absence of any theoretical reason for limiting the number of features in a class. If an operation has a well-defined semantics and is logically related to a data abstraction, then no soul-searching is required: you may include it in the corresponding class, even if you are not certain that many clients will need it. (In the Eiffel implementation, the overhead on clients which do not use the facility is negligible; see 15.4.4.)

The only potential limitation is one of complexity: any class should remain of manageable size. The limits, however, are not as strict as with classical approaches. Software engineering textbooks often tell you to limit the size of any program unit to one or two pages to enable a reader to comprehend it quickly. This applies to traditional methods, where program units are routines. A routine is a unit of algorithmic decomposition; in general, you must grasp the whole routine to understand any of its elements. With classes, the situation is different: if a class is viewed as a shopping list of features, a client programmer only needs information on the features that he actually uses, plus some general properties of the class such as the invariant. In general, features you do not know about cannot harm you.

The features themselves must remain easy to understand individually and thus short. In a good object-oriented design, each routine does one well-defined job. Routines are usually shorter than in functional design and seldom reach one page.

Although a class may be much longer than a program unit in traditional decompositions, its size must still remain within reasonable bounds. These bounds may be expressed in terms of number of features, rather than text length.

Absolute figures are hardly meaningful. It is safe to say, however, that 20 features (attributes and routines) is a good size for a class; at about twice that number, the programmer responsible for the class should start wondering whether all these features really belong to the same conceptual level. If, as is usually the case, two or more levels of abstraction may be identified, inheritance should be used to ensure that every class remains manageable. The fundamental features will be described in a first class; the next logical set of features will be handled by an heir to that class; and so on.

14.1.4   Bottom-up design

Although one may envision top-down object-oriented design techniques, bottom-up design seems to blend much better with the approach.

"Top-down" and "bottom-up" are, of course, extreme characterizations. One never sets out to build a system without considering available facilities; conversely, one never builds software components without some preconceived idea of their future use. The difference is that the top-down designer concentrates on the specific problem at hand, whereas his bottom-up colleague works as much as possible from existing components and, when finding out that a new component must after all be produced, tries to make it general so that future developments may use it.

Classes naturally lend themselves to bottom-up reuse, extension and combination. The more software you develop in this way, the easier it becomes to develop new products, as you can build on your previous tools. Here inheritance is fundamental.

> "Top-down" and "bottom-up" have been used here in their general meaning for software design, as studied in chapter 4. You may wonder how these terms apply to inheritance. Is the process of adding new descendants to existing classes top-down or bottom-up? As a matter of fact, both qualifiers would apply: top-down because a class describes a more abstract notion than its descendants; bottom-up since a class builds on the basis provided by its ancestors. We already encountered this duality when noting that inheritance was specialization from the type perspective and extension from the module perspective.

14.1.5   Influence on the software design process

The various aspects of object-oriented design seen so far, if practiced properly, considerably affect the software process. Traditional approaches are characterized by the extreme difficulty of the first design steps: the decisions taken then are crucial; any mistake will have far-reaching consequences.

In this respect, top-down development appears as an almost impossible recipe. Since the architecture is hierarchical, and built from the top, you are asked to make the most important decisions at the very beginning – when you have the least information at your disposal to avoid design errors! This is typically the time when the picture is still vague; many elements are missing and designers often have the impression of being overwhelmed with complexity and unable to sort the essence from the details. And yet it is then that you have to make the key choices, with the knowledge that any error will be catastrophic! Only a genius could do this.

In contrast, object-oriented design spreads out the decisions more evenly over the development cycle. Initially, you must find the key data abstractions. Of course, it is better not to make mistakes, but if (for example) you forget an important abstraction, there is nothing irreparable: you will add the missing class later. Because of the highly decentralized nature of object-oriented architectures, this is often achieved without much impact on other classes developed in the meantime. When it comes to refining individual classes, the shopping list approach gives a smooth design process, in which features are added in an incremental, progressive fashion.

These remarks should not be construed as meaning that the problems of software design vanish if you use the object-oriented method. Building quality software has always been and will remain a difficult task. But with object-oriented design, because the difficult decisions are not concentrated at the beginning, there is less of the tension in design meetings, feeling of helplessness against complexity and fear of making disastrous mistakes which are so characteristic of the first stages of a traditional project. You still have to work hard and to pay for your errors; but you can approach problems in a more decentralized, more balanced, calmer way.

14.2 FINDING THE CLASSES

When introducing the object-oriented approach, we briefly discussed the question "how does one find the objects?" (4.6). As we now know, the proper question is about finding **classes** of objects with a common behavior.

There is, of course, no absolute answer, which would amount to an infallible technique for designing software – which is no more likely to exist than an infallible method to prove theorems or design buildings. Talent and experience are an inevitable part of any success in design. But some general insights may be given.

14.2.1 External objects

Perhaps the most useful technique for finding classes, introduced in 4.6, is to look for meaningful external objects. Many classes just describe the behavior of objects from the abstract or concrete reality being modeled – missiles and radars, books and authors, figures and polygons, windows and mice, cars and drivers.

This idea often yields the fundamental classes of a system, obtained directly from their external counterparts. This is one of the key ideas of object-oriented design: consider software construction as operational modeling, and use the object classes of the modeled world as basis for the classes in the software system.

14.2.2 Existing classes

Another naive yet fruitful way to find classes is simply to look at what is available. As recalled above, the object-oriented approach favors bottom-up design. A good object-oriented environment will offer a number of predefined classes implementing important abstractions. Designers will naturally look into these to see if there is anything they can reuse. For example, the classes offered by the Eiffel library cover much of the routine of software development – lists, trees, stacks, queues, files, strings, hash tables, binary trees etc. – and get constantly reused.

14.2.3   Previous developments

The advice of looking first at what is available applies to user-developed classes, not just to general-purpose libraries. As you write applications, you will accumulate classes which, if properly designed, should facilitate later developments.

Not all reusable software was born reusable. Often, the first version of a class is produced to meet some immediate requirement rather than for posterity. If reusability is a concern, however, it pays to devote some time, after the development, to making the class more general and robust, improving its documentation, adding any missing assertions. This is different from the construction of software meant from the start to be reusable, but no less fruitful. Having evolved from components of actual systems, the resulting classes have passed the first test of reusability, namely *usability*: they serve at least one useful purpose.

14.2.4   Adaptation through inheritance

When you discover a potentially useful existing class, you will sometimes find that it does not exactly suit your present need: some adaptation may be necessary.

Unless the adaptation addresses a deficiency which should be corrected in the original as well, it is generally preferable to leave the class undisturbed, thus preserving its clients according to the open-closed principle (2.2.5). Instead, you may use inheritance and redefinition to tune the class to your new need.

14.2.5   Evaluating decompositions

Criticism is said to be easier than art, and you can learn to analyze existing designs as a way to learn design. In particular, when a certain set of classes has been proposed for solving a certain problem, you should study them from the criteria and principles of modularity (chapter 2): do they constitute autonomous, coherent modules, with strictly controlled communication channels?   Often, the discovery that two modules are too tightly coupled, that a module communicates with too many others, that an argument list is too long, will pinpoint design errors and lead to a better solution

In a similar vein, the example of full-screen entry systems (12.3) highlighted a frequent mistake: complex data flow in a system, which almost always points to the presence of a neglected data abstraction, which should be made into a class (*STATE* in the example). This occurs in particular in object-oriented systems written by designers who – like most people – were initially trained in classical methods, and will often leave a dose of function-oriented design in their system architectures.

The rule "criticize and improve existing designs" is not by itself a solution to the design problem. But good object-oriented design, as good design in any discipline, must be taught in part by apprenticeship and experience.

14.2.6 What is not a class

Some authors have suggested that a good way to find the classes for the object-oriented design of a system is to start from its requirements document and to underline the nouns – whereas a functional method would result from concentrating on the verbs. For example, a sentence from the requirements document in the form "the radar must track the position and speed of incoming airplanes" would lead a function-oriented designer to detect the need for a tracking function, whereas the object-oriented designer will see two classes, radar and airplane.

This is only a simple-minded technique, however, and it can only give rough first results. If followed to the letter, it is likely to yield **too many** candidate classes. For example it is not clear that two of the nouns in the above sentence, "position" and "speed", should yield classes.

Creating unneeded classes is a typical novice's mistake. But again, there is no sure method for avoiding such mistakes. After all, several of the successful designs discussed in previous chapters resulted from elevating a seemingly unimportant notion to the status of class: think of the "state", "interactive application" and "command" examples in chapter 12. The general guideline is the theory of data abstraction: a notion should only be made into a class if it describes a set of objects characterized by interesting operations (the functions of the underlying abstract data type), with meaningful properties (the axioms).

So, should the "position" of airplanes yield a class? It depends. If there is no specific operation on positions, then just let class *AIRPLANE* have three real attributes representing a plane's position. If, on the other hand, a position is a meaningful entity, with associated operations (distance to another position, measurement error, conversion to another coordinate system etc.), then it is worthwhile to define a class *POSITION* and let *AIRPLANE* include an attribute of this type. The same goes for speed: if a plane's speed is just a real number, or a vector, use one of these types; if it has useful properties of its own, define a specific class (perhaps a descendant of class *VECTOR*).

14.2.7 The grand mistake

The practice of object-oriented design shows that the most common and most damaging mistake is also the most obvious one: designing classes that aren't.

The fundamental rule of object-oriented design is to build modules around object types, not functions. This is the first key to the reusability and extendibility benefits of the approach. Yet beginners will fall time and again into the most obvious pitfall: calling "class" something which is in fact a routine. Writing a module as **class**... **export**... **feature**... **end** does not make it a class; it may just be a routine in disguise. Typical symptoms of the disease are an export clause containing just one routine, and the designer's inability to explain the role of the class other than by saying things like "This class does...". In contrast with a routine, a class should not *do* something but offer a number of services (features) on objects of a certain type.

This mistake is easy to avoid once you are conscious of the risk. The remedy is as before: make sure that each class corresponds to a meaningful data abstraction.

14.3   INTERFACE TECHNIQUES

Module interfaces are as important as what the modules do. Let us review some techniques for designing good modular interfaces.

14.3.1   State machines and active data structures

As pointed out in chapter 9, it is often useful, when writing classes that implement data abstractions, to settle on "active" versions of these abstractions: instances are viewed not just as passive collections of information, but as machines with an internal state, and a local memory. The lists of the Eiffel library, which keep a "cursor", or memory of the target position of the last operation, are a typical example.

14.3.2   Queries vs. commands

The strict distinction between procedures and functions has been advocated (7.7.2) as a healthy design principle.

14.3.3   One interface, several implementations

Another interface technique is made possible by inheritance. When a certain notion admits more than one implementation, it is appropriate to define two or more levels: a general class that describes the interface, and descendant classes that provide various implementations, all with the same **export** clause. Examples abound in the Eiffel library: lists, with class *LIST*, and its descendants (*FIXED_LIST, LINKED_LIST, TWO_WAY_LIST*); various implementations of stacks, queues etc.

Often, the top-level class will be a deferred class, as in the examples mentioned. This is not always the case, however, as the most abstract level may be able to provide a default implementation of the various routines needed. An example was the class *POLYGON* (10.1), which was not deferred even though several more specialized versions (*RECTANGLE* etc.) were available.

The advantages of inheritance for describing implementation variants are in particular that two or more variants may be present in the same system, that a given entity may switch representation at run-time (thanks to polymorphism and dynamic binding), and that the mechanism is progressive, as variants may be organized in a multi-level inheritance hierarchy (as in the case of various table implementations).

14.3.4   One implementation, several interfaces

Inheritance also serves to achieve a symmetric aim: providing several interfaces to an underlying notion. This is made possible by the orthogonality of the inheritance and export mechanisms. The general notion may be described by a class that exports nothing; descendants differ by their export clauses. We saw (11.5) the example of a class describing bank accounts, with heirs providing various interfaces to this notion.

14.4 INHERITANCE TECHNIQUES

Inheritance, a major benefit of object-oriented design, should be put to good use.

14.4.1 Redefinition for more efficiency

One major technique is redefinition, which should be used in particular when a better implementation of a general technique may be found in a special case. The *perimeter* function (10.1) provided a typical example. Appendix A includes many more, such as *back*, a costly operation for one-way lists, redefined more efficiently for two-way lists.

14.4.2 Redefining functions as attributes

A particular form of redefinition occurs when an attribute is available to implement a service originally rendered by a function. An example is *last*, a function on linked lists, which in two-way lists may be implemented as an attribute since a two-way list keeps a reference not only to its first element but also to its last one. Such a function may be redefined as an attribute (11.3.3). Recall that the reverse is not permitted.

14.4.3 Preserving semantics

Routine redefinition is a semantics-preserving transformation: the redefined implementation should satisfy the same specification as the original. Whenever possible, the specification is expressed by assertions; the rules on "subcontracting" (11.1) express how semantics is preserved in this case.

Similarly, any class is bound by the invariants of its parents. This is another expression of the same principle: any instance of the heir must satisfy the constraints imposed on instances of the parents.

Sometimes, it is tempting to override these rules – especially since, in the current Eiffel implementation, assertions are only checked on explicit request, and only at run-time. If, for example, you need a class describing circular lists, you may be tempted to build it as an heir to *LINKED_LIST* as found in the library (A.5). *LINKED_LIST* indeed provides the basic implementation mechanisms.

But some of the properties of *LINKED_LIST* would be violated by circular lists: for example, one clause in the invariant of *LINKED_LIST* is

   previous.Void = (*offleft* or *isfirst*);

which implies that *previous.Void* must be satisfied whenever *isfirst* is true, that is to say, whenever the current *position* index has value 1. This is true for sequential linked lists, but not for circular lists, as shown on the figure below.

The temptation to reuse a class for its implementation only, violating some of its semantic constraints, must always be resisted. Reusability should not be attained at the expense of correctness; inheritance loses its meaning if classes are allowed to reject arbitrary parts of their ancestors' properties.

The situation may be different when inheritance is used for knowledge representation, as in artificial intelligence. In an archaeological knowledge base, a property of the class of amphorae might be that amphorae have either one or two handles. If one day you discover a new kind with three handles, you may still want to treat it as heir to the original class. But in software engineering correctness and robustness are essential, and there can be no exception to the rule about preserving semantics.

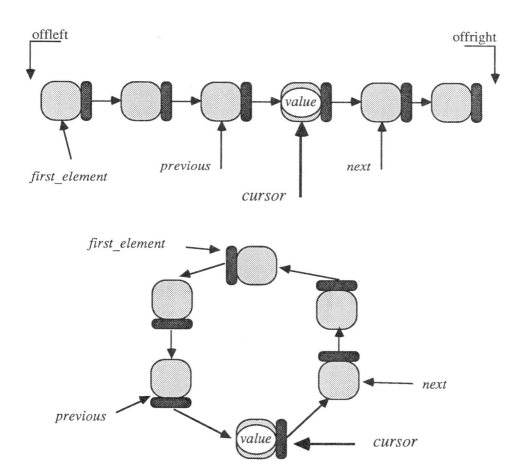

Figure 14.1   Sequential list, circular list

14.4.4   Specialization vs. generalization

Inheritance has been presented as the *is-a* relation, that is to say, specialization. Sometimes, however, development goes the other way around: we do not necessarily conceive the most general abstraction first. You may realize after a while that a certain class is too specific. The example just seen is typical: the notion of list used in *LINKED_LIST* and *TWO_WAY_LIST* is too constrained to be applicable to other similar structures, for example circular lists.

Once this has been recognized, you will usually want to correct the error by designing a new, more general class. Here we may introduce *CHAIN*, describing a more abstract notion of list, generalizing both *LINKED_LIST* and *CIRCULAR_LIST* (exercise 10.5). What is needed in such a case is a way to describe a class as generalization of another. One may fancy a language mechanism that would be the reverse of inheritance: a **generalize** clause, mirroring **inherit**.

No such mechanism exists in Eiffel; it would require techniques for specifying what to keep and what to remove in a generalization. But help is provided by the tools of the environment. One option of the **short** class abstracter (9.5) is the **-e** option (for "Eiffel output"), which will generate the class interface in the form of a correct Eiffel deferred class, where all routines are deferred. If the original class was too specific, applying **short -e** to it is a good way to generate a completely deferred class with the same specification. The result may then be edited to remove unwanted properties.

Once the more general class has been obtained, the initial, too specific class should be redefined as one of the heirs of that new class. This is easily done by adding one item to its inheritance clause, for example adding *CHAIN* to the parents of *LINKED_LIST*. Note that here the original must be modified; the open-closed principle is not satisfied, even though the modification is minimal.

The underlying assumption is that specialization is a normal design process, which should work smoothly and should not impact the classes being specialized, whereas generalization is more the correction of design omissions: the realization that a certain notion had initially been understood in a way that was too restricted, or too dependent on one among several possible implementations. In this view, a certain amount of superficial modification is acceptable when an existing class is redefined as a specialized version of a new, more abstract notion.

14.4.5   Inherit general-purpose facilities

One use of inheritance, although more elementary than the above techniques, is worth recalling. A set of general-purpose facilities may be packaged into a class and inherited by any class that needs them. These facilities may be routines (as the routines of a mathematical library) or constants (as a group of related physical constants).

A standard use of this technique in Eiffel is for input and output. Class *STD_FILES* (see Appendix E) provides basic facilities on the predefined files *input*, *output* and *error*. A simple class needing these facilities will simply inherit from *STD_FILES*, as in

> **class** *SIMPLE* **inherit** *STD_FILES* **feature**
> > *Create* **is**
> > > **do** *output.putstring_nl* (*"Hello Mary!"*) **end**
> **end** -- class *SIMPLE*

(Recall that an equivalent class was given in 5.7.4, where *SIMPLE* was a client of *STD_FILES* rather than an heir. The recommended form is the one given here.) No redefinition or polymorphism is involved in such cases, which use classes not as abstract data type implementations but just as a packaging mechanism.

This technique is only possible because of multiple inheritance: with single inheritance, a class such as *STD_FILES* would conflict with the "true" parents.

14.5   WOULD YOU RATHER BUY OR INHERIT?

In some cases when a class B needs a facility from A, there may be some hesitation as to the relation that should be used: should B be an heir of A, or a client?

The general answer is that inheritance and the client relation correspond to different needs. Put simply, inheritance means "is", client means "has". Inheritance is appropriate if every instance of B may also be viewed as an instance of A. The client relation is appropriate when every instance of B simply possesses one or more attributes of type A.

This simple criterion suffices in cases where only one answer is acceptable. For example, novices sometimes use inheritance improperly. A typical mistake is to declare, say, *HOUSE* as heir to both *DOOR* and *FLOOR*. Of course, this is wrong, as no stretch of imagination will convince anyone that a house *is-a* door or a floor. A house merely **has** these components.

There are cases in which the answer is less clear-cut. The following two examples are typical:

- When a class *STACK2* describing stacks implemented by arrays was defined before the introduction of inheritance (7.3.2), it used an attribute *implementation*: *ARRAY* [T]. Later we rewrote a class *FIXED_STACK* that inherits from *ARRAY*, using multiple inheritance.

- Assume you want to write a window-oriented text editor, that acts on a window. Should it have an attribute *current_window* of type *WINDOW*, or should *WINDOW_EDITOR* inherit from *WINDOW*?

Here the second example appears to favor the client relation, as it seems that an editor "has" (acts on) a window, rather than "is" a window. But only a slight change of perspective is needed to reverse this view: instead of calling the class *WINDOW_EDITOR*, call it *EDITABLE_WINDOW*, representing windows that may be subjected to editing operations (adding or deleting lines, words, characters etc.).

In such cases, there may be arguments in favor of both approaches. Inheritance yields a simpler and more efficient access to features of the original class. For example, class *STACK2* must access all array features through attribute *implementation*, so that its function *top* needs to use *implementation.entry* (*nb_elements*) where the version based on inheritance can use just *entry* (*nb_elements*), which is better both for simplicity of writing and for efficiency. A further advantage of inheritance is its flexibility: thanks to redefinition, you may reuse operations from the parent without necessarily keeping their implementations; you override any implementation that does not suit you. Types of inherited entities may also be redefined. No such possibilities are offered when you access a class through its interface.

On the other hand, inheriting is a more committing decision than "buying" (becoming a client). In the Eiffel framework, when you buy from A, you only see A from its interface; hence you are protected against future changes in its implementation. When you inherit from A you gain access to its implementation, which gives you more power but no protection. (The rationale for this approach was given in 11.5.)

The decision in each case should be based on your evaluation of the respective importance of these criteria. Contrary to many people who view inheritance with suspicion (especially multiple inheritance), I tend to be quite bold about using it and have seldom regretted it. In the stack example, inheritance seems definitely better; I have also used it in (a more refined version of) the editor example.

14.6 BIBLIOGRAPHICAL NOTES

The literature on object-oriented design (as opposed to just programming) is sparse. Some discussions, regarding in particular the proper use of inheritance, may be found in [Halbert 1987]. [Meyer 1986] describes an object-oriented formal specification method.

A discussion of design techniques that have proved useful in the development of industrial object-oriented software with Eiffel may be found in [Gindre 1988]. Of particular interest are the advice given on how to obtain reusable classes, the recommended software development strategy (by successive layers rather than an overall specify-design-implement lifecycle), and the publication of actual measurements, especially with respect to reusability (70% of the code for the project studied was made of reusable components, more than half of which were simply obtained from the Basic Eiffel Library and the rest from previous developments by the same group).

The advice to look for nouns in requirements documents may be found in [Booch 1983].

EXERCISES

14.1 Generalization: trees
Class *TREE*, as introduced in 10.4.3 (see also A.7, appendix A), is just one possible implementation of trees (linked trees). Introduce, along the same principles, a more general notion of trees, of which *LINKED_TREE* is just one descendant. You may need to define a more abstract notion of "linkable" than given so far. Check the generality of the tree class obtained by defining at least one other implementation by inheritance (for example *FIXED_TREE*).

14.2 Are polygons lists?
In the sketch of class *POLYGON* (10.1), polygons were defined as having an attribute *vertices*, of type *LINKED_LIST* [*POINT*]. Should *POLYGON* be instead be declared as an heir of *LINKED_LIST*?

15

Implementation: the Eiffel programming environment

For a practicing software developer, methods and languages are only as good as their implementation. This chapter describes how the concepts introduced in the previous chapters may be practically applied in the current Eiffel environment. It presents the Eiffel compiler, its practical use, and the associated tools; performance issues and ongoing developments are also discussed.

15.1 THE IMPLEMENTATION

15.1.1 Compiling

Eiffel is implemented by a compiler. The decision to use a compiler rather than an interpreter is an important one. Interpreted systems such as Smalltalk (chapter 20) are useful for quick program modification and debugging. Compilers bring safety (with a typed language) and efficiency. We shall see below how these goals may be reconciled with some of the benefits of interpreted systems.

15.1.2 Intermediate code

The Eiffel compiler uses C as intermediate language, making Eiffel potentially portable to any environment supporting C. The first implementations run on Unix systems (System V, BSD, Xenix), supporting about 25 different machine architectures. A VAX-VMS version is also available.

C was chosen as an intermediate language for its portability and its relatively low level; C is probably the closest existing approximation to a portable assembly language.

The role it plays for the Eiffel compiler is comparable to the role of P-code (a simple low-level code) for Pascal compilers, or of other intermediate representations traditionally used by compilers, such as quadruples or attributed abstract syntax trees. As readers will by now be convinced, Eiffel itself as a language has not been polluted by C.

Although the form of the generated C is such that one may easily trace it to the original Eiffel thanks to simple naming conventions and automatically generated comments, it is not meant to be maintained by itself. (If it was, there would be no need for languages of a higher level than C!)

An option of the Eiffel compiler makes it possible to generate a self-contained C package from an Eiffel system; this is important for cross-development. This possibility is described in 15.3 below.

15.1.3 Run-time structure

At run-time, the Eiffel object structure is mapped onto C data structures. The following aspects are worth noting.

- Apart from their normal fields, representing class attributes, objects must be equipped with some supplementary information. In particular, every object must carry its **dynamic type**, which is needed for the implementation of dynamic binding (see below). Some further fields are needed by the garbage collector, discussed in the next chapter.

    Note that this **self-referent** aspect of objects (every object includes information about its own type) is not just one possible implementation technique; it is necessary in any implementation of object-oriented concepts if dynamic binding is to work properly. The idea is reminiscent of "tagged architectures" in hardware.

- A data structure providing some information about classes must also be present at run-time: **class descriptors** (see below).

- Finally, the Eiffel run-time system is loaded with the executable machine program resulting from a system compilation; it takes care of memory management including, when requested, garbage collection.

The effect of these various requirements on system performance is studied below.

15.2 COMPILATION AND CONFIGURATION MANAGEMENT

15.2.1 Separate compilation

The compiler will generate for each Eiffel class a C file containing a number of declarations and functions. The functions correspond to the Eiffel routines. The C files may be compiled separately to machine code by the resident C compiler, called automatically by the Eiffel compiler.

15.2.2   Connection with the file system

The link between classes and files is simple: there must be one file per class. If the class is called C, the file name must be $c \, . \, e$, where c is the lower-case version of C (on operating systems that distinguish between upper and lower case for file names). Remember that for Eiffel the distinction between upper and lower case is not significant, although the standard is to write class names in upper case.

The compiler produces a number of files for each class: the generated C code; the generated machine code; and some small files for the compiler's own use. These files are kept in a directory managed by the compiler (by default called $c \, . \, E$ for a class C). In addition, when the C package generation option is used (see below), the compiler will produce a set of C files and a "Make file" in the designated directory.

15.2.3   Compilation commands

There are two commands for compiling classes. The first, **ec** (for Eiffel Class) takes a single class as argument:

> **ec** c

This will compile the class contained in file $c \, . \, e$. (The file name itself may also be used as argument.) The more general command is **es** (Eiffel System), which will compile a whole system, that is to say a set of classes. In its basic form, **es** is called without arguments and relies on a **System Description File** in the current directory (see below).

15.2.4   Configuration management

Both **es** and **ec** will compile zero, one or more classes depending on the context in which they are called. This is because both commands include a facility for configuration management; more precisely, they analyze class dependencies and time stamps to decide what classes should be recompiled.

Configuration management relies on the following two definitions:

> **Definition** (*Direct dependency*): Class B depends directly on class A if B is either a client or a proper descendant of A.

> **Definition** (*Dependency*): Class B depends on class A if there is a class C such that B depends directly on C, and C either is A or depends on A.

In other words, "depends" means "depends directly or indirectly". "B needs A" is used as a synonym for "B depends on A". The notion of dependency yields the definition of an up-to-date class:

Definition (*Up-to-date class*): A class is said to be up-to-date if and only if the following three conditions are satisfied:

1. A compiled version of *A* is available, and *A* has not been modified since this version was produced by the compiler.
2. All classes needed by *A* are up-to-date.
3. None of the classes needed by *A* has been modified since *A* was last modified.

With these definitions, we may express precisely the aim of the compilation commands: **ec** ensures that a class is up to date (in the process, it may recompile other classes); **es** ensures that a whole system is up-to-date. The other results produced by **es** are an executable machine program and, if requested, a C package (see below).

To achieve these goals, the commands will analyze dependencies and determine whether the classes considered and those they depend on are up to date. The latter is achieved by considering the **time stamps** kept by the operating system, which indicate the last time a file has been modified.

To find the classes that a class needs directly, it suffices to look at the class text, where parents are found in the inheritance clause, and suppliers are found in entity declarations such as $x: C$, which indicates that the class is a client of C. To find all directly or indirectly needed classes, the same process must be repeatedly applied to the resulting classes. For this to work, the compiler must know where to look for the file containing a class of a given name. Both **es** and **ec** use a list of directories where needed classes are to be found. For **ec**, this list is specified using the -**n** option:

   ec -n *dir1* -**n** *dir2* -**n** *dir3* ...

For **es**, the same information is given in the SOURCE entry of the System Description File (see below).

15.2.5 More than Make

The facilities described above appear similar to those offered by the Make tool under Unix (or its equivalent on other systems). Make is a system configuration tool which will reconstruct a system based on a "Make file" describing dependencies between modules and, for each dependency, a command to be executed when a module has been modified later than modules that depend on it. A Make file is a list of entries of the form

   $x : a\ b\ c$ ...
      command option1 option2 ... a b c x ...

expressing that x depends on a, b, c, ..., and must be reconstructed using the given command if any of a, b, c has been modified more recently than x. Starting from such a Make file, Make will look at time stamps and automatically reconstruct the system by executing only the commands for which x is not up to date.

Commands **es** and **ec** apply the same principle, but in a much improved way since they are specifically adapted to the Eiffel context. In particular:

• There is no need to write Make files, a tedious and error-prone process. (With Make and Make files, there is always the risk of a forgotten dependency, especially when the software has been modified). The corresponding information is automatically extracted from the software itself, a much preferable approach.

• Being tailored to Eiffel, the commands are able to distinguish between different kinds of dependencies. In particular, the dependency is not the same for parents and suppliers: a class depends on the implementation of its parents, but only on the interface of its suppliers. When a class A is modified, **es** and **ec** will recompile it, but will not recompile its clients unless A's interface has been changed. If the change only affected non-exported features, the clients are left undisturbed. Thus **es** and **ec** find a minimal set of classes to be recompiled, in a way Make could not.

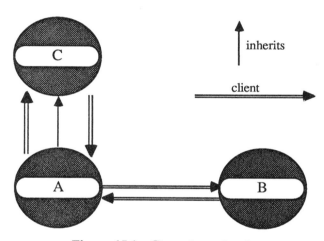

Figure 15.1   Class dependencies

Beyond these advantages, it is important to note that Make is **not** applicable to Eiffel anyway. This is because the relations are more complex than can be handled by Make or similar tools; in particular (see the figure):

• The client relation may be cyclic (A may be a client of B and B a client of A);

• Inheritance is acyclic but may be mixed with the other relation: A may be a client or supplier of one of its ancestors.

Thus class relationships could not be described by the simple non-cyclic dependencies required by Make. In fact, there is no correct compilation order in situations involving cycles. The solution is a four-step, coroutine-like algorithm, in which step i does enough work on all relevant classes to allow step $i+1$ to proceed on the classes that depend on them. The algorithm involved is difficult. (It may be worthwhile to note that at some point during the implementation of Eiffel we started to doubt whether a solution was at all possible in the most general case. We had to produce a formal proof, which in turn suggested the algorithm, providing an example of use of formal methods in software development.)

15.2.6   The open-closed principle

Inheritance is a dependency relation, which affects class compilation and configuration management. To reconstruct a class, information about its proper ancestors (not necessarily in source form) is needed; this is inevitable as the class structure depends on the features declared in its ancestors. As a consequence, the compiled form of a class must keep information about the ancestors. But the reverse is not true: no property of any class, in either source or compiled form, depends on the descendants of the class.

This is in line with our definition of inheritance as an application of the open-closed principle (see 10.2.1). A class is an open structure which must be permanently amenable to new extensions in the form of new descendants. The class has no control over these possible descendants.

These principles are applied not only to the language but to the implementation. When a new class is written that names *A* as one of its parents, *A* and its clients are unaffected; they remain "up to date" if they already were and will not need any recompilation.

15.2.7   The System Description File

Command **es** (the more useful of the two compiling commands) relies on a System Description File, or SDF for short. A template for the SDF is created the first time **es** is called in a certain directory, so that programmers do not need to learn its syntax. The form of an SDF is the following, where elements in italics indicate information to be filled in, if necessary, by the programmer:

ROOT: *Name of the root class*
SOURCE: *Directories where needed classes are to be found*
EXTERNAL: *List of needed external files*
NO_ASSERTION_CHECK (Y\N): *Classes to be compiled with no assertion monitoring*
PRECONDITIONS (Y\N): *Classes to be compiled with precondition monitoring only*
ALL_ASSERTIONS (Y\N): *Classes to be compiled with all assertion monitoring*
TRACE (Y\N): *Classes to be compiled in trace mode*
DEBUG (Y\N): *Classes to be compiled in debug mode*
OPTIMIZE (Y\N): *Classes to be optimized*
GARBAGE_COLLECTION (Y\N) --*Enable garbage collection or not?*
VIRTUAL_MEMORY (Y\N) --*Enable special Eiffel paging or not?*

-- Remaining entries only needed for package generation (next section)

C_PACKAGE (Y\N): *directory where C package will be generated*
C_EXTERNAL: *external .c or .h files*
MAKE: *Make file to compile external files*
VISIBLE (Y\N): *classes whose exported routines will be in the package*

The ROOT entry is the only one that the programmer is required to fill in. Remember (5.6.2) that execution of the system consists in creating an instance of the root class and executing its *Create* procedure (which will normally trigger other object creations and routine executions).

The SOURCE entry lists directories where needed classes are to be found. The generated template initializes this line to contain the directory where the basic Eiffel library resides.

The EXTERNAL entry lists files containing precompiled external routines, used by Eiffel routines through the **external** clause (8.3).

The next few lines list compilation options. For each option, a list of classes is given to which the option applies; the keyword *ALL* may be used in lieu of a list of classes. Each option may be enabled or disabled by typing *Y* or *N* in parentheses (avoiding the need to retype or comment out the list of classes when switching options on and off). In the case of conflicting options, such as the various assertion monitoring levels, the last one specified for each class overrides the other (the order of entries is not significant).

The assertion monitoring options determine the level of run-time assertion checking as defined in 7.10.1: no monitoring, preconditions only or all assertions. PRECONDITIONS is the default.

TRACE enables or disables tracing of routine calls in each class. Routine tracing is a precious tool for debugging and more generally for following the run-time behavior of a system.

The DEBUG entry enables or disables execution of **debug** instructions (8.5.6).

OPTIMIZE governs the optimization option of the C compiler (Eiffel optimization is described below).

The next two entries govern memory management: enable or disable the Eiffel incremental garbage collector and the Eiffel paging system. Memory management issues are discussed in the next chapter.

The last entries are only needed when the C package generator, as described in the next section, is used.

15.3   GENERATING C PACKAGES

In standard Eiffel usage, the C code used internally by the compiler is no more relevant for programmers than any other internal representation maintained by a traditional compiler for any language.

There is another option, however, useful for software developers who must distribute their products to a wide range of users, not all of whom have access to an Eiffel implementation: in such a case, it is possible to produce a complete C package from an Eiffel system. This option is enabled by the Y option in the C_PACKAGE entry of the System Description File.

15.3.1   Contents of a generated package

Remember that an Eiffel system is a set of classes. The C package produced by the package generator will be a set of functions corresponding to the exported routines of certain classes. These classes are selected through the VISIBLE entry of the System Description File.

The package is generated in a directory (a node of the hierarchical file system) and contains:

- The C translation of all classes from the system, in the form of a list of C files, arranged so that only the exported routines (including *Create*) from designated classes are visible (in C form) from other C programs.

- A copy of the Eiffel run-time system, in C form.

- An automatically generated "Make file", or formal dependency list needed to compile the package.

- Some automatically generated documentation.

If external C functions must be included with the package, they are indicated in the C_EXTERNAL entry of the System Description File. Usually, special dependencies must be recorded to compile these (non-Eiffel-generated) functions; a Make file may be given to this effect in the MAKE entry.

The C package generation option thus produces an entirely self-contained package, which may be moved to any machine and recompiled there, independently of any Eiffel tools.

15.3.2   Naming the C functions

When a package is generated, the problem arises of choosing the names under which the generated C functions will be known to the application programmers using them. It would be too tedious for the programmer to have to specify all names; but letting the Eiffel compiler fabricate names would not be very good for clarity. A natural choice is to use the original Eiffel names for the exported routines; but several classes may use the same routine names, which must be disambiguated at the C level. Furthermore, many C compilers only consider the first seven or eight characters of an identifier, whereas there is no such restriction in Eiffel. As a consequence, the following naming policy is used:

- By default, the original Eiffel name is used, truncated to the appropriate number of characters.

- When it detects a conflict, the compiler fabricates names of its own for the second occurrence of an Eiffel name and every subsequent occurrence.

- The compiler produces a correspondence file giving for each Eiffel routine (identified by a class name and a routine name) the corresponding C function name. The programmer is given a chance to edit this file and replace any C name by another; the compiler will then use the names chosen by the programmer. The compiler keeps and updates the correspondence file, so that the programmer will not be forced to retype his choices between successive runs.

The correspondence file is a set of entries such as the following:

Class	Eiffel routine	C name
Window	*display*	*display*
Window	*parent*	*parent*
Window	*height*	*win_height*
Window	*Create*	*win_Create*
....		
Screen	*height*	*scr_height*
Screen	*Create*	*scr_Create*
....		

where the third column has already been edited by the programmer to replace some of the C names generated in cases of conflict.

15.4 PERFORMANCE ISSUES

The Eiffel environment is meant to support the development of serious "production" software, as opposed to just prototyping or experimentation. Hence it was essential to provide efficient compilation and execution.

15.4.1 Compilation speed

As noted above, compilation from Eiffel to C involves four steps. Then **ec** and **es** will call the resident C compiler; **es** will also call the linker.

Typically, the longest part is C compilation and linking. The four Eiffel steps, combined, take about 50% of the time for C compilation and linking when package generation is not invoked. Altogether, thanks to the configuration management facilities described above, the time to recompile a system after a few small changes is usually short – a few minutes on a standard hardware environment – even if the system is very large. Configuration management achieves a good tradeoff between compilation and interpretation: using a compiled approach guarantees safety and speed of the resulting code; configuration management achieves a change-to-retry cycle time which, although longer than an interpreter would permit, is still quite satisfactory.

When the package generator is invoked, it involves three more Eiffel-to-C steps, which bring the Eiffel compilation time to about 80% of the C compilation and linking time. (As seen below, the package generator also performs important optimizations.) Normally, the package generator is only invoked when a system is working and ready for delivery.

15.4.2 Speed of the generated code

A difficult problem arises from the implementation of inheritance and dynamic binding. Assume the call $x.r(\ldots)$, with x declared of class C. The version of r to be used depends on the dynamic type of x, which must be a descendant of C. Let D be this dynamic type; D is known only at run-time and, as we saw, is stored with the object.

To treat the call properly, we must keep a set of class descriptors at run-time; each class descriptor gives access to all the routines of the class. As will be seen in 17.4.2, the class descriptor may be implemented as a list of pointers to routines.

In a naive implementation, the class descriptors are organized into a graph, mirroring the inheritance graph. Then whenever a call of the above form is executed, the graph must be searched for the proper routine, starting at the descriptor for D, continuing (if unsuccessful) with the parents of D, its grandparents etc. This may be called the dynamic routine search method.

Although various "caching" techniques have been described in the literature for speeding up dynamic routine search, the method seems dangerously inefficient. What is particularly worrying is that adding more inheritance levels will make it slower. Inheritance is one of the main object-oriented techniques for reusability; although some overhead is inevitable, a situation of direct conflict between reusability and efficiency is not acceptable. An object-oriented environment in which designers would have to think twice before adding an inheritance level because it would mean degraded performance would be rather unpleasant.

Dynamic routine search seems inapplicable anyway when multiple inheritance is permitted: then a whole graph, not just a list of ancestors, must be searched, leading to unacceptable inefficiencies.

The Eiffel implementation achieves constant-time routine retrieval by representing each class descriptor as an array and using a layout scheme that allows compile-time computation of an index into that array for each routine call. The conflict between more inheritance and more efficiency thus disappears. The mechanism is not free; in our measurements, it adds about 25% to the cost of normal routine calls in standard implementations of classical programming languages such as C. However the price is fixed and, in our experience, acceptable. (See below how the overhead may be totally removed for routines which are never redefined.)

15.4.3   Space

Neither genericity nor multiple inheritance result in code duplication. (Most implementations of Ada duplicate the code of a generic package for every instantiation; published descriptions of how to implement multiple inheritance in Smalltalk require that code for all routines not in the primary lineage be duplicated.) Code may be duplicated, however, in the case of repeated inheritance with feature replication (11.6.3); this is a rare occurrence, in which duplication seems conceptually unavoidable.

A penalty is incurred on both the space occupied by the data – due to the extra fields added to objects, and to the class descriptors – and on the total code size, due to the run-time system.

The overhead on objects amounts to eight bytes per object in our current implementation; if space is a problem, programmers should avoid creating many small objects. The overhead due to class descriptors is usually negligible. The size of the run-time system is about 30 Kbytes.

A further potential penalty on code size, arising from the loading of unused code, is removed by the optimizer, as discussed next.

15.4.4 Optimization

In many implementations of object-oriented languages, two factors contribute serious overhead:

- The mechanism for calling a routine handles possible redefinition; it is too general for routines which are never redefined. This is unfortunate since a significant object-oriented system will usually contain a majority of such routines. Although we have seen that Eiffel avoids variable-time routine search, the penalty cannot be ignored.

- The shopping list approach encouraged by object-oriented design may result in a considerable amount of useless code being loaded together with the routines actually used by an application. This problem may become especially serious with inheritance: designers are tempted to inherit from classes from which they only need a few facilities.

These two problems are solved by an Eiffel optimizer which simplifies calls to non-redefined routines, and removes unneeded code. These optimizations cannot be applied to individual classes: they are only possible on a whole system. For this reason, the optimizer is integrated with the Package Generator (activated when the C_PACKAGE option is enabled in the System Description File for command **es**). The package generator is thus useful not only to produce C packages, but also to obtain optimized code.

If the various optimizations offered by the Eiffel compiler are combined and the appropriate compilation options are selected (NO_ASSERTION_CHECK, OPTIMIZE etc.), the time performance of programs generated by the Eiffel compiler is, using a rough estimate, within 20% of the performance of hand-coded C programs. For space, the figures are those given above.

In highly polymorphic applications, well-written Eiffel systems may actually be smaller than their C counterparts, as complex decision structures repeated in many routines (to test for variants of a data structure, for example whether a figure is a polygon, a circle etc.) are replaced by the simple and uniform mechanism of dynamic binding.

15.5 OTHER ASPECTS OF THE ENVIRONMENT

15.5.1 The library

A key element of Eiffel programming is reliance on the basic library. At the present time, the library covers the common elements of ordinary programming: the fundamental data structures such as lists, trees, stacks, queues, files, strings, hash tables, binary trees etc., encapsulated in classes with the associated algorithms. More library classes (based on the X-Windows graphics package) cover graphical concepts: windows, menus, polygons, circles etc. Others address such applications as parsing, string handling etc. More are under development.

The library classes have been written with great care, using all the mechanisms of the language (multiple inheritance, genericity, assertions, redefinition, renaming), and have been thoroughly exercised. Apart from any other aspect of object-oriented design, transform Eiffel into a much higher-level language where the basic data types would be not just integers, reals etc., but also lists, trees, hash tables and the like – all open to extension and specialization thanks to genericity and inheritance.

One of the most significant practical consequences is that it is not necessary, in everyday Eiffel programming, to explicitly use pointers. Although necessary for non-trivial data structures, pointer manipulations are tricky and error-prone. A look at the internals of the Eiffel library (Appendix A) is sufficient evidence of this; see, for example, deletions in two-way lists, or many other similar operations. But the pointer manipulations in the library are (one may hope) correct, and they have been encapsulated once and for all in the library. In standard situations, the Eiffel programmer will use lists and trees, not pointers and offsets.

15.5.2   Documentation

The documentation tool **short** was presented in 9.5. The command

> **short** c

will yield the interface of class C, contained in file $c.e$. (As with **ec**, the file name may also be used as argument.)

An example output of **short** was given in 9.5.3. It was obtained using the **-t** (troff) option that produces output to be directed to a typesetter for printing with the standard Eiffel conventions regarding indentation, keywords in boldface etc. This is the standard way to produce documentation about Eiffel classes; in particular, the Eiffel library manual [Interactive 1986] is obtained almost entirely from output generated by **short -t** (only the chapter headers are written manually). We have already seen the advantages of such an approach: not only is the documentation obtained essentially for free; more importantly, it is guaranteed to be consistent with the documented software.

15.5.3   Flattening a class

It has already been noted that inheritance is an implementation technique: to the clients of a class, the inheritance structure that led to its design is not relevant.

Thus when a class has been defined through one or more levels of inheritance, it is often useful to present a "flat" version of the class, which shows it as a self-contained module, without reference to any ancestor: all inherited features are copied into the class (taking renaming into account) and the inheritance clause is removed.

To clients of the the class, such a flat version is functionally equivalent to the original. More precisely, the two classes are equivalent as modules, although not as types.

The command

> **flat** c

will produce as output a flat version of class C. (Again, the file name may also be used as argument.) Note that command **flat** must do more than pure textual substitution, since renaming and redefinition must be into account. By injecting the output of **flat** into **short**, which in the Unix command language is done by executing

flat c | **short**

you obtain a complete interface description for C, giving the same type of information for inherited features as for features declared in the class itself. This provides clients with a complete interface description of C.

15.5.4 Graphical exploration of system structures

The above documentation commands apply to individual classes. They are complemented by an important set of tools for controlling the design and analysis of the overall structure of software systems: the **good** (Graphics for Object-Oriented Design) system for graphical creation and exploration of class relationships.

The tools of **good** are based on the graphical conventions used in this book for describing classes and their connections: bubbles for classes, simple arrows for inheritance, double arrows for the client relation. Their user interface uses windows and pop-up menus. Internally, they rely on the graphics classes of the library, mentioned above.

One of the applications of **good** is the analysis of systems: starting with a class, you may see its ancestors, clients etc. This complements at the system level the facilities offered by **short** and **flat** for the analysis of individual classes.

The tools also work in generation mode. You can enter a new class and graphically indicate its ancestors and clients. From the diagrams thus entered, the tools will generate the skeletons of the corresponding Eiffel class texts.

15.5.5 Debugging

Several facilities of the environment support debugging of Eiffel systems. Remember that the C code is not meant for human consumption: all debugging may be done at the Eiffel level. (This is where the Eiffel compiler differs from a C "pre-processor" that would leave programmers in the C world.)

Assertion monitoring has proved to be an invaluable debugging aid if some care is taken to decorate classes and routines with proper assertions. Even when application classes do not include many assertions of their own, the mechanism is useful because of the heavy reliance of typical Eiffel programming on the basic library classes, which have been heavily loaded with assertions (appendix A). Many errors in application classes will give rise to assertions being violated in the basic classes, for example an attempt to insert an element into a list at an illegal position.

The **compiler options** for tracing and debugging are also useful. Tracing, in particular, makes it possible to follow the run-time structure of calls. Output from the tracer will look like

$$In \ r_1, \ class \ c_1, \ object \ n_1$$
$$In \ r_2, \ class \ c_2, \ object \ n_2$$
$$Out \ r_2$$
$$Out \ r_1$$

In r_3, class c_3, object n_3
   In r_4, class c_4, object n_4
      In r_5, class c_5, object n_5
      Out r_5
   Out r_4
Out r_3

showing the hierarchical nesting of calls. The r_i are routine names, the c_i class names. The n_i represent the internal numbers of the objects to which each call applies; the numbers themselves are not directly meaningful, but allow the user to determine whether or not two different calls apply to the same object.

The **viewer** permits run-time exploration of the objects, a particularly important requirement in object-oriented systems. When the viewer is called, the user is given a chance to traverse the object structure, following references. At each step, the contents of an object are displayed; the user may select one of the reference fields by its number, and continue to the corresponding object. A typical session (shown in linear form, although the actual viewer is a full-screen tool), with the user's input in boldface, begins as follows:

Current: TREE_DEMO   Number of fields: 4   Object id: 55f38

   (1)   nb_elements: INTEGER = 5
   (2)   size: REAL = 3.27
   (3)   first_child: reference to TWO_WAY_TREE object (Id: 68e76)
   (4)   active: reference to TWO_WAY_TREE object (Id: 67e31)

   Your command: **3**

Current: TWO_WAY_TREE   Number of fields: 15   Obj_id = 67e31

   (1)   node_value: INTEGER = 0
   (2)   right_sibling: Void reference
   (3)   left_sibling: Void reference
   (4)   position: INTEGER = 1
   (5)   parent: reference to TWO_WAY_TREE object (Obj_id: 55f38)

   ...

(and so on)

The viewer is not just a tool for inspecting objects but in fact a complete interactive debugger, allowing users not only to inspect objects but also to modify them interactively by calling routines, changing values, defining breakpoints, checking invariants etc. The viewer also serves as a testing tool: the **et** (Eiffel Test) command creates an instance of a class and starts the viewer on it; this avoids the need to write a test driver for a simple test that does not have to be kept for later repetition.

The viewer is not built in the compiler but is part of a library class, *VIEWABLE*. To start it, it suffices to call procedure *view (input_file, output_file)* in any class that inherits from *VIEWABLE*. You may also set the viewer to be triggered automatically when a system failure occurs (7.10.3).

15.5.6   Persistent object structures

During their execution, object-oriented systems create and manipulate data (object) structures. It may be necessary to keep these structures between sessions.

Support for storage and retrieval of object structures is offered by the library class *STORABLE*. If the type of x is a descendant of *STORABLE*, and if *fn* is a file name, then

$x.store\ (fn)$

will dump the object structure starting at x, under a specially designed external form, to file *fn*. The object structure may be retrieved, by the same or another system, using

$x.retrieve\ (fn)$

What is stored is the entire object structure referred to by x, directly or indirectly (the shaded objects on the figure below). The external representation preserves the references, and deals correctly with cycles in the data structure. By choosing the right x, you may store the whole object structure of your system, or just part of it.

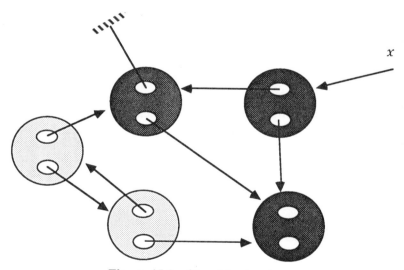

Figure 15.2   Storable structure

Although the system retrieving the objects does not need to be the same as the system that stored them, the classes involved must be the same; otherwise *retrieve* could not make sense of the information it finds in the external form. This is a delicate problem in dealing with persistent object structures, which will be further addressed in chapter 21.

For $x.store$ or $x.retrieve$ to work, the class type of x must be a descendant of *STORABLE*. This is also a sufficient condition: if x refers to an object O, the types of the objects referred to by the fields of O may be arbitrary classes.

15.5.7 Access to internal structures

Normally, the internal object representation is irrelevant to programmers, except for the knowledge that a certain fixed space overhead is incurred for each object.

Special applications, however, may require direct access the internal representation. The case arises in particular in systems that need to manipulate Eiffel objects from other languages; a typical example is an interface with a data base management system, which will be used to store and retrieve Eiffel objects. Existing data base primitives, written in other languages, may be appropriate for this purpose.

Such applications could, of course, use the generated C code directly. But this technique would be difficult to use, and extremely error-prone. Instead, a class *INTERNAL*, encapsulating a set of "clean" primitives for object manipulation, has been included in the Eiffel library.

The primitives of class *INTERNAL* yield such information as the dynamic type of an object and the corresponding class name, the number of fields of the object, the type and value of each field etc. They also provide procedures for dynamically altering this internal structure.

As *VIEWABLE* or *STORABLE*, class *INTERNAL* is meant to be used as an ancestor of any class that needs access to its facilities; such a class may include calls to external (non-Eiffel) routines, to which it may pass internal information about the Eiffel objects.

Class *INTERNAL* is intended for special applications only, and should be used with great care. Since it provides access to internal Eiffel structures, and permits the modification of these structures, it can cause disaster in the run-time behavior of systems if misused.

The following extract from the interface of the class (as generated by **short**) gives an idea of the primitives available in *INTERNAL*.

```
class_name (obj: INTERNAL): STRING
            -- Name of class of object associated with obj
      require
            not obj.Void

field_nb (obj: INTERNAL): INTEGER
            -- Number of fields in obj
      require
            not obj.Void

field_name (i: INTEGER; obj: INTERNAL): STRING
            -- Name of i-th field of obj
      require
            not obj.Void ;
            1 <= i; i <= field_nb (obj)
```

field_type (*i: INTEGER*; *obj: INTERNAL*): *INTEGER*
       -- Type of *i*-th field of *obj*
  require
      not *obj.Void* ;
      1 <= i; i <= field_nb (obj)

  ensure
      -- *Result* gives the type of *i*-th field of *obj*, as follows:
      -- > 0: Reference to object of type *Result* (1 for special object)
      -- 0: Void reference
      -- -1: INTEGER
      -- -2: REAL
      -- -3: BOOLEAN_SET (one or more packed boolean values)
      -- -4: CHARACTER

dynamic_type (*obj: INTERNAL*): *INTEGER*
      -- Dynamic type of *obj* (1 for a special object).
  require
      not *obj.Void*

field (*i: INTEGER*; *obj: INTERNAL*): **like** *Current*
      -- Reference to the object referenced by the *i*-th field of *obj*
  require
      not *obj.Void* ;
      1 <= i; i <= field_nb (obj);
      1 <= field_type (i, obj)
            -- That is to say, the *i*-th field must be an object reference.

free (*obj: INTERNAL*)
      -- Free the memory associated with *obj*
      -- NOTE: use of this facility is at the programmer's risk.
      -- The safe way to handle memory is through garbage collection
      -- (see class *MEMORY*)
  require
      not *obj.Void*

In calls to these primitives, *obj* is usually *Current*. For example, the dynamic type of the current object is given by

dynamic_type (*Current*)

appearing in a class which is a descendant of *INTERNAL* .

The type codes returned by *field_type* and *dynamic_type* include a code (1) for "special objects". Special objects are objects representing arrays or strings; they have to be treated specially because an array or string has a dynamically variable length, whereas instances of any Eiffel class have a fixed size.

The primitives of *INTERNAL* make it possible to write applications that will traverse a complete object structure. Several internal tools of the Eiffel environment indeed rely on *INTERNAL* for this purpose: they include the garbage collector (next chapter), the viewer (procedure *view* in class *VIEWABLE*) and the *store* procedure from class *STORABLE*.

15.5.8   Explicit calls to the garbage collector

The comment introducing procedure *free* above mentions another library class: *MEMORY*. This class enables explicit calls to the public features offered by the Eiffel garbage collector. For example the garbage collector may be triggered, for a limited time, at points where the programmer knows some CPU time will be available, for example during user input. These facilities are described in the next chapter (16.7.1).

The primitives from *MEMORY* are entirely safe. On the other hand, the use of *free* is strongly discouraged in normal situations.

15.5.9   Other tools

Further tools of the environment support various tasks of Eiffel software development. Of particular interest is a specialized syntax-directed editor, which facilitates the development and modification of Eiffel texts.

At the time of writing, a number of other tools are under development.

16

Memory Management

It would be so nice to forget about memory.

Our programs would just create objects as they please. Little by little, objects that are not used would vanish into far-away abysses; those that are needed the most would slowly move closer to the top, as meritorious employees of a large corporation who once in a while manage to get the attention of a higher officer and, by making themselves indispensable to their superiors, will with a bit of luck, at the end of a busy career, be admitted into the inner circle.

But it isn't so. Memory is not infinite; it does not harmoniously organize itself into a continuous spectrum of storage layers with decreasing access speeds, to which objects would naturally distribute. We do need to fire our useless employees, even if we must call it early retirement imposed with regret because of the overall economic situation. This chapter examines who should be thus retired, how, and by whom.

16.1 WHAT HAPPENS TO OBJECTS

Object-oriented programs create objects. Dynamic object creation is one of the most useful features of object-oriented languages.

In Eiffel, creation occurs on execution of an instruction *x.Create* or *x.Clone* (*y*). Other object-oriented languages have equivalent mechanisms.

16.1.1   Models of object management

In the general case – not just object-oriented languages – one may distinguish three models of object creation. Let us stick to the Eiffel terminology and call object an element which exists at run-time, and entity an element of the program text, such as a variable in classical languages, which provides a static (compile-time) handle on such dynamic (run-time) objects.

- In the **static** model, any program entity may be associated with at most one run-time object. This is typical of languages such as Fortran: all entities are allocated once and for all at loading time or at the beginning of execution. This solution precludes recursion, since a recursive subroutine may have several instances active at once, each of which must have its own instances of the entities. It also precludes dynamically created data structures: the exact size of every data structure must be deducible from the program text. Structures that grow and shrink in response to run-time events cannot be accommodated, except by allocating the maximum possible space for each of them.

- In the **stack-based** model, an entity may refer to more than one object; objects associated with a given entity are allocated and deallocated in a last-in, first-out basis. In other words, when an object is deallocated, the corresponding entity becomes associated again with the object it was associated with before allocation of the object (if any). This mode is typical of Algol 60 (which also supports static entities). It enables recursion and arrays with bounds that are only known at run-time, but not dynamic data structures in their full generality.

- Finally, the **free** model (also called heap-based because of the way it is implemented) is the fully dynamic model, whereby all objects are created dynamically by explicit request. An entity may become successively associated with any number of objects; the pattern of object creations is usually not predictable at compile-time. Furthermore, objects may refer to other objects. Thus dynamic data structures of arbitrary behavior may be created.

The last model is clearly the most general. It is often used in conjunction with the first two. Note that it is not specific of object-oriented languages. In fact, it exists in languages as diverse as Pascal (where dynamic objects, whose associated entities must be of pointer types, are created using the *new* procedure), Ada (similar in this respect to Pascal, pointer types being called here "access types"), C (through the *malloc* function), PL/I (for objects of *BASED* mode) and Lisp (where the function *CONS*, used to construct lists, implies the dynamic creation of an object). However it plays a particularly important role in object-oriented languages.

16.1.2   Reclamation

As soon as objects may be created dynamically, the problem arises of what to do when an object becomes useless: is it possible to reclaim the memory space it uses?

In the static model, this is not a pressing issue: every object is associated with an entity; the object's space is needed as long as the entity is active. There is no possibility for reclamation in the proper sense; however, if you are convinced that the objects associated with two entities are never needed together, and each entity need not retain the value of its object between successive uses, you can assign to them the same memory location – if you are really sure of what you are doing. This technique, known as **overlaying** is still, appallingly enough, practiced manually. (If used at all, overlaying should clearly be handled by automatic software tools, as the potential for errors is too high when programmers control it themselves.)

With the stack model, the objects associated with an entity may be allocated on a stack. Things are made particularly simple by block-structured languages: object allocation occurs at the same time for all entities declared in a given block, allowing the use of a single stack for a whole program. The scheme is elegant indeed, as it just involves two sets of concomitant events:

Event	When	How
Allocation	Block entry	Push objects on stack
De-allocation	Block exit	Pop stack

Figure 16.1 Allocation and deallocation in a block-structured language

The simplicity and efficiency of this implementation technique are part of the reason why block-structured languages have been so successful.

With the third model, things cease to be so simple. The problem comes from the very power of the mechanism: as the pattern of object creation is unknown at compile-time, it is not possible to predict when a given object may become useless. (Rather than "useful" and "useless", we shall from now on talk of *live* and *dead* objects.)

16.1.3 Unreachable dynamic objects

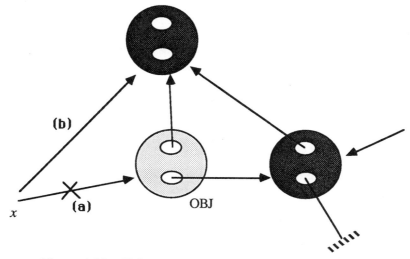

Figure 16.2 Object made dead by *Forget* or reassignment

With the free model, objects may indeed become dead in many ways. In the simplest case, a *Create* followed by a *Forget* or another *Create* on the same entity will render an object dead. The figure shows what happens in this case: after $x.\,Create$ (*a*), x becomes associated with an object OBJ; if this is immediately followed by $e.\,Forget$ or $e := f$, OBJ becomes dead. These two cases are respectively illustrated as (a) and (b) on the figure.

But of course things usually are not that simple. The entity for which an object was initially created may have lost all interest in the object – but this does not suffice to make it a dead object. Because of dynamic aliasing (5.5.3), there may still exist a number of references to it, from program entities or from other live objects.

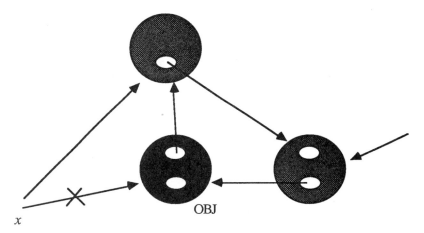

Figure 16.3   Shared object still alive after reference to it is removed

What then are the live objects? In languages such as Pascal, C and Ada which combine stack-based objects (associated with entities of non-pointer types) and fully dynamic objects, the answer is simple: at any point during the execution of a program, any object which is reachable, directly or indirectly, from a stack object, by a chain of references, must be considered live; all others are dead, and will never become live again: the space they occupy may be reclaimed for reuse by other objects. In the figure below, only shaded objects are live.

In Eiffel the situation is slightly different. An Eiffel system is started by creating a root object and executing its *Create* procedure; at any time during the execution of the system, the live objects are of two kinds:

- All objects that are accessible directly or indirectly from the root object are live.

- Since Eiffel routines may have local variables of class types, any object that is referenced by such a variable is also live during the lifetime of a routine.

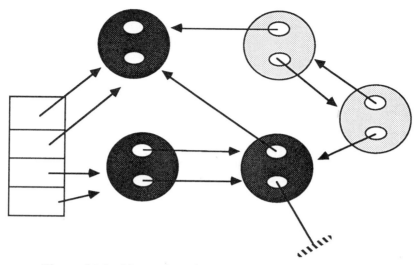

Figure 16.4   Live objects in a Pascal-like run-time model

Note that the terminology used in the second case is not quite correct: an object may not be directly associated with a local variable since a local variable is a program element, not a run-time reference. References corresponding to a local variable of a routine are allocated as a result of calls to this routine on certain objects. Thus the proper terminology is "any object associated with an *instance of* a local variable".

To summarize:

> **Definition** (*Live objects*): At any point during the execution of an Eiffel system, the live objects are those which are reachable directly or indirectly from either the system's root or instances of local variables of a routine currently being executed.

The predefined entity *Result*, used to compute function results, must be included among local variables for this definition.

The Eiffel scheme only differs from that of block-based languages such as Pascal or C by the nature of roots: system root and instances of local routine variables in the object-oriented case, stack entities in the other.

In both cases, we are faced with the problem of certain objects becoming dead at various points during a system's execution, according to a pattern which, in the general case, is unpredictable at compile-time, since object creation and modification of references are purely dynamic phenomena (which may occur, for example, in response to user input).

Note that in specific cases the pattern *may* be predictable to a point. For example, if you are handling linked lists by using the *LINKED_LIST* class sketched in chapter 9, then you have control over the operations that may render *LINKABLE* objects dead (see the *delete* routine given in 9.2.4). In such a case, you might envision a specific reclamation procedure. This idea will be developed below.

In the general case, however, a serious question arises: what should be done about dead elements? Several approaches are possible; the rest of this chapter discusses them.

16.2 THE CASUAL APPROACH

The first approach consists in forgetting about the problem: abandon dead objects to their sad fate. Execute *Create* operations as needed, and do not worry about what may latter happen to those objects that have thus been allocated.

This approach works well in a number of cases. One is small programs that do not create many objects (small-scale tests, for example).

More interesting is the case of programs that may in fact create many objects, but in such a way that none or few of them become dead; this case is similar to static allocation in that no objects are ever retired, the difference being that creation occurs at execution time. In fact static allocation may be viewed as the subcase in which all object creation happens at initialization.

This case provides a good justification for the casual approach, as there is no need for reclamation; the number of objects created may still be too big for the available memory, but no reclamation policy will alleviate the problem if there is nothing to reclaim. Real-time programs often follow this scheme: for efficiency reasons, they usually avoid the complex patterns of dynamic object creation.

Another situation which is used to justify the casual approach is the increasing availability of large memory spaces, and the decreasing cost of memory. The memory involved may be virtual as well as real. On a virtual memory system, both primary and secondary storage are divided into blocks called pages; when primary memory is needed, blocks of primary memory that have not been frequently used are moved to secondary storage ("paged out"). If such a system is used to run object-oriented systems, pages that contain dead objects will tend to be paged out and leave main memory space to frequently used ones. (Of course, if live and dead objects are stored in the same pages, things will not work so well, as pages will tend to move in and out repeatedly; this is known as *thrashing*.)

This approach will only work to a point, however. Even in systems with a large memory, real or virtual, there are limits; it is surprising to see how quickly programmers will reach these limits. Besides, the larger memories made possible by advances in technology are bought to be used, not wasted. So we cannot ignore the issue of storage reclamation if we are to provide support for serious software development.

16.3   RECLAIMING MEMORY: THE ISSUES

If we go beyond the simplistic "casual" approach, we must find how and when to reclaim storage. This in fact involves two issues:

- What level of the system is charged with finding out about dead elements (**detection**).
- How the associated memory is actually reclaimed (**reclamation**).

Each task may be handled at any one of three levels:

- The language implementation level: compiler and run-time system, providing the support common to all software written in a certain language in a certain computing environment.
- The application level: application programs, intended to solve specific problems.
- The **component manufacturing** level: this is an intermediate layer, situated between the previous two, which includes general-purpose software components such as the classes of the Eiffel library, built for reuse by many application programs. Component manufacturing strives for application-independence, as does language implementation, but is comparable to application development because it has only access to the official facilities of the programming language. In contrast, operating system and hardware facilities may be used directly at the language implementation level.

Given two criteria and three possibilities for each, we are in principle faced with nine possibilities. Actually, only four or so make sense. We shall review those which are actually available in existing systems.

16.4   PROGRAMMER-CONTROLLED DEALLOCATION

One all too popular solution is to provide a reclamation facility at the implementation level, while passing the detection problem on to the programmer.

This is certainly the easiest solution for language implementers: all they have to do is to provide a primitive, say *reclaim*, such that *a. reclaim* tells the system that the object associated with *a* is no longer needed and the corresponding space may be recycled.

This is the solution adopted by such (non object-oriented) languages as Pascal (*dispose* procedure), C (*free*), PL/I (*FREE*), Modula-2 and, in certain cases, Ada.

This solution is unacceptable for two reasons: security and complication of program writing.

The security issue is obvious: if, because of a programming mistake, an object is released and recycled while there still are active references to it, further uses of these references will almost certainly result in catastrophes. This is known as the "dangling reference" problem.

The complication issue is just as serious. The problem is that releasing an object is usually not sufficient, as it may itself contain references to other objects. Assume for example a Pascal record type declaration

```
t =
    record
        a1: ↑t1;        {pointer to objects of type t1}
        a2: ↑t2;
        ...
    end
```

Releasing an object x of type t is done in Pascal by the procedure call *dispose* (x). But of course this is not sufficient, as the objects referenced by the fields *a1, a2...* of the object may become dead because of the release of the initial object. This is sometimes called the **recursive dispose** problem: if the release operations are to make any sense, they must apply to a whole data structure, not just to an individual object.

This means that a specific release procedure must be written for any type describing objects that may refer to other objects. The result will be a set of mutually recursive procedures of great complication.

All this is detrimental to the quality of the programming process and the resulting programs. Instead of concentrating on what should be his job – solving an application problem – the programmer turns into a bookkeeper, or garbage collector (whichever metaphor you prefer). The complexity of programs is increased, hampering readability and hence other qualities such as ease of error detection and ease of modification. This further affects security: the more complex a program, the more likely it is to contain errors.

So the role of constructs such as *dispose* is questionable in environments promoting safe programming.

16.5   THE SELF-MANAGEMENT APPROACH

Before we move on to more ambitious schemes such as automatic garbage collection, it is interesting to look at a solution which may be described as a responsible alternative to the previous one, avoiding most of its drawbacks.

This solution is only applicable within an object-oriented, bottom-up approach to software design, where data structures are not developed "on the spot" as programs need them, but built as reusable, general-purpose implementations of abstract data types, with all the associated operations.

We keep the word "class" for such complete data structure implementations, although the technique may to some extent be applied with non-object-oriented languages, using the techniques developed below (chapters 17 to 19) to emulate object-oriented programming.

What characterizes the object-oriented approach with respect to memory management? The most important feature is at first less technical than organizational: between the language implementor and the application programmer, there is now a third person, who will write the data structure implementations. That person may be called a component manufacturer. (He may in practice be one of the previous two, but has a conceptually different role, so that it is convenient to introduce a special name.)

The key point is that the component manufacturer has total control over all uses of a given class, and is thus in a better position to find an acceptable solution to the storage management problem for all instances of that class.

If the pattern of allocation and deallocation for the class is simple enough, the class programmer may thus be able to find an efficient solution which does not even need a specific "dispose" routine from the underlying run-time system; everything may be expressed in terms of higher-level language concepts. This may be called the self-management approach.

16.5.1 Managing space for a linked list

An example will show how this may be achieved. Consider class *LINKED_LIST* [*T*], describing lists consisting of a header and any number of linked cells, which are instances of *LINKABLE* [*T*]. The allocation and deallocation pattern for linked lists is simple. The objects of concern are the "linkable" cells. In this example, the component manufacturer (the person responsible for classes *LINKED_LIST* and *LINKABLE*) knows exactly how linkables are created – by the insertion procedures – and how linkables may become dead – as a result of the deletion procedures. The component manufacturer has full control over these procedures.

The insertion procedures are *insert_right* and *insert_left*. Each of these creates exactly one new live object. The first, for example, has the following form (see 11.4.3, page 269):

```
insert_right (v: T) is
        -- Insert an element of value v to the right of cursor position.
    ...
    local
        new: LINKABLE [T]     -- (like first_element in the original)
    do
        new.Create (v); insert_linkable_right (new)
    ...
    end; -- insert_right
```

The *Create* call directs the language implementation level to allocate memory for a new object.

The deletion procedures are *delete*, *delete_right*, *delete_left*, *delete_all_occurrences* and *wipe_out*. The first three render exactly one linkable dead, the other two an arbitrary number. The code of *delete*, for example, has the following form (9.2.4, page 198):

```
delete is
        -- Delete element at cursor position.
    require
        not offleft; not offright;
    do
        active := next;
        ... Instructions to update previous, next, first_element ...
    end; -- delete
```

The deletion procedures provide the exact context within which dead objects may be detected and, if so desired, put aside for later reuse.

In the absence of any automatic scheme for releasing memory, the component manufacturer may safely conserve memory by avoiding the memory allocation requested by an insertion when previous deletions have created dead objects and made their space available for reuse.

Assume we store these instances of *LINKABLE* in a data structure called *available*; we shall see below how to represent it. Then the calls to *new.Create* (*v*) in *insert_right* and *insert_left* may be replaced by

> *new := fresh* (*v*)

where *fresh* is a new function that will return a ready-for-use linkable; *fresh* will attempt to obtain its result from the *available* list, and will only perform a *Create* if the list is empty. This function, of course, should be secret in class *LINKED_LIST*.

Elements will be fed into *available* by the deletion procedures. For example, the body of *delete* should now be of the form

> **do**
>> *recycle* (*active*);
>>> -- The rest as before:
>>
>> *active := next*;
>> ... Instructions to update *previous, next, first_element* ...

where *recycle*, a new secret procedure of *LINKED_LIST*, plays the opposite role of *fresh*: adding its argument to the list of available objects.

16.5.2   Dealing with recycled elements

To implement *fresh* and *recycle*, note that *available*, the repository of recycled linkables, may be represented as a stack: *fresh* will pop from and *recycle* will push onto the stack. Let us introduce a class *STACK_OF_LINKABLES* for the occasion and add the following secret features to *LINKED_LIST*:

> *available: STACK_OF_LINKABLES* [*T*] **is** ... See below ...;

> *fresh* (*v: T*): *LINKABLE* [*T*] **is**
>> -- A new element with value *v*, for reuse in an insertion
>
> **do**
>> **if** *available.empty* **then**
>>> -- No choice but to perform an actual allocation
>>> *Result.Create* (*v*)
>>
>> **else**
>>> -- Reuse previously discarded linkable
>>> *Result := available.top*; *available.pop*;
>>> *Result.change_value* (*v*)
>
> **end**; -- *fresh*

```
recycle (dead: LINKABLE [T]) is
            -- Return dead to the available list
       require
            not dead.Void
       do
            available.push (dead)
       end -- push
```

Class *STACK_OF_LINKABLES* may be declared as follows:

```
class STACK_OF_LINKABLES [T] export
       top {LINKED_LIST}, empty {LINKED_LIST},
       push {LINKED_LIST}, pop {LINKED_LIST}
feature
       top: LINKABLE [T];

       empty: BOOLEAN is
                  -- Is the stack empty?
            do Result := top.Void end; -- empty

       push (element: like Current) is
                  -- Add element to the stack
            require
                not element.Void
            do
                element.change_right (top); top := element
            end -- push

       pop is
                  -- Remove top of stack
            require
                not empty
            do
                top := top.right
            end
end -- class STACK_OF_LINKABLES
```

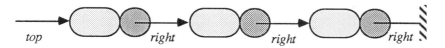

Figure 16.5 Chaining dead elements in a stack

Other structures than a stack are possible, such as a queue, since the order in which available objects are retrieved is irrelevant. Also, the solution could have relied on a reusable, generic implementation of stacks, such as the ones available in the Eiffel library. But here is a case for doing specific programming rather than reusing standard components: the choice of a specific representation makes it possible to take advantage of the "link" field already present in every *LINKABLE* to link together all recycled elements without waste of space, as shown on figure 16.5.

Note that class *LINKABLE* should now export *right* and *change_right* to *STACK_OF_LINKABLES* as well as *LINKED_LIST*. This is acceptable since both *LINKABLE* and *STACK_OF_LINKABLES* are auxiliary classes used for the implementation of *LINKED_LIST*.

16.5.3   Shared lists of available cells

It remains to properly define the *available* list. The simplest way is to introduce it as an attribute:

> *available: STACK_OF_LINKABLES* [T]

With this solution, however, the available list will only hold recycled linkables for one linked list. If a given system contains several lists, it is more efficient to share the pool of recycled linkables over the whole system. This may be done by sharing *available* over all instances of *LINKED_LIST*; in Eiffel, this implies that it should be a once function (13.3.2), which will always return a reference to the same object, created the first time the function is called:

> *available: STACK_OF_LINKABLES* [T] **is**
>   -- Stack of recycled elements
>   **once**
>   *Result.Create*;
>   **end** -- *available*

(See exercise 16.5 for a discussion of the type of this function.)

16.5.4   Discussion

This example is representative of what can be done to alleviate the problem of space reclamation by treating it at the component manufacturing level. It assumes that the underlying language implementation does not offer the automatic mechanisms described in the next section; rather than burdening application programs with memory management problems, which carries all the dangers mentioned above, the solution presented assigns both detection and reclamation to the basic reusable classes.

The advantages and drawbacks of this approach should be carefully weighed. Comparing it to the previous one, we may note that the problems of safety and complication do not magically vanish; coming up with a foolproof memory management scheme for a particular data structure, as done above for linked lists, is hard. But the difference is that this task is not assigned to the application programmer: it is handed over to a component manufacturer, whose job is precisely to chisel out high-quality reusable components. The extra effort involved in solving the storage management problems is justified by the benefits to be expected from the availability of well-crafted components for frequent use by many different application programs.

Both detection and reclamation were treated at the component manufacturing level; the latter is handled by procedures *recycle* and *fresh*. In a language such as Pascal or C offering an interface to the underlying storage management, *recycle* could have been replaced by a call to *dispose* (Pascal) or *free* (C); *fresh* would thus be the standard *Create* (*new* in Pascal, *malloc* in C). Both approaches have pros and cons (exercise 16.4).

The more general question is whether *dispose* is a good facility to have in a language. Although this facility may be properly used at the component manufacturing level, it raises dangers of misuse at the application programming level. The "self-management" approach described here provides an attractive alternative when no automatic storage management is offered by the underlying language system.

16.6   AUTOMATIC STORAGE MANAGEMENT

The above techniques are only partial. A general solution to the problem of storage management for objects involves doing a serious job at the language implementation level.

16.6.1   Reference counting

One technique is known as reference counting. Its principle is simple: every object keeps a count of the number of references to it; when this count becomes null, the object may be recycled.

This solution is not hard to implement (at the language implementation level). When created by $a.Create$ or $a.Clone$ (b), an object will have its reference count initialized to one. In a reference assignment $a := b$, the reference counts of the objects (if any) previously associated with a and b will respectively be decremented and incremented by one; in $a.Forget$, the reference count will be decremented by one. Whenever a count is decremented in the last two cases, it is tested against zero; if it indeed becomes null, the object may be recycled.

Unfortunately, reference counting is not a realistic technique. It is wasteful of both time and space: every operation on a reference, including simple assignment, now involves some arithmetic and tests; and an extra integer field must be added to each object. Furthermore, reference counting is not a general enough technique: it fails to recycle cyclic structures. If an object contains direct or indirect references to itself, its reference count will never become zero even if the object becomes dead, as illustrated on figure 16.6 below.

Cyclic structures are precisely among those for which a "self-management" approach is the most difficult to implement at the component level, and must thus rely on a general-purpose scheme. So reference counting is of little practical interest.

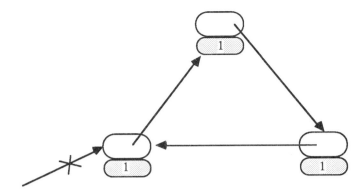

Figure 16.6   Reference counting: dead object space lost forever

16.6.2   Garbage collection

The most general technique is automatic garbage collection. The principle is to run at appropriate times a recycling algorithm that will traverse the whole object structure and reclaim objects that it finds to be dead.

The details of automatic garbage collection algorithms are beyond the scope of this book (see the bibliographical notes). A garbage collector is usually organized in two phases: a **mark** phase which, starting from the roots, traverses the active part of the structure, marking as live all the objects it encounters; and a **sweep** phase that traverses the whole structure linearly, putting all unmarked elements into the list of available cells and unmarking all objects. Here too an extra field is required (for marking purposes), but the space overhead is negligible, as one bit suffices per object.

Classical garbage collectors are activated on demand: when the system runs out of memory, it triggers a whole garbage collection cycle. The advantage of this technique is that no overhead is incurred as long as there is enough memory; the program is only penalized by storage management when it has exceeded available resources. But there is a serious potential drawback: a complete mark-sweep cycle may take a long, long time. While garbage collection is in effect, the program may not proceed.

This is of course unacceptable for real-time applications: imagine a robot manipulation system which, in the middle of computing a trajectory for the robot arm to catch an incoming object, suddenly stops for garbage collection. The result is almost as bad for interactive systems: consider an editor that works speedily most of the time but, once in a while, becomes hung for ten minutes.

In such cases – real-time or interactive systems – users may be expected to accept sacrificing some of the overall performance in order to avoid such unwelcome bursts of storage management activity. It is thus interesting to look for variants of the garbage collection approach which are more "uniformly slow": they should spread out the overhead more evenly, as reference counting does, but at smaller cost and without the other drawbacks of this technique.

A possible solution, on a system that supports multiprocessing, is to assign garbage collection to a separate process. This is known as **on-the-fly** (or **parallel**) garbage collection. The idea is that the collection process should run the mark and sweep cycle continuously, trying to recover what it can from the application program, while interfering with it as little as it can.

Parallel garbage collection turns out to be an extremely difficult problem to solve within these constraints. Interesting algorithms have been published, to which references are given in the bibliographical notes.

One may expect future variants of parallel garbage collection algorithms to run on a separate processor rather than steal time from the processor used by the application program, as is usually the case with the algorithms that have been proposed so far. With a specific garbage collection processor, the overhead on application programs could be reduced to a low level.

16.7 THE EIFFEL APPROACH TO STORAGE MANAGEMENT

Memory management in the Eiffel implementation is a result of the preceding discussion. The aim was to make it possible to write and execute systems that would create a large number of dynamic objects, without burdening the application programmers with the problem of managing storage. On the other hand, it should be possible to write efficient systems; in particular, real-time applications should not be ruled out. (At the time of writing, Eiffel itself does not include direct support for parallel or real-time features, but it is of course possible to encapsulate a set of routines for managing synchronization, communication and other such primitives into a class, the bodies of the routines being coded in some other language such as C. Work on extension of Eiffel for concurrency and real-time is in progress.)

16.7.1 Garbage collection

A garbage collector is part of the environment. Conceptually, this is a parallel collector, which could run as a separate process. Since, however, switching time between processes on an operating system such as Unix would cause too much overhead, the collector is run as a coroutine rather than an actual process. A coroutine (see 20.1.5) is like a routine that does not lose the value of its local data from one activation to the next, and is restarted by each call at the point where its previous activation stopped – as opposed to standard routines, which are always restarted at the beginning. Execution of an Eiffel system may be viewed as a cooperative race between two coroutines: the application, which creates objects as it goes, and renders some dead; and the collector, which chases after the application, collects all the dead objects it can find, and makes them available again to the application.

The collector coroutine is activated when the Eiffel run-time system detects that available space is running low. Since the collector is organized as an infinite loop that may be interrupted at any point, the run-time system controls the activation time of each collector burst, using a self-adapting scheme which attempts to maintain an equilibrium in space occupancy, while ensuring fairness in the race between application and collector for CPU time.

At perfect equilibrium, memory usage is constant: the application renders one object dead for each new object it creates, and the coroutine soon recovers the space. When the equilibrium is broken and the size of occupied memory increases, the coroutine will be called in longer bursts; as it does its job and the size decreases, the bursts are reduced. Below a certain threshold, the collector is not activated at all. At the other extreme, when no memory is left, the coroutine turns into a full sequential mark-and-sweep garbage collector.

Further improvements to the collection mechanism are obtained by treating in a special way any objects that have been live for a long time. This is an application of a technique known as *generation scavenging*, which accelerates collection by "tenuring" objects that have survived a large enough number of collector cycles. Experimental measurements have shown that such objects will often survive for the whole execution; tenuring them, which means removing them from the set of objects to be considered for collection, shortens the detection process. But this raises the problem of tenured objects that become dead after all: with generation scavenging, they may only be reclaimed by a distinct mechanism. Because of this problem, old objects are not kept for the whole execution of a system (as in some implementations of generation scavenging) but they are treated in a special way to accelerate detection and collection.

Thanks to the combination of these various ideas, the overhead for garbage collection may be as small as a few percent. The mechanism may be turned off altogether by specifying **N** on the corresponding line of the System Description File (15.2.7):

GARBAGE_COLLECTION (N)

Further control is available at run-time if the **Y** option has been chosen. Garbage collection may be turned off and on dynamically by the respective calls

collection_off
collection_on

It may be reasonable, for example, to turn collection off during long initialization phases in which the programmer knows that most created objects will be needed. Another interesting possibility is to explicitly trigger garbage collection by either of the two calls

full_collect
collect

These may be used at a point where the programmer knows that CPU time will be available. A typical example occurs in an interactive system when awaiting user input: the time for human actions is several orders of magnitude larger than the time of computer operations.

Routines *collect* and *full_collect* act differently. A call to *full_collect* will direct the collector to find and reclaim all the current dead objects, taking whatever time is necessary. Except in special cases, the recommended primitive is the other one, *collect*, which will activate the collector coroutine for a limited time slot.

Procedure *collect* might be assumed to have an argument, representing the time during which the collector must be activated. But this is not the case: the activation time is determined by the run-time system using the self-adapting scheme mentioned above. The run-time system follows the history of space usage, and is better qualified than the programmer to determine the amount of collection work that is appropriate to maintain efficient storage occupation without wasting CPU time. (Furthermore, it is not clear in which unit a parameter to *collect* should be expressed.)

The above primitives are encapsulated in the library class *MEMORY*. Classes that use them must inherit from this class.

16.7.2   Virtual memory

The parallel garbage collector is complemented in the Eiffel implementation by a specific **Eiffel paging system**. In other words, Eiffel offers its own virtual memory facility for extending the available memory space. Paging is done on the basis of objects; the auxiliary storage used is taken from a temporary file. The replacement policy is "Least Recently Used", meaning that when it is necessary to make room for objects in main memory, the resident objects that have not been used for the longest time are paged out first.

Like garbage collection, virtual memory is an optional facility, controlled by a line in the System Description File:

> **VIRTUAL_MEMORY (Y | N):**

This option should only be enabled in special cases. Eiffel paging is only useful on an operating system that does not offer virtual memory, or as a complement to the operating system's virtual memory. It is appreciable for programs that create many objects. It entails a significant overhead:

- In terms of time, all object accesses are preceded by a test to check whether the object is available in main memory, and, if not, by a page-in operation.

- In terms of space, two extra words of memory are needed in connection with each object in our current implementation.

In normal situations, the benefit is not worth this overhead. In contrast, garbage collection is a highly useful mechanism and should usually be turned on.

Although of limited usefulness at the moment, the paging system is interesting as the first component of a more general mechanism providing for **persistent objects** and object-oriented databases (chapter 21).

16.8   KEY CONCEPTS INTRODUCED IN THIS CHAPTER

- There are three basic models of object creation: static, stack-based and free. The last is characteristic of object-oriented languages but also occurs elsewhere, for example in Lisp, Pascal (pointers and *new*), C (*malloc*), Ada (access types) etc.

- In programs that create many objects, objects may become dead, that is to say unreachable; their memory space is lost, leading to memory waste and, in extreme cases, failure from lack of space even though some space would in fact be available for recycling.

• The issue may be safely ignored in the case of programs that create few dead objects, or few objects altogether as compared to the available memory size.

• When the issue cannot be ignored (highly dynamic data structures, limited memory resources), two problems must be solved: *detection* of dead objects, and *reclamation* of the associated space.

• Either task may be handled by the language implementation, the component manufacturing level or application programs.

• Leaving application programs in charge of detection is cumbersome and dangerous. So is the *dispose* or *free* instruction for releasing storage in a high-level language.

• In some contexts, simple storage management may be achieved at the component level. Detection is handled by the components; reclamation is handled by either the components or the language implementation.

• Component-level management may serve to alleviate a general-purpose mechanism at the language implementation level.

• Reference counting is inefficient and does not work if there are cyclic structures.

• Garbage collection is the most general technique. Its potential overhead on normal system execution may be greatly reduced by running the collector as a parallel process or coroutine.

• Eiffel offers coroutine garbage collection, which may be turned off or, conversely, activated on demand. Built-in paging is also available, although not used in normal cases.

16.9 BIBLIOGRAPHICAL NOTES

A broader perspective on the different models of object creation, discussed at the beginning of this chapter, is provided by the "**contour model**" of programming language execution, which may be found in [Johnston 1971].

A parallel garbage collection algorithm was introduced in [Dijkstra 1978]. Discussion of performance issues of such algorithms may be found in [Cohen 1984].

Generation scavenging is described in [Ungar 1984].

EXERCISES

16.1 Types of stack elements

In the "self-management" version of linked lists, why are the results of *fresh* and *top* and the arguments to *recycle* and *push* (classes *LINKED_LIST* and *STACK_OF_LINKABLES*, see 16.5.2) declared of type *LINKABLE* [*T*] rather than **like** *first_element* or **like** *Current*? (Hint: consider *available* in 16.5.3).

16.2   A function with side-effect

Also in the self-management version of linked lists, function *fresh* calls a procedure, *pop*, and hence produces a side-effect on the data structure. Discuss whether this is acceptable in view of the analysis of side-effects in functions (7.7).

16.3   Declaration by association

In the same context, assume that instead of defining a specific class *STACK_OF_LINKABLES* for the list of available cells, we use a generic implementation of stacks, say *GSTACK*. Then *available* may be declared as *GSTACK* [*LINKABLE* [*T*]]. Could it be declared as *GSTACK* [like *first_element*]? Explain how the two solutions would differ if both were permitted, and the dangers involved. (**Hint**: *available* is a once function.)

16.4   What level of dispose?

As mentioned (page 365), the self-management policy, if implemented in a language like Pascal or C where an operating system *dispose* or *free* facility is available, could use this facility directly rather than managing its own free list for every type of data structure. Discuss the pros and cons of both approaches.

16.5   Once functions and genericity

Examine the *available* once function (page 364) in light of the once function rule (13.3.7). Does the function raise any problem in practice?

PART 3

Applying

object-oriented techniques

in other environments

17

Object-oriented programming in classical languages

Part 2 introduced hand in hand the method of object-oriented design and an associated notation, Eiffel. This chapter and the other chapters of part 3 review how the ideas may be implemented (or in some cases just emulated) in other languages: classical, non-object-oriented languages such as Pascal, Fortran and C; languages offering encapsulation techniques, such as Ada; and other object-oriented languages.

17.1 LEVELS OF LANGUAGE SUPPORT

In assessing how programming languages succeed in supporting object-oriented concepts, we shall encounter three broad categories.

In its most simple form, object-oriented programming is just "programming with abstract data types". A primitive implementation of the idea is to constrain all accesses to a data structure, in any module not owning the structure, to use routines rather than access the fields directly. In the absence of special language support, this is a purely methodological rule, which can be implemented in any language having the notion of routine; it may be called **disciplined data structure access**. But of course this is not object-oriented programming – just a form of information hiding.

The second category includes languages that offer a form of modularity based on data structures. These languages allow the definition of modules that encapsulate a data structure description with the routines that manipulate the data structure. This may be called **encapsulation**. Typical of this category are Ada and Modula-2. A module in such languages may be associated with an abstract data type implementation. However the notions of type and module remain distinct; inheritance is not offered.

The next category (corresponding to levels 4 to 7 of the classification given in section 4.9) covers true object-oriented languages. Classes are used as both modules and types. This opens the way to inheritance, polymorphism, redefinition and dynamic binding.

17.2   OBJECT-ORIENTED PROGRAMMING IN PASCAL?

Assume you have at your disposal a language such as Pascal. How much of the object-oriented approach can you implement?

Not much. The Pascal program structure is based on a totally different paradigm. A Pascal program is made of a sequence of paragraphs, appearing in an immutable order: labels, constants, types, variables, routines (procedures and functions), and executable instructions. The routines themselves have the same structure, recursively.

This simple rule facilitates one-pass compilation of Pascal programs. But it dooms any attempt at using object-oriented techniques in this language. Consider what it takes to implement an abstract data type (say a stack represented as an array): a few constants (such as the array size), one or a few types (such as the record type describing the stack implementation), a few variables (such as the pointer to the stack top), and a few routines representing the operations on the abstract data type. In Pascal, these elements will be scattered all over the program: all the constants for various abstract data types together, all the types together and so on.

The structure of Pascal programs is thus orthogonal to the structure of object-oriented designs. Using Pascal would totally contradict the principle of linguistic modular units (2.2.1), which expressed that any chosen modular policy must be supported by the available language constructs, lest the criteria of composability, decomposability etc. be jeopardized.

So one can do little with Pascal in terms of object-oriented techniques beyond the simple rule of disciplined data structure access, applicable to any language.

Some commercially available versions of Pascal raise the restrictions on order of declarations and include support for some form of module beyond the routine, including separate compilation. These extended modules may contain more than one routine, together with associated constants, types and routines. But such extensions are only Pascal by name; they are not standardized, and in fact resemble more a language like Modula 2. The above discussion refers to standard Pascal.

17.3   FORTRAN

The oldest surviving programming language, Fortran, although very primitive in many respects, provides support for a limited form of encapsulation.

A Fortran system is made of a main program and a number of routines (subroutines or functions). The usual way to implement an abstract data type is to provide a routine for each operation of the specification (as *push*, *pop* etc. for stacks). The data structure implementation may be shared by the routines through COMMON blocks (see 13.5.1). This technique has obvious disadvantages: the routines are not physically related; there is a danger that one will be updated but not the others. This violates the principle of linguistic modular units.

It is possible to emulate encapsulation techniques thanks to a language feature that was made officially part of the language with the 1978 revision (known as Fortran 77), although a number of compilers had offered it before. This feature – multiple entry points to routines – was probably introduced for different purposes, but may be redeemed for the "good cause".

This extension enables Fortran routines to have entry points other than the normal routine header. These entry points may be called by other routines as if they were autonomous routines, and may have different arguments. Calling an entry will start execution of the routine at the entry point. All entries of a routine share the persistent data of the routine; a persistent data item, which in Fortran 77 must appear in a *SAVE* directive, is one whose value is retained from one activation of a routine to the next.

This technique may be used to construct modules that manage abstract objects. Such a module will masquerade as a routine with multiple entries, although the routine itself will never be called under its own name. The entries correspond to the operations on the underlying abstract data type. They must all be of the form

> *ENTRY (arguments)*
> *... Instructions ...*
> *RETURN*

In other words, all entry blocks must be disjoint: control never flows from one entry block to the next. This is a restricted use of entry points, which in general are meant to allow entering a routine at any point and then continuing in sequence.

Below is an example of a function module with multiple entry points, implementing an abstract stack object (stack of reals) and the associated operations. The module might be used as follows by a client – in a style which is indeed reminiscent of the use of a class:

> *LOGICAL OK*
> *REAL X*
> *OK = CREATE ()*
> *OK = PUSH (4.5)*
> *OK = PUSH (–7.88)*
> *X = TOP ()*
> *OK = POP ()*
> *IF (EMPTY ()) A = B*

The module itself may be written as shown on the following page.

A Fortran routine and its entry points must be either all subroutines, or all functions. Here since *EMPTY* and *TOP* have to be functions, all other entries are also declared as functions, including *CREATE* whose result is useless.

```
C   -- IMPLEMENTATION OF
C   -- ONE ABSTRACT STACK
C   -- OF REALS
C
    INTEGER FUNCTION RSTACK ()
    PARAMETER (SIZE=1000)
C
C   -- ARRAY
C   -- AND STACK POINTER
C
    REAL IMPL (SIZE)
    INTEGER LAST
    SAVE IMPL, LAST
C
C   -- DECLARATION
C   -- OF ENTRY POINTS
C
    LOGICAL CREATE
    LOGICAL PUSH
    LOGICAL POP
    REAL TOP
    LOGICAL EMPTY
C
    REAL X
C
C      -- STACK CREATION
C
    ENTRY CREATE ()
      CREATE = .TRUE.
      LAST = 0
    RETURN
C
C      -- PUSHING ELEMENTS
C
    ENTRY PUSH (X)
      IF (LAST .NE. SIZE) THEN
        PUSH = .TRUE.
        LAST = LAST+1
      IMPL (LAST) = X
    ELSE
      PUSH = .FALSE.
    END IF
    RETURN
```

```
C      -- POPPING STACK
C
    ENTRY POP (X)
      IF (LAST .NE. 0) THEN
        POP = .TRUE.
        LAST = LAST-1
      ELSE
        POP = .FALSE.
      END IF
    RETURN
C
C      -- ACCESSING TOP
C
    ENTRY TOP ()
      IF (LAST .NE. 0) THEN
        TOP = IMPL (LAST)
      ELSE
        CALL ERROR
   *        ('TOP: EMPTY STACK')
      END IF
    RETURN
C
C      -- DETERMINING
C      -- IF STACK IS EMPTY
C
    ENTRY EMPTY ()
      EMPTY = (LAST .EQ. 0)
    RETURN
C
    END
```

This style of programming works, and can be applied successfully to emulate the encapsulation techniques of Ada or Modula-2 in contexts when you have no choice but to use Fortran. But of course it suffers from stringent limitations:

- No internal calls are permitted: whereas routines in an object-oriented class usually rely on each other for their implementations, an entry call issued by another entry of the same Fortran routine would be understood as an instance of recursion – anathema to Fortran.

- The mechanism is strictly static: the example shows an implementation of one abstract object, not of an abstract data type with an arbitrary number of dynamically created instances, as with a class. The technique may be generalized to allow for a fixed number of objects (by transforming every variable into a one-dimensional array, and adding a dimension to every array). But there is no support for dynamic object creation.

- Finally, the very fact that the technique uses a language mechanism for purposes other than its probable design objective – cheating, as it were, with the language – raises dangers of confusion and errors.

17.4 OBJECT-ORIENTED PROGRAMMING AND C

17.4.1 Basics

As with any other language, you can apply to C the technique of disciplined data structure access, making sure that data structures are only manipulated through functions. (All routines in C are functions; procedures are viewed as functions with a "void" result type.)

Beyond this, the notion of file may serve to implement higher-level modules. Files are a C notion at the borderline between the language and the operating system. A file is a compilation unit; it may contain a number of functions and some data. Some of the functions may be hidden from other files, and some made public. This achieves encapsulation: a file may contain all the elements pertaining to the implementation of one or more abstract objects, or an abstract data type. With this notion, one can achieve with a C file essentially the same results as with an Ada package, without genericity and the distinction between specification and implementation (see next chapter).

In practice, a commonly used C technique is rather averse to the principles of object-oriented design. Most C programs use "header files", which describe shared data structures. Any file needing the data structures will gain access to them through an "include" directive (handled by the built-in C preprocessor) of the form

>   **#include** <*header.h*>

where *header.h* is the name of the header file (normally terminated by the suffix *.h*, at least on Unix). This is conceptually equivalent to copying the whole header file at the point where the directive appears, and allows the including file to directly access the data structure definitions contained in *header.h*. Client modules are thus encouraged (by the C tradition if not by the language itself) to access data structures by their physical representations – not quite in line with the methods developed in this book.

17.4.2 Self-sufficient objects

Some of the more specialized features of C provide interesting advances towards implementing the true object-oriented approach. They are of more interest to implementors of object-oriented languages than to C programmers, but deserve a discussion.

One of the important aspects of object-oriented programming is that one may view every object as carrying along at run-time the operations applicable to it. This is only an image; but interpreting it literally yields an interesting C technique. As it happens, instances of C "structure types" (the equivalent of records in Pascal) may contain, among their fields, references (pointers) to functions.

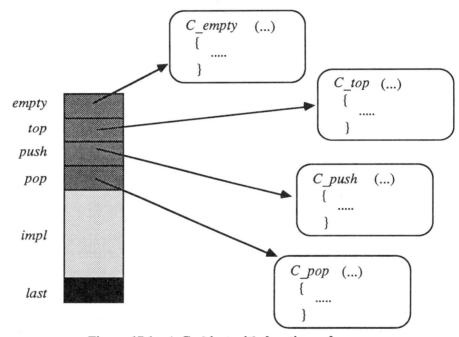

Figure 17.1   A C object with function references

For example, a C structure type *REAL_STACK* may be declared by the type definition

```
typedef struct {
        int last;
        float impl [MAXSIZE];
        void (*pop) ();
        void (*push) ();
        float (*top) ();
        BOOL (*empty) ();
        } REAL_STACK;
```

(The braces serve to delimit the components of the structure type; *float* is the C type for real numbers; procedures are declared as functions with a **void** result type.)

Here the first two components are an integer and an array; the others are references to functions. Each instance of the type must be initialized so that the reference fields will point to appropriate functions. For example, if *a_stack* is a variable of this type and *C_pop* is a popping function, you may assign to the *pop* component of *a_stack* a reference to this function, as follows:

> *a_stack.pop = C_pop*

In the corresponding Eiffel class, *pop* has no argument. Here the *C_pop* function must be given access to the appropriate stack object; hence it needs one argument. It should be declared as

> *C_pop (s)*
> > *REAL_STACK s;*
> > {
> > > ... Implementation of pop operation ...
> > }

so that *pop* may be applied to a stack object *a_stack* under the form

> *a_stack.pop (a_stack)*

More generally, an n-argument Eiffel routine *rout* will yield a C function *C_rout* with $n+1$ arguments. An Eiffel routine call of the form

> $x.rout (arg_1, arg_2, ..., arg_n)$

will be emulated as

> $x.C\_rout (x, arg_1, arg_2, ..., arg_n)$

This technique will work to a certain extent. It can even be extended to emulate inheritance (see exercise 17.3). But it is inapplicable to any serious development: as illustrated in figure 17.1, it implies that every *instance* of every class physically contains references to all the routines that may be applied to it! The space overhead would be prohibitive, especially with inheritance.

This overhead may be brought down to an acceptable level if we notice that routines are common to all instances of a class. We may thus introduce for each class a run-time data structure, the **class descriptor**, containing references to the routines of the class. The class descriptor may be implemented as a linked list or an array. Then instances of the class only need one reference to the class descriptor, rather than individual references to every routine (figure 17.2).

This idea is the basis for the implementation of object-oriented programming languages that use C as target language. Of course, much more advanced techniques are necessary to ensure good performance and to support inheritance – especially multiple inheritance.

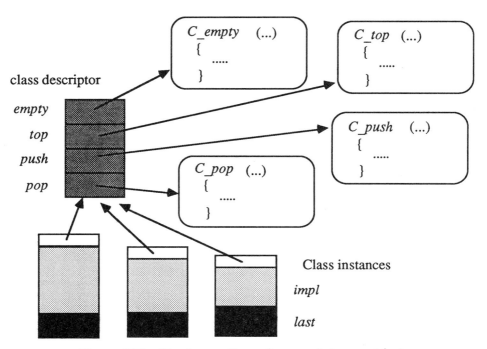

Figure 17.2   Sharing routine references between objects

17.4.3   An assessment

This discussion has shown that implementation techniques may be found to emulate object-oriented programming in C. But it does not mean that programmers should use these techniques. As in the Fortran case, the emulation is only obtained by doing violence to the language.

C is a traditional function-oriented language, a successor to "structured" assembly languages such as PL 360 and BCPL. Because it is based on a small number of concepts, may be used on a wide range of computers, and lends itself to efficient implementation, it has in a few years become the *lingua franca* of systems programming. But few concepts are further from the spirit of C than object-oriented design.

The danger in trying to force object-oriented concepts onto a C base is to get an inconsistent construction, impairing the software development process and the quality of the resulting products. A hybrid approach yields hybrid quality. This is why serious reservations may be voiced about the object-oriented extensions of C described in chapter 20. To benefit from object-oriented techniques, one must use a consistent framework, and overcome the limitations of languages such as Fortran or C which – regardless of their other characteristics – were designed for entirely different purposes.

17.5   BIBLIOGRAPHICAL NOTES

Some techniques for writing Fortran packages based on the principles of data abstraction are described in [Meyer 1982]. They use routines sharing *COMMON* blocks, rather than multiple-entry routines as presented in 17.3.

A discussion of C techniques for the implementation of object-oriented concepts may be found in [Cox 1986].

EXERCISES

17.1   Graphics objects (for Fortran programmers)

Write a set of Fortran multiple-entry routines that implement basic graphics objects (points, circles, polygons). For the specification of the abstractions involved and the associated operations, you may want to refer to the GKS graphics standard.

17.2   Genericity (for C programmers)

How would you transform the C emulation of a "real stack" class declaration (page 380) into an emulated generic declaration, easy to adapt to stacks of any type T rather than just *float*?

17.3   Object-oriented programming in C (term project)

Design and implement a simple object-oriented extension of C using the ideas of section 17.4.2. You may write either a pre-processor, translating an extended version of the language into C, or a function package that does not change the language itself.

Approach the problem through three successive refinements:

• Implement first a mechanism whereby objects carry their own references to available routines.

• Then see how routine references may be factored out at the class level.

• Finally, study how single inheritance may be added to the mechanism.

18

Object-oriented
programming and Ada

In the 1970s, advances in programming methodology brought about a new generation of languages combining the control structures of Algol 60 and the data structuring features of Algol W and Pascal with better system structuring facilities and support for information hiding. Although their precise traits differ, these languages share a common spirit and may be collectively called "the encapsulation languages".

A complete list of languages in this group would be long. Only a few of them have produced a sizable user community; four are particularly worthy of attention: Modula-2, a successor to Pascal, designed by the same author, Niklaus Wirth; CLU, the result of an MIT project under the direction of Barbara Liskov, which among the languages mentioned comes closest to implementing object-oriented concepts with the exception of inheritance; Mesa, a Xerox effort with particular emphasis on describing inter-module relationships of large systems; and Ada, designed by a team led by Jean Ichbiah in response to requirements set by the US Department of Defense.

Our study of how object-oriented techniques may be emulated in the encapsulation languages will be limited to Ada, which, besides having attracted the most attention, is also the most complete (and complex) of these languages, embodying in some form most of the features found in the others. Modula-2, for example, does not offer genericity or overloading; CLU has no support for concurrency. The choice of Ada as vehicle for this discussion does not imply a comparative value judgment.

18.1 PACKAGES

Each of the encapsulation languages offers a construct for grouping logically related program elements. This construct is called a package in Ada; corresponding notions are known as modules in Modula-2 and Mesa, and clusters in CLU.

A class was defined as both a structural system component – a module – and a type. In contrast, a package is only a module.

Another way to characterize this difference is to note that the package is a purely **syntactical** notion. Packages provide a way to distribute system elements (variables, routines etc.) into coherent subsystems; but they are only needed for readability and manageability of the software. The decomposition of a system into packages does not affect its **semantics**: a multi-package Ada system may be transformed into a one-package system producing exactly the same results by a purely syntactical transformation – removing all package boundaries, expanding generic instantiations (see below) and resolving name clashes through renaming. Compare this with classes: besides providing a unit of modular decomposition, a class is also a semantic construct, describing the behavior of a set of objects created at run-time. The semantic effect of classes is made even stronger by dynamic binding.

An Ada package is a free association of program elements and may be used for various purposes. Sensible uses of this notion include writing a package to gather:

- A set of related constants (as done with classes in 13.2).

- A library of routines, for example a mathematical library.

- A set of variables, constants and routines describing the implementation of one abstract object, or a fixed number of abstract objects, accessible only through designated operations, as attempted with Fortran in 17.3.

- An abstract data type implementation.

The last use is the most interesting for this discussion and we shall study it on the example of a stack package, adapted from a similar example given in the Ada reference manual.

18.2 A STACK IMPLEMENTATION

Information hiding is supported in Ada by the two-tier declaration of packages. Every package comes in two parts, officially called "specification" and "body". The former term is too strong for a construct that does not support any formal description of package semantics (in the form of assertions or similar mechanisms), so we shall use the more modest word "interface".

The interface lists the public properties of the package: exported variables, constants, types and routines.[1] The routines are only given by their headers, which give the formal arguments and their types (plus the result type for a function); an example of a routine header is:

---

[1] The standard Ada term for "routine" is "subprogram". We keep the former word for consistency with other chapters.

function *top* (*s: STACK*) **return** *X*;

The body completes the package description by filling in the routine implementations, plus any needed secret elements.

18.2.1   A simple interface

A first version of the interface part of a stack package may be expressed as follows. Note that the keyword **package** by itself introduces a package interface; the body, which will be given later, is introduced by **package body**.

> **package** *REAL_STACKS* **is**
>
>> **type** *STACK_CONTENTS* **is array** (*POSITIVE* **range** <>) **of** *FLOAT*;
>>
>> **type** *STACK* (*max_size: POSITIVE*) **is**
>>> **record**
>>>> *implementation: STACK_CONTENTS* (*1..max_size*);
>>>> *nb_elements: NATURAL* := *0*;
>>> **end record**;
>>
>> **procedure** *push* (*x:* **in** *FLOAT*; *s:* **in out** *STACK*);
>>
>> **procedure** *pop* (*s:* **in out** *STACK*);
>>
>> **function** *top* (*s: STACK*) **return** *FLOAT*;
>>
>> **function** *empty* (*s: STACK*) **return** *BOOLEAN*;
>>
>> *overflow, underflow: EXCEPTION*;
>
> **end** *REAL_STACKS*;

This interface lists exported elements: the type *STACK* used to declare stacks, the auxiliary type *STACK_CONTENTS* used in the definition of *STACK*, the four basic routines on stacks, and two exceptions.

Client packages only rely on the interface (provided their programmers have some idea of the semantics associated with the routines).

The following remarks apply to this simple package interface:

• You will certainly have noted that exporting the whole declaration of *STACK* and *STACK_CONTENTS*, and hence the internal representation, is exporting too much. We shall see below how this may be corrected.

• In contrast with classes of object-oriented languages, a package declaration does not by itself define a type. Here a type *STACK* must be separately defined. One consequence of this separation, for the programmer who builds a package around an abstract data type implementation, is the need to invent two different names – one for the package and one for the type. Another consequence is that the routines have one more argument than their object-oriented counterparts: here they all act on a stack *s*, implicit in the corresponding Eiffel class.

• A declaration may define not only the type of an entity, but also its initial value. Here the declaration of *nb_elements* in type *STACK* prescribes an initial value of 0. It obviates the need for an explicit initialization operation corresponding to *Create*; this would not be the case, however, if a less straightforward initialization was required.

• A few details of Ada are needed to understand the type declarations: *POSITIVE* and *NATURAL* denote the subtypes of *INTEGER* covering positive and non-negative integers, respectively; a type specification of the form **array** (*TYPE* **range** <>), where <> is known as the Box symbol, describes a template for array types, rather than an actual type. An actual type is obtained by choosing a finite subrange of *TYPE*; this is done here in *STACK*, which uses the subrange *1..max_size* of *POSITIVE*. *STACK* is an example of a parameterized type; any declaration of an entity of type *STACK* must specify an actual value for *max_size*, as in

> *s: STACK (1000)*

• In Ada, every routine argument must be characterized by a mode: **in**, **out** or **in out**, defining the routine's rights on the corresponding actual arguments (read-only, write-only or update). In the absence of an explicit keyword, the default mode is **in**.

• Finally, the interface also specifies two exception names: *overflow* and *underflow*. An exception is an error condition that the programmer has decided to treat separately from the normal control flow. Any exceptions that may be propagated to the client packages should, as here, be included in the interface. The Ada exception mechanism is further discussed below.

18.2.2   Using a package

Client code using the package is based on the interface. Here is an example from some package needing real stacks:

> *s: REAL_STACKS.STACK (1000);*
> *REAL_STACKS.push (3.5, s); ...;*
> **if** *REAL_STACKS.empty (s)* **then**...

It is a requirement of Ada support systems that client modules containing such code may be compiled even if only the interface of *REAL_STACKS*, not its body, is available.

Syntactically, note how the name of package *REAL_STACKS* must be repeated, using dot notation, for each use of an entity from this package (where "entities" here include type names such as *STACK* as well as routine names). This somewhat heavy notation may be simplified by including a directive

> **use** *REAL_STACKS*;

at the beginning of the client package. Then the above extract may be written more simply as

> *s: STACK (1000);*
> *push (3.5, s); ...;*
> **if** *empty (s)* **then**...

However the full form must still be used for any entity whose name conflicts with the name of another entity accessible to the client package (that is to say, declared in the client package itself or in another supplier mentioned in a **use** directive).

Some of the Ada literature advises programmers to stay away from the **use** directive altogether on the grounds that it hampers clarity: an unqualified reference such as *empty* (*s*) does not immediately tell the reader what supplier *empty* refers to (*REAL_STACKS* in the example). In contrast, the object-oriented equivalent, *s*. *empty* in Eiffel, is unambiguously bound to a specific supplier class, given by the type of *s*. (In all fairness, however, it must be said that a problem similar to that of the Ada **use** arises with inheritance: when you see a name in a class, it may refer to a feature declared in any of the class's ancestors.)

18.2.3 Implementation

The body of package *REAL_STACKS* might be declared along the following lines. Only one routine is shown in full.

```
package body REAL_STACKS is

        procedure push (x: in FLOAT; s: in out REAL_STACK) is
        begin
            if nb_elements = max_size then
                    raise overflow
            end if;
            nb_elements := nb_elements + 1;
            implementation (nb_elements) := x;
        end push;

        procedure pop (s: in out STACK) is
            ... Implementation for pop ...
        end pop;

        function top (s: STACK) return X is
            ... Implementation for top ...
        end top;

        function empty (s: STACK) return BOOLEAN is
            ... Implementation for empty ...
        end empty;

    end REAL_STACKS;
```

Two aspects are worth noting here. The first is the use of exceptions: a run-time error may be handled by raising a special condition and treating it separately. We shall see below how the exception is caught. The second remark is that most of the interface information (the routine headers) must be repeated in the body. Section 9.6.2 discussed the pros and cons of this approach.

18.2.4 GENERICITY

The package as given is too specific; it should be made applicable to any type, not just *FLOAT*, through genericity. To make the package interface generic, the following syntax will be used:

generic

    type *T* **is private**;

package *STACKS* **is**

    ... As before, replacing all occurrences of *FLOAT* by *T* ...

end *STACKS*;

The syntax for introducing formal generic parameters (using the **generic** ... clause) is heavier than in previously seen notations because more options are offered. In particular, the parameters declared in a **generic** clause may represent not just types but also routines. More will be seen on these possibilities in the next chapter.

The **generic** clause is not repeated in the package body, which will be identical to the version given earlier, except that *T* must be substituted for *FLOAT* throughout.

The "**is private**" specification for *T* prescribes that *T* is to be treated within the package as a private type. This means that entities of the type may only be used in operations applicable to all Ada types: use as source or target of an assignment, as operand of an equality test, as actual argument in a routine, and a few other special operations. This is close to the convention used for formal generic parameters in Eiffel (6.1.3). In Ada, other possibilities are also available. In particular, the operations could be further restricted by declaring the parameter as **limited private**, which essentially bars all uses other than as actual argument to a routine.

Although it is called a package, a generically parameterized module such as *STACKS* is really just a package template, and may not be used directly by clients. Clients must instantiate it with actual generic parameters, for example to provide a more elegant definition of *REAL_STACKS*. The syntax is as follows:

    package *REAL_STACKS* **is new** *STACKS* (*FLOAT*);

Such instances of a generic package are themselves not generic any more. Only they can actually be used by clients. The inflexibility of this mechanism, which only offers parameterized modules (not directly usable) or usable modules (not extendible) should be contrasted with the openness of inheritance, which allows arbitrary extensions to existing modules, according to the "open-closed" principle. This question is discussed in detail in the next chapter.

18.3   HIDING THE REPRESENTATION: THE PRIVATE STORY

Package *STACKS*, as given, fails to implement the principle of information hiding: as noted above, the declarations of types *STACK* and *STACK_CONTENTS* are in the interface, allowing clients to directly access the representation of stacks. For example, a client might include code of the form

/1/

    use *REAL_STACKS*;...
    s: STACK; ...
    s.implementation (*3*) := *7.0*; *s.last* := *51*;

grossly violating the underlying abstract data type specification.

Conceptually, the type declarations belong in the body. Why didn't we put them there in the first place? The reason may only be understood by considering, beyond the language, programming environment issues.

One requirement of the Ada design, already mentioned, is that packages should be separately compilable and, moreover, that it should be possible to compile a client of any package A even though only the interface of A, not its body, is known. This favors top-down design: to proceed with the work on a module, it suffices to know the specification of the facilities it needs; actual implementations may be provided only later.

Thus a client of *REAL_STACKS* may be compiled when only the interface of *REAL_STACKS* (that is to say, the interface of *STACKS*, of which *REAL_STACKS* is an instance) is known. But such a client will contain declarations of the form

> **use** *REAL_STACKS*;...
> *s, s': STACK*; ...
> *s'* := *s*;

which the poor compiler cannot properly handle unless it knows what size is taken up by an object of type *STACK*. But this can only be determined from the type declarations for *STACK* and the auxiliary type *STACK_CONTENTS*.

Hence the dilemma that faced the designers of Ada: conceptually, such declarations belong to the inferno – the body; but implementation concerns seem to require their inclusion in the paradise – the interface.

The solution retained was to create a purgatory: a special section of the package that is physically tied to the interface, and compiled with it, but marked in such a way that clients may not refer to its elements. The purgatory section is called the private part of the interface; it is introduced by the keyword **private** (also used, as we saw above, as a qualifier for protected types). Any declaration appearing in the private part is unavailable to clients. This scheme is illustrated by our final version of the stack package interface:

> **generic**
> > **type** *T* **is private**;
>
> **package** *STACKS* **is**
> > **type** *STACK* (*max_size: POSITIVE*) **is private**;
> >
> > **procedure** *push* (*x:* **in** *T*; *s:* **in out** *STACK*);
> >
> > **procedure** *pop* (*s:* **in out** *STACK*);
> >
> > **function** *top* (*s: STACK*) **return** *T*;
> >
> > **function** *empty* (*s: STACK*) **return** *BOOLEAN*;
> >
> > *overflow, underflow: EXCEPTION*;
>
> **private**
> > **type** *STACK_VALUES* **is array** (*POSITIVE* **range** <>) **of** *T*;

-- (Private clause, continued from previous page)

```
type STACK (max_size: POSITIVE) is
    record
            implementation: STACK_VALUES (1..max_size);
            nb_elements: NATURAL := 0;
    end record
end STACKS;
```

Note how type *STACK* must now be declared twice: first in the non-private part of the interface, where it is only specified as **private**; then again in the private part, where the full description is given. If the first declaration was omitted, a line of the form *s: REAL_STACK* would not be legal in a client, since clients only have access to entities declared in the non-private part. This first declaration only specifies the type as **private**, barring clients from accessing any property of stack objects other than the universal operations (assignment, equality test, use as actual argument). Type *STACK_VALUES*, on the other hand, is purely internal, and irrelevant to clients: thus it need only be declared in the private part.

It must be emphasized again that the information contained in the private part of a package interface is in the interface for language implementation reasons only, and that clients are physically unable to use it. For example, code /1/ above, which directly accessed the representation in a client, is illegal with the new form of the package. The presence of private information in the interface is rather tantalizing for the clients: they see it, but they cannot use it directly. (As a matter of fact, one may imagine that a good Ada programming support environment would as a default hide this part from a client programmer requesting interface information about the class – in the manner of the Eiffel **short** command.) But remember the remark made in the presentation of information hiding (page 23): information hiding is not a security mechanism meant to physically prevent client programmers from reading about the hidden details. The goal is simply to prevent them from using these details.

To summarize at the risk of confusion: the private section of the public part of a package (the interface) lists the implementation of those conceptually private types which must be declared in the public part although their implementation is not publicly available. In the non-private part, these types are declared private.

18.4 EXCEPTIONS

The *STACKS* generic package lists two exceptions in its interface: *overflow* and *underflow*. More generally, programmers may deal with error conditions by defining arbitrary exception names; Ada also includes predefined exceptions, triggered by the hardware or the operating system, for such cases as arithmetic overflow or exhaustion of memory.

18.4.1   Simplifying the control structure

Exceptions as they exist in Ada are a technique for dealing with errors without impairing the control structure of normal processing. If a program performs a series of actions, each of which may turn out to be impossible because of some erroneous condition, the resulting control structure may end up looking like[2]

```
action1;
if error1 then
      error_handling1;
else
      action2;
      if error2 then
            error_handling2;
      else
            action3;
            if error3 then
                  error_handling3;
            else
                  . . .
```

As was mentioned in section 9.3, the Ada exception mechanism is an attempt to fight the complexity of such a scheme – where the elements that perform "useful" tasks sometimes look like a small archipelago in an ocean of error-handling code – by separating the **handling** of errors from their **detection**. There must still be tests to determine whether a certain erroneous condition has occurred; but the only action to take then is to raise a certain signal, the exception, which will be handled elsewhere.

18.4.2   Raising an exception

At a trivial level, the technique may be seen as a replacement of the above **if...then...else...** control structures by simpler **if...then...** constructs, with no nesting, giving more linear code:

```
action1;
if error1 then raise exc1; end;

action2;
if error2 then raise exc2; end;

action3;
if error3 then raise exc3; end;

. . .
```

---

[2] This example uses the Ada syntax where the semicolon is an instruction terminator, rather than a separator as in Eiffel.

18.4.3   Handling an exception

When an instruction **raise** *exc* is executed, control does not flow to the instructions that would normally follow, but is transferred to an **exception handler**. This disruption of the normal flow of control explains why the **else...** clauses are no longer necessary here.

An exception handler is a special paragraph of a block or routine, of the form

> **exception**
>   **when** *exc1* => *treatment1*;
>   **when** *exc2* => *treatment2*;
>   . . .

The handler that will be selected when **raise** *exc* is executed is the first one that handles *exc* in the dynamic chain, that is to say the list of routines beginning with the routine containing the **raise** and continuing with its caller, its caller's caller etc. (If the **raise** is in a **begin... end** block, that block is the first element of the dynamic chain.) Here a handler is said to handle *exc* if *exc* appears in one of its **when** clauses.

If no handler in the dynamic chain handles *exc*, the program terminates and control is returned to the operating system (which presumably will print out an error message and halt execution). If a handler is found, the corresponding right-hand side (after the => symbol) is executed and the enclosing routine returns control to its caller, or terminates if it is the main program. (Ada does have a notion of main program.)

18.4.4   Discussion

Exceptions are a control structure: they do not by themselves provide a technique for handling errors. They allow the programmer to concentrate error handling code in a special section of every routine.

As discussed in the object-oriented context (see 9.3.4), exception mechanisms have a role to play, but in specific cases only. In particular, there is little ground for the hope that exceptions will relieve client programmers from the need to worry about failures. The above stack implementation is particularly illuminating in this respect. How can we handle *underflow*, the exception raised when *pop* or *top* is attempted on an empty stack? There is no clear answer. The routines themselves cannot reasonably contain a handler (*top* does not know what to do when applied to an empty stack); so the responsibility lies with the client, which should include code of the form

/2/
```
    use REAL_STACKS;
    procedure proc (...) is
        s: STACK; ...
    begin
        ... pop (s); ...
    exception
        when underflow => action1;
        ...
    end proc;
```

So the client **must** specify exactly what happens in the erroneous case. The omission of a **when** *underflow* clause would be a serious design error. The above form is to be compared with the classical form for the call (written in Eiffel syntax):

/3/

   if not *s.empty* **then** *s.pop* **else** *action1* **end**

Remember that in some cases the error may be detected after the call rather than before (this is the "a posteriori" scheme described in 9.4.3). But that does not affect this discussion.

The exception form, /2/, differs from /3/ by only two aspects:

* The code for handling the error, *action1*, is textually separate from the calls that may raise the error;

* Error handling is the same for all such calls if more than one.

In this example, the classical approach seems better. The first aspect will not necessarily make the exception form simpler; deeply nested **if**...**then**...**else**... error-handling structures of the form described at the beginning of this section (page 393) will only occur in poorly modularized systems. The second aspect provides an argument in support of the classical form: if a routine contains more than one call to *pop*, the way to deal with empty stacks will almost certainly be different depending on the context of each of these calls.

This leaves little rationale for using programmer-defined exceptions. The previous discussions of exceptions (see 7.10 and 9.3) concluded by distinguishing only three cases in which an exception mechanism seems to play an indispensable role:

* Abnormal cases leading to preemptive action by the hardware or operating system, such as numerical overflow or memory exhaustion.

* Abnormal cases that must lead to termination as early as possible, to avoid potentially catastrophic consequences.

* Software fault tolerance: protection against possible errors in some component of the system itself.

The Ada exception mechanism should be restricted to these cases. Even then, however, it is too general. The problem, already described in 7.11.2, is that this mechanism is not constrained by the notion of contract. The basis of the disciplined exception mechanism studied in chapter 7 is the following rule:

> **First Law of software contracting**: There are only two ways a routine call may terminate: either the routine fulfils its contract, or its fails to fulfil it.

Trivial as it may seem, this rule is not satisfied in Ada. Because an exception handler may perform any operations before it returns control to the caller, it is perfectly possible to hide from the caller the failure to fulfil the contract. This violates the First Law and the following corollary:

> **Second Law of software contracting**: If a routine fails to fulfil its contract, the current execution of its caller also fails to fulfil its own contract.

Note that this rule only states that the current execution must fail, not necessarily the routine as a whole. This keeps open the possibility of retrying to achieve the contract by other means.

These rules, which are satisfied by the exception mechanism of chapter 7, are not enforced by the Ada mechanism. They explain why it is so easy to misuse this mechanism as a generalized goto, and a fairly dangerous one since it crosses routine boundaries.

Any reasonable use of Ada exceptions should abide by these rules, which may be summarized as follows in Ada terms:

> **Ada exception rule**: The execution of every exception handler should end by either executing a **raise** instruction or retrying the enclosing program unit.

In this rule, a program unit is either a block or a routine. The first solution is "organized panic": the exception handler attempts to bring back the environment to a stable state and terminates by a **raise** instruction signaling an exception to the caller (which will be bound by the same rule). Usually, this instruction will be **raise** without an exception name; this form of the instruction raises the original exception again. The second possibility, retrying, may only be implemented in Ada by using gotos, since there is no equivalent to the **retry** instruction of Eiffel.

Application of the above rule is essential to ensure that the exception mechanism of Ada is not misused.

This discussion of exceptions should remove any naive hope that exceptions may be used to duck the issue of errors. With or without an exception mechanism, run-time errors are a fact of (system) life and must be accounted for by the software.

18.5   TASKS

Besides packages, Ada offers another interesting modular construct: the task. Tasks are present to handle concurrency and fall beyond the scope of this book, but they deserve a mention since they actually come closer than packages to supporting object-oriented concepts.

Syntactically, tasks share many aspects of packages. The main difference is that a task is not just a modular unit but the representation of a process, to be executed in parallel with other processes. To use the terms introduced at the beginning of this chapter, a task is more than a syntactical unit; it describes a semantic component of the system. It is thus not surprising that tasks should be more akin to classes than packages are.

Like a package, a task is declared in two parts, interface and body. Instead of routines, a task specification introduces a number of **entries**. To the client, entries look like procedures; for example, the interface of a buffer manager task may be

> **task** *BUFFER_MANAGER* **is**
> **entry** *read* (*x:* **out** *T*);
> **entry** *write* (*x:* **in** *T*);
> **end** *BUFFER_MANAGER*;

(Tasks may not be generic, so that type *T* has to be globally available.) It is only the implementation of entries that distinguishes them from procedures: in the body, "**accept**" instructions will be used to specify synchronization and other constraints on the execution of the entries; here, for example, we might prescribe that only one *read* or *write* may proceed at any point in time, that *read* must wait until the buffer is not empty, and *write* until it is not full.

Although the details of Ada tasking will not be explored here, one point is worth noting for the discussion of object-oriented techniques: Ada permits the definition of **task types**, which may be used to create as many instances (tasks) as needed at run-time.

This makes tasks similar to classes, without inheritance. One can indeed imagine an implementation of object-oriented design in which classes would be represented by task types; at execution-time, objects would be created as tasks, instances of these task types. But this exercise can be of little more than academic interest. Remember that when we define a class, we expect to create a possibly large number of instances at run-time; given the overhead of creating a new parallel process in current operating environments, we could hardly do the same with task types. Perhaps some day, in massively parallel hardware environments....

18.6   KEY CONCEPTS INTRODUCED IN THIS CHAPTER

- Ada, studied as a representative of the class of "encapsulation languages" which also includes Modula-2, offers modular decomposition constructs: packages (and tasks).

- The emphasis is on information hiding: interface and implementation are declared separately.

- Genericity increases the flexibility of packages.

- Conflicts between methodological requirements and language implementation concerns give rise to the "private" problem.

- The package is a purely syntactic mechanism. Modules remain distinct from types. No inheritance mechanism is possible.

- Exceptions separate error detection from error handling, but provide no magic solution to the problem of run-time errors.

- The Ada exception mechanism should only be used in a disciplined fashion; any execution of an exception handler should terminate by either retrying the operation or signaling failure to the caller.

• Task types could in principle be used to implement classes without inheritance, but this solution is not practical in current environments.

18.7 BIBLIOGRAPHICAL NOTES

An influential presentation of how some concepts of object-oriented design may be used in Ada was given in [Booch 1983].

The official reference on Ada is [ANSI 1983]. This is recommended neither as bedtime reading nor as introductory material on the language. Numerous books are now available to fulfill the latter need.

References on the other modular languages mentioned at the beginning of this chapter are [Mitchell 1979] for Mesa, [Wirth 1982] for Modula-2, and [Liskov 1981] for CLU. See also [Liskov 1986], on programming methodology, also based on CLU.

EXERCISES

18.1 Why Eiffel does not need privates

The Ada compilation problem that gives rise to the "private" construct (18.3) might appear to plague object-oriented languages as well if the underlying environment (as in the case of Eiffel) supports separate compilation of classes. In fact, the problem seems to be worse because of inheritance: a variable declared of type C may at run-time refer to instances not only of C but of any descendant class; since any descendant may add its own attributes, the size of these instances is variable. If C is a deferred class, it is not even possible to assign a default size to its instances. Explain why, in spite of these remarks, there is no need in Eiffel for a language construct similar to the **private** mechanism of Ada. Discuss the tradeoffs involved in both solutions. Can you suggest a better approach in the Ada framework?

18.2 Generic routine parameters

Generic parameters to Ada packages may be not just types but also routines. Explain the relevance of this possibility to the implementation of object-oriented concepts, and its limitations. (See also the next chapter.)

18.3 Classes as tasks (for Ada programmers)

Rewrite the Eiffel class *COMPLEX* (7.7.4) as an Ada task type. Show examples of use of the resulting type.

19

Genericity versus inheritance

In part 2 and the previous chapter, we have studied two approaches for making software components more extendible and reusable. One, inheritance, is specific to object-oriented languages; it allows the construction of modules by successive extension and specialization. The other, genericity, is typical of Ada and was originally introduced by Algol 68; it is the ability to define parameterized modules, the parameters being (usually) types.

Both methods rely on *polymorphism* and *overloading*, where polymorphism is the ability to define program entities that may take more than one form, and overloading, a simple form of polymorphism, is the ability to attach more than one meaning to the same name, ambiguities being resolved by looking at the context of each occurrence of the name, either at compile time (static overloading) or at run-time.

On the surface, these techniques seem to address the same need: producing more flexible modules. A question that has intrigued many students of programming is how they compare. Are they redundant? Incompatible? Complementary? Should one choose between them, or does it make sense to combine them?

This chapter addresses these issues through a comparative analysis of genericity and inheritance, in the context of type checking (without which genericity would be meaningless). It assesses their respective strengths and weaknesses, examines which of their components are equivalent and which are truly different, shows how the two approaches complement each other, and explains how they may be reconciled, as exemplified in the design of Eiffel.

19.1   GENERICITY

This review begins by appraising the merits of genericity as it exists in a number of languages. Many of these languages are not object-oriented; the discussion will rely on the form of genericity that exists in Ada. Note that for the rest of section 19.1 we forget about object-oriented languages.

Only the most important form of Ada genericity will be considered: *type parameterization*, that is to say the ability to parameterize a software element (in Ada, a package or routine) by one or more types. Generic parameters have other, less interesting uses in Ada, such as parameterized dimensions for arrays.

One may distinguish between *unconstrained* genericity, whereby no specific requirement is imposed on generic parameters, and *constrained* genericity, whereby a certain structure is required.

19.1.1   Unconstrained genericity

In its simplest form, unconstrained genericity may be seen as a technique to bypass some unnecessary requirements of static type checking.

Consider the example of a simple procedure for exchanging the values of two variables. In a language which is not statically typed, we would write something like the following (using an Ada-like syntax):

/1/
```
procedure swap (x, y) is
     t: local;
begin
     t := x; x := y ; y := t;
end swap
```

The types of the elements to be swapped and of the local variable t do not need to be specified. However this may be too much freedom since a call of the form *swap* (a, b), where a is, say, an integer, and b a character string, will not be prohibited even though it is probably an error.

To address this issue, statically typed languages such as Pascal require programmers to explicitly declare the types of all variables and formal arguments, and enforce a statically checkable type compatibility constraint between actual and formal arguments in calls and between source and target in assignments. In such a language, the procedure to exchange the values of two variables of type T becomes:

/2/
```
procedure T_swap (x, y: in out T) is
     t: T
begin
     t := x; x := y ; y := t;
end swap
```

Demanding that T be specified as a single type averts type incompatibility errors, but has the unpleasant consequence of requiring a new procedure declaration for each type for which a swap operation is needed; in the absence of overloading, a different name must be assigned to each such procedure, for example *int_swap*, *str_swap* and so on. Such multiple declarations lengthen and obscure programs. The example chosen is particularly bad since all the declarations will be identical except for the two occurrences of *T*.

Static typing may be considered too restrictive here: the only real requirement is that the two actual arguments passed to any call of *swap* should be of the same type, and that their type should also be applied to the declaration of the local variable *t*.

A language with genericity provides a tradeoff between too much freedom, as with untyped languages, and too much restraint, as with Pascal. In such a language, one may declare *T* as a generic type parameter to the *swap* procedure. This is possible in Ada; generic routines are declared in the same way as the generic packages studied in the previous chapter. In quasi-Ada, a generic *swap* may be declared as follows:

/3/

```
generic
     type T is private;
procedure swap (x, y: in out T) is
     t: T
begin
     t := x; x := y ; y := t;
end swap
```

This would become correct Ada if the interface and implementation were separated, as explained in the previous chapter. Since information hiding is irrelevant for the discussion in this chapter, interfaces and implementations will be merged for ease of presentation.

The **generic...** clause introduces type parameters. By specifying *T* as "private", the writer of this procedure allows himself to apply to objects of type *T* (*x*, *y* and *t*) operations available on all types, such as assignment or comparison, and these only.

A declaration such as the above does not actually introduce a procedure but rather a procedure pattern; actual procedures are obtained by providing actual type parameters, as in

/4/

```
procedure int_swap is new swap (INTEGER);
procedure str_swap is new swap (STRING);
```

etc. Now assuming that *i* and *j* are variables of type *INTEGER*, *s* and *t* of type *STRING*, then of the following calls

```
int_swap (i, j);
str_swap (s, t);

int_swap (i, s);
str_swap (s, j);
str_swap (i, j);
```

all but the first two are statically incorrect.

More interesting than parameterized routines are parameterized packages. We saw an example in the last chapter: a generic stack package. Consider a queue example for a change. The operations on a queue (first-in, first out collection) are the following: add an element; remove the oldest element added and not yet removed; get the value of this oldest element; test whether the queue is empty. The interface of a queue manipulation package may be written as:

/5/

```
generic
      type T is private;
package QUEUES is
      type QUEUE (max_elements: POSITIVE) is private;
      function empty (s: in QUEUE) return BOOLEAN;
      procedure add (t: in T; s: in out QUEUE);
      procedure remove (s: in out QUEUE);
      function oldest (s: in QUEUE) return T;
private
      type QUEUE (max_elements: POSITIVE) is
                  -- The package uses an array representation for queues
            record
                  implementation: array (0..max_elements) of T;
                  nb_elements: NATURAL;
            end record;
end QUEUES
```

As with generic routines, the above does not define a package but a package pattern; actual packages are obtained by instantiation, as in

/6/

```
package INT_QUEUES is new QUEUES (INTEGER);
package STR_QUEUES is new QUEUES (STRING);
```

You may note again the compromise that generic declarations achieve between typed and untyped languages. *QUEUES* provides a pattern for the declaration of modules implementing queues of elements of all possible types T, while retaining the possibility to enforce type checks: for example it will not be possible to add an integer to a queue of strings.

Both examples above (swap and queue) show a form of genericity which may be called *unconstrained* since there is no specific requirement on the types that may be used as actual generic parameters: one may swap the values of variables of any type and create queues of values of any type – provided all the values in a given queue are of the same type.

Other generic definitions, however, only make sense if the actual generic parameters satisfy some conditions. This form may be called *constrained* genericity.

19.1.2   Constrained genericity

We look at constrained genericity through two examples. As in the unconstrained case, the examples include a routine and a package.

Assume first you need a generic function to compute the minimum of two values. The pattern of *swap* may be applied:

/7/

> **generic**
> > **type** *T* **is private;**
> **function** *minimum* (*x, y: T*) **return** *T* **is**
> **begin**
> > **if** *x* <= *y* **then return** *x*;
> > **else return** *y* **end if;**
> **end** *minimum*

However such a function declaration is not always meaningful: it should only be instantiated for types *T* on which a comparison operator <= is defined. Checking of this property could of course be postponed until run-time, but this is not acceptable in a language that enhances security through static typing. We need a way to specify that type *T* must be equipped with the right operation.

In Ada this will be written by treating the operator <= as a generic parameter of its own. Syntactically it is a function; as a syntactic facility, it is possible to invoke such a function using the usual infix form if it is declared with a name in double quotes, here "<=". Again the following declaration becomes legal Ada if the interface and implementation are taken apart.

/8/

> **generic**
> > **type** *T* **is private;**
> > **with function** "<=" (*a, b: T*) **return** *BOOLEAN* **is** <> ;
> **function** *minimum* (*x, y: T*) **return** *T* **is**
> **begin**
> > **if** *x* <= *y* **then return** *x*;
> > **else return** *y* **end if;**
> **end** *minimum*

The keyword **with** introduces generic parameters representing routines, such as "<=".

You may instantiate *minimum* for any type, say *T1*, such that there exists a function, say *T1_le*, of signature **function** (*a, b: T1*) **return** *BOOLEAN* :

/9/

> **function** *T1_minimum* **is new** *minimum* (*T1, T1_le*);

If, on the other hand, function *T1_le* is in fact called "<=", that is to say if its name and type match those of the corresponding formal routine, then it may be omitted from the list of actual parameters to the generic instance. For example, type *INTEGER* has a predefined "<=" function with the right type, so that you can simply declare

/10/

> **function** *int_minimum* **is new** *minimum* (*INTEGER*);

This use of default routines with matching names and types is made possible by the clause **is** <> in the declaration of the formal routine, here "<=". Operator overloading, as permitted (and in fact encouraged) by the design of Ada, plays an essential role here: many different types may have a "<=" function.

This discussion of constrained genericity for routines readily transposes to packages. Assume you need a generic package for handling matrices of objects of any type T, with matrix sum and product as basic operations. Such a definition only makes sense if type T has a sum and a product of its own, and each of these operations has a zero element; these features of T will be needed in the implementation of matrix sum and product. The public part of the package may be written as follows:

/11/

> **generic**
>> **type** T **is private**;
>> *zero: T*;
>> *unity: T*;
>> **with function** "+" (*a, b: T*) **return** T **is** <>;
>> **with function** "$*$" (*a, b: T*) **return** T **is** <>;
>
> **package** *MATRICES* **is**
>> **type** *MATRIX* (*lines, columns: POSITIVE*) **is private**;
>> **function** "+" (*m1, m2: MATRIX*) **return** *MATRIX*;
>> **function** "$*$" (*m1, m2: MATRIX*) **return** *MATRIX*;
>
> **private**
>> **type** *MATRIX* (*lines, columns: POSITIVE*) **is**
>>> **array** (*1..lines, 1..columns*) **of** T;
>
> **end** *MATRICES*;

Typical instances of the package are:

/12/

> **package** *INT_MATRICES* **is new** *MATRICES* (*INTEGER, 0, 1*);
>
> **package** *BOOL_MATRICES* **is**
>> **new** *MATRICES* (*BOOLEAN, false, true*, "or", "and");

Again, actual parameters corresponding to formal generic routines (here "+" and "$*$") may be omitted for type *INTEGER*, which has matching operations; but they must be included for *BOOLEAN*. (It is convenient to declare such parameters last in the formal list; otherwise keyword notation is required in calls which omit the corresponding actual parameters.)

It is interesting here to show how the implementation part of such a package will look, taking matrix product as an example of function body:

/13/
```
package body MATRICES is

    ... Other declarations ...

    function "*" (m1, m2: T) is
            result: MATRIX (m1' lines, m2' columns);
    begin
        if m1' columns /= m2' lines then
                raise incompatible_sizes;
        end if;
        for i in m1'RANGE(1) loop
                for j in m2'RANGE(2) loop
                        result (i, j) := zero;
                        for k in m1'RANGE(2) loop
                                result (i, j) :=
                                        result (i, j) + m1 (i, k) * m2 (k, j)
                        end loop;
                end loop;
        end loop;
        return result
    end "*";

end MATRICES;
```

This code relies of some specific features of Ada:

- For a parameterized type such as *MATRIX (lines, columns: POSITIVE)*, a variable declaration must provide actual parameters, e.g. *mm: MATRIX (100, 75)*; their values may then be retrieved using the apostrophe notation as in *mm' lines* which in this case has value 100.

- If a is an array, $a'RANGE(i)$ denotes the range of values in its i-th dimension; for example $m1'RANGE(1)$ above is the same as $1..m1'lines$.

- If requested to multiply two dimension-wise incompatible matrices, the program raises an exception. As with the exceptions in the *pop* and *top* routines of the stack package studied in the previous chapter, this exception corresponds to the violation of an implicit precondition.

The minimum and matrix examples are representative of Ada techniques for constrained genericity. They also show a serious limitation of these techniques: only syntactic constraints may be expressed. All that a programmer may require is the presence of certain routines ("<=", "+", "*" in the examples) with given types; but the declarations are meaningless unless some semantic constraints are also satisfied. For example, *minimum* only makes sense if "<=" is a total order relation on T; and the *MATRICES* package should not be instantiated for a type T unless the operations "+" and "*" have not only the right type ($T \times T \rightarrow T$) but also the appropriate properties: associativity, distributivity, *zero* a zero element for "+" and *unity* for "*" etc. We shall use the term **ring** for a structure equipped with operations enjoying these properties.

19.1.3   Implicit genericity

It is important to mention a form of genericity quite different from the above Ada-style explicit parameterization: the implicit polymorphism exemplified by the work on the ML functional language (see bibliographical notes).

This technique is based on the remark that explicit genericity, as seen above, places an unnecessary burden on the programmer, who must give generic types even when the context provides enough information to deduce a correct typing. It may be argued, for example, that the very first version (/1/) given for procedure *swap*, with no type declaration, is acceptable as it stands: with adequate typing rules, a compiler has enough information to deduce that x, y and t must have the same type. Why not then let programmers omit type declarations when they are not strictly needed conceptually, and have the compiler check that all uses of an identifier are consistent?

This approach, sometimes called "unobtrusive type checking", attempts to reconcile the freedom of untyped languages with the security of typed ones. It has been elegantly implemented in ML and other functional languages (see bibliographical notes).

The rest of this chapter relies on the Ada form, which for this discussion has the advantage that generic parameters stand out more visibly.

19.2   INHERITANCE

So much for pure genericity. The other term of the comparison is inheritance, which was studied in detail in chapters 10 and 11. To contrast it with genericity, consider the example of a general-purpose module library for files. First here is the outline of an Eiffel implementation of "special files" in the Unix sense, that is to say, files associated with devices:

/14/
```
    class DEVICE export
            open, close, opened
    feature
            open (file_descriptor: INTEGER) is
                do
                    ...
                end; -- open

            close is
                do
                    ...
                end; -- close

            opened: BOOLEAN
    end -- class DEVICE
```

An example use of this class is:

/15/

> *d1: DEVICE*; *f1: INTEGER*
> *d1.Create*;
> *d1.open (f1)*;
> **if** *d1.opened* **then** ...

Consider next the notion of a *tape* device. For the purposes of this discussion, a tape unit has all the properties of devices, as represented by the three features of class *DEVICE*, plus the ability to rewind its tape. Inheritance comes in handy here. Rather than building a new class from scratch, we may declare class *TAPE* as an extension of *DEVICE*:

/16/

> **class** *TAPE* **export** ... **inherit** *DEVICE* **feature**
> > *rewind* **is**
> > > **do** ... **end**
> **end** -- class *TAPE*

Objects of type *TAPE* automatically possess all the features of *DEVICE* objects, plus their own (here *rewind*). Class *DEVICE* could have more heirs, for example *DISK* with its own specific features such as direct access read and others.

The form of polymorphism associated with inheritance allows assignments of the form

> $x := y$

permitted only, in a typed language such as Eiffel, if the type of x is an ancestor of the type of y. The next associated property is dynamic binding, illustrated in this example by the case in which there is an "open" mechanism for tape devices, warranting redefinition of the corresponding routine:

/17/

> **class** *TAPE* **export** ... **inherit**
> > *DEVICE* **redefine** *open*
> **feature**
> > *open (file_descriptor: INTEGER)* **is**
> > > **do** ... special open for tape devices ... **end**;
> >
> > *rewind* **is**
> > > **do** ... **end**
> **end** -- class *TAPE*

Then if x is a device, the call

> $x.open (f1)$

will be executed differently depending on the assignments performed on x before the call: after $x := y$, where y is a tape, the tape version should be executed.

We have seen the remarkable benefits of the inheritance technique with respect to reusability and extendibility. A key aspect was the application of the open-closed principle: a software element such as *DEVICE* is both usable as it stands (it may be compiled as part of an executable system) and still amenable to extensions (if used as ancestor of new classes). Thus a compromise between usability and flexibility, fundamental for the qualities mentioned, is achieved.

The above properties are complemented by deferred features. Here, for example, devices under Unix are a special kind of files; *DEVICE* should thus be an heir to class *FILE*, whose other heirs may be *TEXT_FILE* (itself with heirs *NORMAL* and *DIRECTORY*) and *BINARY_FILE*. The figure shows the inheritance graph, a tree in this case.

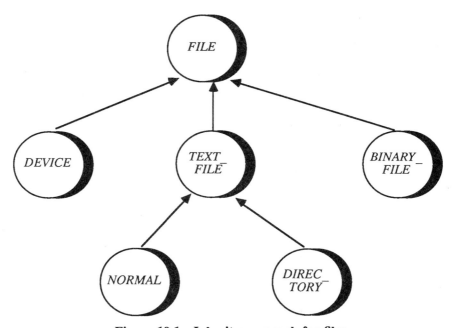

Figure 19.1   Inheritance graph for files

Any file may be opened or closed; but how these operations are performed depends on whether the file is a device, a directory etc. Thus *FILE* will be a deferred class where all corresponding procedures are deferred, passing over the burden of actual implementation to descendant classes:

/18/

```
    deferred class FILE export open, close feature
        open (file_descriptor: INTEGER) is deferred end;
        close is deferred end;
    end -- class FILE
```

Descendants of *FILE* should provide actual definitions of *open* and *close*.

19.3   SIMULATING INHERITANCE WITH GENERICITY

To compare genericity with inheritance, we shall study how, if in any way, the effect of each feature may be simulated in a language offering the other.

First consider a language such as Ada, offering genericity but not inheritance. Can it be made to achieve the effects of inheritance?

The easy part is the overloading. In a language such as Ada or Algol 68 where the same routine name may be reused as many times as needed provided it is applied to operands of different types, there is no difficulty in defining types such as *TAPE*, *DISK* etc., each with its own version of *open*, *close* etc.:

/19/

   procedure *open* (*p:* **in out** *TAPE*; *descriptor:* **in** *INTEGER*);

   procedure *close* (*p:* **in out** *DISK*);

   etc.

Provided the routines are distinguished by the type of at least one operand, as is the case here, no ambiguity will arise.

Yet this solution falls short of providing true polymorphic entities as in languages with inheritance, where, as discussed above, an operation may be executed differently depending on the form of its operand at run-time (even though it is possible, in a statically typed language, to check at compile-time that the operation is defined in all possible cases). A typical example is the call *d. close*, which will be carried out differently after the assignments *d := di* and *d := ta*, where *di* is a *DISK* and *ta* a *TAPE*. The Ada-like form of overloading does not provide anything like this remarkable possibility.

The only feature of Ada which could be used to emulate this property of object-oriented languages is in fact shared with Pascal and has nothing to do with overloading or genericity: it is the record with variant fields. We could for example define something like

/20/

   type *DEVICE* (*unit: DEVICE_TYPE*) **is**
      record
            ... fields common to all device types ...
            case *unit* **is**
                  when *tape* => ... fields for tape devices ...;
                  when *disk* => ... fields for disk devices ...;
                  ... other cases ...;
            end case
      end record

where *DEVICE_TYPE* is an enumeration type with elements *tape*, *disk* etc. Then there would be a single version of each the procedures on devices (*open*, *close* etc.), each containing a case discrimination of the form

/21/

```
case d'unit is
        when tape => ... action for tape devices ...;
        when disk => ... action for disk devices ...;
        ... other cases ...;
    end case
```

But we have seen that such a solution is unacceptable from a software engineering viewpoint: it runs contrary to the criteria of extendibility, reusability and compatibility. It distributes knowledge about possible device types all over the software systems, scattering case discriminations on *DEVICE_TYPE*. Worse yet, it closes the set of possible choices. As opposed to the Eiffel class *DEVICE* which can at any time be used as parent of a new class, the Ada type *DEVICE* has a fixed list of variants, one for each element of the enumeration type *DEVICE_TYPE*. To add a new case, one must change the declaration of *DEVICE*, invalidating any program unit that relied on it.

So the answer to the question posed at the beginning of this section – can inheritance be simulated with genericity? – is no.

19.4 SIMULATING GENERICITY WITH INHERITANCE

We now address the reverse problem: can we achieve the effect of Ada-style genericity in an object-oriented language with inheritance as provided in Eiffel?

As we know from chapter 6, Eiffel does provide a generic parameter mechanism. But since we are comparing pure genericity versus pure inheritance, the rule of the game for some time, frustrating as it may be, is to pretend we have all but forgotten about chapter 6 and genericity in Eiffel. Thus you should consider the following discussion with a grain of salt, since the solutions presented in this section are substantially more complex than those obtainable with full Eiffel, described in 19.5.

The simulation turns out to be easier, or at least less artificial, for constrained genericity – a surprising result since unconstrained genericity is conceptually simpler. Therefore we begin with the constrained case.

19.4.1 Constrained genericity: overview

The idea is to associate a class with a constrained formal generic type parameter. This is a natural thing to do since a constrained generic type may be viewed, together with its constraining operations, as an abstract data type. Consider for example the Ada generic clauses in our two constrained examples, minimum and matrices:

/22/

```
generic
        type T is private;
        with function "<=" (a, b: T) return BOOLEAN is <> ;
```

/23/

> **generic**
>> **type** *T* **is private**;
>> *zero: T*;
>> *unity: T*;
>> **with function** "+" (*a, b: T*) **is** <> ;
>> **with function** "∗" (*a, b: T*) **is** <> ;

We may view these clauses as the definitions of two abstract data types, say *COMPARABLE* and *RING* ; the former is characterized by a comparison operation "<=", and the latter by features *zero, unity,* "+" and "∗".

In an object-oriented language, such types may be directly represented as classes. We cannot define these classes entirely, for there is no universal implementation of "<=", "+" etc.; rather, they are to be used as ancestors of other classes, corresponding to actual generic parameters. Deferred classes provide exactly what is needed:

/24/

> **deferred class** *COMPARABLE* **export** *le* **feature**
>> *le* (*other: COMPARABLE*): *BOOLEAN* **is deferred end**
>
> **end** -- class *COMPARABLE*
>> -- *le* corresponds to "<="; there are no infix functions in Eiffel.

> **deferred class** *RING* **export**
>> *plus, times, zero, unity*
>
> **feature**
>> *plus* (*other: RING*) **is deferred end**;
>> *times* (*other: RING*) **is deferred end**;
>> *zero: RING*;
>> *unity: RING*
>
> **end** -- class *RING*

The comment made page 405 about the lack of semantic specification in Ada constrained genericity would seem to apply here too: none of the required properties on *le*, *plus* etc. has been specified. In Eiffel, however, we can use preconditions and postconditions. Simple examples will be given in 19.4.4.

You will also have noted that *plus* and *times* are defined here as procedures rather than functions; the convention followed in the Eiffel examples below is that *r.plus* (*r1*) is an instruction that performs a side-effect on *r*, adding to its value the value of *r1*, rather than an expression returning the sum of these values (and similarly for *times*). In contrast, the Ada operators "+" and "∗" were functions. The difference is not essential and procedures are used in Eiffel mainly for brevity. Subject to the following discussion, the examples may be changed into functions, as in

> *plus* (*other: RING*): *RING* **is deferred end**

19.4.2   Constrained genericity: routines

A routine such as *minimum* may now be written by specifying its arguments to be of
type *COMPARABLE*. Based on the Ada pattern, the function would be declared as

/25/

> *minimum (one, other: COMPARABLE): COMPARABLE* **is**
> > -- Minimum of *one* and *other*
>
> > **do** ... **end**

In an object-oriented language, however, every routine appears in a class and is
relative to the current instance of that class; thus it seems preferable to include
minimum in class *COMPARABLE*, argument *one* becoming the implicit current
instance. The class becomes:

/26/

> **deferred class** *COMPARABLE* **export** *le, minimum* **feature**
> > *le (other: COMPARABLE): BOOLEAN* **is**
> > > **deferred**
> > > **end**;
>
> > *minimum (other:* **like** *Current): COMPARABLE* **is**
> > > -- Minimum of current element and *other*
> >
> > > **do**
> > > > **if** *le (other)* **then** *Result := Current* **else** *Result := other* **end**
> > >
> > > **end** -- *minimum*
> **end** -- class *COMPARABLE*

To compute the minimum of two elements, you must declare them of some
descendant type of *COMPARABLE*, for which an effective version of *le* has been
defined. For example:

/27/

> **class** *INT_COMPARABLE* **export**
> > *le, value, change_value*
> **inherit**
> > *COMPARABLE*
> **feature**
> > *le (other:* **like** *Current): BOOLEAN* **is**
> > > -- Is current element less than or equal to *other* ?
> > > **do** *Result := (value <= other.value)* **end**;
> >
> > *value: INTEGER*;
> > > -- Value of current element
> >
> > *change_value (new: T)* **is**
> > > -- Assign *new* to value of current element
> > > **do** *value := new* **end**
> **end** -- class *INT_COMPARABLE*

To find the minimum of two integers, you may now apply function *minimum*, not to arguments of type integer, but to arguments of type *INT_COMPARABLE*, say *ic1* and *ic2*, as follows:

/28/

   ic3 := ic1.minimum (ic2)

To use the generic *le* and *minimum* functions, you must renounce direct references to integers, using *INT_COMPARABLE* entities instead; hence the need for attribute *value* and routine *change_value* to access and modify the associated integer values.

Heirs of *COMPARABLE*, say *STR_COMPARABLE*, *REAL_COMPARABLE*, and so on, must be introduced for each type for which a version of *minimum* is desired.

Of course, having to declare similar features *value* and *change_value* for all descendants of *COMPARABLE*, and to sacrifice the direct use of simple types, is unpleasant. But this relatively small price in terms of ease of program writing seems to yield the effect of genericity. (We shall see how to avoid the redundant coding in actual Eiffel.)

Note that the mechanism of declaration by association is essential to ensure type correctness. If the argument to *minimum* in *COMPARABLE* had been declared as a *COMPARABLE*, rather than **like** *Current*, then the following call would be legal:

/29/

   ic1.minimum (c)

even if *c* is a *COMPARABLE* but not an *INT_COMPARABLE*. Clearly, such a call should be disallowed.

> If you do not remember well the details of declaration by association and want to understand the remainder of this chapter properly, please go back to 11.4; declaration by association plays an important part in the following discussion.

19.4.3 Constrained genericity: packages

The previous discussion transposes to packages. The matrix abstraction implemented in Ada by the *MATRICES* package may be emulated by a class:

/30/

```
class MATRIX export
      entry, enter, plus, times
feature

      anchor: RING;

      implementation: ARRAY2 [like anchor];

      entry (i, j: INTEGER): like anchor is
                  -- Value of the (i, j) entry of the matrix
            do Result := implementation.entry (i, j) end;
```

```
    enter (i, j: INTEGER; v: like anchor) is
            -- Assign value v to entry (i, j) of the matrix
        do implementation.enter (i, j, v) end;

    plus (other: like Current) is
            -- Add other to current matrix
        local
            t1: RING
        do
            ... loop
                ...loop
                        t1 := entry (i, j);
                        t1.plus (other.entry (i, j));
                        enter (i, j, t1 )
                    end
                end
        end; -- plus

    times (other: like Current) is
            -- Multiply current matrix by other
        local ... do ... end
end -- class MATRIX
```

Declaration by association is used here too. The type of the argument to *enter* and of the result of *entry* raises an interesting problem: it should be *RING*, but redefined properly in descendant classes. Declaration by association is the solution; but here for the first time no attribute of the class seems to be available to serve as anchor. This is not to stop us, however: we declare an **artificial anchor**, called exactly that – *anchor*. Its only purpose is to be redefined to the proper descendant types of *RING* in future descendants of *MATRIX* (that is to say, to *BOOL_RING* in *BOOL_MATRIX* etc.), so that all associated entities will follow suit.

This technique of artificial anchors is useful to preserve type consistency when, as here, there is no "natural" anchor among the attributes of the class.

We have left out some details (such as how the dimensions of a matrix are set) but outlined the *plus* procedure, exhibiting the object-oriented form of overloading: the internal call to *plus* is the operation on *RING*, not *MATRIX*. Similarly, routines *enter* and *entry* are used in both their *ARRAY2* and *MATRIX* versions. (*ARRAY2* describes two-dimensional arrays.)

To define the equivalent of the Ada generic package instantiation (/12/)

package *BOOL_MATRICES* **is**
        MATRICES (*BOOLEAN, false, true,* "**or**", "**and**");

we must declare the "ring" corresponding to booleans:

/31/

```
class BOOL_RING export
        value, change_value, plus, times, zero, unity
inherit
        RING redefine zero, unity
feature
        value: BOOLEAN;

        change_value (b: BOOLEAN) is
                        -- Assign b to value of current element
                do value := b end;

        plus (other: like Current) is
                        -- Boolean addition: or
                do change_value (value or other.value) end;

        times (other: like Current) is
                        -- Boolean multiplication: and
                do change_value (value and other.value) end;

        zero: like Current is
                        -- Zero element for boolean addition
                once
                        Result.Create;
                        Result.change_value (false)
                end; -- zero

        unity: like Current is
                        -- Zero element for boolean multiplication
                once
                        Result.Create;
                        Result.change_value (true)
                end -- unity
end -- class BOOL_RING
```

Note that *zero* and *unity* are redefined as **once** functions returning constant values of type **like** *Current*.

To obtain an equivalent to the Ada package instantiation for boolean matrices, it suffices to define an heir *BOOL_MATRIX* of *MATRIX*, where only *anchor* needs to be redefined explicitly; the types of arguments or results of *entry*, *enter*, *plus* and ∗, and the type of the elements of array *implementation*, follow automatically.

/32/

```
class BOOL_MATRIX export
        ... same export clause as MATRIX ...
inherit
        MATRIX
                        redefine anchor
feature
        anchor: BOOL_RING;
end -- class BOOL_MATRIX
```

Using inheritance, this construction achieves the effect of constrained genericity.

19.4.4   Unconstrained genericity

The mechanism for simulating unconstrained genericity is the same; this case is simply seen as a special form of constrained genericity, with an empty set of constraints. As above, formal type parameters will be interpreted as abstract data types, but here with no relevant operations. The technique works, but becomes rather heavy to apply since the dummy types do not correspond to any obviously relevant data abstraction.

Let us apply the previous technique to both our unconstrained examples, swap and queue, beginning with the latter. We need a class, say *QUEUEABLE*, describing objects that may be added to and retrieved from a queue. Since this is true of any object, this class has no property beyond its name:

/33/
> **class** *QUEUEABLE* **end**

We may now declare a class *QUEUE*, whose operations apply to *QUEUEABLE* objects. (Remember that this class is not meant as a model to be imitated: we are voluntarily playing with an impoverished version of Eiffel, deprived of genericity.)

As before, it is useful to introduce an artificial anchor, associated here with the type of queue elements. Rather than *anchor*, we choose a more expressive name for the anchor: *a_queue_element*. The routine postconditions have been left out for brevity.

/34/
> **class** *QUEUE* **export**
>   *empty, add, remove, oldest, full*
> **feature**
>   *a_queue_element: QUEUEABLE*; -- Anchor for type of queue elements
>   *implementation: ARRAY* [**like** *a_queue_element*];
>   *max_elements, first, last, nb_elements: INTEGER*;
>
>   *empty: BOOLEAN* **is**
>   -- Is the queue empty?
>   **do** *Result := (nb_elements = 0)* **end**;
>
>   *full: BOOLEAN* **is**
>   -- Is the queue representation full?
>   **do** *Result := (nb_elements = max_elements)* **end**;
>
>   *add (x:* **like** *a_queue_element)* **is**
>   -- Add *x* at end of queue
>   **require**
>   **not** *full*
>   **do**
>   *last := next (last)*;
>   *implementation. enter (last, x)*
>   **end**; -- *add*

remove **is**
>   -- Remove oldest element
>   **require**
>   **not** *empty*
>   **do**
>   *first := next (first)*
>   **end**; -- *remove*

oldest: **like** *a_queue_element* **is**
>   -- Oldest element in queue
>   **require**
>   **not** *empty*
>   **do**
>   *Result := implementation. entry (first+1)*
>   **end**; -- *oldest*

nb_elements: INTEGER **is**
>   -- Number of elements added and not yet removed
>   **do**
>   *Result := (last − first)* **mod** *max_elements*
>   **end**

Create (m: INTEGER) **is**
>   -- Create queue with space for *m* values
>   **do**
>   *implementation.Create (0, m)*;
>   *max_elements := m*   -- One fewer than valid array indices
>   **end** -- *Create*

next (n: INTEGER): INTEGER **is**
>   -- Next value after *n*, modulo *max_elements* (secret)
>   **do**
>   *Result := (n + 1)* **mod** *max_elements*
>   **end**
invariant
>   *0 <= nb_elements*; *nb_elements <= max_elements*;
>   -- An array position is kept free;
>   -- Queued elements appear in array positions
>   -- *first+1, ... last* (cyclically modulo *max_size*)
end -- class *QUEUE*

To instantiate this definition for queues of specific types, you must apply the same techniques as above: define descendants of *QUEUEABLE* , such as

/35/

class *INT_QUEUEABLE* **export**
    value, change_value
inherit
    QUEUEABLE
feature
    value: INTEGER;
    change_value (*n: INTEGER*) **is**
             -- Assign *n* to value of current element
        do *value := n* **end**
end -- *INT_QUEUEABLE*

and similarly *STR_QUEUEABLE* etc.; declare the corresponding descendants of *QUEUE*, redefining the anchor *a_queue_element* appropriately in each.

19.5 GENERICITY AND INHERITANCE IN EIFFEL

It appears from the previous discussion that inheritance is the more powerful mechanism: there is no way to provide a reasonable simulation with genericity. Furthermore:

    • The equivalent of generic routines or packages may be expressed in a language with inheritance, but one does not avoid the need for certain spurious duplications of code. The extra verbosity is particularly hard to justify in the case of unconstrained genericity, for which the simulation mechanism is just as complex as for the conceptually more difficult constrained case.

    • Type checking introduces difficulties in the use of inheritance to express generic objects.

In Eiffel, declaration by association solves the second problem. Let's see how the language's limited form of genericity addresses the first.

19.5.1 Simple genericity

Since unconstrained genericity is both the simpler case and the one for which the pure inheritance solution is least acceptable, it seems adequate to provide a specific mechanism for this case, distinct from the inheritance mechanism. Consequently, Eiffel classes may have unconstrained generic parameters: as we are now (at last) allowed to remember from chapter 6, a class may be defined as

    class *C* [*T1, T2, ..., Tn*] ...

where the parameters represent arbitrary types (basic or class). An actual use of the class will need actual type parameters, as in

    x: C [*INTEGER, RING, ..., DEVICE*]

The examples of the previous sections provide obvious cases where generic parameters are useful if not indispensable. For instance *COMPARABLE* /26/ becomes

/36/

deferred class *COMPARABLE* [*T*] **export**
 le, minimum, value, change_value
feature

 le (*other:* **like** *Current*): *BOOLEAN* **is deferred end**;

 minimum (*other:* **like** *Current*): **like** *Current* **is**
  ... As in /26/ ...;

 value: T;

 change_value (*new: T*) **is do** *value := new* **end**
end -- class *COMPARABLE*

Using a generic parameter makes the class simple and clear. To define *INT_COMPARABLE* all we have to write now is:

/37/

class *INT_COMPARABLE* **export** *le* **inherit**
 COMPARABLE [*INTEGER*]
feature
 le (*other: INT_COMPARABLE*): *BOOLEAN* **is**
   -- Is current element less than or equal to *other* ?
  do *Result :=* (*value <= other.value*) **end**
end -- class *INT_COMPARABLE*

The other examples are treated similarly:

/38/

deferred class *RING* [*T*] **export**
 plus, times, zero, unity, value, change_value
feature
 plus (*other:* **like** *Current*) **is deferred end**;
 times (*other:* **like** *Current*) **is deferred end**;
 zero, unity: **like** *Current*;
 value: T;
 change_value (*new: T*) **is do** *value := new* **end**
end -- class *RING*

/39/

class *MATRIX* [*T*] **export**
 entry, enter, plus, times
feature
 anchor: RING [*T*]
 implementation: ARRAY2 [**like** *anchor*];

 entry (*i, j: INTEGER*): **like** *anchor* **is** ... As before ... (see /30/);

 ... and similarly for *enter, plus* and *times* ...
end -- class *MATRIX*

Note how the use of a generic parameter in two related classes, *RING* and *MATRIX*, makes it possible to ensure type consistency (all elements of a matrix will be of type *RING* [*T*] for the same *T*). As with *COMPARABLE* /36/, the declarations of features *value* and *change_value* have been factored out: they now appear in class *RING* rather than being repeated in all its descendants.

> Clients should be able to look at the matrices as if they contained elements of type *T* even though *RING* [*T*] elements are used internally. With the new definition of the class it becomes possible to write exported functions more appropriate for clients than *entry* and *enter*. See exercise 19.3.

In the unconstrained case, the need for dummy classes disappears; class *QUEUEABLE* and its heirs *INT_QUEUEABLE*, *STR_QUEUEABLE* etc. are not necessary any more, since *QUEUE* may be rewritten as

/40/
>   **class** *QUEUE* [*T*] **export** ... *as before* /34/ ... **feature**
>   *implementation: ARRAY* [*T*];
>
>   ... The rest of the class as in /34/
>   except that *T* is used in lieu of *QUEUEABLE* ...
>
>   **end** -- class *QUEUE*

There is no more use for classes such as *INT_QUEUE, STRING_QUEUE* etc.; simply use *QUEUE* [*INTEGER*], *QUEUE* [*STRING*] and so on. The artificial anchor *a_queue_element* also disappears in this case, since the type of the queue elements, which is also the result type of *oldest*, is now simply *T*.

A remarkable degree of simplification has been achieved. Auxiliary classes are not needed any more for unconstrained genericity. However we do *not* introduce constrained genericity in the language: this feature would be redundant with the inheritance mechanism. To provide the equivalent of a constrained formal generic parameter, we retain the technique introduced in 19.4.1: declare a special class such as *COMPARABLE* [*T*] whose features correspond to the constraints (that is to say, the **with** routines in Ada), and declare any corresponding actual parameters as descendants of this class.

19.6 DISCUSSION

Genericity and inheritance are two important techniques towards the software quality goals mentioned at the beginning of this chapter. The discussion has analyzed which of their features are equivalent, and which are complementary.

Providing a programming language with the full extent of both inheritance and Ada-like genericity would result in a redundant and overly complex design; but including only inheritance would make it too difficult for programmers to handle the simple cases for which unconstrained genericity offers an elegant expression mechanism, as in the queue example.

So in Eiffel the borderline was put at unconstrained genericity. Classes may have unconstrained generic parameters; constrained generic parameters are treated through inheritance. (See exercise 19.5. for a possible extension.)

Declaration by association completes this architecture by permitting completely static type checking, while retaining the necessary flexibility.

This design is meant to achieve a good balance between the facilities offered by two important but very different techniques for the implementation of extendible and reusable software.

19.7   KEY CONCEPTS INTRODUCED IN THIS CHAPTER

• Both genericity and inheritance aim to increase the flexibility of software modules.

• Genericity is a more static technique, not necessarily connected with object-oriented languages.

• Inheritance permits incremental module construction, by extension and specialization.

• Two forms of genericity may be distinguished: unconstrained genericity, whereby no requirements are imposed on the generic parameters, and constrained genericity, whereby the generic parameters are required to be equipped with specific operations.

• The power of inheritance cannot be obtained through genericity in a simple fashion.

• Pure inheritance can be used to simulate genericity, but at the expense of heaviness in expression and violations of type checking constraints.

• A good compromise, as achieved in Eiffel, is to combine the full power of inheritance and redefinition with unconstrained genericity.

• In this framework, the type checking problems are solved through the notion of declaration by association; in some cases, an artificial anchor may be needed.

19.8   BIBLIOGRAPHICAL NOTES

(See also the references in chapter 6.)

An interesting variant of genericity, whereby type parameters are implicit (the language being designed in such a way that when an operation is overloaded, the compiler is able to determine the appropriate variant of the operation from the context of each occurrence) was developed by Robin Milner in connection with the language ML [Milner 1978]. [Cardelli 1987] is an introductory presentation of this approach, which has been integrated into a number of functional languages.

A survey article [Cardelli 1985] on types, data abstraction and polymorphism covers from a mathematical viewpoint some of the issues discussed in this chapter.

EXERCISES

19.1 Artificial anchors

The artificial anchor *anchor* (page 414) is declared as an attribute of class *MATRIX* and thus entails a small run-time space overhead in instances of the class. Is it possible to avoid this overhead by declaring *anchor* as a "once function", whose body may be empty since it will never need to be evaluated?

19.2 Binary trees and binary search trees

Write a generic "binary tree" class *BINTREE*; a binary tree (or binary node) has some root information and two optional subtrees, left and right.

Then consider the notion of "binary search tree" where a new element is inserted on the left of a given node if its information field is less than or equal to the information of that node, and to the right otherwise; this assumes that there is a total order relation on "informations". Write a class *BINSEARCHTREE* implementing this notion, as a descendant of *BINTREE*. Make the class as general as possible, and its use by a client, for an arbitrary type of "informations" with their specific order relation, as easy as possible.

19.3 More usable matrices

Add to the last version obtained for class *MATRIX* /39/ two functions, one for access and one for modification, which in contrast to *entry* and *enter* will allow clients to manipulate a matrix of type *MATRIX* [*T*] in terms of elements of type *T* rather than *RING* [*T*].

19.4 Full queue implementations

Expand the queue example by defining a deferred class *QUEUE*, completing the class of section 19.4.4 (now called *FIXED_QUEUE*, inheriting from *QUEUE* and *ARRAY*, and with proper postconditions), and adding a class *LINKED_QUEUE* for the linked list implementation (based on inheritance from *LINKED_LIST* and *QUEUE*).

19.5 Special support for constrained genericity

(You should answer exercise 19.2 before you attack this one.) A recent extension of the Eiffel generic mechanism allows the declaration of a generic class to include a constraint on generic parameters, expressed under the syntax

> **class** *AA* [*T* –> *BB*] ...

where *BB* is some class; this notation means that any actual generic parameter used for *T* must be a descendant of *BB*. Discuss the usefulness of this extension. Should *BB* be a class type (so that it may have generic parameters, in which case the question arises of whether *T* may be one of them) or just a class name?

20

Other object-oriented languages

Following the introduction of Simula in 1967, a number of object-oriented languages have been designed, highlighting various aspects of the approach. This chapter reviews some of the languages that have attracted the most attention: Simula; Smalltalk; and object-oriented extensions of C, Lisp and Pascal.

Whenever the differences in terminology are unimportant, the Eiffel terms are used. For example, we talk about Simula routines, procedures and functions, although the corresponding terms in standard Simula usage are respectively procedure, untyped procedure and typed procedure.

20.1 SIMULA

20.1.1 Background

Simula was designed in 1967, under the name Simula 67, by Ole-Johan Dahl and Krysten Nygaard from the University of Oslo and the Norwegian Computing Center (Norsk Regnesentral). The name reflects continuity with a previous simulation language, Simula 1; it is somewhat misleading, however, since Simula 67 is really a general-purpose programming language, of which simulation is just one application.

The name was shortened to Simula in 1986.

20.1.2 Availability

Recent converts to the ideas of object-oriented programming sometimes think of Simula as a respectable but defunct ancestor. Quite to the contrary, Simula is still alive and enjoys the support of a small but enthusiastic community. The language definition is maintained by the "Simula Standards Group"

Compilers are available for a variety of hardware environments from a number of companies, mostly Norwegian and Swedish.

20.1.3 Major language traits

Simula is an object-oriented extension of Algol 60. Most correct Algol 60 programs are also correct Simula programs. In particular, the basic control structures are those of Algol 60: loop, conditional, switch (a multiple branch instruction, low-level precursor to Pascal's case instruction). The basic data types (integer, real etc.) are also drawn from Algol 60.

As Algol 60, Simula is a classical language with a notion of main program. An executable program is a main program containing a number of program units (routines or classes). A limited form of separate class compilation is, however, supported.

Simula embodies full block structure in the Algol 60 style: program units such as classes may be nested within one another.

As in Eiffel, entities of non-basic types denote references to class instances. To emphasize this property, such entities are declared as **ref** (C) and operations on them use special symbols: :– rather than := for assignment, == rather than = for equality, =/= rather than /= for inequality. The merits of this convention were discussed in 5.8.3.

As in Eiffel, class instances are created explicitly. Rather than by an instruction, instances are obtained by evaluating **new** expressions, as in

> **ref** (C) a;
>
> ...
>
> a :– **new** C

Evaluation of the **new** expression creates an instance of C and returns a reference to it. A class may have arguments (playing the role of the arguments to *Create* in Eiffel), as in

> **class** C (x, y); *integer x, y*
>
> **begin** ... **end**;

If this is the case, the **new** expression must provide corresponding actual arguments:

> a :– **new** C $(3, 98)$

A class may contain routines, attributes and a sequence of instructions, the body of the class, which is executed as a result of the **new** call.

No assertion mechanism is provided.

Inheritance is offered; B is declared to be an heir of A by

> A **class** B; **begin** ... **end**

The prefix, here A, must be unique; multiple inheritance is not supported.

A feature of a class may be redefined in a descendant class by simply providing a new declaration. (There is no explicit "redefine" clause.)

In the original version of Simula 67, no information hiding was offered. In more recent versions, a feature declared as **protected** will be unavailable to clients; a protected feature which is further declared as **hidden** will also be unavailable to proper descendants. A non-protected feature may be protected by a proper descendant, but a protected feature may not be re-exported by proper descendants.

Deferred features are offered in the form of "virtual routines", appearing in a **virtual** paragraph at the beginning of the class. It is not necessary to declare the arguments of a virtual routine; this means that different effective definitions of a virtual routine may have different numbers and types of arguments. For example, a class *POLYGON* might begin with

> **class** *POLYGON*;
>
> > **virtual:**   **procedure** *set_vertices*;
>
> **begin**
>
> > ...
>
> **end**

allowing descendants to provide a variable number of arguments of type *POINT* for *set_vertices*: three for *TRIANGLE*, four for *QUADRANGLE* etc. This flexibility implies that checking must be done at run-time.

Polymorphism is supported: if B is a descendant of A, the assignment $a1 := b1$ is correct for $a1$ of type A and $b1$ of type B.

By default, binding is static rather than dynamic, except for virtual routines. Thus if f is a non-virtual feature declared at the A level, $a1.f$ will denote the A version of f even if there is a different version in B. Dynamic binding may be forced by using the **qua** construct, as in

> $(a1$ **qua** $B).f$

This, of course, loses the automatic adaptation of every operation to its target, which has been presented as a key feature of the object-oriented approach. This property may be obtained in Simula, however, by declaring polymorphic routines as virtual. In many of the examples that we have studied, a polymorphic routine was not deferred but had a default implementation: this was the case with the first example of dynamic binding, *perimeter* for polygons (10.1). To achieve the same effect, the Simula programmer must add an intermediate class where the routine is virtual.

As an alternative to using **qua**, the **inspect** instruction makes it possible to perform a different operation on an entity $a1$, depending on the actual type of the corresponding object, which must be a descendant of the type A declared for $a1$:

> **inspect** $a1$
> > **when** A do ... ;
> > **when** B do ... ;
> >
> > ...

Using this instruction assumes that the set of descendants of a class is frozen; this contradicts the view of inheritance (open-closed principle) that has been propounded by this book.

20.1.4   An example

The following class extracts will serve to illustrate the general flavor of Simula. They are drawn from the solution to the problem of full-screen entry systems (12.3). It is instructive to compare them with the corresponding Eiffel classes (12.3.5 and 12.3.6).

```
class STATE;
    virtual:
            procedure display;
            procedure read;
            boolean procedure correct;
            procedure message;
            procedure process;

    begin
            ref (ANSWER) user_answer;
            integer next_choice;
        procedure do_one_state;
            begin
                    boolean ok;

                ok := false;

                while not ok do
                    begin
                            display;
                            read;
                            ok := correct;

                            if not ok then
                                    message (a)
                        end checking;
                    process;
            end do_one_state
    end STATE
```

```
class APPLICATION (n, m);
            integer n, m;
    begin
                ref (STATE) array transition (1:n, 0:m−1);
                ref (STATE) array associated_state (1:n);
                integer first_number;

            procedure session;
                begin
                            integer st_number;

                        st_number := first_number;

                        while st_number /= 0 do
                            begin
                                        ref (STATE) st;
                                st := associated_state (st_number);
                                st.do_one_state;
                                st_number :=
                                        transition (st_number, st.next_choice)
                            end Loop

                    end session

        ...


    end APPLICATION
```

20.1.5 Coroutines

The above is a brief description of how Simula implements the basic concepts of object-oriented programming. Simula also offers an interesting addition to these concepts: coroutines.

Coroutines are modeled after parallel processes as they exist in operating systems or real-time software. A process has more conceptual autonomy than a classical routine; a printer driver, for example, is entirely responsible for what happens to the printer it manages. Such a driver is in charge of an abstract data type implementation (the printer, with operations such as switch the printer on, print a line, advance by one page etc.). But it also has a strong process aspect and may be characterized by a well-defined lifecycle, often conceptually infinite. The rough form of the printer process could be something like

```
initialization ;
loop forever
    obtain a file to be printed ;
    print it
end -- loop
```

In sequential programming, the relationship between program units is asymmetric: a program unit calls another, which will execute completely and return to the caller at the point of call. Communication between processes is more a relation between equals: each process pursues its own life, interrupting itself to provide information to, or get information from another.

A

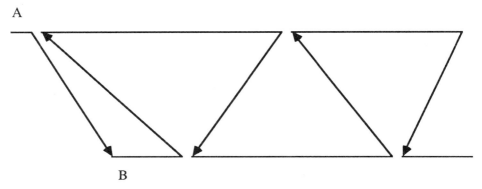

B

Figure 20.1   Coroutine sequencing

Coroutines are designed after this model; the only difference with parallel processes is that coroutines are meant to be executed on a sequential computer. This emulation of parallel execution in a sequential environment is called **quasi-parallelism**. A coroutine may be viewed as a routine which would have a symmetric relation with its caller: the "call" and "return" operations are merged into a single pattern, the **resume** instruction. A coroutine that "resumes" another interrupts its own execution and restarts its colleague at its last point of interruption. The interrupted coroutine may itself be later resumed.

Coroutines are particularly useful when each of several related activities has its own logic; each may be described as a sequential process, and the master-slave relationship implied by routines is not adequate. A frequent example is an input-to-output transformation in which different constraints are placed on the structure of the input and output files. Such a case will be discussed below.

In Simula, coroutines are represented by instances of classes. This is appropriate since coroutines almost always need persistent data, and may often be viewed not just as processes but also as abstract data type implementations. Remember that a Simula class has a body, which is a sequence of instructions. In a class representing a pure data abstraction, this body only serves as initialization of the class instances (the equivalent of the Eiffel *Create*); but in a coroutine it will be the description of a process.

The body of a coroutine is usually a loop of the form

```
while continuation_condition do
    begin
        ... actions;
        resume other_coroutine;
        ...actions
    end
```

where the loop body contains one or more **resume** applied to other coroutines with a similar structure. The *continuation_condition* is often **true** since it may be appropriate, as in the case of the printer driver, to view the coroutine as a conceptually infinite process; when the execution of a system terminates, the coroutine will simply not be resumed. Of course, at least one coroutine should have a continuation condition other than **true** if the execution is to terminate.

A problem that arises with coroutines is how to start the overall execution of a system. A system based on coroutines usually has a main program that first creates a number of coroutine objects, and then resumes one of them:

   corout1 :– **new** *C1*; *corout2* :– **new** *C2*; *corout3* :– **new** *C3*; ...

   resume *corout$_i$*

The evaluation of a **new** expression creates an object and starts executing its body.

In an environment implementing true parallelism rather than quasi-parallelism, the body of a coroutine would be executed as a parallel process; **new** would start such a process and return control immediately to the calling program, allowing it to proceed with the creation of other coroutine objects and the **resume** on one of them. But with a quasi-parallel process only one coroutine may be active at any given time. If every coroutine started to execute its body immediately upon creation, *corout1*, for example, would immediately engage in a **while** loop of the form shown above, without ever allowing the main program to continue.

A solution this problem is provided in Simula by the **detach** instruction, which, in a coroutine, gives control back to the unit that created the coroutine through a **new**. A coroutine body almost always begins with a **detach**, preceding a loop of the above form. This instruction allows the main program to terminate initialization and to start effective system operation by **resume** *corout$_i$*.

As an example of the use of coroutines, consider the following simple problem. We are requested to print a sequence of real numbers, given as input; however every eighth number (the eighth, the sixteenth, the twenty-fourth etc.) is to be omitted from the output. Furthermore, the output is to be organized as a sequence of lines, with six numbers per line (except for the last line which may have fewer). So if i_n denotes the n-th input item, the output will start as

i_1 i_2 i_3 i_4 i_5 i_6
i_7 i_9 i_{10} i_{11} i_{12} i_{13}
i_{14} i_{15} i_{17} etc.

Finally, only the first 1000 numbers are to be printed.

This problem is representative of coroutine use because it conceptually involves three processes, each with its specific logic: the input, where the constraint is to skip every eighth item; the output, where the constraint is to go to the next line after every seventh item; and the main program, which is required to process 1000 items. Traditional control structures are not good at combining such processes with widely different constraints.

A coroutine solution, on the other hand, is well adapted. It will use three coroutines: the producer (input), the printer (output) and the controller. The general structure is the following:

```
begin
        class PRODUCER begin ... see below ... end PRODUCER;
        class PRINTER begin ... see below ... end PRINTER;
        class CONTROLLER begin ... see below ... end CONTROLLER;

        ref (PRODUCER) a_producer;
        ref (PRINTER) a_printer;
        ref (CONTROL) a_controller;

        a_producer :- new PRODUCER;
        a_printer :- new PRINTER;
        a_controller :- new CONTROLLER;

        resume a_controller
end
```

Each coroutine must be created as an instance of a class, for example *a_producer* as instance of *PRODUCER* etc. Recall that Simula has a traditional Algol block structure: the above is a main program, in which various class declarations are embedded.

These classes describe the behavior of the coroutines:

```
class CONTROLLER;
      begin
                        integer i;
                detach;
                for i := 1 step 1 until 1000 do
                        resume a_printer
      end CONTROLLER;

class PRINTER;
      begin
                        integer i;
                detach;
                while true do
                        for i := 1 step 1 until 8 do
                                begin
                                        resume a_producer;
                                        outreal (a_producer.last_input);
                                        resume a_controller
                                end;
                                next_line
                end
      end PRINTER;
```

```
class PRODUCER;
    begin
                integer i;
                real last_input, discarded;
        detach;
        while true do
            begin
                for i := 1 step 1 until 6 do
                    begin
                        count := inreal;
                        resume a_printer
                    end;
                discarded := inreal
            end
    end PRODUCER;
```

Each class body begins with **detach** to allow the main program to proceed with the initialization of other coroutines. Procedure *outreal* prints a real number; function *inreal* reads and returns the next real on input; we have assumed a procedure *next_line* that outputs a line feed character.

Coroutines are a valuable addition to the basic concepts of object-oriented design. Note how decentralized the above scheme is: each process "minds its own business", with limited interference from the others. The producer takes care of the input; the printer takes care of the output; the controller takes care of the overall session. We have repeatedly observed that decentralization was the key to flexible architectures; here decentralization is carried one step further.

Still more decentralized architectures are possible. In particular, the processes in the above structure must activate each other; in a perfectly decentralized world, they would not need to know about each other except to communicate requested information (as when the printer obtains *last_input* from the producer). This may be achieved using the simulation primitives described below. But the full extent of decentralization is obtained by going beyond quasi-parallelism to actual parallelism, as discussed briefly in the next chapter.

20.1.6 Sequencing and inheritance

The potential double role of classes – data types and processes – is apparent even for classes that do not use coroutine primitives since these classes may still have a body. This aspect of the language must be combined with inheritance.

The rule is the following. For any class C, we denote by $body_C$ the sequence of instructions declared as body of C and *actual_body sub C* the sequence of instructions executed for every creation of an instance of C. If C has no parent, $actual\_body_C$ is just $body_C$. If C has a parent A (remember that multiple inheritance is not supported), then $actual\_body_C$ is by default the sequence of instructions

$actual\_body_A$;
$body_C$

In other words, the bodies of the ancestors are executed in the order of inheritance. This default order may be superseded by use of the **inner** construct, used in a class body to denote the heir's body; the default policy is equivalent to having an **inner** at the end of the parent's body. For example, the body of A may be of the form

> *instructions* $_1$; **inner**; *instructions* $_2$

in which case (assuming A itself has no parent) the actual body of C is

> *instructions* $_1$;
> *body* $_C$;
> *instructions* $_2$

This convention is rather awkward, if only because in many cases instances of subclasses should be created in a manner totally different from instances of their ancestors (hence the Eiffel Create rule of 10.1.3). Furthermore, it would be hard to extend the Simula convention to the case of multiple inheritance. Almost all object-oriented languages after Simula, including Eiffel and the other languages discussed in this chapter, have departed from the Simula convention and have treated object initialization as a procedure such as the Eiffel *Create*.

In so doing, however, these languages lose the process aspect of Simula classes, which complements the data aspect emphasized in this book. If you are only concerned with sequential programming, the loss is not irreparable; you will only miss coroutines, an elegant programming technique but one you can usually do without or emulate (exercise 20.1). The process aspect is needed, however, if the object-oriented approach is to be extended to concurrent programming (chapter 21).

20.1.7 Simulation

Simula also includes a set of primitives for discrete-event simulation. Simulation is one of the applications that most directly benefit from object-oriented techniques; the "operational modeling" approach to programming (4.6) promoted by the object-oriented method is directly relevant here.

The general aim of a simulation program is to analyze and predict the behavior of some external reality – an assembly line, a chemical reaction, an computer operating system, a ship etc. This external reality will be called the "physical system".

A discrete event simulation model describes physical systems as changing their states in response to individual events occurring at discrete instants. This is to be contrasted with *continuous simulation*, which views the state as continuously evolving. Both are modeling techniques; which one is applicable to a given physical system depends not so much on whether the physical system is "inherently" continuous or discrete (often a meaningless question) as on whether it may realistically be modeled by either technique.

Another competitor to discrete event simulation is analytical modeling, which simply consists in providing a mathematical model of the physical system under study, and solving the model's equations. In contrast, a discrete event model is a program which executes instructions simulating the events of the modeled physical system: the longer the simulated part of the physical system's lifecycle, the longer the execution of the program. Since longer simulations yield more significant results, a long computing time may be required. This is why analytical models are usually more efficient. But many physical systems are too complex to admit realistic yet tractable mathematical models; then simulation is the only possibility.

Many physical systems lend themselves to discrete event simulation. An example is an assembly line, where typical events may include a new part being entered into the line, a worker or machine performing a certain operation on one or more parts, a finished product being removed from the line, a failure causing the line to stop etc. The simulation may be used to answer questions about the modeled physical systems; for example: how long does it take (average, minimum, maximum, standard deviation) to produce a finished product? How long does a given piece of machinery remain unused? What is the optimum inventory level? How long does it take to recover from a power failure?

The input to a simulation is a sequence of events with their occurrence times. The sequence may be obtained from measurements on the actual physical systems (when the simulation is used to reconstruct and analyze past phenomena, for example a physical system failure); more commonly, it is produced by random number generators according to some chosen statistical laws.

An important feature that a discrete event model must capture is physical system time, also called **simulated time**. Operations in the physical system, such as performing a certain task on a certain part, take time; certain events, such as equipment failure, will occur at specified time intervals. This must be accounted for by the simulation.

This simulated time is not to be confused with the computing time needed to execute the simulation program. From the simulation program's viewpoint, simulated time is simply a non-negative real variable, which the simulation program may only increase by discrete leaps. In Simula, this variable is called *time*; it is a global variable managed by the run-time system and modified by the program through some of the procedures seen below.

Simula supports these concepts through a class *SIMULATION*, which may be used as parent by another class. Let us call "simulation class" any class which is a descendant of *SIMULATION*.[1]

First, *SIMULATION* contains the declaration of a class *PROCESS*. (Remember that in Simula class declarations may be nested). *PROCESS* describes processes of the physical system. In any simulation class, we can declare descendants of *PROCESS*, which we shall call "process classes", and their instances just "processes". Among other properties, a process may be linked to other processes in a linked list (which means that *PROCESS* is a descendant of the Simula equivalent of class *LINKABLE*). A process may be in one of the following four states:

- Active, or currently executing.
- Suspended, or waiting to be resumed.

---

[1] In Simula, inheritance may also be applied to blocks: a block written under the form *C* **begin** ... **end** has access to all the features declared in class *C*. *SIMULATION* is often used in this way as parent of a complete program rather than just a class. Thus we can also talk of a "simulation program".

- Idle, or not part of the system.
- Terminated.

Any simulation (that is to say, any instance of a descendant of *SIMULATION*) maintains a list of event notices, or event list. An event notice is a pair [process, activation_time], where the activation time indicates when the process must be activated. Here and in the rest of this section any mention of time, as well as words such as "when" or "currently", refer to simulated (physical system) time, as controlled by the variable *time*. The event list is sorted by increasing activation time; the first process is active, all others are suspended. Non-terminated processes which are not in the list are idle.

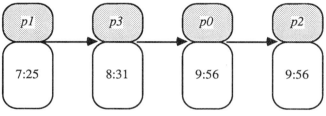

Figure 20.2   Event list

The main operation on processes is activation, which schedules a process to become active at a certain time by inserting a suitable event notice into the event list. Apparently for syntactical reasons, this operation is not a call to a procedure of class *SIMULATION*, but a specific instruction using the keyword **activate** or the variant **reactivate**. (A procedure call would seem to be a more consistent approach; in fact the semantics of **activate** is officially defined by such a procedure.) The basic form of the instruction is

> **activate** *a_process scheduling_clause*

where *a_process* is a non-void entity of type *PROCESS* (or a descendant class). The optional *scheduling_clause* is of one of the following forms:

> **at** *a_time*
> **delay** *a_period*
> **before** *some_process*
> **after** *some_process*

The first two forms specify the position of the new event notice for *a_process* by its activation time (remember that the event list is sorted by activation time); the new activation time is *max(time, a_time)* in the **at** form and *max (time, time + a_period)* in the **delay** form. The new event notice will be inserted after any other already present in the list with the same activation time, unless **prior** is specified. The last two forms specify the position with reference to another process *some_process* in the list. A missing scheduling clause is equivalent to **delay** *0*.

A process may activate itself at a later time by specifying itself as the target process *a_process* of the activate instruction. In this case the keyword should be **reactivate**. This is an important technique for representing a system task that takes some system time but, of course, no computer time. For example, to represent the fact that a worker carries out a 180-second task, the corresponding process, say *worker*, may contain the instruction

> **reactivate** *worker* **delay** *180*

This case is important enough that a specific syntax is provided, avoiding the need for explicit self-reference: the procedure call

> *hold* (*180*)

has exactly the same effect as the above. Procedure *hold* is part of class *SIMULATION*.

Processes are coroutines and the simulation primitives are implemented using the coroutine primitives. The effect of *hold* (*a_period*), for example, may be approximately described (in Eiffel-like syntax extended with **resume**) as

```
        -- Insert a new event notice into the event list,
        -- at the position determined by its time:
my_new_time := max (time, time + a_period);
my_reactivation_notice.Create (Current, my_new_time);
event_list.insert (my_reactivation_notice);

        -- Get the first element of the event list and remove it:
next := event_list.first;
event_list.remove_first;

        -- Activate the chosen process, advancing time if necessary:
time := max (time, next.when);
resume next.what
```

This equivalence assumes the following declarations:

```
my_new_time: REAL;
my_reactivation_notice, next: EVENT_NOTICE;

class EVENT_NOTICE export when, what feature
        when: REAL; -- i.e. time
        what: PROCESS;

        Create (t: REAL; p: PROCESS) is
                do
                        when := t; what := p
                end -- Create

end -- class EVENT_NOTICE
```

Note how a process may become suspended by reactivating itself at a later time. When this happens, the first suspended process (with the earliest reactivation time) in the event list is resumed; if its reactivation time is after the current time, the current time is correspondingly advanced.

As this example shows, the simulation primitives, based on the coroutine primitives, are of a higher level; they should be used whenever there is a choice. In particular, *hold* (0) may be viewed as a form of **resume** that lets the underlying event list mechanism pick the process to be resumed, rather than specifying it explicitly (exercise 20.3).

Many real-world processes are modeled elegantly by process classes. A typical example would be a worker that may be asked to do either one of two tasks. Both tasks may take a variable amount of time; the second task requires that the worker switch on a machine *m*, which takes 300 seconds, and wait for the machine to have done its job.

```
PROCESS class WORKER
    begin
        while true do
            begin
                "get next task type i and task duration d";
                if i = 1 then
                    hold (d)
                else
                    begin
                        activate m delay 300;
                        reactivate this WORKER after m;
                        hold (d)
                    end
            end while
    end WORKER
```

The Simula notation **this** *C*, within a class *C* (here **this** *WORKER*), is the equivalent of the Eiffel *Current*.

The operation "get next task type and task duration" will usually be implemented by obtaining the requested value from a pseudo-random number generator, using a specified statistical distribution. The Simula library includes a number of generators for common statistical laws.

The type of *m* is assumed to be some process class *MACHINE* representing the behavior of machines. All actors of a simulation will be similarly represented by process classes.

20.1.8   Implementation

Simula implementations all support garbage collection. Other facilities vary with the implementations. Several include good source-level debugging facilities. The language definition does not include a standard class library beyond a few important classes for describing two-way linked lists, which are used by the simulation primitives.

20.2   SMALLTALK

The ideas for Smalltalk were laid out around 1970 at the University of Utah by Alan Kay, then a graduate student and part of a group that was particularly active in graphics, when he came across a Simula compiler and realized that the concepts were directly applicable to this graphics work. When Kay later joined Xerox, he used the same principles as the basis for an advanced personal computing environment. The other two persons generally credited with key contributions are Adele Goldberg and Daniel H. H. Ingalls.

Smalltalk evolved into Smalltalk-76, then Smalltalk-80, and versions were developed for a number of machines by Xerox as well as other companies. ParcPlace Systems, a Xerox subsidiary, was created in 1986 in an attempt to turn Smalltalk into a "mainstream" software product.

20.2.1   Language style

As a language, Smalltalk combines the influence of Simula with the free, typeless style of Lisp. The emphasis is on dynamic binding. No type checking is performed: in contrast with the approach emphasized in this book, the determination of whether a routine may be applied to an object only occurs at run-time.

This, by the way, is not the standard Smalltalk terminology. A routine is called a "method" in Smalltalk; applying a routine to an object is called "sending a message" to the object (whose class must find the appropriate method to handle the message).

Another important feature that distinguishes the Smalltalk style from the approach used in the rest of this book is the lack of a clear-cut distinction between classes and objects. Everything in the Smalltalk system is an object; this includes classes themselves. A class is viewed as an instance of a higher-level class called a "metaclass". This allows the class hierarchy to encompass all elements in the system; at the root of the hierarchy is the highest-level class, called *object*. The root of the subtree containing only classes is the metaclass *class*. Three advantages may be claimed for this approach:

- It yields conceptual consistency, a single concept (object) being applicable to all Smalltalk notions.

- It contributes to the quality of the programming environment by making classes part of the run-time context, facilitating the development of symbolic debuggers, tools for finding available classes, and other tools that need access to the class text at run-time. This is appropriate in an interpreted environment.

- Considering a class as an instance of a more abstract metaclass makes it possible to define **class methods** which apply to the class rather than to its instances. Class methods may be used to provide special implementations for standard operations like **new** which allocates instances of the class.

Arguments for the static approach in which classes are *not* objects were discussed in 5.8.5.

20.2.2 Messages

There are three main forms of messages (and associated methods): unary, keyword and binary. Routines without parameters are represented by unary messages, as in

acc1 balance

which sends the message *balance* to the object associated with *acc1*. This is equivalent to the Eiffel or Simula *acc1.balance*. Messages may, as here, return values.

Keyword messages are used for messages with arguments, as in

point1 translateBy: vector1
window1 moveHor: 5 Vert: –3

(The use of upper-case letters in the middle of a word is part of the established Smalltalk style.) Note how the keyword for the first argument is collapsed with the message name. The corresponding Eiffel or Simula syntax would have been *point1.translate (vector1)* and *window1.move (5, –3)*.

Binary messages are used as a clever syntactic device to reconcile the "everything is an object" approach with more traditional arithmetic notations. In a pure object-oriented world, the addition of two integers would be denoted by

2 addMeTo: 3

which is still considered less telling than *2+3* by those survivors of older generations that learned elementary arithmetic before computer programming. Smalltalk provides a solution by essentially allowing the latter form as a synonym for the first; + and similar operators are treated as the keywords for binary messages. The snag is precedence: *a + b * c* means *(a + b) * c*. Parentheses may be used to re-establish standard precedence. Unary messages take precedence over binary messages, so that

window1 height + window2 height

has the expected meaning.

In contrast with Eiffel and Simula, Smalltalk classes may only export methods (routines). An attribute may only be exported through a function that gives access to its value. A typical example is

```
...
x | |
    ↑ xx
y | |
    ↑ yy
scale: scaleFactor | |
    xx ← xx * scaleFactor
    yy ← yy * scaleFactor
...
```

Methods *x* and *y* respectively return the values of the instance variables (attributes) *xx* and *yy*. The up arrow ↑ means that the following expression is the value to be returned by the method to the sender of the corresponding message. The method *scale* takes an argument, *scaleFactor*. A method may use local variables, declared between vertical bars |...|, although in this example no local variables are needed.

As described in [Goldberg 1983], Smalltalk only supports single inheritance. Some recent versions have included multiple inheritance, implemented, however, at the expense of code duplication. Dynamic binding plays an important role in the approach.

As noted in chapter 10, it may be necessary, when a method is redefined, to be able to call the original version, if only because the implementation of the redefined version internally relies on it. This is achieved in Smalltalk by explicitly sending a message to the superclass, denoted by *super*, as in

> *aFunction: anArgument* |...|
> ... *super aFunction: anArgument* ...

This is to be contrasted with the Eiffel approach, which made the original version available, if necessary, through renaming, based on the idea that clients of a class should not need to know about its inheritance structure (10.4.7).

As there is no notion of typing, errors resulting from sending a message to an object that is not equipped with a proper method to handle it are only caught at run-time. (In Eiffel, all such errors are detected by the compiler.)

The typeless approach also renders irrelevant some of the concepts developed earlier in this book: language support for genericity is not needed, as a generic structure such as a stack may contain elements of any type without any static checks on coherence; neither are deferred routines meaningful in this context, as a routine may be freely redefined anyway. A run-time mechanism is provided, however, to ensure that an error is raised if a message is sent to an instance of a class C even though effective definitions of the corresponding method are only provided in proper descendants of C. (In Eiffel, C would be a deferred class, and instances would only be created for non-deferred descendants of C.) For example, we could implement *rotate* in a class *FIGURE* by

> *rotate: anAngle around: aPoint* | |
> *self shouldNotImplement*

The method *shouldNotImplement* is included in the general class *object* and returns an error message.

20.2.3 The environment

Smalltalk is not just a language but a programming environment, covering many of the aspects traditionally addressed by the hardware and the operating system. This environment is Smalltalk's most significant contribution.

The environment is characterized by a distinctive user interface. It introduced or popularized many of the advances in this area: multiple windows, icons, integration of text and graphics, pull-down menus, and use of the mouse as a pointing and selecting device.

These interface techniques are blended in the Smalltalk environment with the techniques of object-oriented programming and made the "objects" of object-oriented programming visible and tangible for a large audience.

As with Simula, the environment supports garbage collection.

Included in the environment is a library of basic classes, covering important abstractions such as "collections" and "dictionaries", and a number of graphics concepts. An important window-based tool is the **browser**, which allows potential users of existing classes to retrieve and view them at various levels of abstraction. The browser addresses an important concern of object-oriented design and, more generally, of techniques emphasizing reusability: once you have produced reusable software components, how do you make them known to the rest of the world? More discussion of this topic may be found in the next chapter.

20.3   C EXTENSIONS

Two separate efforts have attempted to make some of the benefits of object-oriented design available to programmers trained in the C language: C++ and Objective-C. C has become in a few years one of the most widespread languages in industry; these efforts are directed at managers who want to protect their team members from experiencing too much of a culture shock when subjected to the object-oriented method. This "hybrid" approach has been compared by Brad Cox (the designer of Objective-C) to the attempts made in the 1970s to add "structured programming" constructs to Fortran through preprocessors.

Although the aims are similar, the two languages differ significantly. C++ shows a clear Simula influence, while Objective-C is more a preprocessor for Smalltalk-like constructs added to the C stem.

20.3.1   C++

Designed by Bjarne Stroustrup of AT&T, C++ is distributed by AT&T and other companies. The language design is an attempt at "a better C". It extends C with various facilities, not all of which have to do with object-orientedness. Almost any correct C program is a correct C++ program.

The structure of a class is illustrated by the following example:

```
class POINT {
  float xx, yy;
public:
    void translate (float, float);
    void rotate (float);
      float x ();
      float y ();

    friend void p_translate (POINT *, float, float);
    friend void p_rotate (POINT *, float);
      friend float p_x (POINT *);
      friend float p_y (POINT *);
};
```

The first four routines are the normal, object-oriented interface of the class. As shown by this example, the class declaration only shows the headers of these routines, not their implementations (somewhat as in the output of the Eiffel "short" command). The routine implementations must be defined separately, which raises questions of scope for both compilers and human readers.

The other four routines are examples of "friend" routines. This notion is peculiar to C++ and makes it possible to call C++ routines from normal C code. Friend routines will need an extra argument representing the object to which an operation is applied; this argument is here of type *POINT* *, meaning pointer to *POINT*.

Operator overloading makes it possible to use the same name for different operations, in the Ada style. For example, addition functions on different data types (vectors, matrices etc.) may all be called using the + symbols.

The published descriptions of C++ (see bibliographical notes) only provide for single inheritance; multiple inheritance is announced for future versions.

Dynamic binding is also available, but only for routines that have explicitly been marked as "virtual" in their original class. This is not the same as the "virtual" concept of Simula (corresponding to deferred routines), as a virtual C++ routine must be provided an effective definition in its original class: declaring the class as virtual simply makes it amenable to redefinition in descendant classes. This is different from the approach developed in this book, based on the open-closed principle (a class should always remain open for extensions, which implies that it is not its business to decide which of its classes are redefinable by descendants). Requiring that routines may not be redefined unless specifically marked as virtual makes it easier to implement calls efficiently, as static binding may be used for calls to non-virtual routines. (In Eiffel, the corresponding optimization is done by the compiler, as described in 15.4.4).

No garbage collection is provided; object creation and deallocation may be controlled by writing constructor and destructor functions.

20.3.2   Objective-C

Designed by Brad Cox of Productivity Products International, Objective-C is another C extension that grafts Smalltalk concepts onto a C base. As in Smalltalk, the emphasis is on polymorphism and dynamic binding; the object-oriented part of the language is typeless: entities of any class type are simply defined with the type *ID*, a special type added to C. Typical Objective-C syntax looks like the following:

---

[2] Routines are called functions in C and C++; procedures are viewed as functions of type "void". Since "function" has been used in the rest of this book to denote routines other than procedures, we stick to the previous terminology to avoid any confusion.

```
= Proceedings: Publication {
    id date, place;
    id articles;
}
+ new { return [[super new] initialize]}
- initialize { articles = [OrderedCollection new]; return self;}
- add: anArticle { return [contents add: anArticle]; }
- remove: anArticle { return [contents remove:anArticle]; }
- (int)size { return [contents size]; }
=:
```

Class *Proceedings* is defined here as heir to *Publication* (Objective-C supports single inheritance). In curly brackets are attributes (called instance variables in accordance with the Smalltalk terminology). As in Smalltalk, only routines, not attributes, may be exported. The next lines describe routines; *self* is the Smalltalk term for referring to the current instance of the class.

Objective-C is equipped with a library of available classes designed after their Smalltalk counterparts.

20.4 LISP EXTENSIONS

Object-oriented concepts have raised much interest in the artificial intelligence community. The language of choice in this community (with some competition from Prolog) is Lisp, at least in academic circles. Thus it is not surprising that Lisp has been used as a basis for a number of object-oriented languages. But the role of Lisp is due to more than historical coincidence: much of the technical base provided by good Lisp environments (with garbage collection, readily available implementations of tree-like data structures, uniform representation for programs and data, and a number of tools for editing and debugging) is directly applicable to the implementation of object-oriented concepts.

The style of the resulting languages is quite different from the typed approach emphasized in the rest of this book. For example, conventions for the resolution of name conflicts in multiple inheritance (which is usually supported in these languages) are based not on renaming, but on run-time routine search; the first appropriate routine is selected, based on the order in which the parents have been listed. The order may be superseded by explicit requests.

The foremost languages in this category are:

- Loops, developed at Xerox, initially for the Interlisp environment.
- Flavors, developed at MIT, also available on several Lisp-oriented architectures.
- Ceyx, developed at INRIA.

An interesting concept introduced by Loops is "data-oriented programming", where a routine may be attached to a data item (such as an attribute). Execution of the routine will be triggered not only by an explicit call, but also whenever the item is accessed or modified. This opens the way to **event-driven computation**, a further step towards decentralizing software architectures.

20.5 OTHER LANGUAGES

A number of languages have been proposed in recent years. They include Apple's Object Pascal, a successor to the Clascal language used to develop some of the Lisa and Macintosh software, DEC's Trellis/Owl, supporting multiple inheritance and genericity, and numerous language proposals in the area of artificial intelligence.

20.6 BIBLIOGRAPHICAL NOTES

Simula

[Dahl 1966] describes Simula 1 and is of historical interest only. The current Simula, long known as Simula 67, was initially described by [Dahl 1970], which assumed Algol 60 as a basis and only described the Simula extensions. (The 1984 revision describes the complete language.) The most up-to-date official reference is the Swedish national standard [SIS 1987].

The best-known book on Simula is [Birtwistle 1973]. It remains an excellent introduction. A more recent text is [Pooley 1986]. [Nygaard 1981] is an account of Simula's history.

Smalltalk

References on the first two versions of Smalltalk (-72 and -76) are [Goldberg 1976] and [Ingalls 1978].

An introduction to Smalltalk-80 may be found in a special issue of *Byte* devoted to Smalltalk [Goldberg 1981]. [Goldberg 1983] is the basic reference on the language, serving both as pedagogical description and reference, and is complemented by [Goldberg 1985] which describes the programming environment.

C extensions

Objective-C is described in an article [Cox 1984] and a book [Cox 1986]. The same holds for C++: [Stroustrup 1984] and [Stroustrup 1986]. Implementation issues for C++ are described in [Dewhurst 1987].

Lisp extensions

Loops: [Bobrow 1982]; Flavors: [Cannon 1980], [Moon 1986]; Ceyx: [Hullot 1984].

EXERCISES

20.1 Emulating coroutines

Devise a mechanism for emulating coroutines in a language such as Eiffel that does not provide explicit support for this construct. (**Hint:** write a *resume* procedure, implemented as a loop containing a conditional instruction with a branch for every **resume**). Apply this technique to the producer-printer example (page 430).

20.2 Simulation

Write a set of Eiffel classes for discrete-event simulation, patterned after the Simula classes *SIMULATION*, *PROCESS* and *EVENT_NOTICE* as described in 20.1.7. (Use the techniques developed for the previous exercise.)

20.3 Implicit resume

(This is a exercise on Simula concepts, but you may use the Eiffel notation extended with the simulation primitives described in 20.1.7.) Rewrite the producer-printer example in such a way that each coroutine does not need to explicitly resume one of its colleagues when it has finished its current job; the coroutine classes should be declared as descendants of *PROCESS*, and explicit **resume** instructions should be replaced by *hold* (0) instructions. (**Hints:** recall that event notices with the same activation time are kept in the order in which they are generated. Associate with each process a condition that needs to be satisfied for the process to be resumed.)

21

Further issues

This book has introduced a number of design and implementation techniques that may significantly improve both the software we produce and the production process. Many avenues of further research are still open. In this last chapter, we take a brief look at some of the most pressing issues, with only hints as to where possible solutions lie.

21.1 IMPLEMENTING REUSABILITY

Assume everybody embraces object-oriented design, and software factories around the world start churning out reusable software components based on the most advanced technology – classes, programming as contracting, assertions, disciplined exceptions, genericity, multiple inheritance, polymorphism, dynamic binding, and so on. Will reusability automatically work?

Not necessarily. Even disregarding the economical, political and psychological problems involved, software will only be reused if the potential beneficiaries know about available components. This is the whole issue of component databases. Chapter 3 mentioned this issue and added that the right technical level – object-oriented design with the full extent of its techniques – must be reached before it becomes crucial. But once this level is attained, the issue must be addressed.

A first attempt at component databases is the Smalltalk browser (20.2.3), which allows Smalltalk users to interactively explore the class hierarchy, all the way down to the actual code of each class. This tool, which relies on the Smalltalk windowing facilities, is well suited to an environment where classes are contributed by a small number of people, and the total number of classes does not exceed a few tens or perhaps a few hundreds. For large-scale reusability, it is no longer sufficient.

What is needed is a system permitting potential users to find out about existing classes not only through their names (too vague) or their actual text (too detailed) but also through their characteristics; in other words, a database of classes, with an associated query language.

Standard database technology is, to a certain extent, appropriate; a class and its features may be stored in a database in the same way as, say, a customer record. There are further requirements:

- Relationships between classes (inheritance, client) should be recorded in the database. For obvious reasons, they should be extracted automatically from the class texts themselves rather than entered manually.

- The context of each class (remember the SOURCE line in the Eiffel System Description File) should be described precisely, so that references to the names of other classes (parents or suppliers) are unambiguous, even though many classes in the database may share the same name.

- Some support should be provided for version management.

- Some class texts will be available in the database; others may not be available, if only for protection of proprietary information. In all cases, an interface version (as produced in Eiffel by the "short" command) should be available.

- It must be possible to attach supplementary information to a class stored in the database: keywords to facilitate retrieval (describing the application category, such as signal processing, compiler construction etc.), performance data, developer, price, any special restrictions.

- It must be possible to implement access controls and integrity protection.

Only a few of these goals are addressed by existing database systems. A software component database system should probably be based on a database management system, extended by specific mechanisms.

21.2 PERSISTENCY

Object-oriented programming raises another database issue. The objects considered so far exist for the duration of a computing session. There is also a need for objects with a longer time span.

A form of such persistency is offered by the Eiffel class *STORABLE*, with its primitives *store* and *retrieve* (15.5.6), providing for file storage and retrieval of entire data structures. Beyond such facilities, it should be possible to store individual objects and retrieve them through queries on to their attributes. This is clearly a fundamental extension to the approach.

A delicate problem must be addressed by any scheme for dealing with persistent objects: how to retrieve previously stored objects even if the corresponding class descriptions have been slightly changed. Any solution must ensure the preservation of data integrity, as described in Eiffel by class invariants.

More generally, data abstraction and the object-oriented paradigm provide an attractive alternative for the models underlying current database systems – hierarchical, network, relational, entity-relation. As compared to existing relational databases, for example, an object-oriented database would not need to be "normalized": the attributes of an object may be references to other objects.

Database researchers have shown increasing interest in the object-oriented model in recent years. It is hardly questionable that object-oriented concepts provide a potential basis for database systems more effective than those of today; the challenge is to build object-oriented databases that will be at least as efficient and easy to use as databases built with current technology.

21.3 CONCURRENCY

Object-oriented design promotes decentralized software architectures. The full extent of decentralization requires that control also be decentralized: parallelism must be supported.

Simula has shown how classes may be used to implement not just data structures but processes. However Simula processes are meant for execution on a sequential processor.

Not all objects may be viewed as processes. But the view of processes as objects is attractive. Processes have attributes and may execute routines; what distinguishes them from other objects is that they also have a prescribed behavior, going through successive phases. Furthermore, processes communicate with each other, and are subject to synchronization constraints.

The communication aspect seems to be adequately covered by the basic mechanism of object-oriented program execution: calling a routine on an object (or sending a message to that object), possibly with arguments. The Actors model (see bibliographical notes) is based on this idea: describing concurrent computation by a generalization of the message passing paradigm. Other efforts have attempted to add traditional synchronization primitives, such as semaphores or monitors, to an object-oriented base; this may be done, but the elegance of the simple "processes as objects with a scenario" idea is lost.

> At the time of writing, an effort is under way to provide Eiffel with support for concurrent computation on the basis of the Eiffel exception mechanism (7.10); the language's composition facilities (classes, genericity, inheritance) are used to offer support for various high-level models such as rendez-vous, monitors etc. The design is not complete enough, however, to be reported in this book.

The challenge for researchers in this area is to come up with an scheme for parallelism which will blend well with the rest of the object-oriented approach, while matching the convincing simplicity of the most successful concurrency concepts, from monitors to CSP and CCS.

21.4   BIBLIOGRAPHICAL NOTES

A survey of persistency issues in object-oriented systems is given in [Wiederhold 1986]. [VLDB 1987], a conference proceedings volume, contains several articles on this topic.

A set of articles on concurrency in object-oriented systems may be found in [Yonezawa 1987]. One of these articles describes Hewitt's Actors model, which is presented in more detail in [Agha 1986].

A number of articles on research issues in object-oriented techniques may be found in [Shriver 1987]. The OOPSLA (Object-Oriented Programming, Systems, Languages and Applications) and ECOOP (European Conference on Object-Oriented Programming) conferences reflect current progress in the field [OOPSLA 1986] [OOPSLA 1987] [ECOOP 1987].

PART 4

Appendices

A

Extracts from the Eiffel library

The classes given below are extracted from the basic library that constitutes one of the fundamental assets of designing software in Eiffel. They have been somewhat simplified and some aspects have been omitted, but they remain faithful to the original. Some details have been left for the reader to complete.

A.1 ARRAYS

One-dimensional arrays in Eiffel are not a primitive notion but a generic class of which an implementation is given below. Similar classes exist for two- and three-dimensional arrays.

An array may be allocated with arbitrary bounds through the procedure *Create*; routines *entry* and *enter* are used to access and modify array elements.

The implementation shown here relies on low-level, machine-dependent primitives for dynamic memory management: *allocate* for dynamically allocating memory areas, *dynget* to access data from such areas, *dynput* to change these data. These low-level primitives have been assumed to be available in C form. They directly manipulate addresses; since "address" is not, of course, a valid Eiffel type, addresses are encoded as positive integers. The encoding and decoding are the responsibility of the low-level routines; the Eiffel level only sees "abstract" integers.

The example contains little actual Eiffel code, but shows how an Eiffel class may be used to encapsulate a group of related low-level primitives and present it to the outside world as a coherent abstraction, complete with its preconditions, postconditions and class invariant.

class *ARRAY* [*T*] **export**

> *lower, size, upper, entry, enter*

feature

> *lower, size, upper: INTEGER*;

> *area: INTEGER*; -- Secret

> *Create* (*minb, maxb: INTEGER*) **is**
>> -- Allocate array with bounds *minb* and *maxb*.
>> -- (Empty if *minb* > *maxb*.)
>
> **external**
>> *allocate* (*length: INTEGER*): *INTEGER*
>> **name** "*allocate*" **language** "*C*";
>>> -- Reserve an area of *length* integers
>>> -- and return its address (0 if impossible)
>
> **do**
>> *lower := minb*;
>> *upper := maxb*;
>>
>> **if** *minb* >= *maxb* **then**
>>> *size := maxb − minb + 1*;
>>> *area := allocate* (*size*)
>>
>> **else**
>>> *size := 0*
>>
>> **end**;
>
> **end**; -- *Create*

> *entry* (*i: INTEGER*): *T* **is**
>> -- Entry of index *i*
>
> **require**
>> *lower <= i; i <= upper; area > 0*
>
> **external**
>> *dynget* (*address, index: INTEGER*): *T*
>> **name** "*dynget*" **language** "*C*";
>>> -- Value of *index*-th element in area of address *address*
>
> **do**
>> *Result := dynget* (*area, i*)
>
> **end**; -- *entry*

enter (i: INTEGER, value: T) **is**
                    -- Assign *value* to *i*-th entry
           require
                    lower <= i; i <= upper; area > 0
           external
                    dynput (address, index: INTEGER; val: T)
                    name *"dynput"* **language** *"C"*;
                            -- Replace with *val* the value of *index*-th element
                            -- in area of address *address*
           do
                    dynput (area, i, value)
           end; -- *enter*

invariant
      size = upper – lower + 1; size >= 0;
      -- *area > 0* if and only if array has been allocated
end -- class *ARRAY [T]*

A.2   GENERAL LISTS

This section and those that follow introduce classes corresponding to lists of various brands:

• *LIST [T]* (General notion of list)

• *FIXED_LIST [T]* (lists represented by arrays; no insertion or deletion)

• *LINKED_LIST [T]* (linked representation; insertions and deletions possible)

• *TWO_WAY_LIST [T]* (like *LINKED_LIST* but doubly linked for more efficient right-to-left traversal).

These classes are built according to the principles of 9.2 as describing active data structures, with position information remembered from one routine call to the next. Every list includes a "cursor" which may be moved by various procedures.

                    -- General lists, without commitment as to their representation
class *LIST [T]* **export**
      nb_elements, empty,
      position, offright, offleft, isfirst, islast,
      value, i_th, first, last,
      change_value, change_i_th, swap,
      start, finish, forth, back, go, search,
      mark, return,
      index_of, present,
      duplicate

feature

-- Number of list elements

    nb_elements: INTEGER;

    empty: BOOLEAN **is**
                -- Is the list empty?
        do *Result* := (*nb_elements* = *0*) **end**; -- *empty*

-- Inquiring about the cursor position

    position: INTEGER;

    offright: BOOLEAN **is**
                -- Is cursor off right edge?
        do *Result* := *empty* **or** (*position* = *nb_elements* + *1*) **end**; -- *offright*

    offleft: BOOLEAN **is**
                -- Is cursor off left edge?
        do
            Result := *empty* **or** (*position* = *0*)
                -- This formulation is for symmetry with *offright*:
                -- *empty* implies (*position* = *0*), so the second condition
                -- is equivalent to the entire "or" expression
        end; -- *offleft*

    isfirst: BOOLEAN **is**
                -- Is cursor on first element?
                -- (If so, the list is not empty)
        do
            Result := (*position* = *1*)
        ensure
            not *Result* **or else not** *empty*
        end; -- *isfirst*

    islast: BOOLEAN **is**
                -- Is cursor on last element?
                -- (If so, the list is not empty)
        * Left to the reader

-- Accessing list values

    value: T **is**
                -- Value of element at cursor position
        require
            not *offleft*; **not** *offright* -- This implies **not** *empty*
        deferred
        end; -- *value*

i_th (i: INTEGER): T **is**
                -- Value of *i*-th element
        require
                1 <= i; i <= nb_elements -- This implies **not** *empty*
        do
                mark; *go (i)*; *Result := value*; *return*
        ensure
                -- *Result* = value of *i*-th element
        end; -- *i_th*

first: T **is**
                -- Value of first element
        require
                not *empty*
        do
                Result := i_th (1)
        end; -- *first*

last: T **is**
                -- Value of last element
        * Left to the reader

-- Changing list values

change_value (v: T) **is**
                -- Assign *v* to element at cursor position
        require
                not *offleft*; **not** *offright* -- This implies **not** *empty*
        deferred
        ensure
                value = v
        end; -- *change_value*

change_i_th (i: INTEGER, v: T) **is**
                -- Assign *v* to *i*-th element
        * Left to the reader

swap (i: INTEGER) **is**
                -- Exchange values of elements at cursor position and position *i*.
                -- Do not move cursor.
        require
                not *offleft*; **not** *offright*; *1 <= i; i <= nb_elements*
                        -- This implies **not** *empty*
        local
                thisvalue, thatvalue: T;
        do
                thisvalue := value; *mark*;
                go (i); *thatvalue := value*; *change_value (thisvalue)*;
                return; *change_value (thatvalue)*
        end; -- *swap*

-- Moving along the list

```
start is
            -- Move cursor to first element (no effect if list is empty)
        deferred
        ensure
            (empty and Nochange) or else isfirst
        end; -- start
forth is
            -- Move cursor to next element
        require
            not offright
        deferred
        ensure
            position = old position + 1
        end; -- forth
go (i: INTEGER) is
            -- Move cursor to position i
        require
            0 <= i; i <= nb_elements + 1
        do
            if empty or i = 0 then
                    go_offleft
            else
                    from
                            if position > i then start end
                    invariant
                            1 <= position; position <= i
                    variant
                            i - position
                    until position = i loop
                            check not offright end;
                        forth
                    end -- loop
            end -- if
        ensure
            (i = 0 and offleft) or
            (i = nb_elements + 1 and offright) or
            (1 <= i and i <= nb_elements and position = i)
        end; -- go
back is
            -- Move cursor to previous element
        require
            not offleft
        do
                    check position >= 1 end;
                go (position - 1)
        end; -- back
```

finish **is**

-- Move cursor to last element (no effect if list is empty)
do

go (nb_elements)
ensure

(*empty* **and** *Nochange*) **or else** *islast*
end; -- *finish*

go_offleft **is**

-- Move cursor off left edge
-- (Secret procedure; use *go (0)* in clients)
deferred
ensure

offleft
end; -- *go_offleft*

search (v: T; i: INTEGER) **is**

-- Move cursor to *i*-th element of value *v* in the list
-- if there are at least *i* such elements; else go offright.
require

i > 0
local

k: INTEGER
do

from

start; *k := 1*
invariant

position >= 0;
-- *k* − 1 elements to the left of cursor position
-- have a value equal to *v*
variant

nb_elements − position
until

offright **or else** (*value = v* **and** *k = i*)
loop

if *value = v* **then** *k := k + 1* **end**;
forth
end -- loop
ensure

offright **or else** *value = v*;
-- *offright* **or else** *cursor is at i*-th element of value *v*
end; -- *search*

-- Secret attributes for mark and return
backup: **like** *Current*;
no_change_since_mark: BOOLEAN;

-- Marking positions and returning (return will be last-in, first-out)
mark **is**

>   -- Mark cursor position
> **do** *backup.Clone (Current)*; **end**; -- *mark*

return **is**
>   -- Move cursor to last marked position
> **require**
> > **not** *backup.Void*;
> > *no_change_since_mark*
>
> **do**
> > *position := backup.position*;
> > *no_change_since_mark := backup.no_change_since_mark*;
> > *backup := backup.backup*
>
> **end**; -- *return*

-- Finding information about occurrences of given elements.

index_of (v: T; i: INTEGER): INTEGER **is**
>   -- Index of the *i*-th element of value *v* (0 if fewer than *i*)
> **require**
> > *i > 0*
>
> **do**
> > *mark*; *search (v, i)*;
> > **if not** *offright* **then** *Result := position* **end**;
> > *return*
>
> **ensure**
> > -- (*Result > 0* **and then**
> > --   *Result* is the index of the *i*-th element of value *v* in the list)
> > -- **or else**
> > --   (*Result = 0* **and**
> > --   there are fewer than *i* elements of value *v* in the list)
>
> **end**; -- *index_of*

present (v: T): BOOLEAN **is**
>   -- Does *v* appear in the list?
> **do**
> > *Result := index_of (v, 1) > 0*
>
> **ensure**
> > -- *Result* = (*v* appears in the list)
>
> **end**; -- *present*

-- Duplicating a list

duplicate: **like** *Current* **is**
>   -- Complete clone of the list
> **deferred**
> **end**; -- *duplicate*

invariant
> *0 <= position; position <= nb_elements + 1*;
> **not** *empty* **or else** (*position = 0*);

$empty = (offleft$ **and** $offright)$;
$offright = (empty$ **or** $(position = nb\_elements + 1))$;
$offleft = (empty$ **or** $(position = 0))$;
   -- Note that $empty$ implies $(position = 0)$, so that also:
$offleft = (position = 0)$;

$isfirst = (position = 1)$;
$islast = ($**not** $empty$ **and** $(position = nb\_elements))$;
 not $empty$ **or else** (**not** $isfirst$ **and not** $islast)$;
end -- class $LIST$

A.3 ARRAY LISTS

Class $FIXED\_LIST$ $[T]$ provides an array implementation of lists; only limited operations are available (no insertions or deletions). The array is created with fixed bounds, given as arguments to the version of procedure $Create$ redefined for this class.

   -- Lists with a fixed number of elements
class $FIXED\_LIST$ $[T]$ **export**
 ... Same exported features as in $LIST$ ...

inherit
 $ARRAY$ $[T]$
  rename $Create$ **as** $array\_Create$;
 $LIST$ $[T]$
  redefine $i\_th,$ $change\_i\_th,$ $swap,$ go;

feature
 $Create$ $(n: INTEGER)$ **is**
    -- Allocate fixed list with n elements
  do
   $array\_Create$ $(1, n)$;
    check $n = size$ **end**;
   $nb\_elements := n$;
  end; -- $Create$

 $value: T$ **is**
   -- Value of element at cursor position
  do $Result := entry$ $(position)$ **end**; -- $value$

 $change\_value$ $(v: T)$ **is**
   -- Assign v to element at cursor position
  do
   $enter$ $(position, v)$
  ensure
   $value = v$; $entry$ $(position) = v$
  end; -- $change\_value$

i_th (i: INTEGER): T **is**
               -- Value of *i*-th element
          * Left to the reader

change_i_th (i: INTEGER, v: T) **is**
               -- Assign *v* to *i*-th element
          * Left to the reader

swap (i: INTEGER) **is**
               -- Exchange values of elements at cursor position and position *i*.
               -- Do not move cursor.
          * Left to the reader

start **is**
               -- Move cursor to first element (no effect if list is empty)
          do
               position := min (nb_elements, 1)
          end; -- *start*

forth **is**
               -- Move cursor to next element
          require
               not *offright*
          do
               position := position + 1
          ensure
               position = **old** *position + 1*
          end; -- *forth*

go (i: INTEGER) **is**
               -- Move cursor to *i*-th element
          * Left to the reader

go_offleft **is**
               -- Move cursor off left edge
               -- (Secret procedure; use *go (0)* in clients)
          * Left to the reader

duplicate: **like** *Current* **is**
               -- Complete clone of the list
          do
               Result.Create (nb_elements);
                    -- *Result.Clone* would be inappropriate
               mark;
               from *start*; *Result.start* **invariant**
                    -- *position − 1* values
                    -- have been copied
               variant *nb_elements − position* **until**
                    offright
                         -- Thus *Result.offright* too

```
        loop
                Result.change_value (value);
                forth; Result.forth
        end; -- loop

        return; Result.go (position)
    end; -- duplicate
```

invariant
    -- The class invariant adds nothing to the invariant of class *LIST*
end -- class *FIXED_LIST*

A.4   LINKABLE ELEMENTS

This section introduces classes *LINKABLE* [*T*] and *BI_LINKABLE* [*T*] corresponding to "linkable" list components of two different brands: right-linked only and doubly-linked. Objects of such types have two fields: a value and a "right" pointer to another similar object. Bi-linkable objects also have a "left" field. Such component structures are designed for use in connection with classes representing linked lists: *LINKED_LIST* [*T*] and *TWO_WAY_LIST* [*T*].

        -- Linked list elements
        -- (for use in connection with [T] and *TWO_WAY_LIST* [*T*])
class *LINKABLE* [*T*] **export**

    value {*LINKED_LIST*}, *change_value* {*LINKED_LIST*},
    right {*LINKABLE, LINKED_LIST*},
    change_right {*LINKABLE, LINKED_LIST*},
    forget_right {*LINKABLE, LINKED_LIST*},
    put_between

feature
    Create (*initial: T*) **is**
                -- Initialize with value *initial*
        do *value := initial* **end**; -- *Create*

    value: T;

    change_value (*new: T*) **is**
                -- Assign value *new* to current list element
        do *value := new* **end**; -- *change_value*

    right: **like** *Current*;

    change_right (*other:* **like** *Current*) **is**
                -- Put *other* to the right of current element
        do *right := other* **end**; -- *change_right*
```
```

put_between (before, after: **like** *Current)* **is**
>   -- Insert current element between *before* and *after* (if it makes sense)
>   -- This procedure is used in *LINKED_LIST*
>   -- every time an insertion is performed.

>   **do**
>   **if not** *before.Void* **then**
>   *before.change_right (Current)*
>   **end**;
>   *change_right (after)*;
>   **end**; -- *put_between*
end -- class *LINKABLE* [*T*]

                        -- Same as *LINKABLE* [*T*], plus "left" field
class *BI_LINKABLE* [*T*] **export**

>   *value, right, left,*
>   *change_value {TWO_WAY_LIST}*,
>   *change_right {BI_LINKABLE, TWO_WAY_LIST}*,
>   *change_left {BI_LINKABLE, TWO_WAY_LIST}*
inherit

>   *LINKABLE* [*T*]
>   **redefine** *right, change_right*

feature

>   *left, right:* **like** *Current*;

>   *change_right (other:* **like** *Current)* **is**
>   -- Put *other* to the right of current element
>   **do**
>   *right := other*;
>   **if not** *other.Void* **then**
>   *other.change_left (Current)*
>   **end**
>   **end** -- *change_right*;

change_left (*other:* **like** *Current*) **is**
              -- Put *other* to the left of current element
        do
              left := other;
              if *not other.Void*
                    -- Avoid infinite recursion with *change_right*!
              and then *other.right /= Current*
              then
                    other.change_right (*Current*)
              end
        end -- *change_left*
invariant
      right.Void **or else** *right.left = Current;*
      left.Void **or else** *left.right = Current;*
end -- class *BI_LINKABLE* [*T*]

A.5   LINKED LISTS

Class *LINKED_LIST* [*T*] introduces singly-linked lists. All operations of insertion and deletion are possible; however, since the lists are chained one way only, operations such as *back*, implying a complete traversal, are inefficient.

The representation keeps references not only to the element at cursor position but also to its left and right neighbors (*active, left, right*). This allows, for example, efficient insertions both just before and just after the cursor.

A note to the courageous reader: an excellent test of your understanding of the present set of basic classes and the general principles of Eiffel design is to write two procedures patterned after *insert_right* and *insert_left* below, namely

      merge_after (*l:* **like** *Current*)
      merge_before (*l:* **like** *Current*)

which insert a linked list *l* to the right and left (respectively) of the current cursor position. The precise conditions (**require**...) under which they are applicable should be spelled out. The guiding criteria should be simplicity (no auxiliary procedure is necessary), preservation of the class invariant, perfect symmetry between left and right, and elegance. It will be even better if the procedures also apply to two-way lists (next section) without redefinition.

-- One-way linked lists
class *LINKED_LIST* [*T*] **export**
-- Features from *LIST:*
nb_elements, empty,
position, offright, offleft, isfirst, islast,
value, i_th, first, last,
change_value, change_i_th, swap,
start, finish, forth, back, go, search,
mark, return,
index_of, present,
duplicate,
-- Plus new features permitted by linked list representation:
insert_right, insert_left,
delete, delete_right, delete_left,
delete_all_occurrences, wipe_out
inherit
LIST [*T*]
redefine *first*

feature

first: T;
-- Value of first element (redefined here as attribute)

-- Secret attributes specific to linked list representation
first_element: LINKABLE [*T*];
active, previous, next: **like** *first_element*;

-- Linked list implementations of features deferred in *LIST*

value: T **is**
-- Value of element at cursor position
require
not *offleft*; **not** *offright* -- This implies **not** *empty*
do
Result := active.value
end; -- *value*

change_value (*v: T*) **is** .
-- Assign *v* to element at cursor position
require
not *offleft*; **not** *offright* -- This implies **not** *empty*
do
active.change_linkable_value (*v*)
ensure
value = v
end; -- *change_value*

start **is**
> -- Move cursor to first element (no effect if list is empty)

    do
> **if not** *empty* **then**
>> *previous.Forget;*
>> *active := first_element;*
>>> **check not** *active.Void* **end**;
>> *next := active.right;*
>> *position := 1*
> **end**

    ensure
> *empty* **or else** *isfirst*

    end; -- *start*

forth **is**
> -- Move cursor to next element

    require
> **not** *offright*

    do
> **if** *offleft* **then**
>>> **check not** *empty* **end**;
>> *start*
> **else**
>>> **check not** *active.Void* **end**;
>> *previous := active; active := next;*
>> **if not** *active.Void* **then** *next := active.right* **end**;
>> *position := position + 1*
> **end**

    ensure
> *position =* **old** *position + 1*

    end; -- *forth*

go_offleft **is**
> -- Move cursor off left edge
> -- (Secret procedure; use *go (0)* in clients)

    do
> *active.Forget; previous.Forget; next := first_element;*
> *position := 0*

    ensure
> *offleft*

    end; -- *go_offleft*

duplicate: **like** *Current* **is**
> -- Complete clone of the list
> * Left to the reader
> * (Go through list, duplicating every list element)
> * (See corresponding procedure for *FIXED_LIST*)

-- Deletion and insertion procedures specific to linked lists

insert_right (*v: T*) **is**
                    -- Insert an element of value *v* to the right of cursor position
                    -- if there is one. Do not move cursor.
          require
                    empty **or else not** *offright*
          local
                    new: **like** *first_element*
          do
                    new.Create (*v*);
                    insert_linkable_right (*new*)
          ensure
                    nb_elements = **old** *nb_elements* + *1*;
                    active = **old** *active*;
                    position = **old** *position*;
                    not *next.Void*; *next.value* = *v*
          end; -- *insert_right*

insert_left (*v: T*) **is**
                    -- Insert an element of value *v* to the left of cursor position
                    -- if there is one. Do not move cursor.
          * Left to the reader

delete **is**
                    -- Delete element at cursor position and move cursor to right neighbor.
                    -- (List becomes offright if no right neighbor)
          require
                    not *offleft*; **not** *offright*
          do
                    active := *next*;
                    if not *previous.Void* **then** *previous.change_right* (*active*) **end**;
                    if not *active.Void* **then** *next* := *active.right* **end**;
                          -- else *next* is void already
                    nb_elements := *nb_elements* – *1*;
                    no_change_since_mark := **false**;
                          check
                                position – *1* >= *0*; *position* – *1* <= *nb_elements*;
                                empty **or else** *position* – *1* > *0* **or else not** *active.Void*;
                          end;
                    update_after_deletion (*previous, active, position* – *1*);
          ensure
                    nb_elements = **old** *nb_elements* – *1*;
                    empty **or else** (*position* = **old** *position*)
          end; -- *delete*

delete_right **is**
            -- Delete element immediately to the right of cursor position.
            -- Do not move cursor.
            -- (No effect if cursor position is last in list.)
        * Left to the reader (imitate *delete*)

delete_left **is**
            -- Delete element immediately to the left of cursor position.
            -- Do not move cursor.
            -- (No effect if cursor position is first in list)
            -- Inefficient for one-way lists: included for completeness
        * Left to the reader (use *back* and *delete*)

delete_all_occurrences (*v: T*) **is**
            -- Delete all occurrences of *v* from the list
        do
            from *start* **until** *offright* **loop**
                    if *value* = *v* **then** *delete* **else** *forth* **end**
            end;
            no_change_since_mark := **false**
        end; -- *delete_all_occurrences*

wipe_out **is**
            -- Empty the list
        do
            nb_elements := *0*; *position* := *0*;
            active.Forget; *first_element.Forget*; *previous.Forget*; *next.Forget*;
            no_change_since_mark := **false**
        ensure
            empty
        end -- *wipe_out*

-- Secret routines for implementing insertion and deletion

insert_linkable_right (*new:* **like** *first_element*) **is**
            -- Insert *new* to the right of cursor position if there is one.
            -- Do not move cursor. (Secret procedure.)
        require
            not *new.Void*; *empty* **or else not** *offright*
        do
            new.put_between (*active, next*);
            next := *new*; *nb_elements* := *nb_elements* + *1*;
            no_change_since_mark := **false**;
                    check *1* <= *position* + *1*; *position* + *1* <= *nb_elements* **end**;
            update_after_insertion (*new, position* + *1*)
        ensure
            nb_elements = **old** *nb_elements* + *1*;
            position = **old** *position*;
            previous = *new*
        end; -- *insert_linkable_right*

insert_linkable_left (*new:* **like** *first_element*) **is**
        -- Insert *new* to the left of cursor position if there is one.
        -- Do not move cursor. (Secret procedure.)
    require
        not *new.Void; empty* **or else not** *offleft*
    do
        if *empty* **then** *position := 1* **end**;
        new.put_between (*previous, active*);
        previous := new; nb_elements := nb_elements + 1;
        position := position + 1; no_change_since_mark := **false**
                check *1 <= position − 1; position − 1 <= nb_elements* **end**;
        update_after_insertion (*new, position − 1*);
    ensure
        nb_elements = **old** *nb_elements + 1*;
        position = **old** *position + 1*;
        previous = new
    end; -- *insert_linkable_left*

update_after_insertion (*new:* **like** *first_element; index: INTEGER*) **is**
        -- Check consequences of insertion of element *new*
        -- at position *index*: does it become the first element?
    require
        not *new.Void*;
        index >= 1; index <= nb_elements
    do
        if *index = 1* **then**
                first_element := new; first := new.value
        end
    end; -- *update_after_insertion*

update_after_deletion (*one, other:* **like** *first_element; index: INTEGER*) **is**
        -- Check consequences of deletion of element between *one*
        -- and *other*, where *one* is at position *index*.
        -- Update *first_element* if necessary.
    require
        index >= 0; index <= nb_elements;
        empty **or else** *index > 0* **or else not** *other.Void*;
        -- The element deleted was between *one* and *other*
    do
        if *empty* **then**
                first_element.Forget; position := 0
        elsif *index = 0* **then**
                        check not *other.Void* **end**; -- See precondition
                first_element := other; first := other.value
        -- else do nothing special
        end
    end; -- *update_after_deletion*

invariant
          -- The invariant of class *LIST*, plus the following:
     empty = *first_element.Void*;
     empty **or else** *first_element.value* = *first*;
     active.Void = (*offleft* **or** *offright*);
     previous.Void = (*offleft* **or** *isfirst*);
     next.Void = (*offleft* **or** *islast*);
     previous.Void **or else** (*previous.right* = *active*);
     active.Void **or else** (*active.right* = *next*);
          -- (*offleft* **or** *offright*) **or else** *active* is the *position*-th element
end -- class *LINKED_LIST*

A.6   TWO-WAY LISTS

     Class *TWO_WAY_LIST* [*T*] introduces doubly linked lists. Features *back* and *forth*
now have the same efficiency; in fact the whole class is almost entirely-symmetric with
respect to "left" and "right".

          -- Two-way linked lists
class *TWO_WAY_LIST* [*T*] **export**
     ... Same exported features as in *LINKED_LIST* ...

inherit

     LINKED_LIST [*T*]
          rename
               go **as** *reach_from_left*,
               wipe_out **as** *simple_wipe_out*,

          redefine
               first_element, *last*, *back*, *go*, *wipe_out*, *last*,
               update_after_deletion, *update_after_insertion*

feature

     first_element: BI_LINKABLE [*T*];
          -- Redefined from *LINKED_LIST*

          -- Two-way lists also keep a reference to the last element, and its value:
     last_element: **like** *first_element*;

     last: T;
          -- Redefined as attribute (was function in *LINKED_LIST*)

```
back is
        -- Move cursor to previous position
    require
        not offleft
    do
        if offright then
                check not empty end;
            finish
        else
                check not active.Void end;
            next := active; active := previous;
            if not active.Void then previous := active.left end;
            position := position - 1
        end
    ensure
        position = old position - 1
    end; -- back

go (i: INTEGER) is
        -- Move cursor to position i
    require
        i >= 0; i <= nb_elements + 1
    do
        if i = nb_elements + 1 then -- Go offright:
            active.Forget; next.Forget; previous := last_element;
            position := nb_elements + 1
        elsif
            i <= position/2 or
                (i >= position and i <= (position + nb_elements)/2)
        then
            reach_from_left (i)
        else -- Reach from right:
            from
                if position < i then
                        -- Finish (revised for two-way lists)
                        active := last_element; previous := active.left;
                        next.Forget
                end
            invariant
                    i <= position; position <= nb_elements
            variant position - i
            until position = i loop
                        check not offleft end;
                    back
            end -- loop
        end -- if
    ensure
        position = i
    end; -- go
```

update_after_insertion (*new:* **like** *first_element; index: INTEGER*) **is**
          -- Check consequences of insertion of element *new*
          -- at position *index*: does it become the first element?
   * Redefinition left to the reader
   * Hints: make the routine symmetric with respect to right and left;
   * *last_element* and *last* may need to be updated
   * as well as *first_element* and *first*

update_after_deletion (*one, other:* **like** *first_element; index: INTEGER*) **is**
          -- Check consequences of deletion of element
          -- between *one* and *other*, where *one* is at position *index*.
          -- Update *first_element* if necessary.
   * Redefinition left to the reader
   * Hints: see *update_after_insertion*

wipe_out **is**
          -- Empty the list
   do
          simple_wipe_out; last_element.Forget
   ensure
          empty
   end -- *wipe_out*

invariant
          -- The invariant of *LINKED_LIST*, plus the following:
   empty = last_element.Void;
   empty **or else** *last_element.value = last;*
   active.Void **or else** (*active.left = previous*);
   next.Void **or else** (*next.left = active*);
   -- (*offleft* **or** *offright*) **or else** *active* is the *position*-th element
end -- class *TWO_WAY_LIST*

A.7   TREES AND NODES

The following class is an implementation of trees, using linked representation. Note that no distinction is made between trees and tree nodes.

As explained in 10.4.3, tree nodes are implemented as a combination of lists and list elements. The list features make it possible to obtain the children of a node; the list element features make it possible to access the value associated with each node and its right sibling (the class may be redefined using two-way lists and "bi-linkable" elements to allow access to the left sibling as well). The added feature *parent* makes it possible to access the parent of each node.

Since each node of the tree is – among other things – a list in the sense defined above, it keeps a record of the child on which the "cursor" is. To move the cursor of a node, procedures inherited from *LIST* (through *LINKED_LIST*) are available: *back, forth, go* etc.

class *TREE* [*T*] **export**
   position, offright, offleft, isfirst, islast,
   start, finish, forth, back, go,
   mark, return,
   is_leaf, arity,
   node_value, change_node_value,
   child_value, change_child_value,
   child, change_child,
   right_sibling, first_child,
   insert_child_right, insert_child_left,
   delete_child,
   delete_child_left, delete_child_right
   parent, is_root

inherit
   LINKABLE [*T*]
      rename
         right **as** *sibling,*
         value **as** *node_value,*
         change_value **as** *change_node_value,*
         put_between **as** *linkable_put_between;*

      redefine *put_between;*

   LINKED_LIST [*T*]
      rename
         empty **as** *is_leaf, nb_elements* **as** *arity,*
         value **as** *child_value, change_value* **as** *change_child_value,*
         active **as** *child, first_element* **as** *first_child,*
         insert_linkable_right **as** *insert_child_right,*
         insert_linkable_left **as** *insert_child_left,*
         delete **as** *delete_child,*
         delete_left **as** *delete_child_left, delete_right* **as** *delete_child_right,*
         update_after_insertion **as** *linked_update_after_insertion;*

      redefine *first_child, update_after_insertion*

feature
   first_child: TREE [*T*];

   parent: **like** *first_child;*

   attach_to_parent (*n:* **like** *first_child*) **is**
                  -- Make *n* the parent of current node.
                  -- Secret procedure.
      do
         parent := n
      ensure
         parent = n
      end; -- *attach_to_parent*

```
update_after_insertion (new: like first_element; index: INTEGER) is
            -- Check consequences of insertion of element new
            -- at position index: does it become the first element?
            -- Secret procedure redefined from LINKED_LIST
      require
            not new.Void; index >= 1;
            index <= nb_elements
      do
            linked_update_after_insertion (new, index);
            if index = 1 then new.attach_to_parent (Current) end
      end; -- update_after_insertion


change_child (n: like first_child) is
                  -- Replace by n the child at cursor position
      require
            not n.Void;
            not offleft; not offright -- Thus not child.Void
      do
            insert_child_right (n);
                  check n.parent = Current end;
                  -- Because of the redefinition of put_between
            delete_child;
                  check child = n end

            -- A direct implementation (not using insert and delete)
            -- is also possible
      ensure
            child = n;
            n.parent = Current
      end; -- change_child


is_root: BOOLEAN is
                  -- Is current node a root?
      do
            Result := parent.Void
      end; -- is_root


put_between (before, after: like first_child) is
            -- Insert current element between before and after (if it makes sense)
            -- Redefined from LINKABLE
            -- to give Current the same parent as its new siblings.
      require
            (before.Void or after.Void) or else (before.parent = after.parent)
      do
            linkable_put_between;
            if not before.Void then attach_to_parent (before.parent) end;
            if not after.Void then attach_to_parent (after.parent) end;
      end; -- put_between
```

invariant

      -- The invariants of the parent classes, plus the following:

    is_root = parent.Void;

    sibling.Void **or else** *sibling.parent = parent;*

    child.Void **or else** *child.parent = Current;*

    previous.Void **or else** *previous.parent = Current;*

    next.Void **or else** *next.parent = Current;*

    first_child.Void **or else** *first_child.parent = Current;*

end -- class *TREE*

B

Eiffel: a quick overview

This appendix gives a fast-paced review of the Eiffel language and environment.

B.1 DESIGN PRINCIPLES

The design principles behind Eiffel follow from the discussion in chapters 1 to 4: software reusability, extendibility and compatibility were deemed essential. Other design goals also played a significant part. Helping programmers ensure *correctness* and *robustness* of their software is of course a prime concern. *Portability* was one of the requirements on the implementation. Finally, *efficiency* cannot be neglected in a tool that is aimed at practical, medium- to large-scale developments.

To achieve these aims, the language is based on the principles of object-oriented design. Object-oriented design is defined as the construction of software systems as structured collections of abstract data type implementations, with the following comments:

- The emphasis is on structuring a system around the classes of objects it manipulates rather than the functions it performs on them, and on reusing whole data structures, together with the associated operations, rather than isolated procedures.

- Objects are described as instances of abstract data types – that is to say, data structures known from an official interface rather than through their representation.

- The basic modular unit, called the class, describes an implementation or a group of implementations of an abstract data type – not the abstract data type itself, whose specification would not necessarily be executable. (Some classes, called "deferred classes", represent a group of implementations rather than just one.)

• The word *collection* reflects how classes should be designed: as units which are interesting and useful on their own, independently of the systems to which they belong, and may be reused by many different systems. Software construction is viewed as the assembly of existing classes, not as a top-down process starting from scratch.

• Finally, the word *structured* reflects the existence of important relationships between classes, particularly the **multiple inheritance** relation.

B.2   CLASSES

A class that represents an implementation of an abstract data type describes a set of potential run-time objects characterized by the operations available on them (the same for all instances of a given class), and the properties of these operations. These objects are called the **instances** of the class. Classes and objects should not be confused: "class" is a compile-time notion, whereas objects only exist at run-time. This is similar to the difference that exists in classical programming between a program and one execution of that program.

The basic structure and properties of classes are described in chapter 5. Consider the example of a simple class *ACCOUNT* describing bank accounts. Before studying the class itself, it is helpful to look at how it would be used by another class, say *X*. To use *ACCOUNT*, class *X* may introduce an entity and declare it of this type:

> *acc1: ACCOUNT*

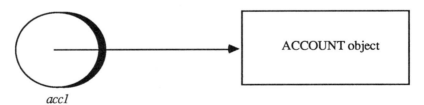

acc1

Figure B.1   Entity and object

The term "entity" is preferred here to "variable" as it denotes a more general notion. An entity declared of a class type, such as *acc1*, may at any time during execution refer to an object; as Eiffel is a typed language, this object must be an instance of *ACCOUNT* (or, as seen below, of a "descendant class" of *ACCOUNT*). An entity which does not refer to any object is said to be void. By default (at initialization) entities are void; objects must be created explicitly, by an instruction

> *acc1.Create*

which associates *acc1* with the newly created object. *Create* is a predefined "feature" of the language.

Once *acc1* has been associated with an object, the features defined in class *ACCOUNT* may be applied to it. Examples are:

acc1.open ("*John*");
acc1.deposit (*5000*);

if *acc1.may_withdraw* (*3000*) **then**
        acc1.withdraw (*3000*)
end;
print (*acc1.balance*)

All feature applications use the dot notation: *entity_name.feature_name* . There are two kinds of features: **routines** (as *open*, *deposit*, *may_withdraw* or *withdraw*), that is to say operations; and **attributes**, that is to say data items associated with objects of the class.

Routines are further divided into procedures (actions, which do not return a value) and functions (which return a value). Here *may_withdraw* is a function with an integer parameter, returning a boolean result; the other three routines invoked are procedures.

The above extract of class *X* does not show whether, in class *ACCOUNT*, *balance* is an attribute or a function without parameters. This ambiguity is intentional. A class such as *X*, said to be a **client** of *ACCOUNT*, does not need to know how a balance is obtained: it could be stored as an attribute of every account object, or recomputed by a function, whenever requested, from other attributes such as the list of previous deposits and withdrawals. Deciding on one of these implementations is the business of class *ACCOUNT*, not anybody else's. This is the principle of *uniform reference*, explained in 2.1.4.

Here now is a first sketch of how class *ACCOUNT* itself might look. Line segments beginning with -- are comments.

class *ACCOUNT* **export**
        open, deposit, may_withdraw, withdraw, balance, owner
feature
        balance: INTEGER ;

        minimum_balance: INTEGER **is** *1000* ;

        owner: STRING ;

        open (*who: STRING*) **is**
                -- Assign the account to owner *who*
        do *owner := who* **end**; -- *open*

        add (*sum: INTEGER*) **is**
                -- Add *sum* to the balance (secret procedure)
        do *balance := balance+sum* **end**; -- *deposit*

deposit (sum: INTEGER) **is**
                -- Deposit *sum* into the account
   do *add (sum)* **end**; -- *deposit*

withdraw (sum: INTEGER) **is**
                -- Withdraw *sum* from the account
   do *add (–sum)* **end**; -- *withdraw*

may_withdraw (sum: INTEGER): BOOLEAN **is**
                -- Is it permitted to withdraw *sum* from the account?
   do *Result := (balance >= minimum_balance)* **end**; -- *deposit*
end -- class *ACCOUNT*

This class includes two clauses: **feature**, which describes the features of the class, and **export**, which lists the names of features available to clients of the class. Non-exported features are said to be secret. Here procedure *add* is secret, so that *acc1.add* (*–3000*) would be illegal in *X*. Attribute *minimum_balance* is also secret.

Routines are distinguished from attributes by a clause of the form **is...do...end**. Thus *balance* is in fact an attribute. The clause **is** *1000* introduces *minimum_balance* as a constant attribute, which will not occupy any physical space in objects of the class (constants are studied in chapter 13). Non-constant attributes such as *balance* use space for each object of the class; they are similar to components of a record in Pascal.

Attributes *balance* and *minimum_balance* are declared of type *INTEGER*. Eiffel is strongly typed: every entity is declared of a certain type. A type is either simple, that is to say one of *INTEGER*, *REAL*, *CHARACTER* and *BOOLEAN*, or a class. Arrays and strings belong to the second category; they are described by predefined system classes, *ARRAY* and *STRING*, treated exactly as user-defined classes with one exception: a special notation, as in *"John"*, is available to denote literal string constants.

Automatic initialization (5.3.6) is ensured by the language definition, so that the initial *balance* of an account object will be zero after a *Create*. Numeric attributes are initialized to zero, booleans to false, characters to the null character; those of class types are initially void.

The other five features are straightforward routines. The first four are procedures, the last one (*may_withdraw*) a function returning a boolean value; note that the special variable *Result* denotes the function result. It is initialized on function entry to the default value of the appropriate type, as defined above.

To understand the routines, it is necessary to remember that in an object-oriented languages any operation is relative to a certain object. In a client class invoking the operation, this object is specified by writing the corresponding entity on the left of the dot, as *acc1* in *acc1.open ("John")*. Within the class, however, the "current" object to which operations apply usually remains implicit: unqualified references, such as *owner* in procedure *open* or *add* in *deposit*, mean "the *owner* attribute or *add* routine relative to the current object". The special variable *Current* may be used, if needed, to explicitly denote this object. Thus the unqualified occurrences of *add* appearing in the above class are equivalent to *Current. add*.

B.3 ASSERTIONS

An abstract data type is not just defined by a set of operations, but also by the formal properties of these operations, which do not appear in the above class example.

Eiffel enables and encourages programmers to express formal properties of classes by writing **assertions** (chapter 7), which may in particular appear in the following positions:

- Routine **preconditions** express conditions that must be satisfied whenever a routine is called. For example withdrawal might only be permitted if it keeps the account's balance on or above the minimum. Preconditions are introduced by the keyword **require**.

- Routine **postconditions**, introduced by the keyword **ensure**, express conditions that are guaranteed to be true on routine return (if the precondition was satisfied on entry).

- Class **invariants** must be satisfied by objects of the class at all times, or more precisely after object creation and after any call to a routine of the class. They are described in the **invariant** clause of the class and represent general consistency constraints that are imposed on all routines of the class.

Assertions are one of the traits that reflect the concern for correctness in the language design. Remarkable as object-oriented techniques are for producing extendible and reusable components, they are of little interest unless we can convince ourselves that these components are also correct and robust.

The *ACCOUNT* class may be rewritten with appropriate assertions:

class *ACCOUNT* **export** ... (as before) **feature**

    ... Attributes *balance, minimum_balance, owner* as before

    ... Routines *open, may_withdraw* and *add* as before

    deposit (sum: INTEGER) **is**
                -- Deposit *sum* into the account
        require
            sum >= 0
        do
            add (sum)
        ensure
            balance = **old** *balance + sum*
        end; -- *deposit*

    withdraw (sum: INTEGER) **is**
                -- Withdraw *sum* from the account
        require
            0 <= sum; sum <= balance – minimum_balance
        do
            add (–sum)
        ensure
            balance = **old** *balance – sum*
        end; -- *withdraw*

```
Create (initial: INTEGER) is
    require
        initial >= minimum_balance
    do
        balance := initial
    end -- Create

invariant
    balance >= minimum_balance
end -- class ACCOUNT
```

The **old...** notation may be used in an **ensure** clause, with a self-explanatory meaning.

This class now includes a specific *Create* procedure, as needed when the default initializations are not sufficient. With the previous version of the class, an account was created by, say, *acc1.Create*, which initialized all attributes to the default values. But this is now incompatible with the class invariant, since *balance* would be initialized to zero. When non-default initialization is required, possibly (as here) calling for client-supplied arguments, the class should include a procedure called *Create*. The effect of

acc1.Create (5500)

is to allocate the object and perform the default initializations (as in the default *Create*), then to call the procedure called *Create* in the class, with the given argument. This call is correct as it satisfies the precondition and ensures the invariant. (Procedure *Create*, when provided, is recognized as special; it is automatically exported and should not be included in the **export** clause.)

Syntactically, assertions are boolean expressions, with a few extensions (such as the **old** notation). The semicolon (see the precondition to *withdraw*) is equivalent to an "and", but permits individual identification of the components.

Assertions should primarily be viewed as powerful tools for documenting correctness arguments: they serve to make explicit the assumptions on which programmers rely when they write program fragments that they believe are correct. Writing assertions, in particular preconditions and postconditions, amounts to spelling out the terms of the **contract** that binds a routine and its callers. The precondition binds the callers; the postcondition binds the routine. This metaphor of *programming as contracting* is a general and fruitful paradigm, extended in the case of inheritance by the notion of subcontracting (see below and chapter 11).

B.4 EXCEPTIONS

If, at run-time, an assertion is violated, it means that the system contains a programming error: some element of the system has not observed part of its contract.

A disciplined exception mechanism (7.10) is provided to deal with such cases. A compilation option, set separately for each class, makes it possible to monitor assertions at run-time. Three levels of monitoring (none, preconditions only, all assertions) are offered. When a violation is detected, an **exception** is raised. Exceptions are also raised as a result of abnormal conditions detected by the hardware or operating system (numerical overflow, memory exhaustion etc.); formally, these cases may be viewed as violations of implicit assertions (for example the precondition, implicit on any arithmetic addition, that operands are not too large).

An exception occurring during the execution of a routine normally causes the routine to **fail**. Failure of a routine in turn causes an exception in the routine's caller.

A routine may, however, contain a **rescue clause** which will be activated whenever an exception is raised during the execution of the routine. The aim of the rescue clause is to put the object to which the routine was applied back into a stable state (one satisfying the class invariant). If the rescue clause is executed to its end, the routine fails, causing an exception in its caller. The rescue clause may also terminate by executing a **retry** instruction which will attempt to re-execute the routine; this assumes that the rescue clause has corrected the cause of the exception and re-ensured the routine precondition. If this new attempt succeeds, no exception will be raised in the calling routine.

As an example, the following routine attempts to write an integer onto a tape. If the operation fails, for example because the tape is off-line, the routine outputs an error message and tries again, but will fail after three unsuccessful attempts. A failure to write is assumed to raise an exception.

```
attempt_to_write (x: INTEGER) is
            -- Attempt (at most three times) to write x onto tape
    do
        actual_write (x)
            -- actual_write is a physical write operation
            -- which may raise an exception
    rescue
        attempts := attempts + 1;
        if failed <= 3 then
            message ("Tape write failed. Check if unit is on-line.");
            message ("Type any character when ready to try again.");
            read_a_character;
            retry
        end
    end -- attempt_to_write
```

Exceptions should be used sparingly (7.10.3). They are not a technique for dealing with cases other than the most common ones for an algorithm. They should be reserved for unpredictable abnormal events, untestable preconditions and fault tolerance (protection against remaining errors in the software).

B.5   GENERIC CLASSES

Building software components (classes) as implementations of abstract data types yields systems with a solid architecture but does not in itself suffice to ensure reusability and extendibility. This section and the next two describe Eiffel techniques for making the components as general and flexible as possible.

The first technique is genericity. Classes may have generic parameters representing types. The following examples come from the Eiffel class library (appendix A):

> *ARRAY* [*T*]
> *LIST* [*T*]
> *LINKED_LIST* [*T*]

They respectively describe one-dimensional arrays, general lists (without commitment as to a specific representation) and lists in linked representation. Each has a formal generic parameter *T* representing an arbitrary type. To use these classes, you provide actual generic parameters, which may be either simple or class types, as in the following declarations:

> *il: LIST* [*INTEGER*];
> *aa: ARRAY* [*ACCOUNT*];
> *aal: LIST* [*ARRAY* [*ACCOUNT*]] --etc.

Eiffel's generic facility is described in detail in chapter 6. Chapter 19 is a precise comparison of this facility with inheritance (see next section), explaining their combination in the context of strict type checking.

B.6   MULTIPLE INHERITANCE

Inheritance (chapters 10 and 11) is a key technique for reusability. The basic idea is simple: when defining a new class, it is often fruitful to introduce it by combination and specialization of existing classes rather than as a new entity defined from scratch.

The following simple example, from the Eiffel library, is typical. *LIST*, as indicated, describes lists of any representation. One possible representation for lists with a fixed number of elements uses an array. Such a class will be defined by combination of *LIST* and *ARRAY*, as follows:

> **class** *FIXED_LIST* [*T*] **export** ...
> **inherit**
> > *LIST* [*T*];
> > *ARRAY* [*T*]
>
> **feature**
> > ... Specific features of fixed-size lists ...
>
> **end** -- class *FIXED_LIST*

The **inherit**... clause lists all the "parents" of the new class, which is said to be their "heir". (The "ancestors" of a class include the class itself, its parents, grandparents etc.; the reverse term is "descendant".) Declaring *FIXED_LIST* as shown ensures that all the features and properties of lists and arrays are applicable to fixed lists as well.

Multiple inheritance yields remarkable economies of programming effort and has a profound effect on the software development process.

The very power of the mechanism demands adequate means to keep it under control. In Eiffel, no name conflict is permitted between inherited features. Since name conflicts inevitably arise in practice, especially for software components contributed by independent developers, the language provides a technique to remove them: **renaming** (10.4.6), as in

> **class** *C* **export... inherit**
> *A* **rename** *x* **as** *x1, y* **as** *y1*;
> *B* **rename** *x* **as** *x2, y* **as** *y2*
> **feature...**

Here the **inherit** clause would be illegal without renaming, since the example assumes that both *A* and *B* have features named *x* and *y*.

Renaming also serves to provide more appropriate feature names in heirs. In another example from the library (10.4.3), class *TREE* [*T*], is defined as a descendant of *LINKED_LIST*, since a tree, or tree node, may be viewed as a list of its subtrees, to which the usual list operations of insertion, change, deletion, traversal etc. apply. (*TREE* is also a descendant of *LINKABLE*, describing linked list elements, as a tree may itself be inserted as subtree into another tree; this use of multiple inheritance yields a simple, yet general and powerful definition of trees.) In the inheritance clause, the feature *empty* of linked lists, a boolean-valued function which determines whether a list is empty, is renamed *is_leaf* to conform to tree terminology. Feature *nb_elements* of lists is similarly renamed *arity*, the standard term for trees.

To further ensure that the multiple inheritance mechanism is not misused, the invariants of all parent classes automatically apply to a newly defined class. Thus classes may not be combined if their invariants are incompatible. Routine preconditions and postconditions are also applicable to descendants (see below).

B.7 POLYMORPHISM

One important aspect of inheritance (10.1.5) is that it enables the definition of flexible program entities that may refer to objects of various forms at run-time (hence the name "polymorphic").

This possibility is one of the distinctive features of object-oriented languages. In Eiffel, it is reconciled with static typing. The type compatibility rule (11.3.1) permits an assignment of the form *a := b* not only if *a* and *b* are of the same type, but more generally whenever *a* and *b* are of class types *A* and *B* such that *B* is a descendant of *A*.

This corresponds to the intuitive idea that a value of a more specialized type may be assigned to an entity of a less specialized type – but not the reverse. (As an analogy, consider the fact that if I request vegetables, getting green vegetables is fine, but if I ask for green vegetables, receiving a dish labeled just "vegetables" is not acceptable, as it could include, say, carrots.)

What makes this possibility particularly powerful is the complementary facility: **feature redefinition**. A feature of a class may be redefined in any descendant class; the type of the redefined feature (if an attribute or a function) may be redefined as a descendant type of the original feature, and, in the case of a routine, its body may also be replaced by a new one.

Assume for example that a class *HOUSE*, describing houses, has among its features a real attribute *space*, representing the floor space occupied by a house, and a function *tax* returning a real result, the annual tax to be paid for the house, as computed from *space* and other attributes. An heir of *HOUSE*, describing a house rented to some tenant, may be:

> **class** *RENTED_HOUSE* **export** ... **inherit**
>   *HOUSE* **redefine** *tax*
> **feature**
>   -- Specific features of rented houses, such as:
>   *monthly_rental_fee: REAL*;
>
>   *tax: REAL* **is**
>   -- Version taking into account special tax rules for rented houses
>   **do**
>   ... Some computation involving *monthly_rental_fee* ...
>   **end**; -- *tax*
>   ... other *RENTED_HOUSE* features ...

Here it is necessary to redefine *tax* for rented houses as there is a specific algorithm in this case. Note the explicit **redefine** subclause (which would come after the **rename** if present).

Other descendants of *HOUSE*, such as *UNOCCUPIED_HOUSE* (if a special rule is applicable in this case) may also have their own redefinitions of *tax*. The version to use in any call is determined by the run-time form of the parameter. Consider the following class fragment:

> *h: HOUSE*; *r: RENTED_HOUSE*;
> ... *h.Create*; *r.Create*; ...
> **if** *c* **then** *p* := *r* **end**;
> *print* (*h.tax*)

The assignment *h* := *r* is valid because of the type compatibility rule. If condition *c* is false, *h* will refer to an object of type *HOUSE* when *h.tax* is evaluated, so the *HOUSE* algorithm will be used; in the opposite case, however, *h* will dynamically refer to a rented house, so that the redefined version of the feature will be applied. This property is known as dynamic binding (10.1.8).

This technique provides a high degree of flexibility and generality. The remarkable advantage for clients is the ability to request an operation (here the computation of the tax on a house) without knowing what version of the operation will be selected; the selection only occurs at run-time. This is essential in large systems, where many variants of operations may be available, and each component of the system needs to be protected against variant changes in other components.

There is no equivalent to this possibility in non-object-oriented languages. For example, discrimination on records with variants, as permitted by Pascal or Ada, is of a much more restrictive nature, as the list of variants of a record type is fixed: any extension may invalidate existing code. In contrast, inheritance is open and incremental: an existing class may always be given a new heir (with new and/or redefined features) without itself being changed. This facility is of great importance in software development, an activity which (whether by design or circumstance) is invariably incremental.

Neither do the generic and overloading facilities of Ada (see 3.6.3 and chapters 18-19) offer the kind of polymorphism shown here, as they do not support a programming style in which a client module may issue a request meaning: "compute the tax on h, using the algorithm appropriate for whatever form h happens to have when the request is executed".

The inheritance mechanism is present in Eiffel in a disciplined form. First, feature redefinition, as seen above, is explicit. Second, because the language is typed, the compiler may always check statically whether a feature application $a.f$ is correct.

A third tool for controlling the power of the redefinition mechanism is provided in Eiffel by assertions. If no precautions are taken, redefinition may be dangerous: how can a client be sure that evaluation of $h.tax$ will not in some cases return, say, the height of h? One way to maintain the semantic consistency of routines throughout their redefinitions is to use preconditions and postconditions, which are binding on redefinitions. More precisely (11.1.2), any redefined version must satisfy a weaker or equal precondition and ensure a stronger or equal postcondition than in the original. Thus, by making the semantic constraints explicit, routine writers may limit the amount of freedom granted to eventual redefiners.

These rules should be understood in light of the contracting metaphor introduced above. Redefinition and dynamic binding introduce subcontracting (11.1.4): *HOUSE*, for example, subcontracts the implementation of *tax* to *RENTED_HOUSE* when applied to any entity that refers at run-time to a rectangle object. An honest subcontractor is bound by the contract accepted by the prime contractor: it may not impose stronger requirements on the clients (but may accept more general requests, hence the possibility for the precondition to be weaker); and it must achieve at least as much as promised by the original contractor (but may achieve more, hence the possibility for the postcondition to be stronger).

B.8   DEFERRED CLASSES

An important extension of the inheritance mechanism is provided by deferred classes (10.3). A deferred class is one in which at least one routine is declared as deferred, to express that actual implementations are only provided in descendants. For example, a system used by the Department of Motor Vehicles to register vehicles could include a class of the form

```
deferred class VEHICLE export
        dues_paid, valid_plate, register, ...
feature
        dues_paid (year: INTEGER): BOOLEAN is ... end;

        valid_plate (year: INTEGER): BOOLEAN is ... end;

        register (year: INTEGER) is
                        -- Register vehicle for year
                require
                        dues_paid (year)
                deferred
                ensure
                        valid_plate (year)
                end; -- register
        ... Other features ...
end -- class VEHICLE
```

This example assumes that there is not a single registration algorithm; the exact procedure to follow depends on the type of vehicle considered: passenger car, motorcycle, truck etc. However the same precondition and postcondition are applicable in all cases. The solution is to treat *register* as a deferred routine, making *VEHICLE* a deferred class. Effective versions of this routine are given in descendants of class *VEHICLE*, for example *TRUCK* etc. They are similar to redefined versions of a routine; but here there is no effective definition in the original class, only a specification in the form of a deferred routine.

Deferred classes may be viewed as describing a group of implementations of an abstract data type rather than a single implementation. A deferred class may not be instantiated: *v. Create* is illegal if *v* is an entity declared of type *VEHICLE*. But such an entity may be assigned a reference to an instance of a non-deferred descendant of *VEHICLE*. For example, assuming *CAR* and *TRUCK* provide effective definitions for all deferred routines of *VEHICLE*, the following will be correct:

        ... v: VEHICLE; c: CAR; t: TRUCK; ... c. Create (...); t.Create (...); ...
        if "some test" then v := c else v := t end;
        v.register (1990)

The mechanism of polymorphism and dynamic binding are fully exploited here: depending on the outcome of "some test", *v* will be treated as a car or a truck, and the appropriate registration algorithm will be applied. Note that "some test" may depend on some event whose outcome is impossible to predict until run-time, for example the mouse selection by the user of one vehicle icon among several displayed ones.

Deferred classes are particularly useful for the application of Eiffel as high-level design language. The first version of a module, obtained at the global design stage, may be a deferred class, which will later be refined into one or more effective (non-deferred) classes. Particularly important for this application is the possibility to associate a precondition and a postcondition to a routine even though it is deferred (as with routine *register* above), and an invariant to a class even though it is a deferred class. This enables the designer to attach a precise semantics to a module long before any implementation is provided.

B.9   THE IMPLEMENTATION

The Eiffel implementation (chapter 15) runs on various versions of Unix (System V, 4.2/4.3 BSD, Xenix); at the time of writing it has been ported to about 20 different machine architectures. A Vax-VMS version is in progress.

The compiler uses C as intermediate language, making Eiffel potentially portable to any environment supporting C. As a language, Eiffel is in no way an extension of C; but the use of a widely available assembly language such as C as intermediate code has obvious portability advantages.

Great care has been taken to provide efficient compilation and execution, so that the environment would support the development of serious software. The following points are particularly worth noting.

- Redefinition implies that a qualified routine reference, say $h.tax$, may have many different interpretations depending on the value of h at run-time. A run-time search for the appropriate routine, would carry a heavy performance penalty, especially with multiple inheritance. The Eiffel implementation solves this problem through a technique that always finds the appropriate routine in constant time, with only a small penalty over a standard procedure call, and no significant space overhead.

- There is almost never any code duplication. Code is only duplicated in a special case, "repeated" inheritance with renaming (11.6).

- The run-time system handles object creation and memory deallocation. It includes an incremental garbage collector, implemented as a coroutine which continuously cooperates with application programs. Automatic garbage collection is an essential component of the object-oriented approach: programmers of object-oriented applications, which typically create many objects, should not be charged with the tedious and error-prone task of storage management. Garbage collection may be turned off; the collector coroutine may also be explicitly activated for a certain time at points where the programmer knows some CPU time is available, for example while awaiting user input. Memory management is discussed in chapter 16.

- Compilation is performed on a class-by-class basis, so that large systems can be changed and extended incrementally. The Eiffel to C translation time is usually about half of the time for the next step, C to machine code.

- The implementation is highly open: classes are meant to be interfaced with code written in other languages. This concern is reflected in the language by the optional **external** clause which, in a routine declaration, lists external subprograms used by the routine but written in other languages (8.3). This mechanism makes it possible to use external routines – an important requirement for making reuse practical – without impacting the conceptual consistency of Eiffel classes. Thanks to this facility, Eiffel may be used as a "programming-in-the-large" language for integrating components written in other languages.

B.10   THE ENVIRONMENT

The construction of systems in Eiffel is supported by a set of development tools.

Most important are the facilities for automatic configuration management integrated in the compilation command **es**, for Eiffel System (15.2). When a class C is compiled, the system automatically looks for all classes on which C depends directly or indirectly (as client or heir), and recompiles those whose compiled versions are obsolete.

This problem is made difficult by the complexity of the dependency relations: a class may be a client of one of its descendants or ancestors, and the client relation may be cyclic. Its solution completely frees programmers from having to keep track of changed modules to maintain the consistency of their systems. The algorithm avoids many unneeded recompilations by detecting modifications that do not impact class interfaces.

The environment also contains debugging tools (15.5.5): tools for run-time checking of assertions; a tracer and symbolic debugger; a viewer for interactive exploration of the object structure at run-time.

An important documentation tool is **short** (9.5), which produces a summary version of a class showing the interface as available to clients: the exported features only and, in the case of routines, only the header, precondition and postcondition. Such documentation is essentially obtained "for free" and is guaranteed to be consistent with the documented software, as it is extracted from it rather than maintained separately as in classical approaches. The **flat** tool (15.5.3) produces a version of a class functionally equivalent to the original, but without any inheritance clause: all inherited features are reproduced from their versions in parents, renaming and redefinition being taken into account.

A postprocessor integrated within **es** optionally performs important optimizations on the generated C code (15.4.4): removal of unneeded routines and simplification of calls to non-polymorphic routines. One of its main options (15.3) is the generation of a stand-alone **C package** from an Eiffel system; the package comes complete with its make file and a copy of the run-time system. It may be ported to any environment supporting C and some primitive functions. This facility is particularly interesting for cross-development: developers may use Eiffel to design and implement their software but deliver it to their customers in standard C form. Eiffel need not be available on the target environments.

Finally the environment includes a library of classes (appendix A) covering many of the most important data structures and algorithms of everyday programming. Use of this library is one of the elements that give Eiffel programming its distinctive flavor, enabling programmers to think and write in terms of lists, trees, stacks, hash tables etc. rather than arrays, pointers, flags and the like.

C

Eiffel grammar

This appendix describes the grammar of Eiffel. Lexical conventions are introduced in section C.1. The syntactical specification is given in section C.2. In this specification, the syntax for expressions does not take operator precedence into account; precedence is given separately in section C.3.

Note that the syntax may also be found in diagram form in Appendix F.

C.1 LEXICAL CONVENTIONS

The syntactical specification given in the next section uses the following lexical elements as primitive constructs:

- *Integer*: unsigned integers, such as 345 or 1987.
- *Real*: unsigned real numbers, such as 34. or 34.56.
- *Character*: characters, such as A or /.
- *String*: sequences of characters, such as ABCD/?00+eee.
- *Identifier*: identifiers.

An Eiffel identifier is a sequence made of letters, digits and underlined blank (_) characters. The first character must be a letter (it may not be an underlined blank). There is no limitation on the length of identifiers, with one exception: class names must not exceed 12 characters (because of limitations on file names in common operating systems).

Eiffel has 53 reserved words, which may not be used as identifiers. These reserved words, listed in appendix D, include keywords (such as **class**), names of predefined routines (such as *Create*) and predefined entities (such as *Result*, denoting the result of a function).

Letter case is **not** significant in Eiffel identifiers. *AB, aB, aB* and *ab* all denote the same identifier. Thus you may not, for example, call an identifier *result*, as this would be confused with the predefined entity *Result*.

Certain standard conventions are, however, recommended to enhance clarity:

• Class names and other types (*INTEGER* etc.) in upper case letters.

• Predefined entities and routines (*Result, Create, Void* etc.) start with an upper-case letter.

• Names of symbolic constant also start with an upper-case letter.

• All other identifiers in lower-case.

C.2 SYNTACTICAL SPECIFICATION

Class_declaration	=	Class_header
		[Formal_generics]
		[Exports]
		[Parents]
		[Features]
		[Class_invariant]
		end ["--" **class** Class_name]
Class_header	=	[Deferred_mark] **class** Class_name
Deferred_mark	=	**deferred**
Class_name	=	Identifier
Formal_generics	=	"[" Formal_generic_list "]"
Formal_generic_list	=	{Formal_generic ","...}
Formal_generic	=	Identifier
Exports	=	**export** Export_list
Export_list	=	{Export_item "," ...}
Export_item	=	Feature_name [Export_restriction]
Feature_name	=	Identifier
Export_restriction	=	"{" Class_list "}"
Class_list	=	{Class_name "," ...}
Parents	=	**inherit** Parent_list
Parent_list	=	{Parent ";" ...}
Parent	=	Class_type [Rename_clause] [Redefine_clause]

Class_type	=	Class_name [Actual_generics]
Actual_generics	=	"[" Type_list "]"
Type_list	=	{Type "," ...}
Type	=	*INTEGER* | *BOOLEAN* | *CHARACTER* | *REAL* |
		Class_type | Formal_generic | Association
Association	=	**like** Anchor
Anchor	=	Feature_name | *Current*
Rename_clause	=	**rename** Rename_list
Rename_list	=	{Rename_pair "," ...}
Rename_pair	=	Feature_name **as** Feature_name
Redefine_clause	=	**redefine** Feature_list
Feature_list	=	{Feature_name "," ...}
Features	=	**feature** {Feature_declaration ";" ...}
Feature_declaration	=	Feature_name
		[Formal_arguments]
		[Type_mark]
		[Feature_value_mark]
Formal_arguments	=	Entity_declaration_list
Entity_declaration_list	=	{Entity_declaration_group ";" ...}
Entity_declaration_group	=	{Identifier "," ...}+ Type_mark
Type_mark	=	":" Type
Feature_value_mark	=	**is** Feature_value
Feature_value	=	Constant | Routine
Constant	=	Integer_constant | Character_constant |
		Boolean_constant | Real_constant | String_constant
Integer_constant	=	[Sign] Integer
Sign	=	'+' | '–'
Character_constant	=	"'" Character "'"
Boolean_constant	=	**true** | **false**
Real_constant	=	[Sign] Real
String_constant	=	'"' String '"'
Routine	=	[Precondition]
		[Externals]
		[Local_variables]
		Body
		[Postcondition]
		[Rescue]
		end ["--" Feature_name]

Precondition	=	**require** Assertion
Assertion	=	{Assertion_clause ";" ...}
Assertion_clause	=	[Tag_mark] Unlabeled_assertion_clause
Tag_mark	=	Tag ":"
Tag	=	Identifier
Unlabeled_assertion_clause	=	Boolean_expression | Comment
Boolean_expression	=	Expression
Comment	=	"--" String
Externals	=	**external** External_list
External_list	=	{External_declaration ";" ...}
External_declaration	=	Feature_name [Formal_arguments] [Type_mark] [External_name] Language
Language	=	**language** String_constant
External_name	=	**name** String_constant
Local_variables	=	Entity_declaration_list
Body	=	Full_body | Deferred_body
Deferred_body	=	**deferred**
Full_body	=	Normal_body | Once_body
Normal_body	=	**do** Compound
Once_body	=	**once** Compound
Compound	=	{Instruction ";" ...}
Instruction	=	Call | Assignment | Conditional | Loop | Check | Retry | Debug
Call	=	Qualified_call | Unqualified_call
Qualified_call	=	Expression "." Unqualified_call
Unqualified_call	=	Feature_name [Actuals]
Actuals	=	"(" Expression_list ")"
Expression_list	=	{Expression Separator ...}
Separator	=	"," | ";"
Assignment	=	Entity ":=" Expression
Entity	=	Identifier | *Result*
Expression	=	{Unqualified_expression "." ...}
Unqualified_expression	=	Constant | Entity | Unqualified_call | *Current* | Old_value | Nochange | Operator_expression
Old_value	=	**old** Expression
Nochange	=	**nochange**

Operator_expression	=	Unary_expression | Binary_expression | Multiary_expression | Parenthesized
Unary_expression	=	Unary Expression
Unary	=	**not** | "+" | "–"
Binary_expression	=	Expression Binary Expression
Binary	=	^ | = | /= | < | > | <= | >=
Multiary_expression	=	{Expression Multiary ...}⁺
Multiary	=	"+" | "–" | "*" | "/" | **and** | **and then** | **or** | **or else**
Parenthesized	=	"(" Expression ")"
Conditional	=	**if** Then_part_list [Else_part] **end**
Then_part_list	=	{Then_part **elsif** ...}⁺
Then_part	=	Boolean_expression **then** Compound
Else_part	=	**else** Compound
Loop	=	Initialization [Loop_invariant] [Loop_variant] Exit_clause Loop_body **end**
Initialization	=	**from** Compound
Loop_invariant	=	**invariant** Assertion
Loop_variant	=	**variant** Integer_expression
Integer_expression	=	Expression
Exit_clause	=	**until** Boolean_expression
Loop_body	=	**loop** Compound
Check	=	**check** Assertion **end**
Retry	=	**retry**
Debug	=	**debug** Compound **end**
Postcondition	=	**ensure** Assertion
Rescue	=	**rescue** Compound
Class_invariant	=	**invariant** Assertion

C.3 OPERATOR PRECEDENCE

Operators are listed below in order of decreasing precedence (from closest to furthest binding). Operators at the same level associate from left to right, except for the relational operators of level 4 which are not associative.

Level	Operators
10	. (Dot notation for qualified features)
9	**old**
8	ˆ (Power)
7	**not** + − (unary)
6	* / **mod div**
5	+ − (binary)
4	= /= < > <= >=
3	**and** **and then**
2	**or** **or else**
1	; (lower precedence ''and'' in assertions)

D

Eiffel reserved words and special symbols

D.1 RESERVED WORDS

and	debug	*Equal*	invariant	not	*Result*
as	deferred	external	is	old	retry
BOOLEAN	div	false	language	once	*STRING*
check	do	feature	like	or	then
class	else	*Forget*	local	*REAL*	true
CHARACTER	elsif	from	loop	redefine	until
Clone	end	if	mod	rename	variant
Create	ensure	inherit	name	require	*Void*
Current	export	*INTEGER*	nochange	rescue	

D.2 SPECIAL SYMBOLS

```
--
; ,
: .
:=
= /= < > <= >=
+ – * / ^
( ) [ ] { }
```

E

Input, output and strings

This appendix shows how to handle input-output and strings in Eiffel, as handled by classes from the basic library. Their use is explained by the class interfaces produced by command **short** (see 9.5).

Also important for practical usage of Eiffel is the handling of arrays. The corresponding class, *ARRAY*, was given in appendix A (A.1).

E.1 STANDARD INPUT AND OUTPUT

Class *STD_FILES* describes the three basic files (input, normal output and error output). Any class inheriting from this class may perform file operations (as described by features of class *FILE*, given in the next section) on any of the files denoted by *input*, *output* and *error*.

class interface *STD_FILES* **exported features**

    input, output, error

feature specification

    input: FILE

    output: FILE

    error: FILE

end interface -- class *STD_FILES*

The three features of this class are internally defined as once functions performing the necessary initializations. Thus it is not necessary to initialize the corresponding files: they will be automatically opened in the correct mode the first time an I/O operation is applied.

E.2   FILES

The attributes of class *STD_FILES* are of type *FILE*, described by the following class.

class interface *FILE* exported features

> *exists, readable, writable, executable, date, creatable,*
> *open_read, open_write, open_append, close, putint, putreal,*
> *putchar, putstring, putbool, putint_nl, putreal_nl, putchar_nl,*
> *putstring_nl, putbool_nl, lastint, lastreal, lastchar, laststring,*
> *next_line, error, set_error_output, unset_error_output*

feature specification

> *Create (fn: STRING)*
> > -- Create file with *fn as file name.*

> *error: INTEGER*
> > -- Error code returned by last file operation

> > -- Error codes:
> *No_error: INTEGER*
> *Incorrect_file: INTEGER*
> *Read_error: INTEGER*
> *Write_error: INTEGER*
> *End_of_file: INTEGER*

> *set_error_output*
> > -- Enable writing of error messages on error output
> > -- in case of input-output errors.
> > -- (This is the default.)

> *unset_error_output*
> > -- Disable writing of error messages on error output
> > -- in case of input-output errors.
> > -- (This is not the default.)

> *exists: BOOLEAN*
> > -- Does file exist?

> *readable: BOOLEAN*
> > -- Is file readable?

executable: BOOLEAN
            -- Is file executable?

writable: BOOLEAN
            -- Is file writable?

creatable: BOOLEAN
            -- Can file be created in parent directory?

date: INTEGER
            -- Date stamp

open_read
            -- Open file in read-only mode.

open_write
            -- Open file in write-only mode.

open_append
            -- Open file in append-only mode.

putint_nl (n: INTEGER)
            -- Write *n* at end of file, followed by new line.

putbool_nl (b: BOOLEAN)
            -- Write *b* at end of file, followed by new line.

putreal_nl (r: REAL)
            -- Write *r* at end of file, followed by a new line.

putstring_nl (s: STRING)
            -- Write *s* at end of file, followed by new line.

putchar_nl (c: CHARACTER)
            -- Write *n* at end of file, followed by new line.

putint (n: INTEGER)
            -- Write *n* at end of file

putbool (b: BOOLEAN)
            -- Write *b* at end of file

putreal (r: REAL)
            -- Write *r* at end of file

putstring (s: STRING)
            -- Write *s* at end of file.

putchar (c: CHARACTER)
            -- Write *c* at end of file.

readchar
> -- Advance input by one character, if possible

readitem
> -- Read next item, if possible

itemtype: INTEGER
> -- Code for type of last item read

> -- Type codes:

Integer_type: INTEGER
Real_type: INTEGER
String_type: INTEGER
Unknown_type: INTEGER

add_delimiter (c: CHARACTER)
> -- Add *c* to delimiters for *readitem*
> -- (default: only blank and new line)

remove_delimiter (c: CHARACTER)
> -- Remove *c* from delimiters for *readitem*

lastchar: CHARACTER
> -- Last character read by *readchar*

lastint: INTEGER
> -- Last integer read by *readitem*

lastreal: REAL
> -- Last real read by *readitem*

laststring (size: INTEGER): STRING
> -- Last string read by *readitem*

next_line
> -- Move to next input line

close
> -- Close file.

end interface -- class *FILE*

E.3 STRINGS

The following class describes operations on strings. Note that this class may also be used to declare manifest string constants (13.5.2).

class interface *STRING* **exported features**

> *size, length, resize, enter, entry, append, prepend,*
> *substring, duplicate, to_upper, to_lower, share, shared_with,*
> *same_as, le, gt, string_char, to_integer, clear, fill_blank,*
> *remove_char, remove_all_occurrences, tail, head, char_string,*
> *left_adjust, right_adjust, hash_code, to_c*

inherit

> *INDIRECT* [*CHARACTER*]

feature specification

> *size: INTEGER*
>
> *length: INTEGER*
> > -- Actual dynamic length.
> > **ensure**
> > *Result >= 0*
>
> *Create* (*n: INTEGER*)
> > -- Allocate approximate space for string with *n* characters
> > **require**
> > *non_negative_size: n >= 0*
> > **ensure**
> > *size = n*
>
> *resize* (*newsize: INTEGER*)
> > -- Reallocate string if needed.
> > **require**
> > *new_size_non_negative: newsize >= 0*
>
> *entry* (*i: INTEGER*): *CHARACTER*
> > -- Character at position *i*.
> > **require**
> > *index_large_enough: i > 0;*
> > *index_small_enough: i <= length*
>
> *enter* (*i: INTEGER, c: CHARACTER*)
> > -- Replace character at position *i* by *c*
> > **require**
> > *index_large_enough: i > 0;*
> > *index_small_enough: i <= length*
> > **ensure**
> > *entry* (*i*) = *c*

clear
          -- Clear out string
     ensure
          length = 0

fill_blank
          -- Fill string with blanks
     ensure
          -- *forall i: 1..length, entry (i) = ' '*

append (s: STRING)
          -- Append a copy of *s* at end of current string
     require
          argument_not_void: **not** *s.Void*
     ensure
          length = old length + s.length

prepend (s: STRING)
          -- Prepend a copy of *s* at front of current string
     require
          argument_not_void: **not** *s.Void*
     ensure
          length = old length + s.length

substring (n1: INTEGER, n2: INTEGER): **like** *Current*
          -- Substring starting at position *n1* and ending at *n2*
     require
          st_argument_large_enough: 1 <= n1;
          t_no_greater_than_second: n1 <= n2;
          nd_argument_small_enough: n2 <= length
     ensure
          Result.length = n2 − n1 + 1
          -- forall i: 1..n2-n1, Result.entry (i) = entry (n1+i-1)

duplicate: STRING
          -- Copy of current string
     ensure
          Result.length = length;
          -- forall i: 1..length, Result.entry (i) = entry (i)

to_lower
          -- Convert string to lower case

to_upper
          -- Convert string to upper case

share (other: STRING)
>   -- Make current string share the text of *other*
>   **require**
>   *argument_not_void:* **not** *other.Void*
>   **ensure**
>   *other.length = length*;
>   -- forall *i: 1..length, Result.entry (i) = entry (i)*;
>   -- Subsequent changes to the characters of current string will
>   -- also affect *other*, and conversely

shared_with (other: STRING): BOOLEAN
>   -- Does current string share the text of *other*?

same_as (other: STRING): BOOLEAN
>   -- Does current string have the same content as *other*?

le (other: STRING): BOOLEAN
>   -- Is current string lexicographically smaller than *other*?

gt (other: STRING): BOOLEAN
>   -- Is current string lexicographically greater than *other*?

to_integer: INTEGER
>   -- Integer value of current string, assumed to contain digits only.
>   -- Example: when applied to "123", will yield 123
>   **require**
>   -- String only contains digits

char_string (c: CHARACTER)
>   -- Add *c* at front
>   **ensure**
>   -- length = old length + 1

string_char (c: CHARACTER)
>   -- Add *c* at end
>   **ensure**
>   *length =* **old** *length + 1*

hash_code: INTEGER
>   -- Hash code value of current string

to_c: INTEGER
>   -- Corresponding C string

remove_all_occurrences (c: CHARACTER)
    -- Remove all occurrences of *c*
  ensure
    -- forall i: 1..length, entry (i) /= c
    -- length = old length - (number of occurrences of c in initial string)

remove_char (i: INTEGER)
    -- Remove *i*-th character
  require
    index_large_enough: i >= 1;
    index_small_enough: i <= length
  ensure
    length = **old** *length – 1*

tail (n: INTEGER)
    -- Remove all characters except for the last *n*.
    -- If n >= length, do nothing.
  require
    non_negative_argument: n >= 0
  ensure
    -- length = min (n, old length)

head (n: INTEGER)
    -- Remove all characters except for the first *n*.
    -- If n >= length, do nothing.
  require
    non_negative_argument: n >= 0
  ensure
    -- length = min (n, old length)

left_adjust
    -- Remove leading blanks
  ensure
    (length = 0) **or else** *(entry (1) /= ' ')*

right_adjust
    -- Remove trailing blanks
  ensure
    (length = 0) **or else** *(entry (length) /= ' ')*

invariant

    0 <= length;
    length <= size
end interface -- class *STRING*

F

Eiffel syntax diagrams

Class_declaration

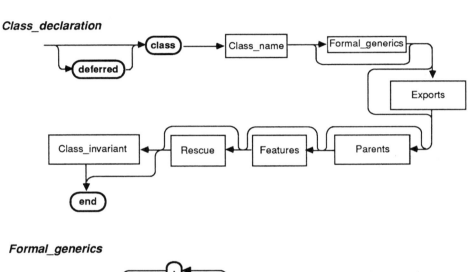

Formal_generics

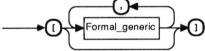

Exports

Parents

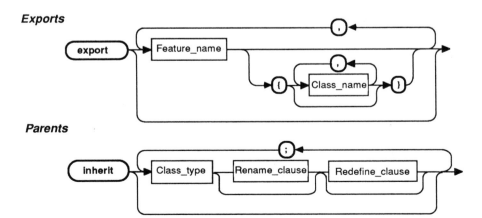

Class_type

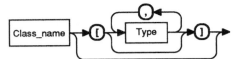

Type

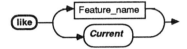

Association

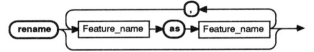

Rename_clause

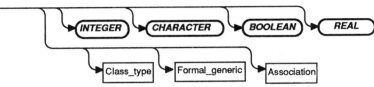

Redefine_clause

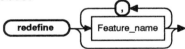

Features

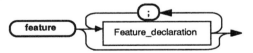

Feature_declaration

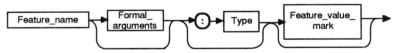

Formal_arguments

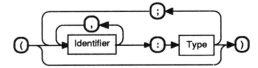

Feature_value_mark

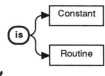

Constant

Integer_constant   *Real_constant*   *Boolean_constant*

String_constant   *Character_constant*

Routine   *Precondition*

Postcondition

Assertion

Boolean_expression,
Integer_expression

Rescue

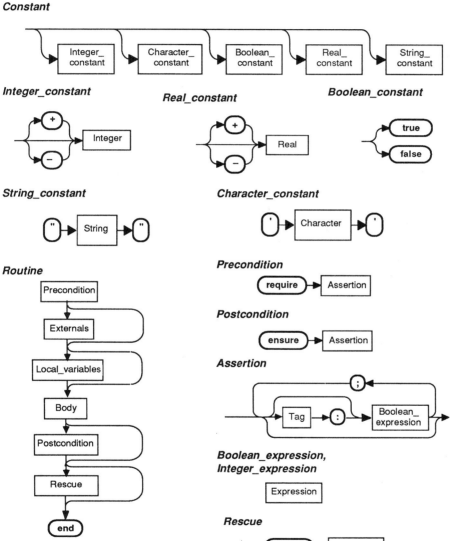

Externals

External_declaration

Language   ***External_name***

Local_variables

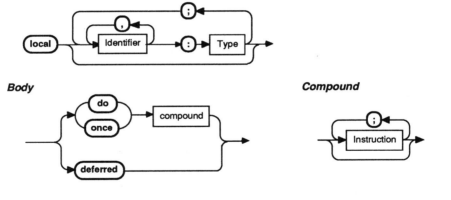

Body   ***Compound***

Instruction

Call

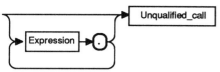

Unqualified_call

Actuals

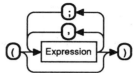

Expression

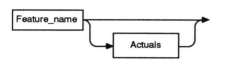

Unqualified_expression

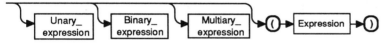

Operator_expression

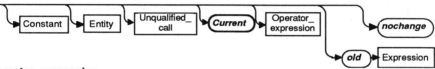

Unary_expression

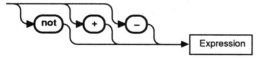

Binary_expression

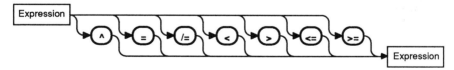

Multiary_expression

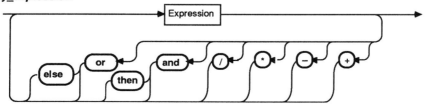

Assignment

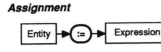

Conditional

Loop

Class_invariant, Loop_invariant

Loop_variant

Check

Debug

Class_name, Formal_generic,
Feature_name, Tag

Entity

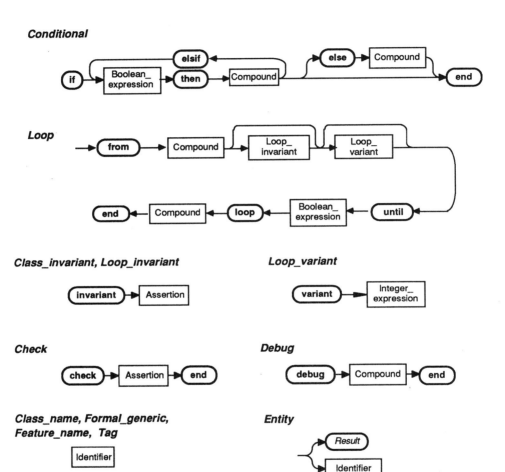

Bibliography

Abrial 1980.

Jean-Raymond Abrial, Stephen A. Schuman and Bertrand Meyer, "A Specification Language," in *On the Construction of Programs*, ed. R. McNaughten and R.C. McKeag, Cambridge University Press, 1980.

ANSI 1983.

ANSI and AJPO, "Military Standard: Ada Programming Language (Am. Nat. Standards Inst. and US Gov. Dept. of Defense, Ada Joint Program Office)," ANSI/MIL-STD-1815A-1983, Feb. 17, 1983.

Agha 1986.

Gul Agha, *A Model of Concurrent Computation in Distributed Systems,* MIT Press, 1986.

Avižienis 1985.

Algirdas Avižienis, "The N-version aproach to Fault-Tolerant Software," *IEEE Trans. on Software Engineering*, vol. SE-11, no. 12, pp. 1491-1501, Dec. 1985.

Bert 1983.

Didier Bert, "Manuel de Référence du Langage LPG, Version 1.2," Rapport R-408, IFIAG, IMAG Inst. (Grenoble University), Grenoble, Dec. 1983.

Biggerstaff 1984.

Ted J. Biggerstaff and Alan J. Perlis (eds.), "Special Issue on Software Reusability," *IEEE Trans. on Software Engineering*, vol. SE-10, no. 5, pp. 474-609, Sept. 1984.

Birtwistle 1973.

Graham Birtwistle, Ole-Johan Dahl, Bjorn Myrhaug and Kristen Nygaard, *Simula Begin,* Studentliteratur (Lund) and Auerbach Pub. (New York), 1973.

Bobrow 1982.

Daniel G. Bobrow and Mark J. Stefik, *LOOPS: an Object-Oriented Programming System for Interlisp,* Xerox PARC, 1982.

Boehm 1978.

Barry W. Boehm, J.R. Brown, G. McLeod, Myron Lipow and M. Merrit, "Characteristics of Software Quality," TRW Series of Software Technology, North-Holland Publishing Co., Amsterdam, 1978.

Boehm 1979.

Barry W. Boehm, "Software Engineering - As It Is," in *Proc. 4th International Conf. on Software Engineering,* pp. 11-21, Munich, Sept. 1979.

Booch 1983.

Grady Booch, *Software Engineering with Ada,* Benjamin/Cummings Publishing Co., Menlo Park (Calif.), 1983.

Booch 1986.

Grady Booch, "Object-Oriented Development," *IEEE Trans. on Software Engineering,* vol. SE-12, no. 2, pp. 211-221, Feb. 1986.

Brachman 1983.

Ronald J. Brachman, "What IS-A and Isn't: An Analysis of Taxonomic Links in Semantic Networks," *IEEE Computer,* vol. 16, no. 10, pp. 67-73, Oct. 1983.

Cannon 1980.

H.I. Cannon, "Flavors," Tech. Report, MIT Artificial Intelligence Laboratory, Cambridge (Mass.), 1980.

Cardelli 1984.

Luca Cardelli, "A Semantics of Multiple Inheritance," in *Semantics of Data Types* (eds. Gilles Kahn, David B. McQueen and Gordon Plotkin), Lecture Notes in Computer Science 173, pp. 51-67, Springer-Verlag, New York, 1984.

Cardelli 1985.

Luca Cardelli and Peter Wegner, "On Understanding Types, Data Abstraction and Polymorphism," *Computing Surveys,* vol. 17, no. 4, pp. 471-522, December 1985.

Cardelli 1987.

Luca Cardelli, "Basic Polymorphic Typechecking," , 1987. (Revised version of 1984 AT&T Bell Laboratories Comp. Sc. Tech. Report, to appear.)

Cohen 1984.

Jacques Cohen and Tim Hickey, "Performance Analysis of On-the-Fly Garbage Collection," *Communications of the ACM,* vol. 27, no. 11, pp. 1143-1154, Nov. 1984.

Cox 1984.

Brad J. Cox, "Message/Object Programming: An Evolutionary Change in Programming Technology," *IEEE Software,* vol. 1, no. 1, pp. 50-69, Jan. 1984.

Cox 1986.

Brad J. Cox, *Object-Oriented Programming: An Evolutionary Approach,* Addison-Wesley, Reading (Mass.), 1986.

Cristian 1985.

Flaviu Cristian, "On Exceptions, Failures and Errors," *Technology and Science of Informatics,* vol. 4, no. 1, Jan. 1985.

Curry 1984.

Gael A. Curry and Robert M. Ayers, "Experience with Traits in the Xerox Star Workstation," *IEEE Trans. on Software Engineering*, vol. SE-10, no. 5, pp. 519-527, Sept. 1984.

Dahl 1966.

Ole-Johan Dahl and Kristen Nygaard, "SIMULA - An Algol-based Simulation Language," *Communications of the ACM*, vol. 9, no. 9, pp. 671-678, Sept. 1966.

Dahl 1970.

Ole-Johan Dahl, Bjørn Myrhaug and Kristen Nygaard, "(Simula 67) Common Base Language," Publication N. S-22, Norsk Regnesentral (Norwegian Computing Center), Oslo, Oct. 1970. (Revised version, Feb. 1984.)

DeMarco 1978.

Tom DeMarco, *Structured Analysis and System Specification,* Yourdon Press, New York, 1978.

DeRemer 1976.

Frank DeRemer and Hans H. Kron, "Programming-in-the-Large Versus Programming-in-the-Small," *IEEE Trans. on Software Engineering*, vol. SE-2, no. 2, pp. 80-86, June 1976.

Dewhurst 1987.

Stephen C. Dewhurst, "Object Representation of Scope during Translation," in [*ECOOP 1987*], pp. 79-86, 1987.

Dijkstra 1976.

Edsger W. Dijkstra, *A Discipline of Programming,* Prentice-Hall, Englewood Cliffs (N.J.), 1976.

Dijkstra 1978.

E. W. Dijkstra, L. Lamport, A.J. Martin, C.S. Scholten and E.F.M. Steffens, "On-the-Fly Garbage Collection: An Exercise in Cooperation," *Communications of the ACM*, vol. 21, no. 11, pp. 966-975, Nov. 1978.

ECOOP 1987.

ECOOP, *First European Conference on Object-Oriented Programming*, AFCET, Paris, June 15-17, 1987, published as BIGRE 54, June 1987.

Feldman 1979.

Stuart I. Feldman, "Make - A Program for Maintaining Computer Programs," *Software, Practice and Experience*, vol. 9, pp. 255-265, 1979.

Floyd 1967.

Robert W. Floyd, "Assigning Meanings to Programs," in *Proc. Am. Math. Soc. Symp. in Applied Mathematics*, vol. 19, pp. 19-31, 1967.

Futatsugi 1985.

Kokichi Futatsugi, Joseph A. Goguen, Jean-Pierre Jouannaud and José Messeguer, "Principles of OBJ2," in *Proc. ACM Symp. on the Principles of Programming Languages*, vol. 12, pp. 52-66, 1985.

Geschke 1975.

C.M. Geschke and J.G. Mitchell, "On the Problem of Uniform References to Data Structures," *SIGPLAN Notices*, vol. 10, no. 6, pp. 31-42, June 1975.

Gindre 1988.
> Cyrille Gindre and Frédérique Sada, "A Development in Eiffel: Design and Implementation of a Network Simulator," *Journal of Object-Oriented Programming*, 1988. To appear.

Goguen 1978.
> Joseph A. Goguen, J. W. Thatcher and E. G. Wagner, "An Initial Algebra Approach to the Specification, Correctness and Implementation of Abstract Data Types," in *Current Trends in Programming Methodology,* vol. 4, ed. Raymond T. Yeh, pp. 80-149, Prentice-Hall, Englewood Cliffs (N.J.), 1978.

Goguen 1984.
> Joseph A. Goguen, "Parameterized Programming," *IEEE Trans. on Software Engineering*, vol. SE-10, no. 5, pp. 528-543, Sept. 1984.

Goldberg 1976.
> Adele Goldberg and Alan Kay (eds.), "Smalltalk-72 Instruction Manual," Tech. Report SSL-76-6, Xerox Palo Alto Research Center, March 1976.

Goldberg 1981.
> Adele Goldberg and others, "Special issue on Smalltalk-80," *Byte Magazine*, August 1981.

Goldberg 1983.
> Adele Goldberg and David Robson, *Smalltalk-80: The Language and its Implementation,* Addison-Wesley, Reading (Mass.), 1983.

Goldberg 1985.
> Adele Goldberg, *Smalltalk-80: The Interactive Programming Environment,* Addison-Wesley, Reading (Mass.), 1985.

Guttag 1977.
> John V. Guttag, "Abstract Data Types and the Development of Data Structures," *Communications of the ACM*, vol. 20, no. 6, pp. 396-404, June 1977.

Halbert 1987.
> D.C. Halbert and P.D. O'Brien, "Using Types and Inheritance in Object-Oriented Languages," in [*ECOOP 1987*], pp. 23-34, 1987.

Hoare 1969.
> C.A.R. Hoare, "An Axiomatic Basis for Computer Programming," *Communications of the ACM*, vol. 12, no. 10, pp. 576-580, 583, Oct. 1969.

Hoare 1972.
> C.A.R. Hoare, "Proof of Correctness of Data Representations," *Acta Informatica*, vol. 1, pp. 271-281, 1972.

Horowitz 1984.
> Ellis Horowitz and John B. Munson, "An Expansive View of Reusable Software," *IEEE Trans. on Software Engineering*, vol. SE-10, no. 5, pp. 477-487, Sept. 1984.

Hullot 1984.
> Jean-Marie Hullot, "Ceyx, Version 15: I - une Initiation," Rapport Technique no. 44, INRIA, Rocquencourt, Eté 1984.

Ingalls 1978.
> Daniel H. H. Ingalls, "The Smalltalk-76 Programming System: Design and Implementation," in *Proc. ACM Symp. on the Principles of Programming Languages*, Jan. 1978.

Interactive 1986.
Interactive Software Engineering Inc., "Eiffel Library Manual," Tech. Report TR-EI-7/LI, 1986.

Jackson 1975.
Michael A. Jackson, *Principles of Program Design,* Academic Press, London, 1975.

Jackson 1983.
Michael A. Jackson, *System Development,* Prentice-Hall International, Hemel Hempstead, 1983.

Johnston 1971.
J.B. Johnston, "The Contour Model of Block Structured Processes," *SIGPLAN Notices*, vol. 6, no. 2, pp. 55-82, Feb. 1971.

Jones 1980.
Cliff B. Jones, *Software Development: A Rigorous Approach,* Prentice-Hall International, Hemel Hempstead, 1980.

Jones 1984.
T. Capers Jones, "Reusability in Programming: A Survey of the State of the Art," *IEEE Trans. on Software Engineering*, vol. SE-10, no. 5, pp. 488-494, Sept. 1984.

Jones 1986.
Cliff B. Jones, *Systematic Software Development Using VDM,* Prentice-Hall International, Hemel Hempstead, 1986.

Knuth 1984.
Donald E. Knuth, "Literate Programming," *The Computer Journal*, vol. 27, no. 2, pp. 97-111, May 1984.

Lampson 1977.
Butler W. Lampson, Jim J. Horning, Ralph L. London, J. G. Mitchell and Gerard L. Popek, "Report on the Programming Language Euclid," *SIGPLAN Notices*, vol. 12, no. 2, pp. 1-79, Feb. 1977.

Lientz 1979.
B.P. Lientz and E.B. Swanson, "Software Maintenance: A User/Management Tug of War," *Data Management*, pp. 26-30, Apr. 1979.

Liskov 1974.
Barbara H. Liskov and Stephen N. Zilles, "Programming with Abstract Data Types," Computation Structures Group, Memo no. 99, MIT, Project MAC, Cambridge (Mass.), 1974. (See also SIGPLAN Notices, 9, 4, pp. 50-59, Apr. 1974.)

Liskov 1979.
Barbara H. Liskov and Alan Snyder, "Exception Handling in CLU," *IEEE Trans. on Software Engineering*, vol. SE-5, no. 6, pp. 546-558, Nov. 1979.

Liskov 1981.
Barbara H. Liskov, Russel Atkinson, T. Bloom, E. Moss, J. Craig Schaffert, R. Scheifler and Alan Snyder, *CLU Reference Manual,* Springer-Verlag, New York, 1981.

Liskov 1986.
Barbara H. Liskov and John Guttag, *Abstraction and Specification in Program Development,* MIT Press, Cambridge (Mass.), 1986.

McCall 1977.

James McCall (ed.), *Factors in Software Quality,* General Electric, 1977.

McIlroy 1976.

M.D. McIlroy, "Mass-produced Software Components," in *Software Engineering Concepts and Techniques (1968 NATO Conf. on Software Engineering),* eds. J. M. Buxton, P. Naur and B. Randell, pp. 88-98, 1976.

McMenamin 1984.

Stephen M. McMenamin and John F. Palmer, *Essential Systems Analysis,* Yourdon Press, New York, 1984.

Meyer 1976.

Bertrand Meyer, "La Description des Structures de Données," *Bulletin de la Direction des Etudes et Recherches d'Electricité de France, Série C (Informatique),* no. 2, Clamart (France), 1976.

Meyer 1978.

Bertrand Meyer and Claude Baudoin, *Méthodes de Programmation,* Eyrolles, Paris, 1978. New edition, 1984.

Meyer 1979.

Bertrand Meyer, "Quelques concepts importants des langages de programmation modernes et leur expression en Simula 67," *Bulletin de la Direction des Etudes et Recherches d'Electricité de France, Série C (Informatique),* no. 1, pp. 89-150, Clamart, France, 1979. Also in GROPLAN 9, AFCET, 1979.

Meyer 1982.

Bertrand Meyer, "Principles of Package Design," *Communications of the ACM,* vol. 25, no. 7, pp. 419-428, July 1982.

Meyer 1986.

Bertrand Meyer, "M: A System Description Method," Tech. Report TRCS85-15, University of California, Santa Barbara, Computer Science Department, Aug. 1986.

Meyer 1986a.

Bertrand Meyer, "Cépage: A Software Design Tool," *Computer Language,* vol. 3, no. 9, pp. 43-53, Sept. 1986.

Meyer 1987.

Bertrand Meyer, "Reusability: the Case for Object-Oriented Design," *IEEE Software,* vol. 4, no. 2 , pp. 50-64, March 1987.

Meyer 1988.

Bertrand Meyer, "Eiffel: A Language and Environment for Software Engineering," *The Journal of Systems and Software.* To appear.

Meyer 1988a.

Bertrand Meyer, "Genericity, static type checking and inheritance," *The Journal of Pascal, Ada and Modula-2,* 1988. To appear (Revised version of paper in [*OOPSLA 1986*], pp. 391-405).

Milner 1978.

Robin Milner, "A Theory of Type Polymorphism in Programming," *Journal of Computer and System Sciences,* vol. 17, pp. 348-375, 1978.

Mitchell 1979.

J.G. Mitchell, W. Maybury and R. Sweet, "Mesa Language Manual (Version 5.0)," Report CSL-79-3, Xerox Research Center, Palo Alto (Calif.), Apr. 1979.

Moffat 1981.

David V. Moffat, "Enumerations in Pascal, Ada and Beyond," *SIGPLAN Notices*, vol. 16, no. 2, pp. 77-82, Feb. 1981.

Moon 1986.

David A. Moon, "Object-Oriented Programming with Flavors," in [*OOPSLA 1986*], 1986.

NSIA 1985.

NSIA (National Security Industry Association), *Proc. First Joint DoD-Industry Symp. on the STARS program*, San Diego (Calif.), Apr. 30-May 2 1985.

Nygaard 1981.

Kristen Nygaard and Ole-Johan Dahl, "Simula 67," in *History of Programming Languages*, ed. Richard W. Wexelblat, 1981.

OOPSLA 1986.

OOPSLA, *ACM Conference on Object-Oriented Programming, Systems, Languages and Applications*, Portland (Oreg.), Sept. 29-Oct. 2, 1986, published as SIGPLAN Notices, 21, 11, Nov. 1986.

OOPSLA 1987.

OOPSLA, *ACM Conference on Object-Oriented Programming, Systems, Languages and Applications*, Orlando (Flor.), Oct. 4-8, 1987, published as SIGPLAN Notices, 22, 12, Dec. 1987.

Orr 1977.

Ken T. Orr, *Structured Systems Development,* Yourdon Press, New York, 1977.

Page-Jones 1980.

Meillir Page-Jones, *The Practical Guide to Structured Systems Design,* Yourdon Press, New York, 1980.

Parnas 1972.

David Lorge Parnas, "On the Criteria to Be Used in Decomposing Systems into Modules," *Communications of the ACM*, vol. 5, no. 12, pp. 1053-1058, Dec. 1972.

Pooley 1986.

Robert J. Pooley, *An Introduction to Programming in SIMULA,* Blackwell Scientific, Oxford, 1986.

Randell 1975.

Brian Randell, "System Structure for Software Fault Tolerance," *IEEE Trans. on Software Engineering*, vol. SE-1, no. 2, pp. 220-232, June 1975.

Shaw 1981.

Mary Shaw and others, *Alphard: Form and Content,* Springer-Verlag, New York, 1981.

SIS 1987.

SIS, *Data Processing- Programming Languages – SIMULA,* Svensk Standard SS 63 61 14, Standardiseringskommissionen i Sverige (Swedish Standards Inst.), 20 May 1987.

Schaffert 1986.
Craig Schaffert, Topher Cooper, Bruce Bullis, Mike Kilian and Carrie Wilpolt, "An Introduction to Trellis-Owl," in [*OOPSLA 1986*], pp. 9-16, 1986.

Shriver 1987.
Bruce Shriver and Peter Wegner (eds.), *Research Directions in Object-Oriented Programming*, MIT Press, 1987.

Snyder 1986.
Alan Snyder, "Encapsulation and Inheritance in Object-Oriented Programming Languages," in [*OOPSLA 1986*], pp. 38-45, 1986.

Standish 1984.
Thomas A. Standish, "An Essay on Software Reuse," *IEEE Trans. on Software Engineering*, vol. SE-10, no. 5, pp. 494-497, Sept. 1984.

Stroustrup 1984.
Bjarne Stroustrup, "Data Abstraction in C," *AT&T Bell Laboratories Tech. Journal*, vol. 63, no. 8, Part 2, pp. 1701-1732, Oct. 1984.

Stroustrup 1986.
Bjarne Stroustrup, *The C++ Programming Language*, Addison-Wesley, Menlo Park (Calif.), 1986.

Tabourier 1986.
Yves Tabourier, *De l'autre côté de Merise - Systèmes d'Information et Modèles d'Entreprise*, Les Editions d'Organisation, Paris, 1986.

Tardieu 1984.
Hubert Tardieu, Arnold Rochfeld and René Colletti, *La Méthode Merise, Principes et Outils* (2nd Edition), Les Editions d'Organisation, Paris, 1984.

Tesler 1985.
Larry Tesler, "Object Pascal Report," *Structured Language World*, vol. 9, no. 3, 1985.

Ungar 1984.
David Ungar, "Generation Scavenging: A Non-disruptive High Performance Storage Reclamation Algorithm," in *Proc. ACM SIGSOFT/SIGPLAN Software Engineering Symp. on Practical Software Development Environments* (Pittsburgh, Pennsylvania, Apr. 23-25, 1984), pp. 157-167, ACM Software Engineering Notes, 9, 3 and SIGPLAN Notices, 19, 5, May 1984.

VLDB 1987.
VLDB, *Very Large Databases Conference, 1987*, London, Sept. 1987.

Waters 1985.
Richard C. Waters, "The Programmer's Apprentice: A Session with KBEmacs," *IEEE Trans. on Software Engineering*, vol. SE-11, no. 11, pp. 1296-1320, Nov. 1985.

Wegner 1984.
Peter Wegner, "Capital-Intensive Software Technology," *IEEE Software*, vol. 1, no. 3, July 1984.

Welsh 1977.
J. Welsh, W. Sneeringer and C.A.R. Hoare, "Ambiguities and Insecurities in Pascal," *Software, Practice and Experience*, vol. 7, pp. 685-696, 1977.

Wiederhold 1986.

Gio Wiederhold, "Views, Objects and Databases," *IEEE Computer*, vol. 19, no. 2, pp. 37-44, Dec. 1986.

Wirth 1971.

Niklaus Wirth, "Program Development by Stepwise Refinement," *Communications of the ACM*, vol. 14, no. 4, pp. 221-227, 1971.

Wirth 1982.

Niklaus Wirth, *Programming in Modula-2,* Springer-Verlag, New York, 1982.

Yonezawa 1987.

Akinori Yonezawa and Mario Tokoro (eds.), *Object-oriented Concurrent Programming,* MIT Press, Cambridge (Mass.), 1987.

Yourdon 1979.

Edward Nash Yourdon and Larry L. Constantine, *Structured Design: Fundamentals of a Discipline of Computer Program and Systems Design,* Prentice-Hall, Englewood Cliffs (N.J.), 1979.

van Wijngaarden 1975.

Aad van Wijngaarden, B. J. Mailloux, J.E.L Peck, C.H.A. Koster, Michel Sintzoff, Charles H. Lindsey, Lambert G.L.T. Meertens and R.G. Fisker, "Revised Report on the Algorithmic Language Algol 68," *Acta Informatica*, vol. 5, pp. 1-236, 1975.

Index